THE COMPLETE
WORLD
ATLAS

THE COMPLETE
WORLD
ATLAS

**An up to date Atlas
for the 21st Century**

MAES & ZEIJLSTRA

This edition is published in 2000 for Grange Book an
imprint of Grange Books PLC. The Grange Kingsnorth
Industrial Estate, Hoo, Nr. Rochester Kent Me3 9ND.

Cartography:
M & Z MapProduction, Oosterbeek, The Netherlands

Geography:
Hans de Jong, Goesbeek, The Netherlands

Cover design:
Minkowsky Graphics, Enkhuizen, The
Netherlands

Editing and production:
TextCase, Groningen, The Netherlands

ISBN 1840134038

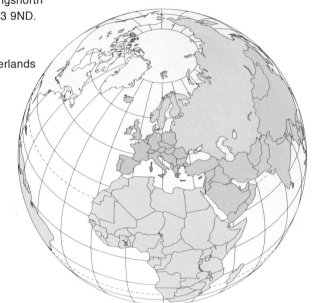

FOREWORD

The *Complete World Atlas* has been compiled according to the principle of 'a separate map for every country of the world'. There is a good reason for doing so. You will find a map of France with quite a lot of information in just about every atlas, but if you want to find out something about Bhutan then that is a very different kettle of fish. You will then have to make do with a tiny section somewhere on the map of South East Asia, which does not tell you a great deal more than the name of the capital and that it is a rather mountainous country.

Detailed
This *Complete World Atlas* provides you with considerably more information. Even in the case of small and remote countries it gives a detailed representation of the most important cities, roads, rivers and lakes, regions, bays and islands. The maps of the archipelago in the Pacific Ocean even give the names of the smaller islands. A map has been included for each of the states of the United States of America. You will find an explanation of the presentation on page 14.

Relief
On most of the maps the colours indicating the different heights have a set value, which is shown on page 15. In the case of maps on which the height differences are negligible, the colours have different values. Separate mention has been made of this on these maps.

Legends
Per country the legends state the official name of the country, the capital, the population, the surface area in square kilometres, the currency, the language or most important languages spoken by the population and finally information about the degree of their welfare and well-being: gross domestic product (GDP) or average income, and the life expectancy of the inhabitants. All this information was updated in 1999.

Order of the maps
Wherever possible the maps have been arranged per continent, in the order of their position from West to East, starting in from the North. Europe therefore commences with Iceland, Africa with Morocco.

Looking up information
You can find the things that you are looking for in various ways:
- index arranged in alphabetical order according to country/state names - in alphabetical order, on pages 11 to 13;
- index arranged according to continent, showing the order of the maps;
- world map on pages 6-7 provides an overview of the sequence of page numbers of the continents;
- index of geographical names on pages 296–329.

We hope you will enjoy using this *Complete World Atlas* as much as we enjoyed putting it together.

The compilers

WORLD

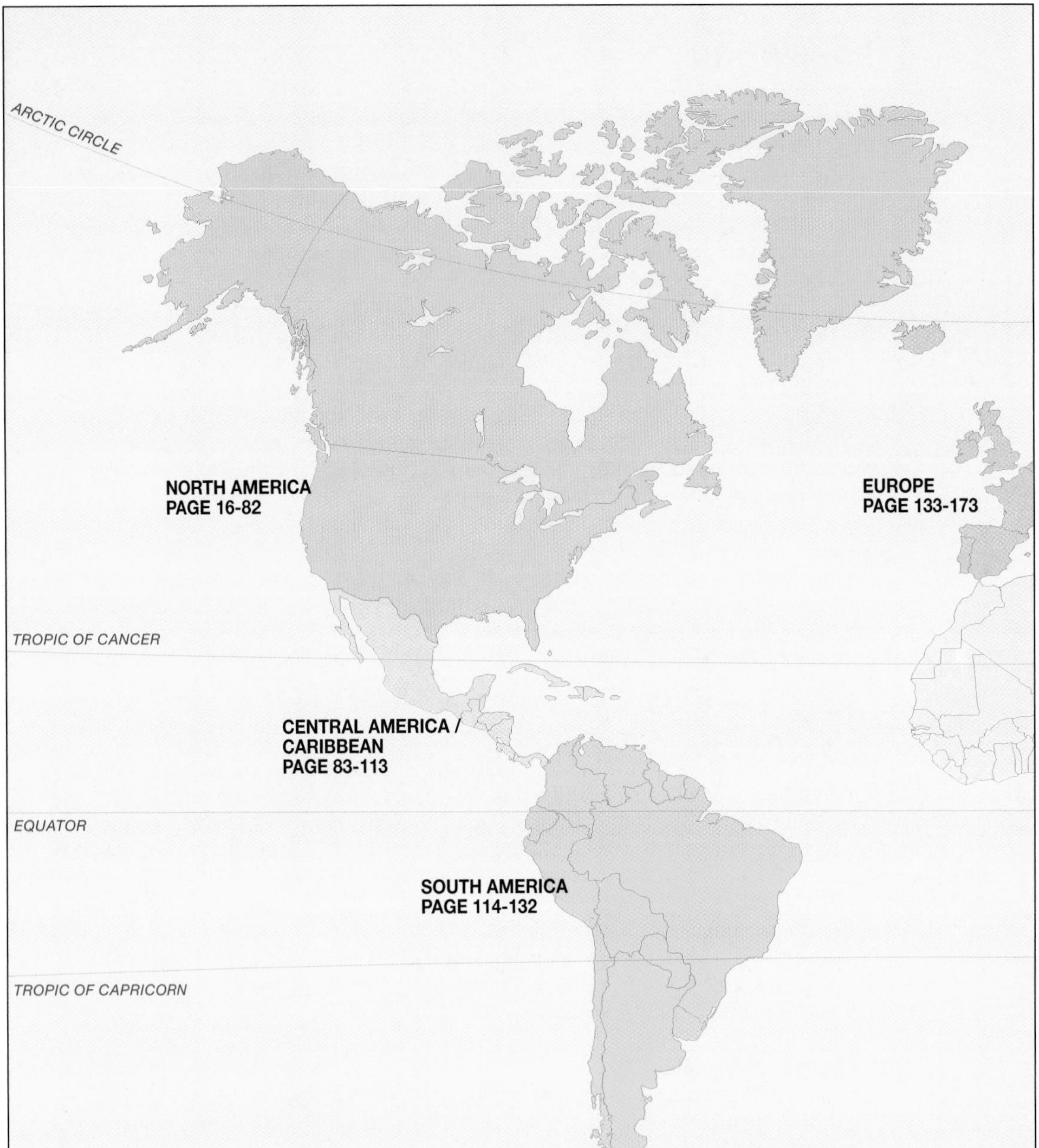

ARCTIC CIRCLE
NORTH AMERICA
PAGE 16-82
EUROPE
PAGE 133-173
TROPIC OF CANCER
CENTRAL AMERICA /
CARIBBEAN
PAGE 83-113
EQUATOR
SOUTH AMERICA
PAGE 114-132
TROPIC OF CAPRICORN

ASIA
PAGE 221-281

AFRICA
PAGE 174-220

AUSTRALIA /
OCEANIA
PAGE 282-293

TOWN AND VILLAGES

■   > 100,000 inhabitants

●   < 25,000 inhabitants

•   25,000 - 100,000 inhabitants

■——   The name of the capital is underlined.

●——

•—

HYDROGRAPHIC INFORMATION

 LAKE CLAIRE   Lake

 SEPIK   River

KUSKOKWIM BAY   BAY OF BENGAL   Bay

MINDORO STRAIT   Strait

 LAGON D'OUVÉA   Reef

GULF OF HONDURAS   Sea

INDIAN OCEAN   Ocean

 DRANGA-JÖKULL   Glacier

TOPOGRAPHIC INFORMATION

▲ KULA KANGRI 7 554   Mountain

GISSARSKIJ CHREBET   Mountain range

SÃO TOMÉ EN PRÍNCIPE   Country

AR RUB'AL KHALI   Region

PULAU NUMFOOR   Island

CABO TRES PUNTAS   Cape

ROADS AND BORDERS

————   Main road

————   National border

— — — —   National border across water

FURTHER INFORMATION

 International airport

 Arrow indicating the nNorth

▲ AMBOSELI NATIONAL PARK

▲ CASTLE CRAGS STATE PARK   National park, reserve or state park

RELIEF INFORMATION

All heights on the maps all heights are shown in metres; the colours represent the following heights.

Sea/ocean	< 0	0 - 200	200 - 500	500 - 1000	1000 - 2000	2000 - 5000	> 5000

(In certain a number of maps where the difference in height range is less than 200 m the same colours are also used to introduce some relief features. These values are then indicated on the relevant maps.)

SAMPLE MAP

Name of the country

National flag

Scale of the map

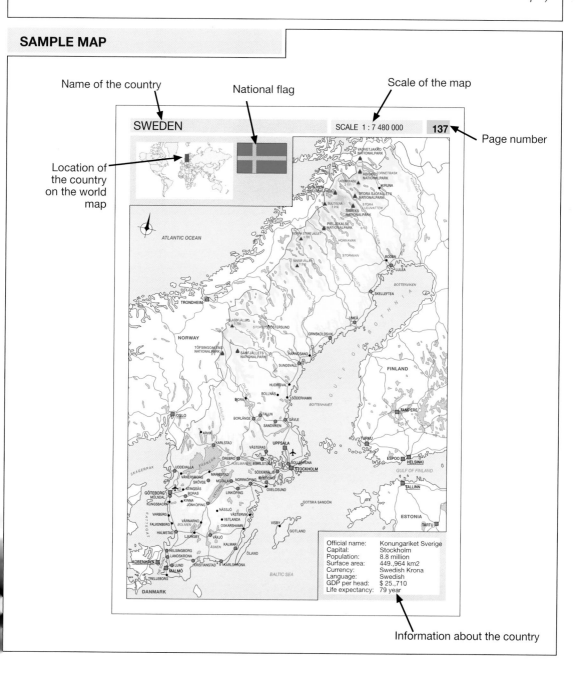

SWEDEN

SCALE 1 : 7 480 000

137

Page number

Location of the country on the world map

ATLANTIC OCEAN

NORWAY

FINLAND

GULF OF FINLAND

ESTONIA

BALTIC SEA

DANMARK

SKAGERRAK

KATTEGAT

Official name:	Konungariket Sverige
Capital:	Stockholm
Population:	8.8 million
Surface area:	449.,964 km2
Currency:	Swedish Krona
Language:	Swedish
GDP per head:	$ 25.,710
Life expectancy:	79 year

Information about the country

RUSSIA

ARCTIC OCEAN

ARCTIC CIRCLE

ICELAND

GREENLAND

ALASKA

ANCHORAGE

NUUK

YUKON

MACKENZIE

C A N A D A

HUDSON BAY

EDMONTON

SASKATCHEWAN

NELSON

CALGARY

VANCOUVER

QUEBEC

WINNIPEG

MONTREAL

OTTAWA

SEATTLE

TORONTO

MISSOURI

BOSTON

PORTLAND

PACIFIC OCEAN

U N I T E D   S T A T E S

CHICAGO

NEW YORK

CLEVELAND

PHILADELPHIA

WASHINGTON

SAN FRANCISCO

DENVER

COLORADO

OHIO

ST. LOUIS

ATLANTIC OCEAN

LOS ANGELES

ATLANTA

SAN DIEGO

PHOENIX

MISSISSIPPI

RIO GRANDE

DALLAS

NEW ORLEANS

HOUSTON

M E X I C O

GULF OF MEXICO

MIAMI

ARCTIC OCEAN

WANDEL SEA

KONG FREDERIK VIII LAND

DANMARKSHAVN

LINCOLN SEA

PEARY LAND

DANEBORG

KONG CHRISTIAN X LAND

ITTOQQORTOORMIIT

MESTERS VIG

ICELAND

KNUD RASMUSSEN LAND

NARES STRAIT

DANMARK STRAIT

KONG CHRISTIAN IX LAND

SIORAPALUK   QAANAAQ

PITUFFIC

SAVISSIVIC

KAPUTITEEQ

KULLORSUAQ

KAP GUSTAV HOLM

BAFFIN BAY

TASIUSAQ

NUUGAATSIAQ

MONT FOREL 3 360

ANGMAGSSALIK

UMANAK

QUTDLIGSSAT   DISKO

ILULISSAT

QUASIGIANNGUIT

QEQERTARSUAQ   DISKO BUGT

AASIAAT

KANGERLUSSUAQ

KANGAATSIAQ

KONG FREDERIK IX LAND

KAP MØSTING

KONG FREDERIK VI LAND

SISIMIUT

DAVIS STRAIT

KAP CORT ADELAER

MALITSOQ

NUUK (GODTHÅB)

J.A.D. JENSENS NUNATAKKER 1 680

CANADA

NARSSAQ

KAP FARVEL

QEQERTARSUATSIAAT

PAAMIUT

NARSSAQ KUJALLEQ

IVIGTUT   QAQORTOQ

LABRADOR SEA

ATLANTIC OCEAN

Official name:	Kalaallit nunaat
Capital:	Nuuk (Godthåb)
Population:	55,863
Surface area:	2,166,086 km^2
Currency:	Danish Krone
Languages:	Eskimo, Danish, English
GDP per head:	$ 19,020
Life expectancy:	75 years

CANADA

RUSSIA

ARCTIC OCEAN

PRINCE PATRICK ISLAND

M'CLURE STRAIT

BEAUFORT SEA

BANKS
ISLAND

UNITED STATES
(ALASKA)

AMUNDSEN GULF

VICTORIA ISLAND

ANCHORAGE

YUKON TERRITORY

GREAT BEAR LAKE

NUNAVUT

MACKENZIE

MACKENZIE MOUNTAINS

MOUNT LOGAN
5 951

PELLY

WHITEHORSE

NORTHWEST TERRITORIES

YELLOWKNIFE

JUNEAU

GREAT SLAVE LAKE

PACIFIC OCEAN

BRITISH COLUMBIA

R O C K

PEACE

LAKE
ATHABASCA

QUEEN CHARLOTTE ISLAND

ALBERTA

SAKATCHEWAN

EDMONTON

VANCOUVER ISLAND

SASKATOON

VANCOUVER

CALGARY

REGINA

LETHBRIDGE

SEATTLE

U N I T E D   S T A T E S

Official name:	Canada
Capital:	Ottawa
Population:	30.0 million
Surface area:	9,958,319 km²
Currency:	Canadian Dollar
Languages:	English, French
GDP per head:	$ 19,020
Life expectancy:	79 years

ARCTIC OCEAN

ELLESMERE ISLAND

GREENLAND

AXEL HEIBERG ISLAND

BAFFIN BAY

DEVON ISLAND

ATLANTIC OCEAN

BAFFIN ISLAND

NUUK

FOXE BASSIN

IQALUIT

LABRADOR SEA

NUNAVUT

UNGAVA BAY

HUDSON BAY

NEW FOUNDLAND

ST. JOHN'S

MANITOBA

SEVEN

JAMES BAY

QUEBEC

GULF OF ST. LAWRENCE

ST. PIERRE ET MIQUELON (FR.)

ONTARIO

ALBANY

PRINCE EDWARD ISLAND

LAKE WINNIPEG

CHICOUTIMI

FREDERICTON

QUEBEC

HALIFAX

NOVA SCOTIA

WINNIPEG

MONTREAL

THUNDER BAY

OTTAWA

SAULT STE. MARIE

KINGSTON

LAKE SUPERIOR

UNITED STATES

LAKE HURON

TORONTO

LAKE ONTARIO

NIAGARA FALLS

MINNEAPOLIS

LAKE MICHIGAN

LONDON

DETROIT

LAKE ERIE

NEW YORK

CHICAGO

ATLANTIC OCEAN

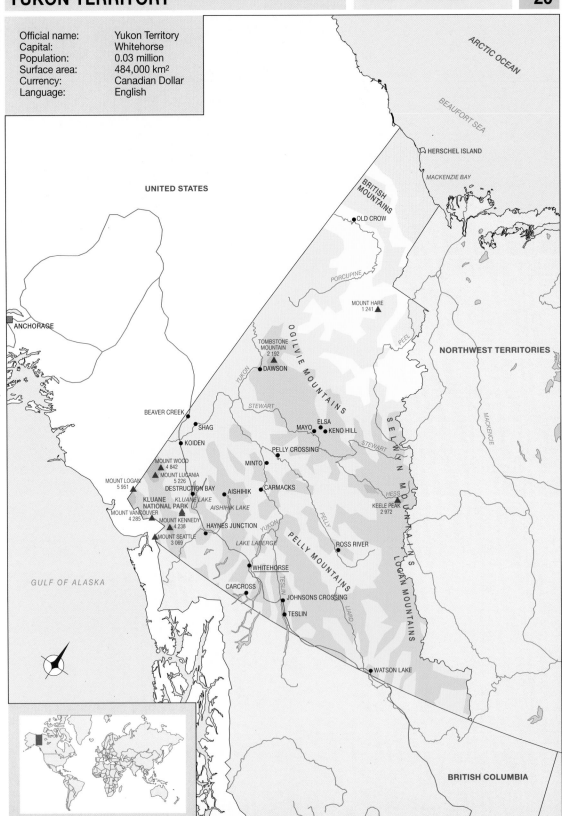

YUKON TERRITORY

SCALE 1 : 8 000 000

20

Official name: Yukon Territory
Capital: Whitehorse
Population: 0.03 million
Surface area: 484,000 km²
Currency: Canadian Dollar
Language: English

ARCTIC OCEAN

BEAUFORT SEA

HERSCHEL ISLAND

MACKENZIE BAY

BRITISH
MOUNTAINS

OLD CROW

UNITED STATES

PORCUPINE

MOUNT HARE
1 241

NORTHWEST TERRITORIES

PEEL

O G I L V I E   M O U N T A I N S

TOMBSTONE
MOUNTAIN
2 192

DAWSON

YUKON

STEWART

MACKENZIE

S E L W Y N   M O U N T A I N S

ANCHORAGE

BEAVER CREEK

SHAG

KOIDEN

MAYO
ELSA
KENO HILL

STEWART

PELLY CROSSING

MINTO

CARMACKS

MOUNT WOOD
4 842
MOUNT LUCANIA
5 226

DESTRUCTION BAY

AISHIHIK

HESS

KEELE PEAK
2 972

MOUNT LOGAN
5 951

KLUANE
NATIONAL PARK

KLUANE LAKE

AISHIHIK LAKE

MOUNT VANCOUVER
4 285

MOUNT KENNEDY
4 238

HAYNES JUNCTION

YUKON

PELLY

ROSS RIVER

MOUNT SEATTLE
3 069

LAKE LABERGE

P E L L Y   M O U N T A I N S

L O G A N   M O U N T A I N S

GULF OF ALASKA

WHITEHORSE

CARCROSS

TESLIN

JOHNSONS CROSSING

TESLIN

LIARD

WATSON LAKE

BRITISH COLUMBIA

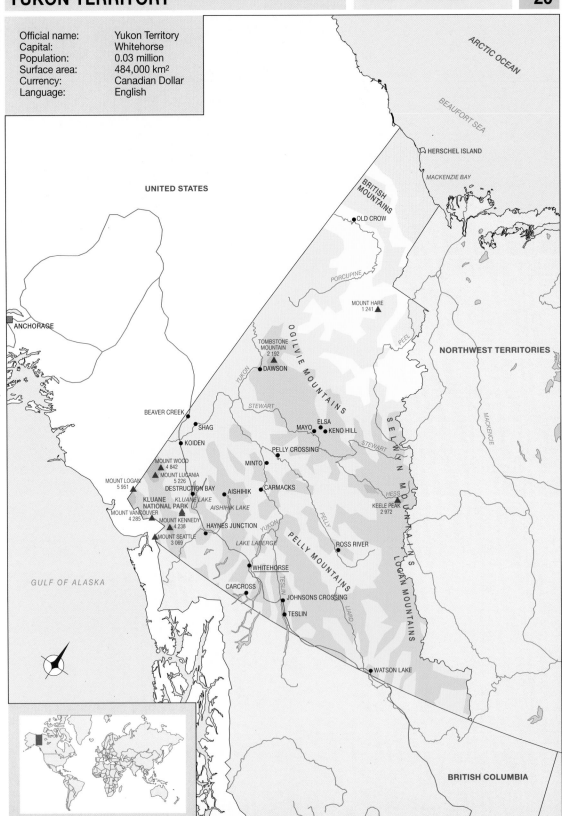

NORTHWEST TERRITORIES / NUNAVUT

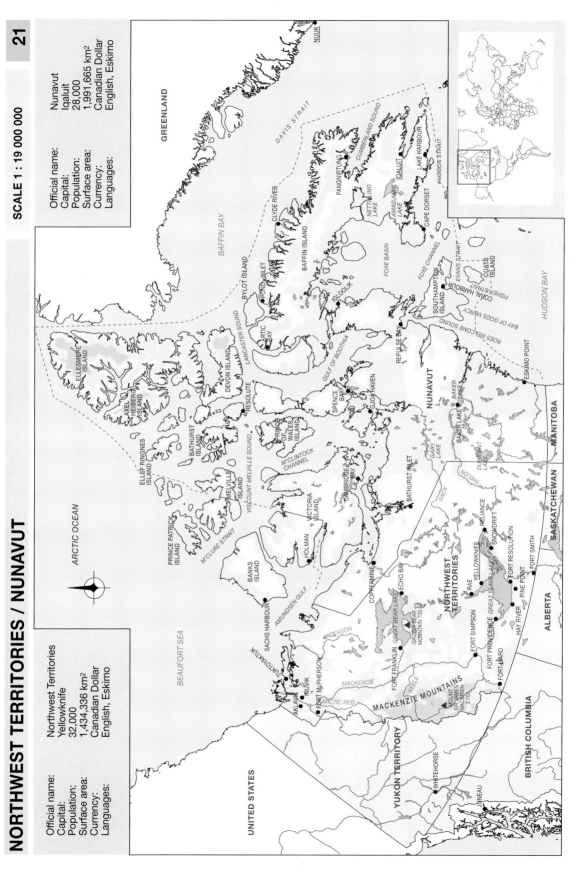

Official name: Northwest Territories
Capital: Yellowknife
Population: 32,000
Surface area: 1,434,336 km²
Currency: Canadian Dollar
Languages: English, Eskimo

Official name: Nunavut
Capital: Iqaluit
Population: 28,000
Surface area: 1,991,665 km²
Currency: Canadian Dollar
Languages: English, Eskimo

ARCTIC OCEAN

GREENLAND

BAFFIN BAY

DAVIS STRAIT

NUUK

HUDSON BAY

HUDSON STRAIT

BEAUFORT SEA

UNITED STATES

YUKON TERRITORY

BRITISH COLUMBIA

ALBERTA

SASKATCHEWAN

MANITOBA

NORTHWEST TERRITORIES

NUNAVUT

ELLESMERE ISLAND

AXEL HEIBERG ISLAND

ELLEF RINGNES ISLAND

PRINCE PATRICK ISLAND

BATHURST ISLAND

DEVON ISLAND

BYLOT ISLAND

BAFFIN ISLAND

CUMBERLAND SOUND

LANCASTER SOUND

MELVILLE ISLAND

VISCOUNT MELVILLE SOUND

M'CLURE STRAIT

BANKS ISLAND

AMUNDSEN GULF

PRINCE OF WALES ISLAND

M'CLINTOCK CHANNEL

VICTORIA ISLAND

GULF OF BOOTHIA

FOXE BASIN

FOXE CHANNEL

SOUTHAMPTON ISLAND

COATS ISLAND

FISHER STRAIT

EVANS STRAIT

CORAL HARBOUR

ROES WELCOME SOUND

BAY OF GODS MERCY

NETTILLING LAKE

AMADJUAK LAKE

IQALUIT

CAPE DORSET

LAKE HARBOUR

PANGNIRTUNG

CLYDE RIVER

POND INLET

ARCTIC BAY

IGLOOLIK

RESOLUTE

SPENCE BAY

GJOAHAVEN

CAMBRIDGE BAY

BATHURST INLET

REPULSE BAY

ESKIMO POINT

BAKER LAKE

GARY LAKE

DUBAWNT LAKE

THELON

BACK

HOLMAN

SACHS HARBOUR

TUKTOYAKTUK

AKLAVIK

INUVIK

FORT McPHERSON

ARCTIC RED

MACKENCIE

ANDERSON

KEELE

COPPERMINE

ECHO BAY

GRIZZLE BEAR MOUNTAIN 700

GREAT BEAR LAKE

FORT FRANKLIN

FORT SIMPSON

FORT PROVIDENCE

FORT LIARD

MACKENZIE MOUNTAINS

MOUNT SIR JAMES MACBRIEN 2 762

RAE

YELLOWKNIFE

GREAT SLAVE LAKE

SNOWDRIFT

RELIANCE

FORT RESOLUTION

PINE POINT

HAY RIVER

FORT SMITH

WHITEHORSE

JUNEAU

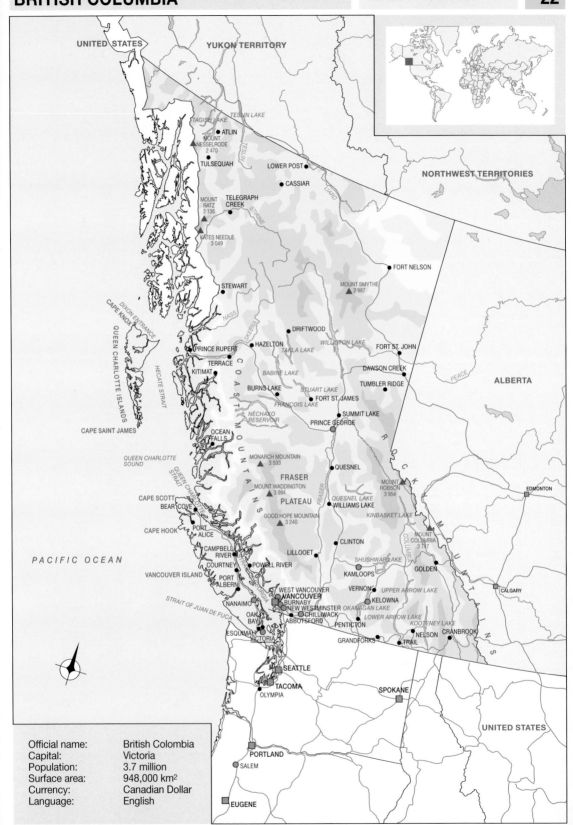

UNITED STATES

YUKON TERRITORY

NORTHWEST TERRITORIES

TAGISH LAKE

TESLIN LAKE

ATLIN

MOUNT
NESSELRODE
2 470

TULSEQUAH

LOWER POST

CASSIAR

TESLIN

LIARD

STIKINE

MOUNT
RATZ
3 136

TELEGRAPH
CREEK

KATES NEEDLE
3 049

STEWART

FORT NELSON

MOUNT SMYTHE
2 987

NASS

CAPE KNOX

CAPE SANTRANCE

DIXON ENTRANCE

QUEEN CHARLOTTE ISLANDS

HECATE STRAIT

DRIFTWOOD

SKEENA

HAZELTON

TAHLA LAKE

WILLISTON LAKE

FORT ST. JOHN

PRINCE RUPERT

TERRACE

KITIMAT

BABINE LAKE

DAWSON CREEK

TUMBLER RIDGE

ALBERTA

BURNS LAKE

STUART LAKE

FORT ST. JAMES

FRANÇOIS LAKE

PEACE

CAPE SAINT JAMES

*NÉCHAKO
RESERVOIR*

OCEAN
FALLS

SUMMIT LAKE

PRINCE GEORGE

*QUEEN CHARLOTTE
SOUND*

MONARCH MOUNTAIN
3 533

QUESNEL

MOUNT
ROBSON
3 954

EDMONTON

QUEEN CHARLOTTE STRAIT

FRASER

MOUNT WADDINGTON
3 994

PLATEAU

FRASER

QUESNEL LAKE

WILLIAMS LAKE

KINBASKET LAKE

MOUNT
COLUMBIA
3 747

CAPE SCOTT

BEAR COVE

GOOD HOPE MOUNTAIN
3 240

CLINTON

COLUMBIA

CAPE HOOK

PORT
ALICE

SHUSHWAP LAKE

GOLDEN

CALGARY

PACIFIC OCEAN

CAMPBELL
RIVER

LILLOOET

COURTNEY

POWELL RIVER

KAMLOOPS

VANCOUVER ISLAND

PORT
ALBERNI

VERNON

UPPER ARROW LAKE

STRAIT OF JUAN DE FUCA

NANAIMO

WEST VANCOUVER
VANCOUVER
BURNABY
NEW WESTMINSTER
CHILLIWACK
ABBOTSFORD

KELOWNA

OKANAGAN LAKE

LOWER ARROW LAKE

OAK
BAY

KOOTENEY LAKE

ESQUIMALT

PENTICTON

NELSON

CRANBROOK

VICTORIA

GRANDFORKS

TRAIL

SEATTLE

TACOMA

SPOKANE

OLYMPIA

MOUNTAINS

COAST MOUNTAINS

ROCKY MOUNTAINS

UNITED STATES

PORTLAND

SALEM

EUGENE

Official name:	British Colombia
Capital:	Victoria
Population:	3.7 million
Surface area:	948,000 km²
Currency:	Canadian Dollar
Language:	English

NORTHWEST TERRITORIES

BISTCHO LAKE

CAMERON HILLS

STEEN RIVER

MEANDER RIVER

CARIBOU MOUNTAINS

SLAVE

PEACE POINT

LAKE ATHABASCA

HIGH LEVEL

PEACE

FORT CHIPEWYAN

FORT VERMILION

LAKE CLAIRE

PEACE RIVER

FORT MACKAY

FORT McMURRAY

BRITISH COLUMBIA

LESSER SLAVE LAKE

PRIMROSE LAKE

GRANDE-PRAIRIE

SWAN HILLS

ATHABASCA

BEAVER

COLD LAKE

R
O
C
K
Y

WILLMORE WILDERNESS PROVINCIAL PARK

BARRHEAD

WESTLOCK

ST. PAUL

EDSON

ST. ALBERT

FORT SASKATCHEWAN

NORTH SASKATCHEWAN

SASKATCHEWAN

HINTON

SPRUCE-GROVE

EDMONTON

VEGREVILLE

DRAYTON VALLEY

SHERWOOD PARK

JASPER NATIONAL PARK

LEDUC

MOUNT ALBERTA 3 619

CAMROSE

MOUNT COLUMBIA 3 747

PONOKA

WAINWRIGHT

M
O
U
N
T
A
I
N
S

LACOMBE

RED DEER

STETTLER

BANFF NATIONAL PARK

INNISFAIL

OLDS

HANNA

BANFF

DRUMHELLER

SASKATOON

MOUNT ASSINIBOINE 3 618

CALGARY

BOW

BROOKS

FORT MACLEOD

TABER

MEDICINE HAT

PINCHER CREEK

LETHBRIDGE

CYPRESS HILLS

CARDSTON

Official name:	Alberta
Capital:	Edmonton
Population:	2.7 million
Surface area:	661,000 km²
Currency:	Canadian Dollar
Language:	English

UNITED STATES

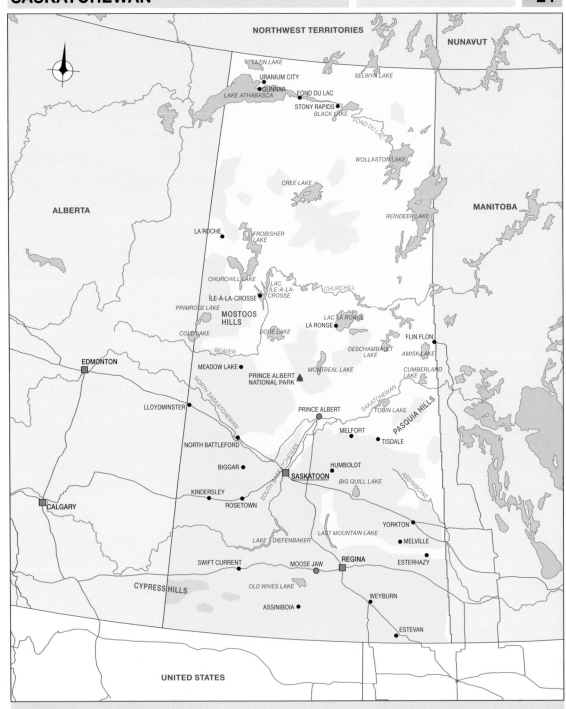

NORTHWEST TERRITORIES

NUNAVUT

TAZIN LAKE

SELWYN LAKE

URANIUM CITY

GUNNAR

FOND DU LAC

LAKE ATHABASCA

STONY RAPIDS

BLACK LAKE

FOND DU LAC

WOLLASTON LAKE

CREE LAKE

REINDEER LAKE

ALBERTA

MANITOBA

LA ROCHE

FROBISHER LAKE

CHURCHILL LAKE

LAC ÎLE-À-LA-CROSSE

CHURCHILL

ÎLE-À-LA-CROSSE

PRIMROSE LAKE

MOSTOOS HILLS

LAC LA RONGE

LA RONGE

COLD LAKE

DORE LAKE

BEAVER

DESCHAMBAULT LAKE

FLIN FLON

AMISK LAKE

EDMONTON

MEADOW LAKE

PRINCE ALBERT NATIONAL PARK

MONTREAL LAKE

CUMBERLAND LAKE

LLOYDMINSTER

NORTH SASKATCHEWAN

SASKATCHEWAN

TOBIN LAKE

PASQUIA HILLS

PRINCE ALBERT

MELFORT

NORTH BATTLEFORD

TISDALE

SOUTH SASKATCHEWAN

BIGGAR

HUMBOLDT

SASKATOON

ASSINIBOINE

BIG QUILL LAKE

KINDERSLEY

ROSETOWN

YORKTON

LAST MOUNTAIN LAKE

MELVILLE

LAKE DIEFENBAKER

CALGARY

SWIFT CURRENT

MOOSE JAW

REGINA

ESTERHAZY

CYPRESS HILLS

OLD WIVES LAKE

WEYBURN

ASSINIBOIA

ESTEVAN

UNITED STATES

Official name: Saskatchewan
Capital: Regina
Population: 1.0 million
Surface area: 652,000 km²
Currency: Canadian Dollar
Language: English

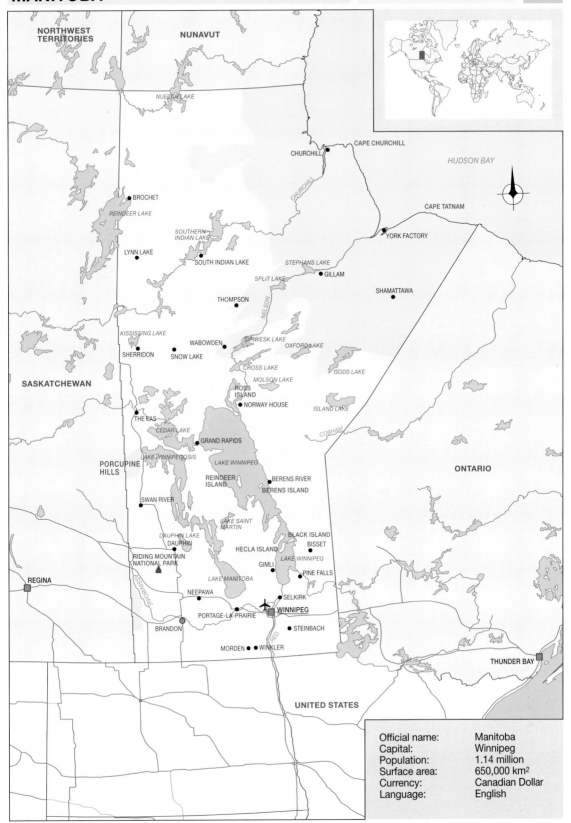

MANITOBA

SCALE 1 : 8 000 000

25

NORTHWEST TERRITORIES

NUNAVUT

NUELTIN LAKE

CAPE CHURCHILL

CHURCHILL

HUDSON BAY

CHURCHILL

CAPE TATNAM

BROCHET

REINDEER LAKE

YORK FACTORY

SOUTHERN INDIAN LAKE

LYNN LAKE

SOUTH INDIAN LAKE

STEPHANS LAKE

GILLAM

SPLIT LAKE

SHAMATTAWA

THOMPSON

NELSON

KISSISSING LAKE

WABOWDEN

SIPIWESK LAKE

OXFORD LAKE

SHERRIDON

SNOW LAKE

CROSS LAKE

GODS LAKE

SASKATCHEWAN

MOLSON LAKE

ROSS ISLAND

NORWAY HOUSE

ISLAND LAKE

THE PAS

CEDAR LAKE

COBHAM

GRAND RAPIDS

ONTARIO

LAKE WINNIPEGOSIS

LAKE WINNIPEG

PORCUPINE HILLS

REINDEER ISLAND

BERENS RIVER

BERENS ISLAND

SWAN RIVER

LAKE SAINT MARTIN

DAUPHIN LAKE

DAUPHIN

BLACK ISLAND

BISSET

HECLA ISLAND

LAKE WINNIPEG

RIDING MOUNTAIN NATIONAL PARK

GIMLI

PINE FALLS

REGINA

ASSINIBOINE

LAKE MANITOBA

NEEPAWA

SELKIRK

WINNIPEG

PORTAGE-LA-PRAIRIE

BRANDON

STEINBACH

RED

MORDEN

WINKLER

THUNDER BAY

UNITED STATES

Official name:	Manitoba
Capital:	Winnipeg
Population:	1.14 million
Surface area:	650,000 km²
Currency:	Canadian Dollar
Language:	English

ONTARIO

SCALE 1 : 10 800 000

Official name:	Ontario
Capital:	Toronto
Population:	10.8 million
Surface area:	1,069,000 km²
Currency:	Canadian Dollar
Language:	English

26

QUEBEC

HARTFORD

NEW YORK

ALBANY

ALLENTOWN

UNITED STATES

SYRACUSE

ROCHESTER

BUFFALO

ERIE

CLEVELAND

LAKE ONTARIO

QUEBEC

MONTREAL

CORNWALL

VANIER

BROCKVILLE

St. Lawrence

OTTAWA

KINGSTON

PETERBOROUGH

SCARBOROUGH

TORONTO

MISSISSAUGA

NIAGARA FALLS

HAMILTON

LONDON

WINDSOR

DETROIT

LANSING

PEMBROKE

MADAWASKA HIGHLANDS

NORTH BAY

LAKE NIPISSING

BARRIE

NORTH YORK

ETOBICOKE

WATERLOO

KITCHENER

STRATFORD

CHATHAM

SARNIA

ORILLIA

MIDLAND

OWEN SOUND

LAKE SIMCOE

GEORGIAN BAY

MANITOULIN ISLAND

BRUCE PENINSULA NATIONAL PARK

LAKE HURON

LAKE ERIE

MILWAUKEE

CAPREOL

SUDBURY

BLIND RIVER

ELLIOT LAKE

SAULT SAINTE MARIE

KIRKLAND LAKE

TIMMINS

NIGHT HAWK LAKE

LAKE ABITIBI

MATTAGAMI

HEARST

TIPTOP MOUNTAIN 640

PUKASKWA NATIONAL PARK

WAWA

MICHIPICOTEN ISLAND

LAKE SUPERIOR

MOOSONEE

JAMES BAY

AKIMISKI ISLAND

CAPE HENRIETTA MARIA

FORT ALBANY

ATTAWAPISKAT

ALBANY

HUDSON BAY

WINISK

MARATHON

SCHREIBER

BEARDMORE

GERALDTON

NAKINA

NIPIGON

RED ROCK

THUNDER BAY

LAKE NIPIGON

ARMSTRONG STATION

ATIKOKAN

DRYDEN

KENORA

FORT FRANCES

RAINY LAKE

SIOUX LOOKOUT

LAC SEUL

LAKE ST. JOSEPH

PICKLE CROW

NORTH CARIBOU LAKE

WUNNUMMIN LAKE

ATTAWAPISKAT LAKE

BIG TROUT LAKE

TROUT LAKE

RED LAKE

FORT SEVEN

SEVERN

WINNIPEG

LAKE OF THE WOODS

MANITOBA

UNITED STATES

MINNEAPOLIS

NUNAVUT

LABRADOR SEA

HUDSON STRAIT

CHARLES ISLAND

BUTTON ISLAND
KILLING ISLAND

CAPE HOPES ADVANCE

DIGGES ISLAND

SALLUIT   KANGIQSUJUAQ

AKPATOK ISLAND

IVUJIVIK

KANGIRSUK

UNGAVA BAY

MANSEL ISLAND

KANGIQSUATUJJUAQ

POVUNGNITUK   LAC PAYNE   KUUJJUAQ

CANIAPISCAU

LAC AUX GOÉLANDS

OTTAWA ISLANDS

INUKJUAK

LAC MINTO

SCHEFFERVILLE

NEW FOUNDLAND

HUDSON BAY

LAC GUILLAUME DELISLE

LAC À L'EAU CLAIRE

LAC BIENVILLE

ST.-AUGUSTIN -SAGUENAY

BELCHER ISLANDS

POSTE-DE-LA-BALEINE

GRANDE RIVIÈRE DE LA BALEINE

FERMONT

LONG ISLAND

LA GRANDE RIVIÈRE

GAGNON

HAVRE-ST.-PIERRE

DÉTROIT DE JACQUES-CARTIER

RÉSERVOIR MANICOUAGAN
MONT DE BABEL
957

ÎLE D'ANTICOSTI

DÉTROIT D'HONGUEDO

GULF OF ST. LAWRENCE

CHISASIBI

JAMES BAY

LAC SAKAMI

SEPT-ÎLES

ÎLES DE LA MADELEINE

PORT-CARTIER

GASPÉ

MANICOUAGAN

EASTMAIN

LAC MISTASSINI

PÉRIBONCA

HAUTERIVE

MATANE

PRINCE EDWARD ISLAND

WASKAGANISH

MISTASSINI

ST. LAWRENCE

RIMOUSKI

HARRICANA

CHIBOUGAMAU

CHICOUTIMI

ALMA   LA BAIE
JONQUIÈRE

RIVIÈRE-DU-LOUP

NEW BRUNSWICK

MATAGAMI

RÉSERVOIR GOUIN

LAC ST.-JEAN

BAIE-ST.-PAUL

ONTARIO

LA SARRE   AMOS
NORANDA
ROUYN

SENNETERRE

PARENT   LA TUQUE

BEAUFORT

MONTMAGNY

HALIFAX

QUÉBEC

RÉSERVOIR DOZOIS

TROIS-RIVIÈRES   THETFORD-MINES

NOVA SCOTIA

SOREL   DRUMMONDVILLE

MONT TREMBLANT

JOLIETTE

LAC KIPAWA

SAINT-JÉRÔME   LAVAL

GRANBY

MONTRÉAL

OTTAWA

SAINT-JEAN-SUR-RICHELIEU

HULL

SALABERRY- DE-VALLEYFIELD

OTTAWA

ATLANTIC OCEAN

UNITED STATES

Official name:	Quebec
Capital:	Quebec
Population:	7.1 million
Surface area:	1,541,000 km²
Currency:	Canadian Dollar
Languages:	English, French, Eskimo

NEW BRUNSWICK

SCALE 1 : 3 860 000

Official name:	New Brunswick
Capital:	Fredericton
Population:	0.7 million
Surface area:	73,000 km²
Currency:	Canadian Dollar
Language:	English

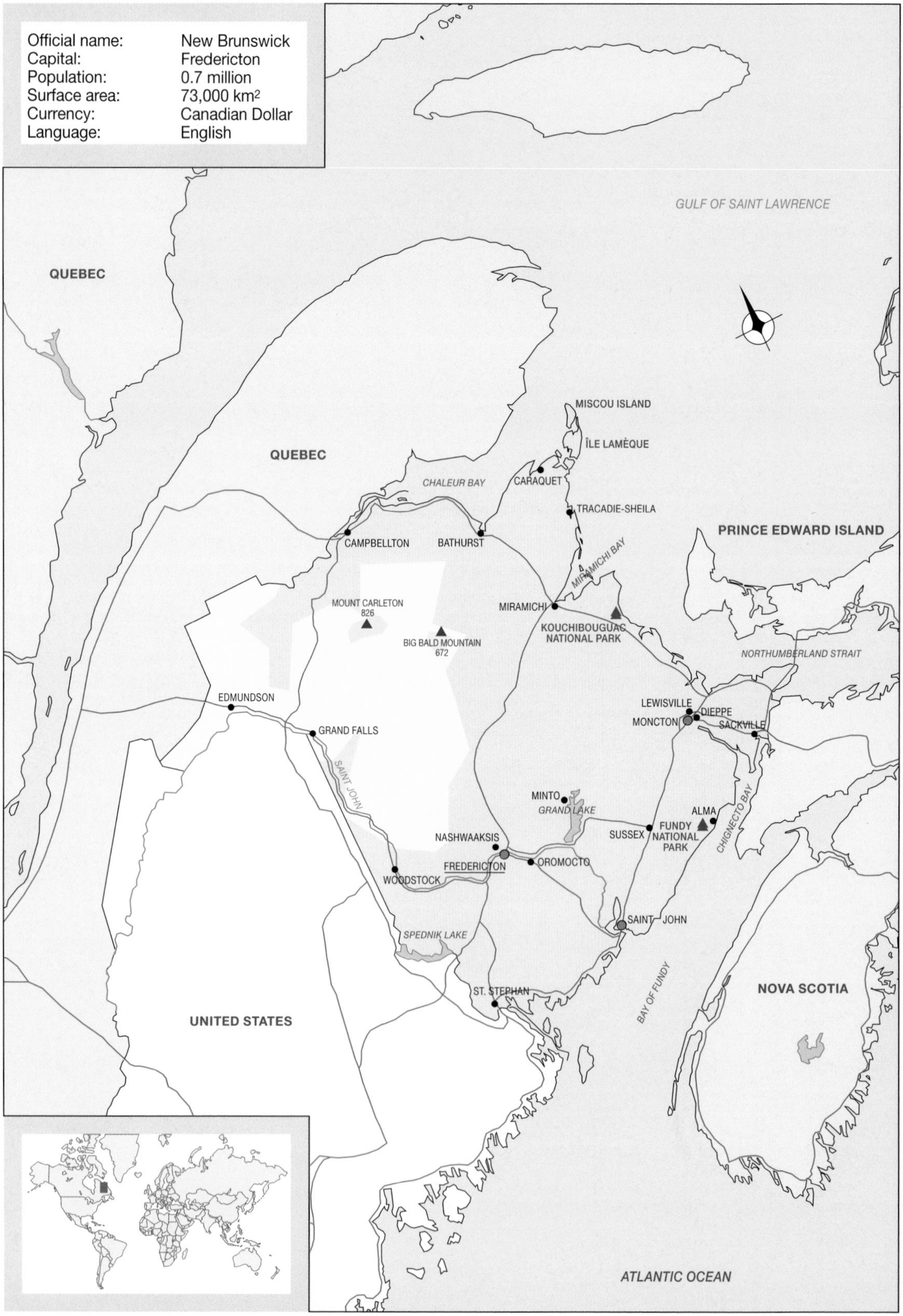

GULF OF SAINT LAWRENCE
QUEBEC
QUEBEC
MISCOU ISLAND
ÎLE LAMÈQUE
CARAQUET
CHALEUR BAY
TRACADIE-SHEILA
CAMPBELLTON
BATHURST
PRINCE EDWARD ISLAND
MIRAMICHI BAY
MIRAMICHI
MOUNT CARLETON
826
BIG BALD MOUNTAIN
672
KOUCHIBOUGUAC
NATIONAL PARK
NORTHUMBERLAND STRAIT
EDMUNDSON
GRAND FALLS
LEWISVILLE
DIEPPE
MONCTON
SACKVILLE
SAINT JOHN
MINTO
GRAND LAKE
ALMA
SUSSEX
FUNDY
NATIONAL
PARK
CHIGNECTO BAY
NASHWAAKSIS
FREDERICTON
OROMOCTO
WOODSTOCK
SAINT JOHN
SPEDNIK LAKE
ST. STEPHAN
BAY OF FUNDY
NOVA SCOTIA
UNITED STATES
ATLANTIC OCEAN

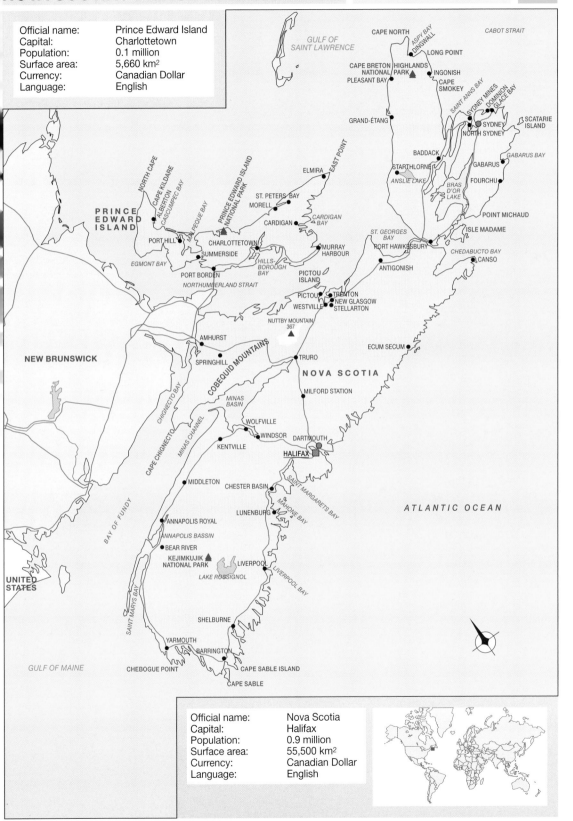

Official name: Prince Edward Island
Capital: Charlottetown
Population: 0.1 million
Surface area: 5,660 km²
Currency: Canadian Dollar
Language: English

GULF OF SAINT LAWRENCE

CAPE NORTH
ASPY BAY
DINGWALL
LONG POINT
CABOT STRAIT

CAPE BRETON HIGHLANDS
NATIONAL PARK
PLEASANT BAY
INGONISH
CAPE SMOKEY

SAINT ANNS BAY
SYDNEY MINES
DOMINION
GLACE BAY
NORTH SYDNEY
SYDNEY
SCATARIE ISLAND

GRAND-ÉTANG

BADDACK
GABARUS BAY

STARTHLORNE
ANSLIE LAKE
BRAS D'OR LAKE
GABARUS
FOURCHU

NORTH CAPE
CAPE KILDARE
CASCUMPEC BAY
ALBERTON

ELMIRA
EAST POINT

ST. PETERS BAY
MORELL

POINT MICHAUD

PRINCE EDWARD ISLAND

PRINCE EDWARD ISLAND NATIONAL PARK

CARDIGAN
CARDIGAN BAY

ST. GEORGES BAY

ISLE MADAME

MALPEQUE BAY
PORT HILL
CHARLOTTETOWN
PORT HAWKESBURY
CHEDABUCTO BAY
CANSO

SUMMERSIDE
MURRAY HARBOUR

EGMONT BAY
HILLS-BOROUGH BAY
PICTOU ISLAND
ANTIGONISH

PORT BORDEN
NORTHUMBERLAND STRAIT

PICTOU
TRENTON
NEW GLASGOW
WESTVILLE
STELLARTON

NUTTBY MOUNTAIN
367

AMHURST

NEW BRUNSWICK

ECUM SECUM

SPRINGHILL
COBEQUID MOUNTAINS
TRURO

NOVA SCOTIA

CHIGNECTO BAY
MILFORD STATION

CAPE CHIGNECTO
MINAS CHANNEL
MINAS BASIN

WOLFVILLE
WINDSOR
DARTMOUTH
KENTVILLE
HALIFAX

SAINT MARGARETS BAY

ATLANTIC OCEAN

MIDDLETON
CHESTER BASIN
MAHONE BAY

BAY OF FUNDY
LUNENBURG

ANNAPOLIS ROYAL
ANNAPOLIS BASSIN
BEAR RIVER
KEJIMKUJIK NATIONAL PARK
LAKE ROSSIGNOL
LIVERPOOL
LIVERPOOL BAY

UNITED STATES

SAINT MARYS BAY

SHELBURNE

YARMOUTH
BARRINGTON
CHEBOGUE POINT
CAPE SABLE ISLAND
CAPE SABLE

GULF OF MAINE

Official name: Nova Scotia
Capital: Halifax
Population: 0.9 million
Surface area: 55,500 km²
Currency: Canadian Dollar
Language: English

ST. PIERRE-ET-MIQUELON

Official name:	Saint-Pierre-et-Miquelon
Capital:	Saint-Pierre
Population:	6,392
Surface area:	242 km²
Currency:	French Franc
Language:	French

NEWFOUNDLAND

SCALE 1 : 9 820 000

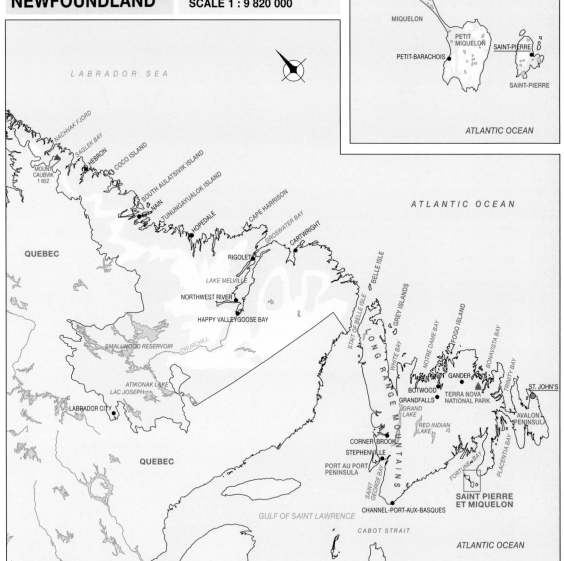

Official name:	Newfoundland
Capital:	St. John's
Population:	0.6 million
Surface area:	406,000 km²
Currency:	Canadian Dollar
Languages:	English, French

UNITED STATES OF AMERICA/ states

SCALE 1 : 23 600 000

MAINE (ME)

NEW HAMPSHIRE (NH)

MASSACHUSETTS (MA)

RHODE ISLAND (RI)

CONNECTICUT (CT)

NEW JERSEY (NJ)

DELAWARE (DE)

MARYLAND (MD)

WASHINGTON D.C.

VERMONT (VT)

NEW YORK (NY)

PENNSYLVANIA (PA)

VIRGINIA (VA)

WEST VIRGINIA (WV)

NORTH CAROLINA (NC)

SOUTH CAROLINA (SC)

FLORIDA (FL)

OHIO (OH)

KENTUCKY (KY)

GEORGIA (GA)

INDIANA (IN)

TENNESSEE (TN)

ALABAMA (AL)

MICHIGAN (MI)

ILLINOIS (IL)

MISSISSIPPI (MS)

WISCONSIN (WI)

MISSOURI (MO)

ARKANSAS (AR)

LOUISIANA (LA)

MINNESOTA (MN)

IOWA (IA)

OKLAHOMA (OK)

NORTH DAKOTA (ND)

SOUTH DAKOTA (SD)

NEBRASKA (NE)

KANSAS (KS)

TEXAS (TX)

MONTANA (MT)

WYOMING (WY)

COLORADO (CO)

NEW MEXICO (NM)

IDAHO (ID)

UTAH (UT)

ARIZONA (AZ)

WASHINGTON (WA)

OREGON (OR)

NEVADA (NV)

CALIFORNIA (CA)

PUERTO RICO (PR)

HAWAII (HI)

ALASKA (AK)

UNITED STATES OF AMERICA

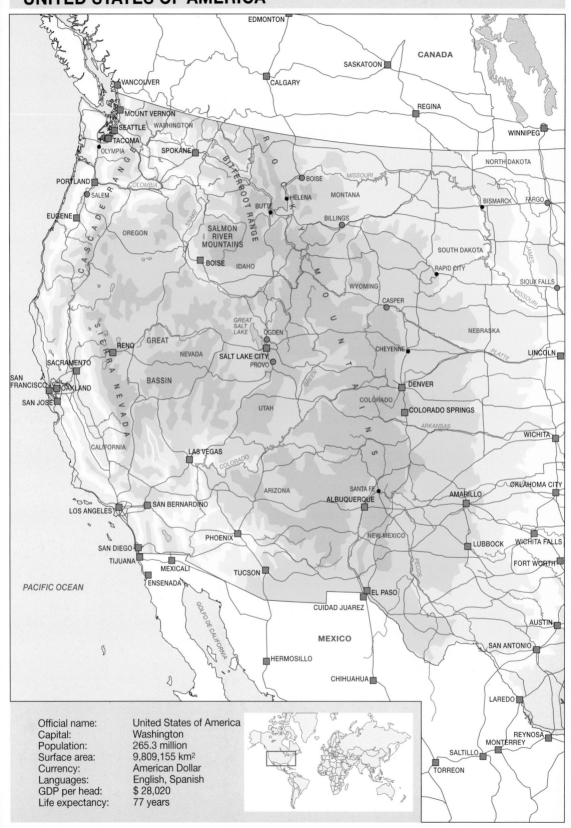

Official name:	United States of America
Capital:	Washington
Population:	265.3 million
Surface area:	9,809,155 km²
Currency:	American Dollar
Languages:	English, Spanish
GDP per head:	$ 28,020
Life expectancy:	77 years

RUSSIA

BERING SEA

CHUKCHI SEA

ARTIC OCEAN

RAT ISLANDS

A L E U T I A N   I S L A N D S

ADAK ISLAND
ADAK

ATKA ISLAND

AMLIA ISLAND

ISLANDS OF FOUR
MOUNTAINS

UMNAK ISLAND

UNALASKA ISLAND

UNIMAK ISLAND

SANAK ISLANDS

COLD BAY
PORT MOLLER

SHUMAGIN
ISLANDS

PACIFIC OCEAN

SAINT MATTHEW
ISLAND

SAINT LAWRENCE
ISLAND

BERING STRAIT

PRIBILOF
ISLAND

NUNIVAK
ISLAND

KUSKOKWIM
BAY

BETHEL

TIKCHIK LAKES

BRISTOL
BAY

ILIAMNA LAKE

LAKE CLARK

SHELIKOF STRAIT

AKHIOK

KODIAK

KODIAK ISLAND

NOME

NORTON SOUND

YUKON

UNALAKLEET

NULATO

KOZEBUE SOUND

LEDYARD BAY

KOYUKUK

YUKON

ALASKA   RANGE

MOUNT
McKINLEY
6 194

DENALI
NATIONAL
PARK

COLLEGE

WILLOW

KENAI

COOK INLET

PALMER
ANCHORAGE

STEWART

VALDEZ

CORDOVA

FAIRBANKS

NORTH POLE

BIG DELTA

TANANA

GATES OF THE ARTIC
NATIONAL PARK

B R O O K S   R A N G E

MEADE

TESHEKPUK
LAKE

COLVILLE

NOATAK

KOBUK

BARROW

KAKTOVIK

BEAUFORT SEA

FORT YUKON

PORCUPINE

YUKON

WRANGLER
MOUNTAINS

WRANGLER SAINT ELIAS NATIONAL PARK

MOUNT LOGAN
5 951

MOUNT VANCOUVER
4 785

MOUNT SEATTLE
3 069

GULF OF ALASKA

SKAGWAY

CHICHAGOF
ISLAND

MOUNT EDGECUMBE
SITKA

BARANOF ISLAND

ALEXANDER ARCHIPELAGO

PRINCE OF WALES
ISLAND

JUNEAU

PETERSBURG

METLAKATLAG

CANADA

Official name:	Alaska
Capital:	Juneau
Population:	0.6 million
Surface area:	1,700,138 km²
Currency:	American Dollar
Language:	English

WASHINGTON

SCALE 1 : 3 660 000

Official name:	Washington
Capital:	Olympia
Population:	5.5 million
Surface area:	184,672 km²
Currency:	American Dollar
Language:	English

MONTANA

IDAHO

PEND OREILLE

MOUNT SPOKANE
STATE PARK

VERADALE

OPPORTUNITY

SPOKANE

CHENEY

PULLMAN

CLARKSTON

FRANKLIN D. ROOSEVELT LAKE

COLUMBIA

SPOKANE

SNAKE

WALLA WALLA

CANADA

COLUMBIA

MOSES LAKE

POTHOLES RESERVOIR

COLUMBIA
BASIN

PASCO

RICHLAND

KENNEWICK

LAKE WALLULA

MOUNT LAGO
2 665

JACK MOUNTAIN
2 785

SILVER STAR MOUNTAIN
2 705

LAKE CHELAN

WENATCHEE

EPHRATA

SUNNYSIDE

GRANDVIEW

COLUMBIA

ELDORADO PEAK
2 703

MOUNT LOGAN
2 770

ELLENSBURG

YAKIMA

TOPPENISH

GOLDENDALE

YAKIMA

MOUNT SHUKSAN
2 782

ROSS LAKE

MOUNT BAKER
3 285

GLACIER PEAK
3 213

SKAGIT

R A N G E

C A S C A D E

BELLINGHAM

SEDRO
WOOLLEY

MOUNT VERNON

EVERETT

LYNNWOOD

EDMONDS

SHORELINE

REDMOND

KIRKLAND

BELLEVUE

RENTON

KENT

AUBURN

ENUMCLAW

MT. RANIER
NATIONAL PARK

MOUNT RAINIER
4 392

MOUNT ST HELENS
2 510

VANCOUVER

SAN JUAN
ISLANDS

ANACORTES

OAK HARBOR

WHIDBY ISLAND

PUGET SOUND

SEATTLE

BURIEN

TACOMA

LACEY

CENTRALIA

CHEHALIS

BEACON ROCK
STATE PARK

VANCOUVER

PORTLAND

OREGON

VICTORIA

STRAIT OF JUAN DE FUCA

PORT ANGELES

MOUNT OLYMPUS
2 428

OLYMPIC
NATIONAL
PARK

OLYMPIC MOUNTAINS

BREMERTON

SHELTON

OLYMPIA

COWLITZ

LONGVIEW

KELSO

CAPE FLATTERY

CAPE ALAVA

POINT BROWN

GRAYS HARBOR

HOQUIAM

ABERDEEN

WILLAPA BAY

RAYMOND

LEADBETTER POINT

ILWACO

CAPE DISAPPOINTMENT

PACIFIC OCEAN

OREGON

SCALE 1 : 4 950 000

Official name:	Oregon
Capital:	Salem
Population:	3.2 million
Surface area:	254,819 km²
Currency:	American Dollar
Language:	English

IDAHO

■ BOISE

SPOKANE

WASHINGTON

NEVADA

CALIFORNIA

COLUMBIA PLATEAU

BLUE MOUNTAINS

COLUMBIA

CASCADE RANGE

HARNEY BASSIN

PAULINA MOUNTAINS

SACAJAWEA PEAK ▲ 2 997

STRAWBERRY MOUNTAIN ▲ 2 755

PUEBLO MOUNTAIN ▲ 2 831

WARNER PEAK ▲ 2 444

CRANE MOUNTAIN 2 577

DRAKE PEAK ▲ 2 562

GEARHART MOUNTAIN 2 549

MOUNT McLOUGHLIN 2 894

THREE SISTERS 3 157

MALHEUR LAKE

HARVEY LAKE

WICKIUP RESERVOIR

GOOSE LAKE

CRATER LAKE

UPPER KLAMATH LAKE

SPRAGUE

KLAMATH

WILLAMETTE

UMPQUA

COLUMBIA

SNAKE

LA GRANDE

BAKER CITY

ONTARIO

NYSSA

MILTON-FREEWATER

HERMISTON

PENDLETON

BURNS

LAKE VIEW

ALTAMONT

KLAMATH FALLS

THE DALLES

PRINEVILLE

REDMOND

BEND

COVE PALISADES STATE PARK

CRATER LAKE NATIONAL PARK

SILVER FALLS STATE PARK

PORTLAND

GRESHAM

ERROL HEIGHTS

MILWAUKIE

WOODBURN

FOUR CORNERS

LEBANON

ALBANY

SWEET HOME

SPRINGFIELD

EUGENE

SANTA CLARA

KEIZER

SALEM

WEST SLOPE

BEAVERTON

NEW BERG

HILLSBORO

McMINNVILLE

SAINT HELENS

TILLAMOOK

SEASIDE

ASTORIA

CORVALLIS

NEWPORT

TOLEDO

LINCOLN CITY

CAPE LOOKOUT

CAPE FALCON

COTTAGE GROVE

SUTHERLIN

ROSEBURG

GREEN

FLORENCE

REEDSPORT

NORTH BEND

COOS BAY

COQUILLE

MYRTLE POINT

CAPE ARAGO

GRANT PASS

MEDFORD

ASHLAND

CAPE BLANCO

CAPE SEBASTIAN

BROOKINGS

PACIFIC OCEAN

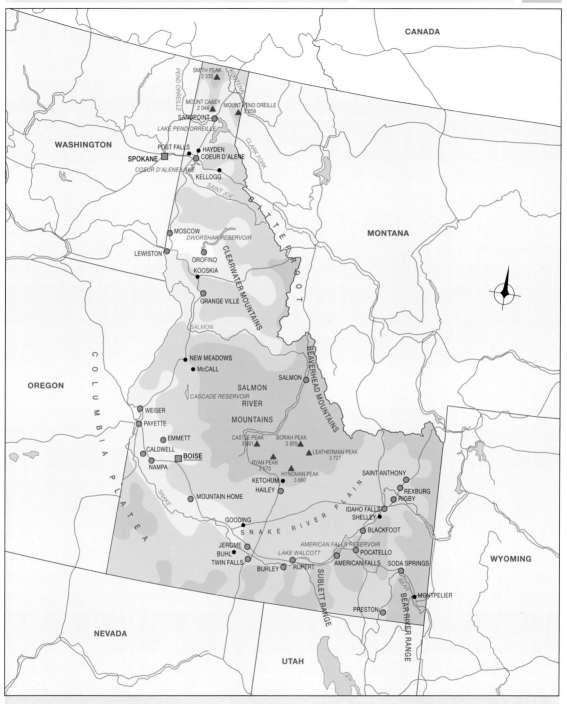

CANADA

SMITH PEAK
2 333 ▲

MOUNT CASEY
2 044 ▲
MOUNT PEND OREILLE
2 059 ▲
SANDPOINT ●

PEND OREILLE

LAKE PEND OREILLE

WASHINGTON

POST FALLS ■
HAYDEN ●
COEUR D'ALENE
SPOKANE ■

CLARK FORK

COEUR D'ALENE LAKE
KELLOGG ●

SAINT JOE

MONTANA

MOSCOW ●
DWORSHAK RESERVOIR

LEWISTON ●
OROFINO ●
KOOSKIA ●

CLEARWATER MOUNTAINS

BITTERROOT

GRANGE VILLE ●

SALMON

NEW MEADOWS ●
McCALL ●

SALMON ●

BEAVERHEAD MOUNTAINS

OREGON

SALMON
RIVER
MOUNTAINS

CASCADE RESERVOIR

COLUMBIA PLATEAU

WEISER ●
PAYETTE ●
EMMETT ●
CALDWELL ●
NAMPA ●
BOISE ■

CASTLE PEAK
3 401 ▲
BORAH PEAK
3 859 ▲
LEATHERMAN PEAK
3 727 ▲

RYAN PEAK
3 670 ▲
HYNDMAN PEAK
3 660 ▲
KETCHUM ●
HAILEY ●

SAINT ANTHONY ●
REXBURG ●
RIGBY ●

SNAKE

MOUNTAIN HOME ●

SNAKE RIVER PLAIN

IDAHO FALLS ●
SHELLEY ●

GOODING ●

BLACKFOOT ●

JEROME ●
BUHL ●
TWIN FALLS ●

AMERICAN FALLS RESERVOIR
LAKE WALCOTT

BURLEY ● RUPERT ●

AMERICAN FALLS ●

POCATELLO ●

SODA SPRINGS ●

SUBLETT RANGE

BEAR RIVER RANGE

MONTPELIER ●

PRESTON ●

WYOMING

NEVADA

UTAH

Official name:	Idaho
Capital:	Boise
Population:	1.2 million
Surface area:	216,456 km²
Currency:	American Dollar
Language:	English

CANADA

WASHINGTON

NORTH DAKOTA

SOUTH DAKOTA

WYOMING

OREGON

IDAHO

SPOKANE

BOISE

LIBBY
WHITE FISH
KALISPELL
EVERGREEN
COLUMBIA FALLS
GLACIER NATIONAL PARK
FLATHEAD
FLATHEAD LAKE
CLARK FORK
CUT BANK
SHELBY
CONRAD
HAVRE
GREAT FALLS
MISSOURI
GLASGOW
FORT PECK LAKE
WOLF POINT
SIDNEY
MISSOURI
GLENDIVE
MAKOSHIKA STATE PARK
BAKER
MILES CITY
YELLOWSTONE
MEDICINE ROCK STATE PARK
COLSTRIP
ROUNDUP
LEWISTOWN
LITTLE BELT MOUNTAINS
BIG BELST MOUNTAINS
CRAZY MOUNTAINS
MISSOULA
CLARK FORK
BITTERROOT
EL CAPITAN 3 043
MOUNT HAGGIN 3 233
TRAPPER PEAK 3 096
FLORAL PARK
ANACONDA
DEER LODGE
HELENA
CANYON FERRY LAKE
BUTTE
JEFFERSON
BELGRADE
BOZEMAN
LEWIS AND CLARCK CAVERN STATE PARK
LIVINGSTON
ABSAROKA RANGE
KOCH PEAK 3 440
TWEEDY MOUNTAIN 3 400
DILLON
HOMER YOUNGS PEAK 3 237
GARFIELD MOUNTAIN 3 341
BILLINGS
LAUREL
YELLOWSTONE
HARDIN
BIGHORN
R O C K Y   M O U N T A I N S

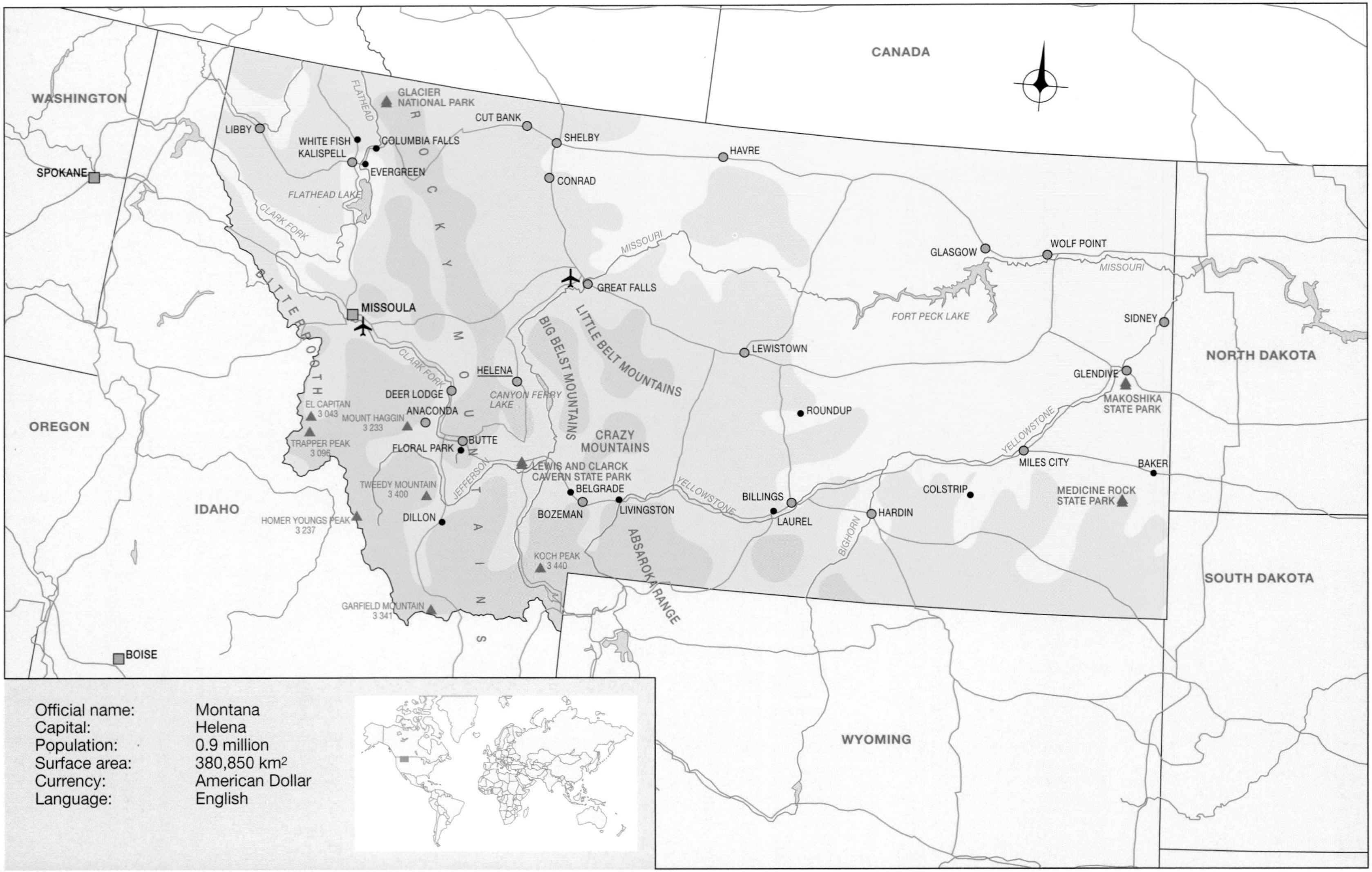

Official name:	Montana
Capital:	Helena
Population:	0.9 million
Surface area:	380,850 km²
Currency:	American Dollar
Language:	English

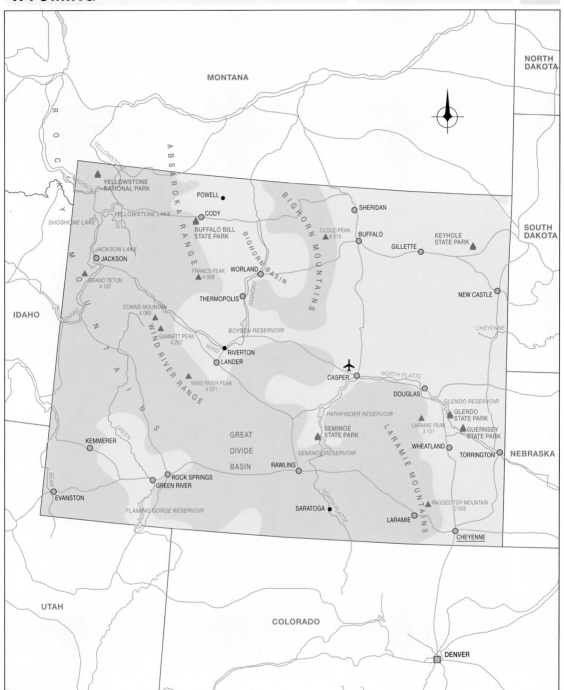

MONTANA

NORTH DAKOTA

SOUTH DAKOTA

IDAHO

NEBRASKA

UTAH

COLORADO

ROCKY

YELLOWSTONE NATIONAL PARK

POWELL

CODY

SHERIDAN

CLOUD PEAK
4 013

BUFFALO

GILLETTE

KEYHOLE STATE PARK

YELLOWSTONE LAKE

SHOSHONE LAKE

BUFFALO BILL STATE PARK

A B S A R O K A   R A N G E

B I G H O R N   M O U N T A I N S

B I G H O R N   B A S I N

JACKSON LAKE

JACKSON

M A D I S O N

GRAND TETON
4 197

FRANCS PEAK
4 009

WORLAND

THERMOPOLIS

NEW CASTLE

CHEYENNE

BIGHORN

DOWNS MOUNTAIN
4 069

GANNETT PEAK
4 207

BOYSEN RESERVOIR

WIND

RIVERTON

LANDER

W I N D   R I V E R   R A N G E

WIND RIVER PEAK
4 021

CASPER

NORTH PLATTE

DOUGLAS

GLENDO RESERVOIR

GLENDO STATE PARK

PATHFINDER RESERVOIR

LARAMIE PEAK
3 131

GUERNSEY STATE PARK

SEMINOE STATE PARK

SEMINOE RESERVOIR

WHEATLAND

TORRINGTON

M O U N T A I N S

GREAT DIVIDE BASIN

SNAKE

GREEN

KEMMERER

RAWLINS

L A R A M I E   M O U N T A I N S

ROCK SPRINGS
GREEN RIVER

BEAR

EVANSTON

FLAMING GORGE RESERVOIR

SARATOGA

NORTH PLATTE

RAGGED TOP MOUNTAIN
2 505

LARAMIE

CHEYENNE

DENVER

Official name:	Wyoming
Capital:	Cheyenne
Population:	0.5 million
Surface area:	253,349 km²
Currency:	American Dollar
Language:	English

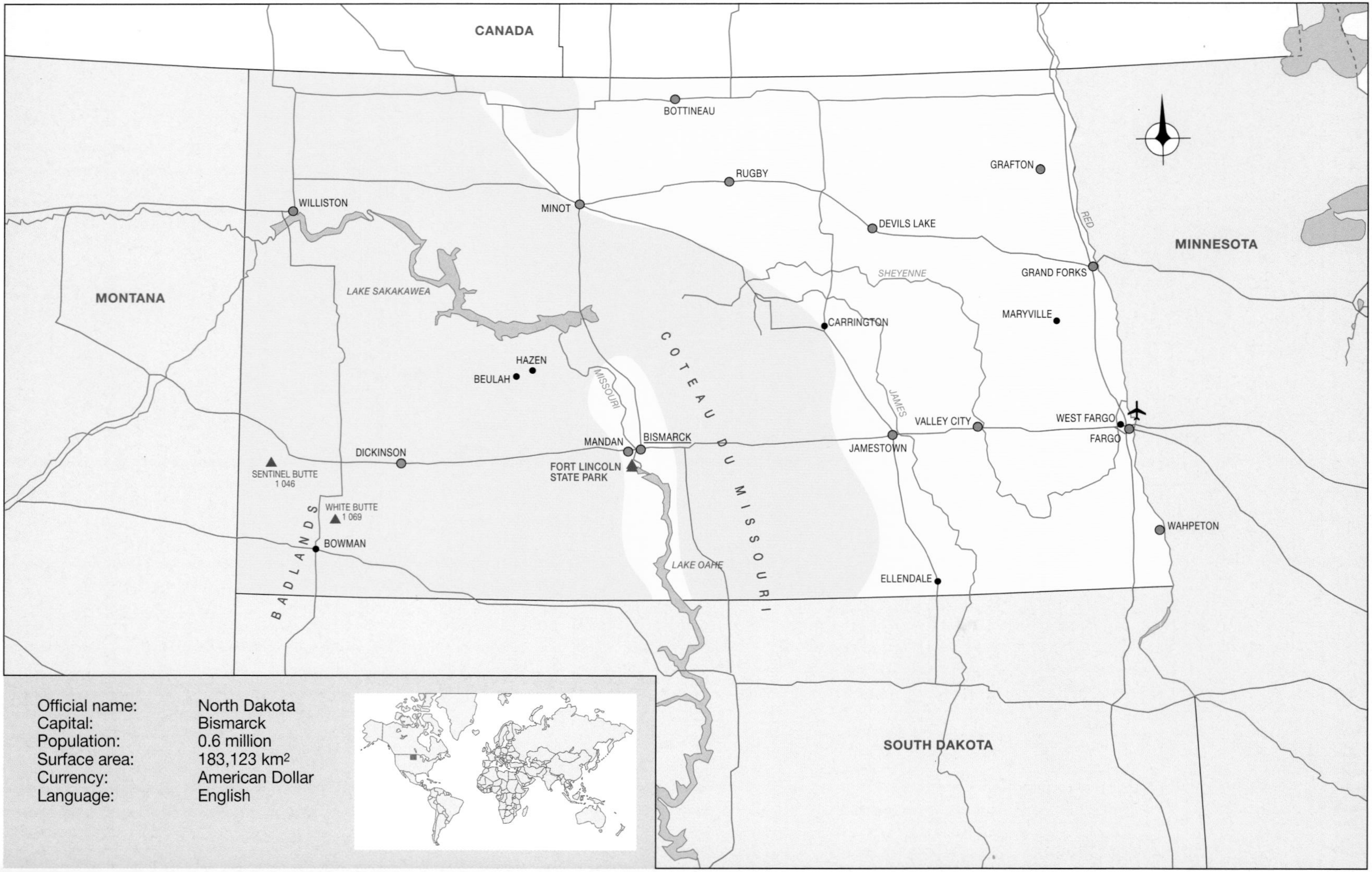

NORTH DAKOTA

SCALE 1 : 3 850 000

CANADA

MONTANA

MINNESOTA

SOUTH DAKOTA

WILLISTON

BOTTINEAU

RUGBY

MINOT

GRAFTON

DEVILS LAKE

GRAND FORKS

MARYVILLE

CARRINGTON

VALLEY CITY

WEST FARGO

FARGO

WAHPETON

JAMESTOWN

ELLENDALE

BISMARCK

MANDAN

FORT LINCOLN
STATE PARK

HAZEN

BEULAH

DICKINSON

WHITE BUTTE
1 069

BOWMAN

SENTINEL BUTTE
1 046

LAKE SAKAKAWEA

MISSOURI

LAKE OAHE

C O T E A U   D U   M I S S O U R I

B A D L A N D S

RED

SHEYENNE

JAMES

Official name: North Dakota
Capital: Bismarck
Population: 0.6 million
Surface area: 183,123 km²
Currency: American Dollar
Language: English

SOUTH DAKOTA

SCALE 1 : 3 850 000

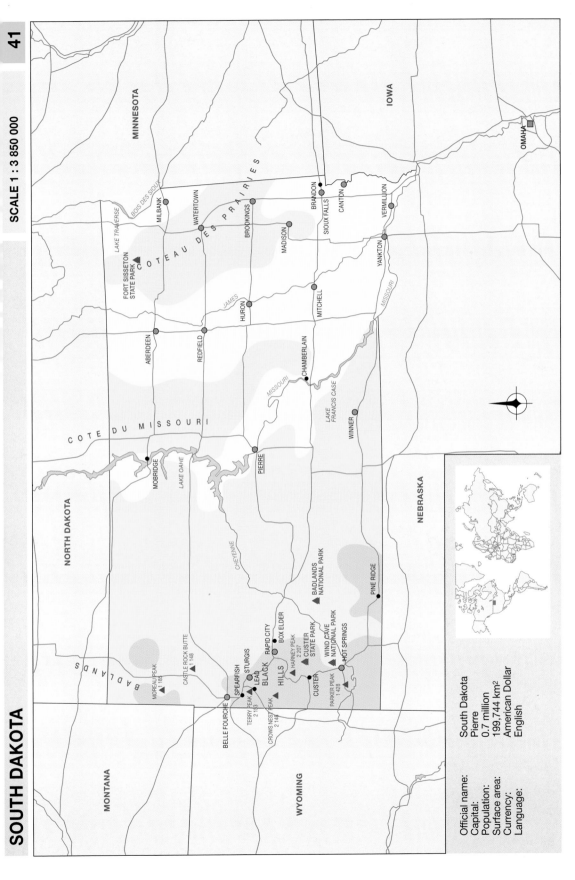

MONTANA

NORTH DAKOTA

MINNESOTA

WYOMING

NEBRASKA

IOWA

BADLANDS

COTE DU MISSOURI

COTEAU DES PRAIRIES

MOREAU PEAK 1 183

CASTLE ROCK BUTTE 1 148

MOBRIDGE

LAKE OAHE

CHEYENNE

BELLE FOURCHE

SPEARFISH

STURGIS
LEAD
TERRY PEAK 2 153
CROWS NEST PEAK 2 148

RAPID CITY
BOX ELDER
BLACK HILLS
HARNEY PEAK 2 207

CUSTER STATE PARK

CUSTER
PARKER PEAK 1 428
WIND CAVE NATIONAL PARK
HOT SPRINGS

BADLANDS NATIONAL PARK

PINE RIDGE

ABERDEEN

REDFIELD

HURON

JAMES

PIERRE

WINNER

LAKE FRANCIS CASE

CHAMBERLAIN

MISSOURI

FORT SISSETON STATE PARK

LAKE TRAVERSE

BOIS DES SIOUX

MILBANK

WATERTOWN

BROOKINGS

MADISON

MITCHELL

YANKTON

MISSOURI

BRANDON
SIOUX FALLS
CANTON
VERMILLION

OMAHA

Official name: South Dakota
Capital: Pierre
Population: 0.7 million
Surface area: 199,744 km²
Currency: American Dollar
Language: English

NEBRASKA

SCALE 1 : 3 960 000

IOWA

MISSOURI

KANSAS CITY

TOPEKA

BELLEVUE

OMAHA

BLAIR

FREMONT

PAPILLION

AUBURN

FALLS CITY

SIOUX CITY

WAYNE

WEST POINT

NEBRASKA CITY

LINCOLN

WAHOO

SCHUYLER

DAVID CITY

CRETE

NORFOLK

SEWARD

BEATRICE

FAIRBURY

COLUMBUS

YORK

MISSOURI

PLATTE

CENTRAL CITY

AURORA

HASTINGS

SUPERIOR

KANSAS

O'NEILL

GRAND ISLAND

KEARNEY

MINDEN

REPUBLICAN

BROKEN BOW

HOLDREGE

VALENTINE

AINSWORTH

GOTHENBURG

COZAD

LEXINGTON

THEDFORD

STAPLETON

NORTH PLATTE

McCOOK

SOUTH DAKOTA

S A N D   H I L L S

LAKE McCONAUGHY

OLGALLALA

CHADRON

ALLIANCE

SYDNEY

P I N E   R I D G E

FORT ROBINSON
STATE PARK

SCOTTSBLUFF

GERING

HOGBACK MOUNTAIN
1 543

KIMBALL

WYOMING

COLORADO

Official name:	Nebraska
Capital:	Lincoln
Population:	1.7 million
Surface area:	200,358 km²
Currency:	American Dollar
Language:	English

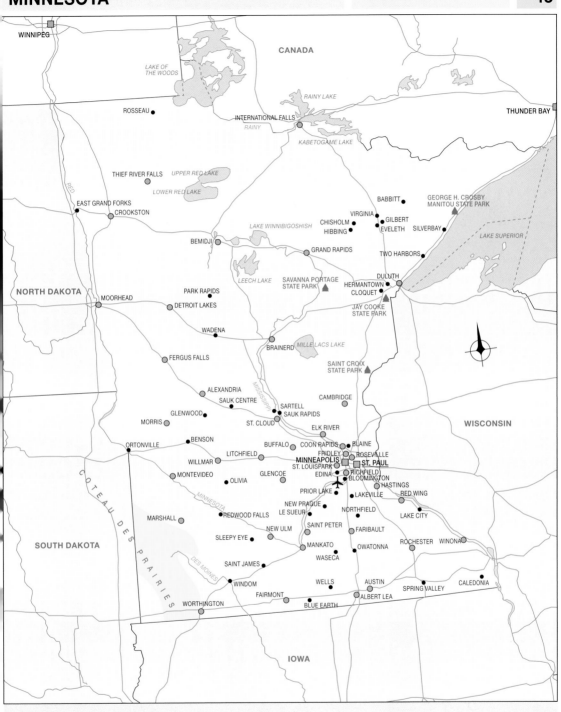

WINNIPEG

CANADA

LAKE OF
THE WOODS

RAINY LAKE

ROSSEAU

INTERNATIONAL FALLS

THUNDER BAY

RAINY

KABETOGAME LAKE

THIEF RIVER FALLS

UPPER RED LAKE

LOWER RED LAKE

BABBITT

GEORGE H. CROSBY
MANITOU STATE PARK

EAST GRAND FORKS

CROOKSTON

VIRGINIA

GILBERT

CHISHOLM

HIBBING

EVELETH

SILVERBAY

LAKE WINNIBIGOSHISH

LAKE SUPERIOR

BEMIDJI

GRAND RAPIDS

TWO HARBORS

RED

NORTH DAKOTA

MOORHEAD

LEECH LAKE

SAVANNA PORTAGE
STATE PARK

DULUTH

HERMANTOWN

CLOQUET

PARK RAPIDS

DETROIT LAKES

JAY COOKE
STATE PARK

WADENA

BRAINERD

MILLE LACS LAKE

FERGUS FALLS

SAINT CROIX
STATE PARK

MISSISSIPPI

ALEXANDRIA

CAMBRIDGE

SAUK CENTRE

SARTELL

GLENWOOD

SAUK RAPIDS

MORRIS

ST. CLOUD

WISCONSIN

ELK RIVER

ORTONVILLE

BENSON

BUFFALO

COON RAPIDS

BLAINE

LITCHFIELD

FRIDLEY

ROSEVILLE

WILLMAR

MINNEAPOLIS

ST. PAUL

MONTEVIDEO

GLENCOE

ST. LOUISPARK

EDINA

RICHFIELD

OLIVIA

BLOOMINGTON

HASTINGS

MINNESOTA

PRIOR LAKE

LAKEVILLE

RED WING

NEW PRAGUE

LE SUEUR

NORTHFIELD

LAKE CITY

REDWOOD FALLS

MARSHALL

SAINT PETER

FARIBAULT

NEW ULM

SLEEPY EYE

MANKATO

OWATONNA

ROCHESTER

WINONA

SAINT JAMES

WASECA

SOUTH DAKOTA

DES MOINES

WINDOM

WELLS

AUSTIN

SPRING VALLEY

CALEDONIA

FAIRMONT

ALBERT LEA

WORTHINGTON

BLUE EARTH

COTEAU DES PRAIRIES

IOWA

Official name: Minnesota
Capital: St. Paul
Population: 4.7 million
Surface area: 225,182 km²
Currency: American Dollar
Language: English

MINNEAPOLIS ST. PAUL

MINNESOTA

WISCONSIN

SOUTH DAKOTA

MADISON

CRESCO
DECORAH

SIBLEY
SPIRIT LAKE
ESTHERVILLE
FOREST CITY
OSAGE
NEW HAMPTON
SHELDON
EMMETSBURG
CLEAR LAKE
MASON CITY
WEST UNION
SPENCER
ALGONA
CHARLES CITY
SIOUX CENTER
BELMOND
WAVERLY
OELWIEN
DYERSVILLE
DUBUQUE
ORANGE CITY
HUMBOLDT
LE MARS
CEDAR FALLS
WATERLOO
MANCHESTER
CHEROKEE
INDEPENDENCE
MONTICELLO
STORM LAKE
IOWA FALLS
SIOUX CITY
ELDORA
MAQUOKETA
SAC CITY
FORT DODGE
VINTON
MARION
CLINTON
MOUNT VERNON
CARROLL
JEFFERSON
AMES
MARSHALLTOWN
CEDAR RAPIDS
TIPTON
ONAWA
DENISON
BOONE
DE WITT
BELLE PLAINE
DAVENPORT
AUDUBON
ANKENY
NEWTON
IOWA CITY
BETTENDORF
HARLAN
URBANDALE
WEST DES MOINES
DES MOINES
MUSCATINE
ATLANTIC
PELLA
WINTERSET
INDIANOLA
OSKALOOSA
WASHINGTON
OMAHA
KNOXVILLE
OTTUMWA
MOUNT PLEASANT
COUNCIL BLUFFS
FAIRFIELD
WEST BURLINGTON
NEBRASKA
RED OAK
OSCEOLA
CHARITON
BURLINGTON
CRESTON
AFTON
BLOOMFIELD
LINCOLN
CLARINDA
CENTERVILLE
FORT MADISON
KEOKUK
ILLINOIS

MISSISSIPPI
DES MOINES
MISSOURI
DES MOINES

MISSOURI

KANSAS

KANSAS CITY   KANSAS CITY

TOPEKA

ST. LOUIS

Official name:	Iowa
Capital:	Des Moines
Population:	2.9 million
Surface area:	145,754 km²
Currency:	American Dollar
Language:	English

WISCONSIN

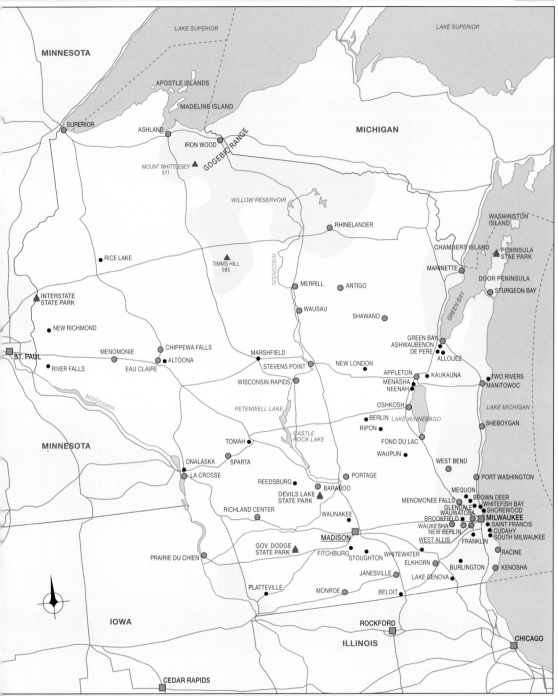

LAKE SUPERIOR

MINNESOTA

LAKE SUPERIOR

APOSTLE ISLANDS

MADELING ISLAND

MICHIGAN

SUPERIOR

ASHLAND

IRON WOOD

GOGEBIC RANGE

MOUNT WHITTLESEY
571

WASHINGTON
ISLAND

WILLOW RESERVOIR

RHINELANDER

CHAMBERS ISLAND

PENINSULA
STAE PARK

MARINETTE

RICE LAKE

TIMMS HILL
595

WISCONSIN

MERRILL

ANTIGO

DOOR PENINSULA

STURGEON BAY

WAUSAU

SHAWANO

INTERSTATE
STATE PARK

NEW RICHMOND

GREEN BAY

CHIPPEWA FALLS

MARSHFIELD

GREEN BAY
ASHWAUBENON
DE PERE

ALLOUEZ

ST. PAUL

MENOMONIE

ALTOONA

STEVENS POINT

NEW LONDON

APPLETON

KAUKAUNA

TWO RIVERS

MANITOWOC

RIVER FALLS

EAU CLAIRE

WISCONSIN RAPIDS

MENASHA
NEENAH

MISSISSIPPI

PETENWELL LAKE

OSHKOSH

LAKE WINNEBAGO

LAKE MICHIGAN

BERLIN

RIPON

SHEBOYGAN

MINNESOTA

CASTLE
ROCK LAKE

TOMAH

ONALASKA

SPARTA

LA CROSSE

REEDSBURG

PORTAGE

BARABOO

DEVILS LAKE
STATE PARK

FOND DU LAC

WAUPUN

WEST BEND

PORT WASHINGTON

MEQUON

MENOMONEE FALLS

BROWN DEER
WHITEFISH BAY
SHOREWOOD

RICHLAND CENTER

WAUNAKEE

GLENDALE
WAUWATOSA

MILWAUKEE

BROOKFIELD

SAINT FRANCIS

WAUKESHA

CUDAHY

NEW BERLIN

SOUTH MILWAUKEE

MADISON

WEST ALLIS

FRANKLIN

GOV. DODGE
STATE PARK

FITCHBURG

PRAIRIE DU CHIEN

STOUGHTON

WHITEWATER

ELKHORN

RACINE

JANESVILLE

LAKE GENOVA

BURLINGTON

KENOSHA

PLATTEVILLE

MONROE

BELOIT

IOWA

ROCKFORD

CHICAGO

ILLINOIS

CEDAR RAPIDS

Official name:	Wisconsin
Capital:	Madison
Population:	1.8 million
Surface area:	169,643 km²
Currency:	American Dollar
Language:	English

WISCONSIN

LAKE MICHIGAN

MICHIGAN

ZION
WAUKEGAN
NORTH CHICAGO
LAKE FOREST
HIGHLAND PARK
HARVARD
McHENRY
WOODSTOCK
DEERFIELD
WINNETKA
MACHESNEY PARK
WILMETTE
LOVES PARK
BELVIDERE
ARLINGTON
HEIGHTS
NILES
EVANSTON
FREEPORT
DES PLAINES
SKOKIE
ROCKFORD
ELGIN
ELMHURST
OAK PARK
CHICAGO
DE KALB
BERWYN
CICERO
NAPERVILLE
SOUTH BEND
AURORA
BLUE ISLAND
DIXON
SANDWICH
BOLLINGBROOK
OAK LAWN
CALDMET CITY
STERLING
HARVEY
ROCK FALLS
JOLIET
CHICAGO HEIGHTS
GARY
PARK FOREST

CEDAR RAPIDS

IOWA

MORRIS
BOURBONNAIS
DAVENPORT
EAST MOLINE
LA SALLE
BRADLEY
ROCK ISLAND
PERU
OTTAWA
MOLINE
KANKAKEE
KEWANEE
STREATOR
CHILLICOTHE
PONTIAC
WATSEKA
GALESBURG
MONMOUTH
PEORIA HEIGHTS
HOOPESTON
PEORIA
WASHINGTON
EAST PEORIA
NORMAL
MACOMB
CANTON
MORTON
BLOOMINGTON
RANTOUL
PEKIN
DANVILLE
CHAMPAIGN
INDIANA
URBANA
LINCOLN
CLINTON
MISSISSIPPI
LINCOLN'S NEW SALEM
STATE PARK
DECATUR
PARIS
BEARDSTOWN
SPRINGFIELD
TAYLORVILLE
CHARLESTON
QUINCY
MATTOON
JACKSONVILLE
PANA
EFFINGHAM
ROBINSON
VANDALIA
JERSEYVILLE

MISSOURI

OLNEY
ALTON
SALEM
FLORA
WOOD RIVER
GRANITE CITY
WABASH
ST. LOUIS
EAST ST. LOUIS
MOUNT CARMEL
CAHOKIA
CENTRALIA
FAIRFIELD
BELLEVILLE
EVANSVILLE
WATERLOO
MOUNT VERNON
CARMI
DU QUOIN
BENTON
WEST FRANKFORT
CHESTER
HERRIN
MURPHYSBORO
MARION
CARBONDALE
HARRISBURG
GIANT CITY
STATE PARK
KENTUCKY

Official name: Illinois
Capital: Springfield
Population: 11.8 million
Surface area: 150,007 km²
Currency: American Dollar
Language: English

CANADA

MINNESOTA

WISCONSIN

ILLINOIS

INDIANA

OHIO

LAKE SUPERIOR

LAKE HURON

LAKE MICHIGAN

LAKE ERIE

LAKE ST. CLAIR

GEORGIAN BAY

GREEN BAY

SAGINAW BAY

KEWEENAW BAY

KEWEENAW PENINSULA

ISLE ROYAL

ISLE ROYAL

SUGAR ISLAND

BOIS BLANC ISLAND

BEAVER ISLAND

STRAITS OF MACKINAC

TAMOUAMENON FALLS STATE PARK

PORCUPINE MOUNTAINS STATE PARK

WILDERNESS STATE PARK

HARTWICK PINES STATE PARK

IRONWOOD
HANCOCK
HOUGHTON
ISHPEMING
MARQUETTE
MUNISING
GRAND ISLE
GLADSTONE
ESCANABA
MANISTIQUE
MENOMINEE
SAULT SAINTE MARIE
ST. IGNACE
CHEBOYGAN
PETOSKEY
TRAVERSE CITY
CADILLAC
ALPENA
BIG RAPIDS
MOUNT PLEASANT
MANISTEE
LUDINGTON
MUSKEGON
MUSKEGON HEIGHTS
NORTON SHORES
GRAND HAVEN
HOLLAND
BENTON HARBOR
ST. JOSEPH
NILES
OTSEGO
PAW PAW
KALAMAZOO
THREE RIVERS
BATTLE CREEK
ALBION
COLDWATER
JACKSON
GRAND RAPIDS
EAST GRAND RAPIDS
WYOMING
HOLT
LANSING
EAST LANSING
ANN ARBOR
ADRIAN
MONROE
ALMA
OWOSSO
SAGINAW
MIDLAND
BAY CITY
CARO
BRIDGEPORT
BURTON
FLINT
PONTIAC
WARREN
ROYAL OAK
MOUNT CLEMENS
ROSEVILLE
DETROIT
WINDSOR
DEARBORN
LIVONIA
LINCOLN PARK
SOUTH GATE
WYANDOTTE
PORT HURON
TOLEDO
ERIE
CLEVELAND
AKRON
YOUNGSTOWN
LONDON
KITCHENER
HAMILTON
MISSISSAUGA
ETOBICOKE
TORONTO
NORTH YORK
SCARBOROUGH
MILWAUKEE
CHICAGO
GARY
ROCKFORD

Official name: Michigan
Capital: Lansing
Population: 9.6 million
Surface area: 250,465 km²
Currency: American Dollar
Language: English

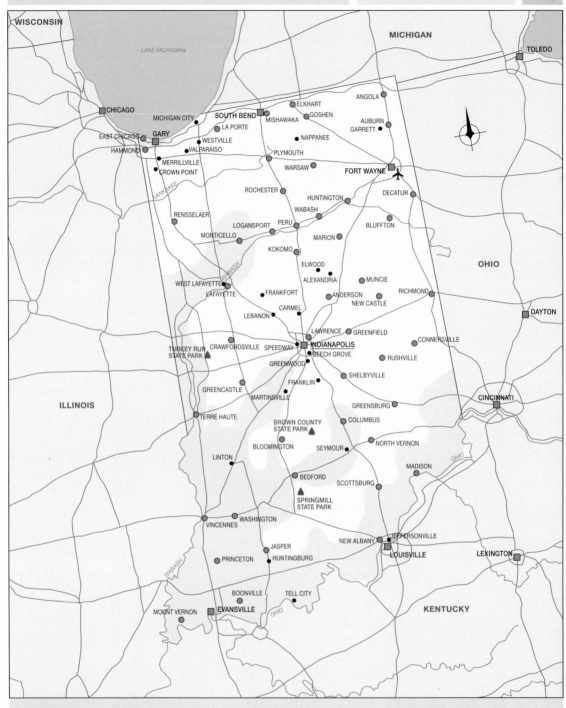

WISCONSIN
MICHIGAN

Lake MICHIGANa

TOLEDO

CHICAGO

ELKHART
ANGOLA
MICHIGAN CITY
SOUTH BEND
GOSHEN
AUBURN
MISHAWAKA
GARRETT
LA PORTE
EAST CHICAGO
WESTVILLE
NAPPANEE
GARY
VALPARAISO
HAMMOND
PLYMOUTH
MERRILLVILLE
WARSAW
FORT WAYNE
CROWN POINT
ROCHESTER
HUNTINGTON
DECATUR

KANKAKEE
RENSSELAER
WABASH
PERU
BLUFFTON
LOGANSPORT
MONTICELLO
MARION
OHIO
KOKOMO

WEST LAFAYETTE
ELWOOD
ALEXANDRIA
MUNCIE
LAFAYETTE
FRANKFORT
ANDERSON
RICHMOND
CARMEL
NEW CASTLE
LEBANON
LAWRENCE
GREENFIELD
CONNERSVILLE
TURKEY RUN
STATE PARK
CRAWFORDSVILLE
SPEEDWAY
INDIANAPOLIS
BEECH GROVE
RUSHVILLE
GREENWOOD

ILLINOIS
GREENCASTLE
FRANKLIN
SHELBYVILLE
MARTINSVILLE
GREENSBURG
CINCINNATI
TERRE HAUTE
COLUMBUS
DAYTON
BROWN COUNTY
STATE PARK
BLOOMINGTON
SEYMOUR
NORTH VERNON
LINTON
MADISON
BEDFORD
OHIO
SCOTTSBURG
SPRINGMILL
STATE PARK
WASHINGTON
VINCENNES
NEW ALBANY
JEFFERSONVILLE
JASPER
LEXINGTON
PRINCETON
HUNTINGBURG
LOUISVILLE
WABASH
BOONVILLE
TELL CITY
MOUNT VERNON
EVANSVILLE
OHIO
KENTUCKY

Official name:	Indiana
Capital:	Indianapolis
Population:	5.8 million
Surface area:	94,328 km²
Currency:	American Dollar
Language:	English

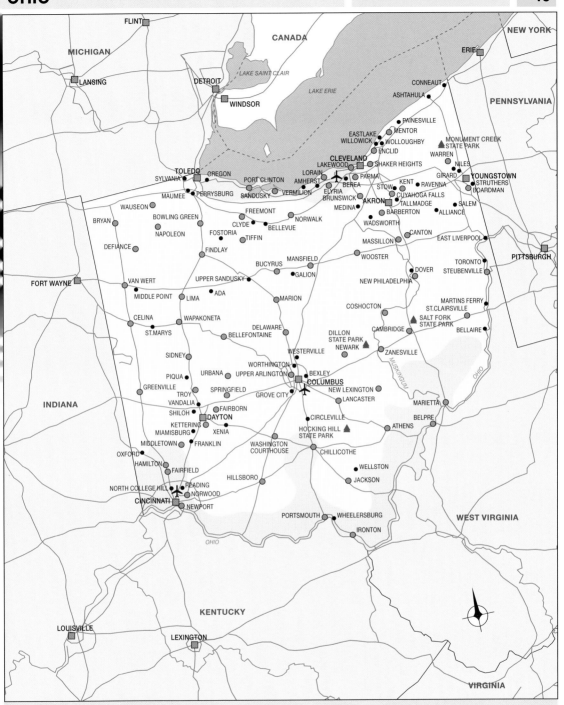

FLINT
MICHIGAN
LANSING
DETROIT
WINDSOR
Lake Saint Clair
Lake Erie
CANADA
NEW YORK
ERIE
PENNSYLVANIA
CONNEAUT
ASHTABULA
PAINESVILLE
MENTOR
EASTLAKE
WILLOWICK
WOLLOUGHBY
ENCLID
MONUMENT CREEK
STATE PARK
WARREN
NILES
CLEVELAND
LAKEWOOD
SHAKER HEIGHTS
GIRARD
YOUNGSTOWN
TOLEDO
OREGON
LORAIN
AMHERST
PARMA
KENT
RAVENNA
STRUTHERS
BOARDMAN
SYLVANIA
PORT CLINTON
VERMILION
ELYRIA
BEREA
STOW
CUYAHOGA FALLS
SALEM
MAUMEE
PERRYSBURG
SANDUSKY
BRUNSWICK
AKRON
TALLMADGE
ALLIANCE
WAUSEON
FREEMONT
MEDINA
BARBERTON
BRYAN
BOWLING GREEN
NORWALK
WADSWORTH
CANTON
EAST LIVERPOOL
NAPOLEON
CLYDE
BELLEVUE
FOSTORIA
TIFFIN
MASSILLON
TORONTO
PITTSBURGH
DEFIANCE
FINDLAY
WOOSTER
DOVER
STEUBENVILLE
BUCYRUS
MANSFIELD
NEW PHILADELPHIA
FORT WAYNE
VAN WERT
UPPER SANDUSKY
GALION
MARTINS FERRY
MIDDLE POINT
LIMA
ADA
MARION
COSHOCTON
ST.CLAIRSVILLE
SALT FORK
STATE PARK
BELLAIRE
CELINA
WAPAKONETA
CAMBRIDGE
ST.MARYS
DELAWARE
BELLEFONTAINE
DILLON
STATE PARK
NEWARK
ZANESVILLE
SIDNEY
WESTERVILLE
PIQUA
URBANA
WORTHINGTON
UPPER ARLINGTON
BEXLEY
MARIETTA
GREENVILLE
TROY
SPRINGFIELD
COLUMBUS
NEW LEXINGTON
BELPRE
VANDALIA
GROVE CITY
LANCASTER
SHILOH
FAIRBORN
DAYTON
CIRCLEVILLE
ATHENS
KETTERING
XENIA
HOCKING HILL
STATE PARK
MIAMISBURG
MIDDLETOWN
FRANKLIN
WASHINGTON
COURTHOUSE
OXFORD
CHILLICOTHE
HAMILTON
FAIRFIELD
HILLSBORO
WELLSTON
INDIANA
NORTH COLLEGE HILL
READING
JACKSON
CINCINNATI
NORWOOD
NEWPORT
PORTSMOUTH
WHEELERSBURG
WEST VIRGINIA
IRONTON
OHIO
KENTUCKY
LOUISVILLE
LEXINGTON
VIRGINIA
MUSKINGUM
OHIO

Official name:	Ohio
Capital:	Columbus
Population:	11.2 million
Surface area:	116,103 km²
Currency:	American Dollar
Language:	English

AKRON

PITTSBURGH

PENNSYLVANIA

WEIRTON

OHIO

WHEELING

MOUNDSVILLE

MARYLAND

MORGANTOWN

CACAPON
STATE PARK

MARTINSBURG

PINE SWAMP KNOB
946

KEYSER

FAIRMONT

GRAFTON

CLARKSBURG

BRIDGEPORT

CANAAN VALLEY
STATE PARK

MOUNT PORTO CRAYON
1 454

ELKINS

BICKLE KNOB
1 225

VIENNA
PARKERSBURG

BUCKHANNON

SPRUCE KNOB
1 482

MONONGAHELA

KANAWHA

OHIO

VIRGINIA

BIG SPRUCE KNOB
1 424

ALLEGHENY MOUNTAINS

NITRO

CHARLESTON

SAINT ALBANS

DUNBAR

HUNTINGTON

OAK HILL

KEENEY KNOB
1 197

BECKLEY

BLUESTONE
STATE PARK

PIPESTEM
STATE PARK

ROANOKE

PRINCETON

KENTUCKY

BLUEFIELD

NORTH CAROLINA

Official name: West Virginia
Capital: Charleston
Population: 1.8 million
Surface area: 62,759 km²
Currency: American Dollar
Language: English

NEW YORK

Official name:	New York
Capital:	Albany
Population:	18.2 million
Surface area:	141,080 km²
Currency:	American Dollar
Language:	English

SCALE 1 : 4 140 000

CANADA

UNITED STATES

GULF OF MAINE

NEW HAMPSHIRE

VERMONT

MASSACHUSETTS

BOSTON

WORCESTER

PROVIDENCE

RHODE ISLAND

SPRINGFIELD

HARTFORD

CONNECTICUT

NEW HAVEN

FISHERS ISLAND

GARDINERS BAY

MONTAUK POINT

LONG ISLAND SOUND

SAINT JAMES

PATCHOGUE

BRENTWOOD

FIRE ISLAND

LONG BEACH

NATIONAL SEASHORE

ATLANTIC OCEAN

WHITE PLAINS

HUNTINGTON

GLEN COVE

OSSINING

FREEPORT

PEEKSKILL

NEW CITY

SPRING VALLEY

PEARL RIVER

NEW ROCHELLE

YONKERS

JERSEY CITY

NEW YORK

PATERSON

NEWARK

ELIZABETH

NEW JERSEY

POUGHKEEPSIE

NEWBURGH

BEACON

MIDDLETOWN

KINGSTON

HUDSON

SLIDE MOUNTAIN 1 277

HUNTER MOUNTAIN 1 234

CATSKILL MOUNTAINS

ALBANY

TROY

COHOES

HUDSON

ROTTERDAM

SCHENECTADY

AMSTERDAM

GLOVERSVILLE

GLOVERSVILLE

SARATOGA SPRINGS

GLENS FALLS

GIANT MOUNTAIN 1 410

MOUNT MARCY 1 629

WHITE FACE MOUNTAIN 1 483

LYON MOUNTAIN 1 159

PLATTSBURGH

LAKE CHAMPLAIN

SARANAC LAKE

SNOWY MOUNTAIN 1 188

ADIRONDACK MOUNTAINS

MALONE

MASSENA

OTTAWA

OGDENSBURG

POTSDAM

CANTON

WATERTOWN

UTICA

ROME

ONEIDA

ONEIDA LAKE

SYRACUSE

FULTON

OSWEGO

LAKE ONTARIO

COBLESKILL

ONEONTA

NORWICH

CORTLAND

BINGHAMTON

JOHNSON CITY

ENDICOTT

ELMIRA

ITHACA

CAYUGA LAKE

AUBURN

NEWARK

GENEVA

SENECA LAKE

WATKINS GLEN STATE PARK

PENN YAN

CANANDAIGUA

BATH

CORNING

SUSQUEHANNA

PENNSYLVANIA

ALLENTOWN

HORNELL

WELLSVILLE

OLEAN

DANSVILLE

LETCHWORTH STATE PARK

GENESEO

BATAVIA

ROCHESTER

BRIGHTON

GREECE

IRONDEQUOIT

WEBSTER

LOCKPORT

TONAWANDA

AMHERST

DEPEW

LACKAWANNA

HAMBURG

BUFFALO

NIAGARA FALLS

DUNKIRK

FREDONIA

JAMESTOWN

LAKE ERIE

ERIE

HAMILTON

KITCHENER

MISSISSAUGA

TORONTO

SCARBOROUGH

NORTH YORK

ETOBICOKE

PENNSYLVANIA

SCALE 1 : 3 590 000

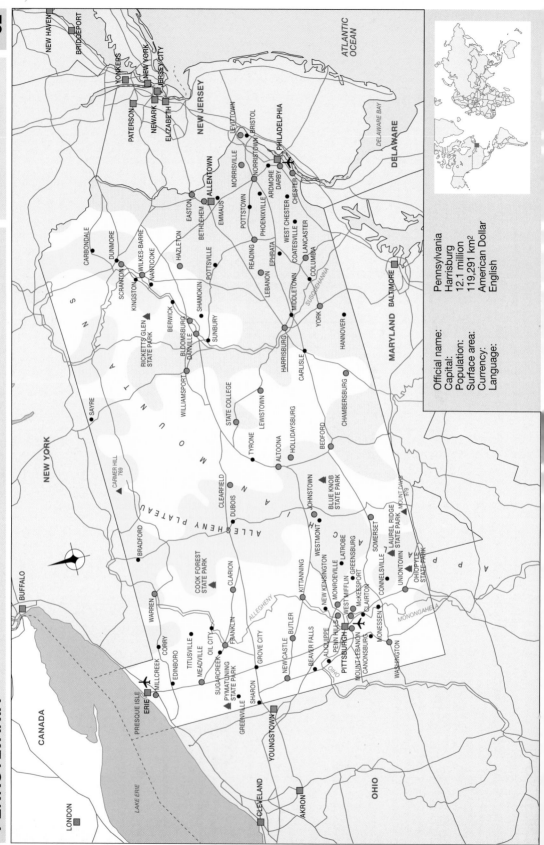

Official name: Pennsylvania
Capital: Harrisburg
Population: 12.1 million
Surface area: 119,291 km²
Currency: American Dollar
Language: English

NEW HAVEN
BRIDGEPORT
YONKERS
NEW YORK
JERSEY CITY
PATERSON
NEWARK
ELIZABETH
NEW JERSEY
ATLANTIC OCEAN
LEVITTOWN
BRISTOL
TRENTON
PHILADELPHIA
ALLENTOWN
MORRISVILLE
NORRISTOWN
ARDMORE
DARBY
CHESTER
DELAWARE
EASTON
BETHLEHEM
EMMAUS
POTTSTOWN
PHOENIXVILLE
WEST CHESTER
COATESVILLE
LANCASTER
DELAWARE BAY
CARBONDALE
DUNMORE
WILKES-BARRE
HAZLETON
POTTSVILLE
READING
EPHRATA
COLUMBIA
BALTIMORE
SCRANTON
KINGSTON
NANTICOKE
SHAMOKIN
LEBANON
MIDDLETOWN
YORK
HANNOVER
MARYLAND
RICKETTS GLEN STATE PARK
BERWICK
BLOOMSBURG
DANVILLE
SUNBURY
HARRISBURG
CARLISLE
SUSQUEHANNA
SAYRE
WILLIAMSPORT
STATE COLLEGE
LEWISTOWN
CHAMBERSBURG
CARMER HILL 769
TYRONE
ALTOONA
HOLLIDAYSBURG
BEDFORD
NEW YORK
CLEARFIELD
DUBOIS
ALLEGHENY PLATEAU
JOHNSTOWN
BLUE KNOB STATE PARK
BRADFORD
COOK FOREST STATE PARK
CLARION
WESTMONT
LATROBE
GREENSBURG
SOMERSET
LAUREL RIDGE STATE PARK
MOUNT DAVIS 979
BUFFALO
WARREN
KITTANNING
NEW KENSINGTON
MONROEVILLE
UNIONTOWN
OHIOPYLE STATE PARK
CORRY
OIL CITY
BUTLER
WEST MIFFLIN
McKEESPORT
CLAIRTON
CONNELLSVILLE
ALLEGHENY
TITUSVILLE
MEADVILLE
FRANKLIN
ALIQUIPPE
PENN HILLS
PITTSBURGH
MONESSEN
EDINBORO
SUGARCREEK
GROVE CITY
BEAVER FALLS
MOUNT LEBANON
CANONSBURG
WASHINGTON
MONONGAHELA
PRESQUE ISLE
MILLCREEK
ERIE
PYMATUNING STATE PARK
NEWCASTLE
OHIO
CANADA
SHARON
GREENVILLE
YOUNGSTOWN
LONDON
LAKE ERIE
CLEVELAND
AKRON
OHIO
MOUNTAINS

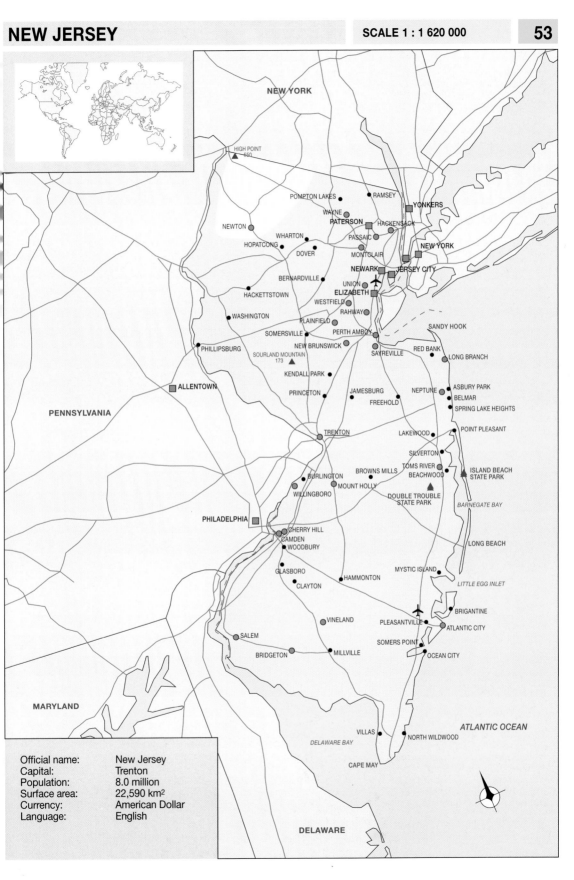

NEW JERSEY

NEW YORK

HIGH POINT
550

POMPTON LAKES   RAMSEY

WAYNE   YONKERS

NEWTON   PATERSON HACKENSACK

WHARTON PASSAIC

HOPATCONG DOVER MONTCLAIR NEW YORK

NEWARK JERSEY CITY

BERNARDVILLE UNION

HACKETTSTOWN ELIZABETH

WESTFIELD

WASHINGTON RAHWAY

PLAINFIELD

SOMERSVILLE PERTH AMBOY SANDY HOOK

PHILLIPSBURG NEW BRUNSWICK SAYREVILLE RED BANK

SOURLAND MOUNTAIN LONG BRANCH
173

KENDALL PARK

ALLENTOWN PRINCETON JAMESBURG NEPTUNE ASBURY PARK

FREEHOLD BELMAR

PENNSYLVANIA SPRING LAKE HEIGHTS

LAKEWOOD POINT PLEASANT

TRENTON

SILVERTON

BROWNS MILLS TOMS RIVER

BURLINGTON BEACHWOOD ISLAND BEACH
STATE PARK

WILLINGBORO MOUNT HOLLY DOUBLE TROUBLE
STATE PARK BARNEGAT BAY

PHILADELPHIA

CHERRY HILL LONG BEACH
CAMDEN
WOODBURY

GLASBORO MYSTIC ISLAND

CLAYTON HAMMONTON LITTLE EGG INLET

BRIGANTINE

VINELAND PLEASANTVILLE ATLANTIC CITY

SALEM SOMERS POINT

BRIDGETON MILLVILLE OCEAN CITY

MARYLAND

VILLAS ATLANTIC OCEAN

DELAWARE BAY NORTH WILDWOOD

CAPE MAY

Official name:	New Jersey
Capital:	Trenton
Population:	8.0 million
Surface area:	22,590 km²
Currency:	American Dollar
Language:	English

DELAWARE

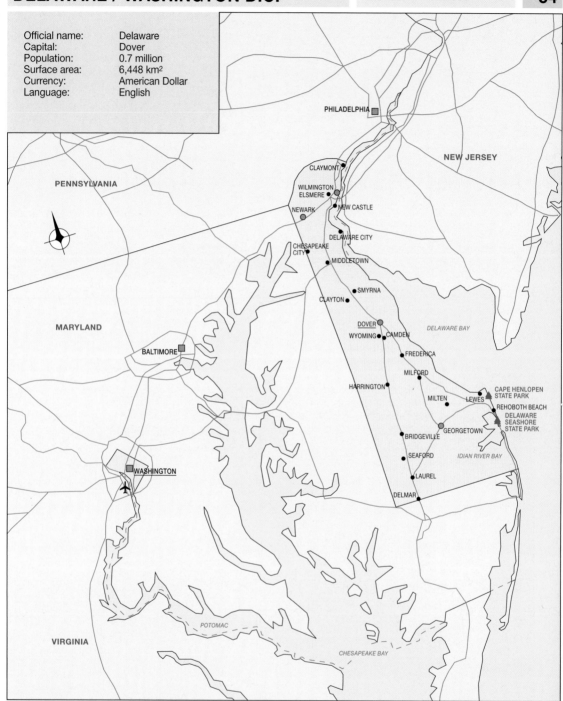

Official name:	Delaware
Capital:	Dover
Population:	0.7 million
Surface area:	6,448 km²
Currency:	American Dollar
Language:	English

PHILADELPHIA

NEW JERSEY

PENNSYLVANIA

CLAYMONT

WILMINGTON
ELSMERE

NEWARK

NEW CASTLE

DELAWARE CITY

CHESAPEAKE
CITY

MIDDLETOWN

SMYRNA

CLAYTON

MARYLAND

DELAWARE BAY

DOVER

WYOMING   CAMDEN

BALTIMORE

FREDERICA

MILFORD

HARRINGTON

MILTEN

LEWES

CAPE HENLOPEN
STATE PARK

REHOBOTH BEACH

DELAWARE
SEASHORE
STATE PARK

GEORGETOWN

BRIDGEVILLE

WASHINGTON

SEAFORD

IDIAN RIVER BAY

LAUREL

DELMAR

POTOMAC

VIRGINIA

CHESAPEAKE BAY

Official name:	Washington D.C.
Capital:	Washington
Population:	0.6 million
Surface area:	177 km²
Currency:	American Dollar
Language:	English

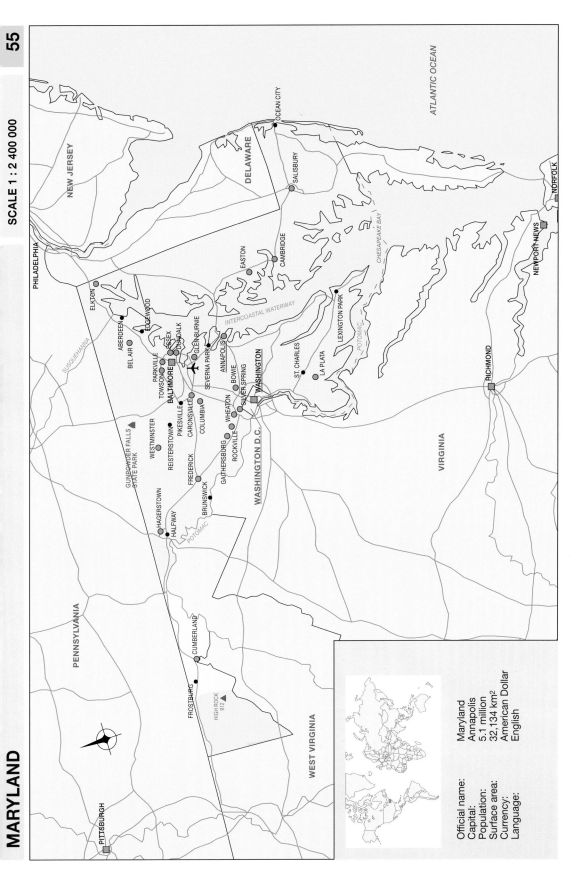

MARYLAND

SCALE 1 : 2 400 000

55

Official name: Maryland
Capital: Annapolis
Population: 5.1 million
Surface area: 32,134 km²
Currency: American Dollar
Language: English

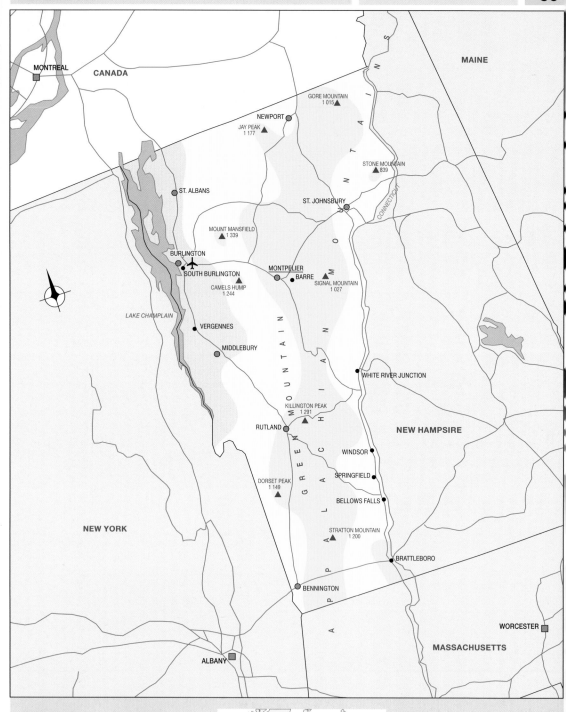

MONTREAL

CANADA

MAINE

GORE MOUNTAIN
1 015 ▲

NEWPORT

JAY PEAK
1 177 ▲

STONE MOUNTAIN
▲ 839

ST. ALBANS

ST. JOHNSBURY

CONNECTICUT

MOUNT MANSFIELD
▲ 1 339

BURLINGTON

MONTPELIER

SOUTH BURLINGTON

BARRE

CAMELS HUMP
1 244 ▲

SIGNAL MOUNTAIN
1 027 ▲

LAKE CHAMPLAIN

VERGENNES

MIDDLEBURY

WHITE RIVER JUNCTION

KILLINGTON PEAK
1 291 ▲

RUTLAND

NEW HAMPSIRE

WINDSOR

SPRINGFIELD

DORSET PEAK
1 149 ▲

BELLOWS FALLS

NEW YORK

STRATTON MOUNTAIN
1 200 ▲

BRATTLEBORO

BENNINGTON

WORCESTER

MASSACHUSETTS

ALBANY

GREEN MOUNTAIN

APPALACHIAN MO

Official name:	Vermont
Capital:	Montpelier
Population:	0.6 million
Surface area:	24,903 km²
Currency:	American Dollar
Language:	English

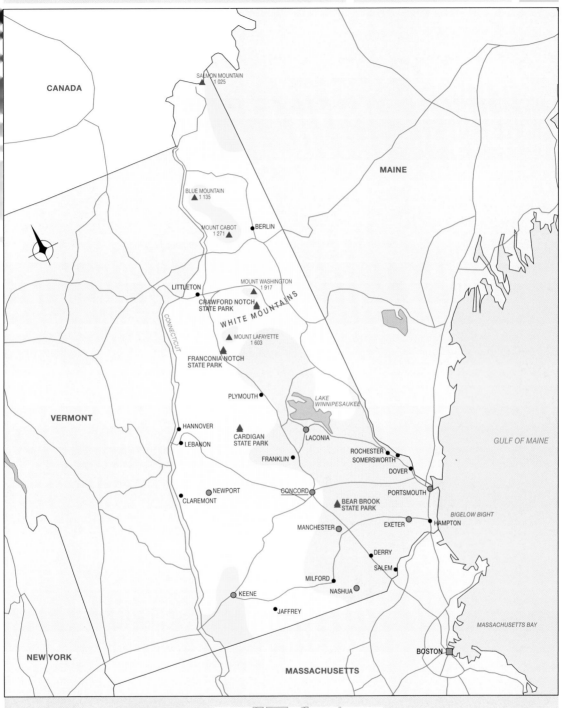

CANADA

SALMON MOUNTAIN
▲ 1 025

MAINE

BLUE MOUNTAIN
▲ 1 135

MOUNT CABOT
1 271 ▲   BERLIN

LITTLETON

MOUNT WASHINGTON
▲ 1 917

CRAWFORD NOTCH
STATE PARK

WHITE MOUNTAINS

CONNECTICUT

MOUNT LAFAYETTE
▲ 1 603

FRANCONIA NOTCH
STATE PARK

PLYMOUTH

LAKE
WINNIPESAUKEE

VERMONT

HANNOVER

CARDIGAN
STATE PARK   LACONIA

LEBANON

FRANKLIN

ROCHESTER
SOMERSWORTH

DOVER

GULF OF MAINE

NEWPORT

CLAREMONT

CONCORD   PORTSMOUTH

BEAR BROOK
STATE PARK

BIGELOW BIGHT

MANCHESTER   EXETER   HAMPTON

DERRY

SALEM

MILFORD

KEENE   NASHUA

JAFFREY

MASSACHUSETTS BAY

BOSTON

NEW YORK

MASSACHUSETTS

Official name:	New Hampshire
Capital:	Concord
Population:	1.2 million
Surface area:	24,219 km²
Currency:	American Dollar
Language:	English

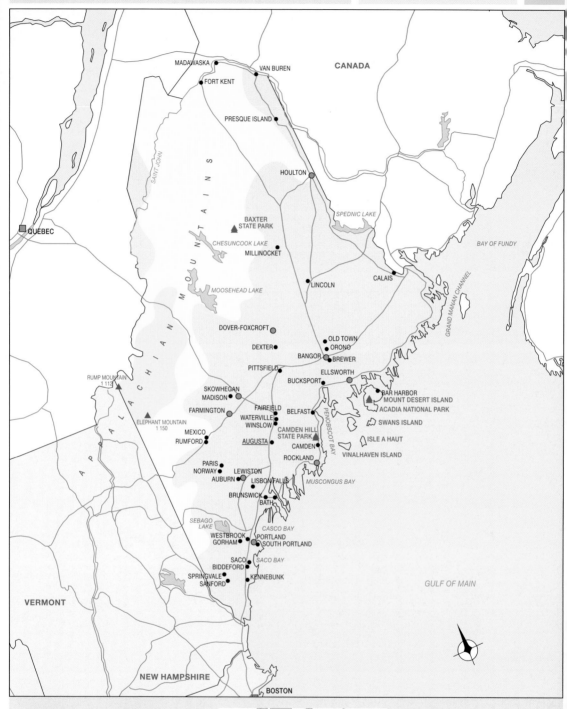

CANADA

MADAWASKA
VAN BUREN
FORT KENT

PRESQUE ISLAND

SAINT JOHN

HOULTON

SPEDNIC LAKE

QUEBEC

BAXTER
STATE PARK

CHESUNCOOK LAKE
MILLINOCKET

BAY OF FUNDY

M O U N T A I N S

MOOSEHEAD LAKE

LINCOLN

CALAIS

GRAND MANAN CHANNEL

DOVER-FOXCROFT

OLD TOWN
ORONO
BANGOR
BREWER

DEXTER

PITTSFIELD

ELLSWORTH
BUCKSPORT

RUMP MOUNTAIN
1 113

A P P A L A C H I A N

SKOWHEGAN
MADISON

FARMINGTON

ELEPHANT MOUNTAIN
1 150

FAIRFIELD

WATERVILLE
WINSLOW

BELFAST

BAR HARBOR
MOUNT DESERT ISLAND
ACADIA NATIONAL PARK

SWANS ISLAND

MEXICO
RUMFORD

CAMDEN HILL
STATE PARK

AUGUSTA

CAMDEN

PENOBSCOT BAY

ISLE A HAUT

VINALHAVEN ISLAND

PARIS
NORWAY
AUBURN

LEWISTON

ROCKLAND

LISBON FALLS

MUSCONGUS BAY

BRUNSWICK
BATH

SEBAGO
LAKE

CASCO BAY

WESTBROOK
GORHAM

PORTLAND
SOUTH PORTLAND

SACO
BIDDEFORD

SACO BAY

GULF OF MAIN

SPRINGVALE
SANFORD

KENNEBUNK

VERMONT

NEW HAMPSHIRE

BOSTON

Official name: Maine
Capital: Augusta
Population: 1.2 million
Surface area: 91,653 km²
Currency: American Dollar
Language: English

MASSACHUSETTS

SCALE 1 : 1 980 000

Official name:	Massachusetts
Capital:	Boston
Population:	6.1 million
Surface area:	27,337 km²
Currency:	American Dollar
Language:	English

ATLANTIC OCEAN

CAPE COD

CAPE COD BAY

MASSACHUSETTS BAY

BIGELOW BAY

NANTUCKET SOUND

VINEYARD SOUND

RHODE ISLAND BAY

MONOMY ISLAND

NANTUCKET ISLAND

MARTHA'S VINEYARD

SOUTH YARMOUTH
WEST YARMOUTH
HYANNIS
EAST FALMOUTH
NANTUCKET
EDGARTOWN

NEW BEDFORD
FAIRHAVEN
FALL RIVER
SOMERSET
PROVIDENCE

RHODE ISLAND

CONNECTICUT

HARTFORD

NEW YORK

ALBANY

VERMONT

NEW HAMPSHIRE

MOUNT GREYLOCK 1,064
NORTH ADAMS
ADAMS
PITTSFIELD
MOUNT EVERETT 793

GREENFIELD
ATHOL
GARDNER
HATFIELD
AMHURST
NORTHAMPTON
EASTHAMPTON
HOLYOKE
CHICOPEE
SPRINGFIELD
WESTFIELD
LONGMEADOW
CONNECTICUT
WARE
SPENCER
WEBSTER
SOUTHBRIDGE
OXFORD
AUBURN
MILFORD
WORCESTER
FRAMINGHAM
SHREWSBURY
MARLBOROUGH
HUDSON
CLINTON
LEOMINSTER
FITCHBURG

AMESBURY
NEWBURYPORT
HAVERHILL
LAWRENCE
DRACUT
LOWELL
ROCKPORT
GLOUCESTER
BEVERLY
SALEM
LYNN
PEABODY
WOBURN
LEXINGTON
WALTHAM
CAMBRIDGE
NEWTON
BOSTON
QUINCY
NORWOOD
STOUGHTON
FRANKLIN
ATTLEBORO
TAUNTON
COHASSET
SCITUATE
WEYMOUTH
BROCKTON
MIDDLEBORO
PLYMOUTH

CONNECTICUT / RHODE ISLAND

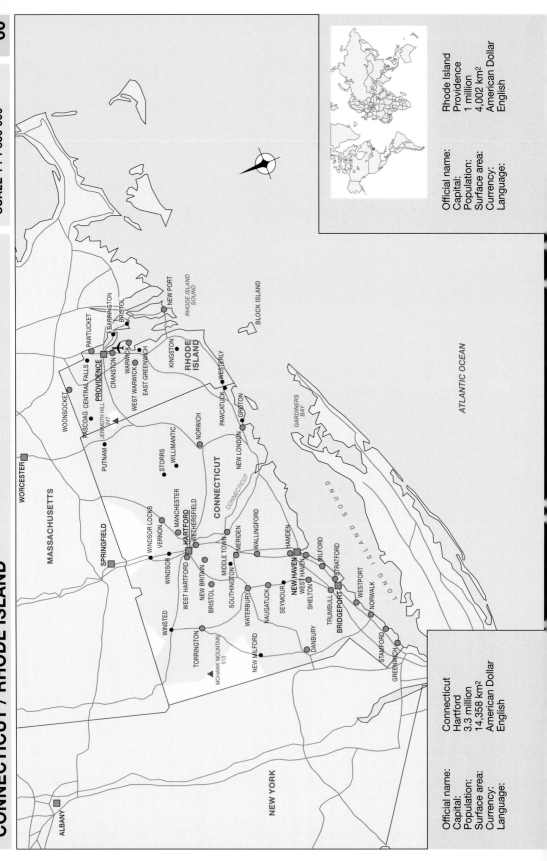

Official name: Connecticut
Capital: Hartford
Population: 3.3 million
Surface area: 14,358 km²
Currency: American Dollar
Language: English

Official name: Rhode Island
Capital: Providence
Population: 1 million
Surface area: 4,002 km²
Currency: American Dollar
Language: English

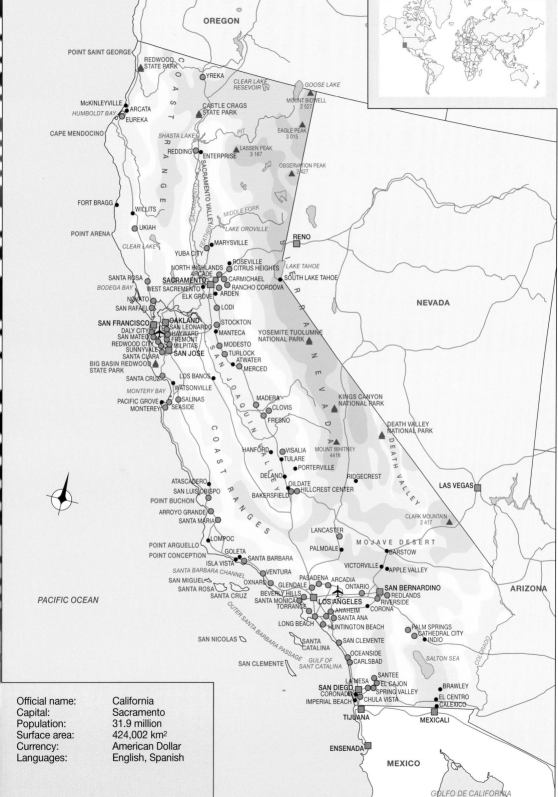

OREGON

POINT SAINT GEORGE

REDWOOD
STATE PARK

McKINLEYVILLE
ARCATA
HUMBOLDT BAY
EUREKA

CAPE MENDOCINO

FORT BRAGG

POINT ARENA

CLEAR LAKE

YREKA

*CLEAR LAKE
RESEVOIR*

GOOSE LAKE

MOUNT BIDWELL
2 527

CASTLE CRAGS
STATE PARK

SHASTA LAKE

EAGLE PEAK
3 015

PIT

REDDING
ENTERPRISE

LASSEN PEAK
3 187

OBSERVATION PEAK
2 427

WILLITS

UKIAH

MIDDLE FORK
LAKE OROVILLE

MARYSVILLE

RENO

NEVADA

YUBA CITY

SANTA ROSA
BODEGA BAY
NOVATO
SAN RAFAEL

SAN FRANCISCO
DALY CITY
SAN MATEO
REDWOOD CITY
SUNNYVALE
SANTA CLARA
BIG BASIN REDWOOD
STATE PARK

SANTA CRUZ

MONTEREY BAY
PACIFIC GROVE
MONTEREY

ROSEVILLE
CITRUS HEIGHTS
NORTH HIGHLANDS
ARCADE
SACRAMENTO
CARMICHAEL
WEST SACRAMENTO
RANCHO CORDOVA
ELK GROVE
ARDEN

LODI

STOCKTON

OAKLAND
SAN LEONARDO
HAYWARD
FREMONT
MILPITAS
SAN JOSE

MANTECA

MODESTO

TURLOCK
ATWATER
MERCED

LOS BANOS

WATSONVILLE
SALINAS
SEASIDE

SOUTH LAKE TAHOE

LAKE TAHOE

YOSEMITE TUOLUMNE
NATIONAL PARK

MADERA

CLOVIS

FRESNO

KINGS CANYON
NATIONAL PARK

DEATH VALLEY
NATIONAL PARK

HANFORD

VISALIA
TULARE

MOUNT WHITNEY
4418

COAST RANGES

ATASCADERO
SAN LUIS OBISPO
POINT BUCHON
ARROYO GRANDE
SANTA MARIA

POINT ARGUELLO
POINT CONCEPTION

SAN JOAQUIN VALLEY

DELANO

BAKERSFIELD

LOMPOC

GOLETA
ISLA VISTA
SANTA BARBARA

PORTERVILLE

OILDATE
HILLCREST CENTER

RIDGECREST

LANCASTER

PALMDALE

CLARK MOUNTAIN
2 417

LAS VEGAS

DEATH VALLEY

MOJAVE DESERT

BARSTOW

VICTORVILLE
APPLE VALLEY

SANTA BARBARA CHANNEL
SAN MIGUEL
SANTA ROSA
SANTA CRUZ

VENTURA
OXNARD

PASADENA
GLENDALE
BEVERLY HILLS
SANTA MONICA
TORRANCE

LONG BEACH

SAN NICOLAS

OUTER SANTA BARBARA PASSAGE

SANTA
CATALINA

SAN CLEMENTE

*GULF OF
SANT CATALINA*

ARCADIA
ONTARIO
LOS ANGELES
ANAHEIM
SANTA ANA
HUNTINGTON BEACH

SAN BERNARDINO
REDLANDS
RIVERSIDE
CORONA

PALM SPRINGS
CATHEDRAL CITY
INDIO

SAN CLEMENTE

OCEANSIDE
CARLSBAD

SALTON SEA

LA MESA
SAN DIEGO
CORONADO
IMPERIAL BEACH

SANTEE
EL CAJON
SPRING VALLEY
CHULA VISTA

BRAWLEY

EL CENTRO
CALEXICO

TIJUANA

MEXICALI

ENSENADA

MEXICO

ARIZONA

COLORADO

PACIFIC OCEAN

Official name:	California
Capital:	Sacramento
Population:	31.9 million
Surface area:	424,002 km²
Currency:	American Dollar
Languages:	English, Spanish

GOLFO DE CALIFORNIA

OREGON

IDAHO

GRANITE PEAK
2 966

MATTERHORN
3 304

BLACK ROCK DESSERT

WINNEMUCCA

RYE PATCH
RESERVOIR

HUMBOLDT

STAR PEAK
2 997

HOLE IN THE MOUNTAIN PEAK
3 446

PYRAMID LAKE

BATTLE MOUNTAIN

ELKO

SPRING CREEK

SPRUCE MOUNTAIN
3 128

RENO

SPARKS

GREAT

RUBY MOUNTAINS

LAKE TAHOE NEVADA
STATE PARK

FALLON

CARSON CITY

LAKE TAHOE

SACRAMENTO

WALKER LAKE

BASSIN

SCHELL CREEK RANGE

ELY

MOUNT MORIAH
3 673

MOUNT GRANT
3 426

HAWTHORNE

WHEELER PEAK
3 982

UTAH

TONOPAH

BOUNDARY PEAK
4 006

SILVER PEAK
RANGE

CALIFORNIA

NORTH LAS VEGAS

SUNRISE MANOR

LAS VEGAS

PARADISE

HENDERSON

BOULDER CITY

LAKE MEAD

ARIZONA

LAUGHLIN

LOS ANGELES

SAN BERNARDINO

Official name:	Nevada
Capital:	Carson City
Population:	1.6 million
Surface area:	286,367 km²
Currency:	American Dollar
Language:	English

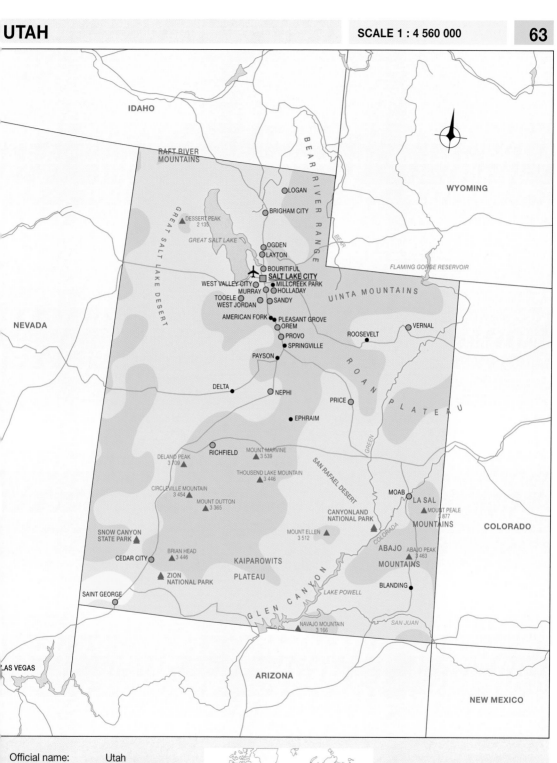

IDAHO

RAFT RIVER MOUNTAINS

GREAT SALT LAKE DESERT

GREAT SALT LAKE

BEAR RIVER RANGE

BEAR

WYOMING

FLAMING GORGE RESERVOIR

UINTA MOUNTAINS

NEVADA

LOGAN

BRIGHAM CITY

▲ DESSERT PEAK 2 135

OGDEN
LAYTON
BOURITIFUL
SALT LAKE CITY
WEST VALLEY CITY   MILLCREEK PARK
MURRAY   HOLLADAY
TOOELE   SANDY
WEST JORDAN
AMERICAN FORK
PLEASANT GROVE
OREM
PROVO
SPRINGVILLE
PAYSON

ROOSEVELT   VERNAL

ROAN PLATEAU

DELTA

NEPHI

PRICE

GREEN

EPHRAIM

RICHFIELD   MOUNT MARVINE ▲ 3 539

DELAND PEAK 3 709 ▲

THOUSEND LAKE MOUNTAIN ▲ 3 446

CIRCLEVILLE MOUNTAIN 3 454 ▲

MOUNT DUTTON ▲ 3 365

SAN RAFAEL DESERT

CANYONLAND NATIONAL PARK ▲

MOAB

LA SAL
▲ MOUNT PEALE 877
MOUNTAINS

COLORADO

COLORADO

SNOW CANYON STATE PARK ▲

BRIAN HEAD ▲ 3 446

MOUNT ELLEN 3 512

ABAJO
MOUNTAINS
ABAJO PEAK ▲ 3 463

CEDAR CITY

ZION NATIONAL PARK ▲

KAIPAROWITS PLATEAU

BLANDING

SAINT GEORGE

GLEN CANYON

LAKE POWELL

NAVAJO MOUNTAIN 3 166

SAN JUAN

LAS VEGAS

ARIZONA

NEW MEXICO

Official name:	Utah
Capital:	Salt Lake City
Population:	2.0 million
Surface area:	219,902 km²
Currency:	American Dollar
Language:	English

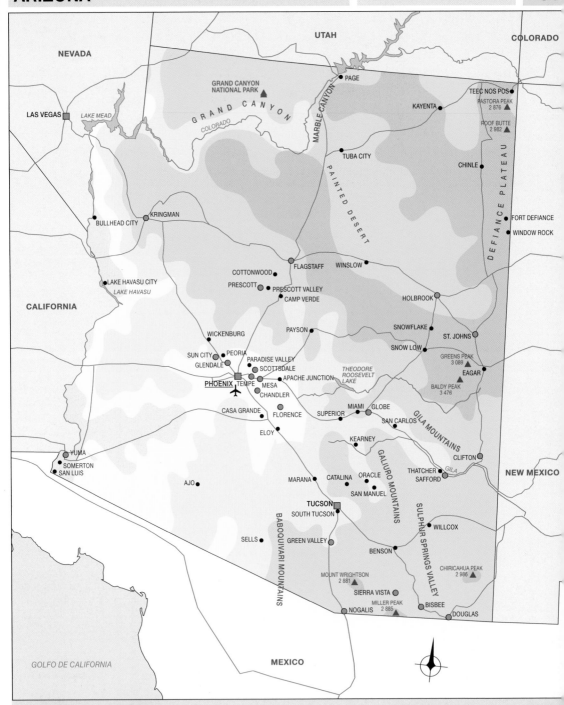

NEVADA

UTAH

COLORADO

GRAND CANYON NATIONAL PARK ▲

PAGE

TEEC NOS POS

PASTORA PEAK
2 876 ▲

LAS VEGAS

Lake Mead

LAKE MEAD

G R A N D   C A N Y O N

COLORADO

M A R B L E   C A N Y O N

KAYENTA

ROOF BUTTE
2 982 ▲

TUBA CITY

CHINLE

D E F I A N C E   P L A T E A U

BULLHEAD CITY

KRINGMAN

P A I N T E D   D E S E R T

FORT DEFIANCE

WINDOW ROCK

CALIFORNIA

LAKE HAVASU CITY
LAKE HAVASU

COTTONWOOD

PRESCOTT

FLAGSTAFF

WINSLOW

PRESCOTT VALLEY
CAMP VERDE

HOLBROOK

WICKENBURG

PAYSON

SNOWFLAKE

SNOW LOW

ST. JOHNS

GREENS PEAK
3 089 ▲

SUN CITY
PEORIA
GLENDALE

PARADISE VALLEY

SCOTTSDALE

EAGAR

BALDY PEAK
3 476 ▲

PHOENIX ✈ TEMPE
MESA
CHANDLER

APACHE JUNCTION

*THEODORE
ROOSEVELT
LAKE*

CASA GRANDE

FLORENCE

SUPERIOR

MIAMI
GLOBE

SAN CARLOS

G I L A   M O U N T A I N S

ELOY

KEARNEY

CLIFTON

GILA

YUMA
SOMERTON
SAN LUIS

AJO

MARANA

CATALINA

ORACLE

SAN MANUEL

G A L U I R O   M O U N T A I N S

THATCHER
SAFFORD

NEW MEXICO

TUCSON
SOUTH TUCSON

S U L P H U R   S P R I N G S   V A L L E Y

WILLCOX

SELLS

GREEN VALLEY

BENSON

CHIRICAHUA PEAK
2 986 ▲

B A B O Q U I V A R I   M O U N T A I N S

MOUNT WRIGHTSON
2 881 ▲

SIERRA VISTA

MILLER PEAK
2 885 ▲

BISBEE

NOGALIS

DOUGLAS

GOLFO DE CALIFORNIA

MEXICO

Official name: Arizona
Capital: Phoenix
Population: 4.4 million
Surface area: 295,276 km²
Currency: American Dollar
Languages: English, Spanish

COLORADO

Official name: Colorado
Capital: Denver
Population: 3.8 million
Surface area: 269,618 km²
Currency: American Dollar
Language: English

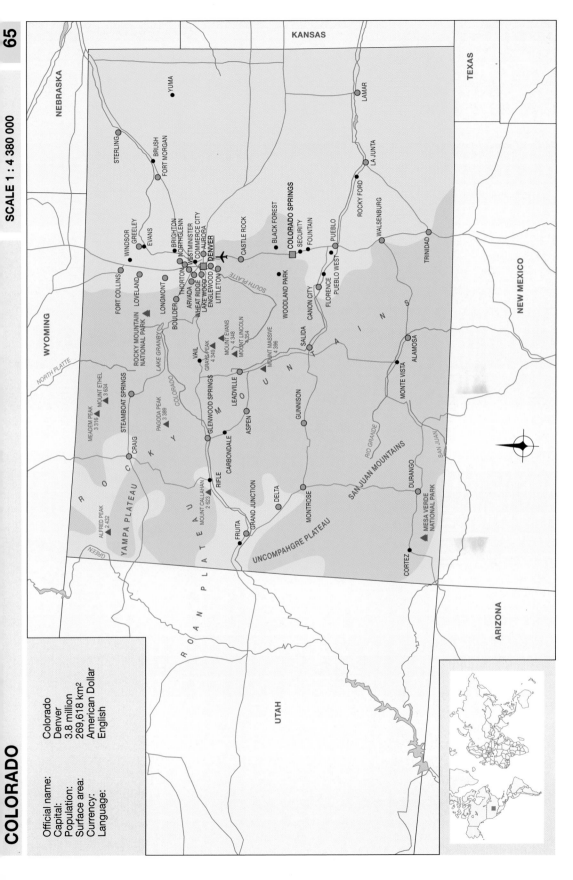

KANSAS

NEBRASKA

TEXAS

NEW MEXICO

WYOMING

UTAH

ARIZONA

YUMA

STERLING

BRUSH
FORT MORGAN

LAMAR

LA JUNTA

ROCKY FORD

WALSENBURG

TRINIDAD

WINDSOR
GREELEY
EVANS

BRIGHTON
NORTHGLENN
WESTMINSTER
COMMERCE CITY
AURORA
DENVER
THORNTON
ARVADA
WHEAT RIDGE
LAKEWOOD
ENGLEWOOD
LITTLETON

CASTLE ROCK

BLACK FOREST

COLORADO SPRINGS
SECURITY
FOUNTAIN

PUEBLO
PUEBLO WEST

WOODLAND PARK

FLORENCE
CANON CITY
SALIDA

FORT COLLINS
LOVELAND
LONGMONT
BOULDER

ROCKY MOUNTAIN
NATIONAL PARK

Lake Granby

VAIL
GRAYS PEAK
4 349

MOUNT EVANS
4 348
MOUNT LINCOLN
4 354

MOUNT MASSIVE
4 396

MEADEM PEAK
3 316
MOUNT ETHEL
3 634

STEAMBOAT SPRINGS

PAGODA PEAK
3 389

CRAIG

NORTH PLATTE

COLORADO

SOUTH PLATTE

LEADVILLE

ASPEN

GLENWOOD SPRINGS

CARBONDALE

RIFLE

GRAND JUNCTION

DELTA

FRUITA

ALFRED PEAK
2 432

MOUNT CALLAHAN
2 623

YAMPA PLATEAU

ROAN PLATEAU

GREEN

GUNNISON

MONTROSE

UNCOMPAHGRE PLATEAU

SAN JUAN MOUNTAINS

RIO GRANDE

SAN JUAN

ALAMOSA

MONTE VISTA

DURANGO

MESA VERDE
NATIONAL PARK

CORTEZ

ROCKY MOUNTAINS

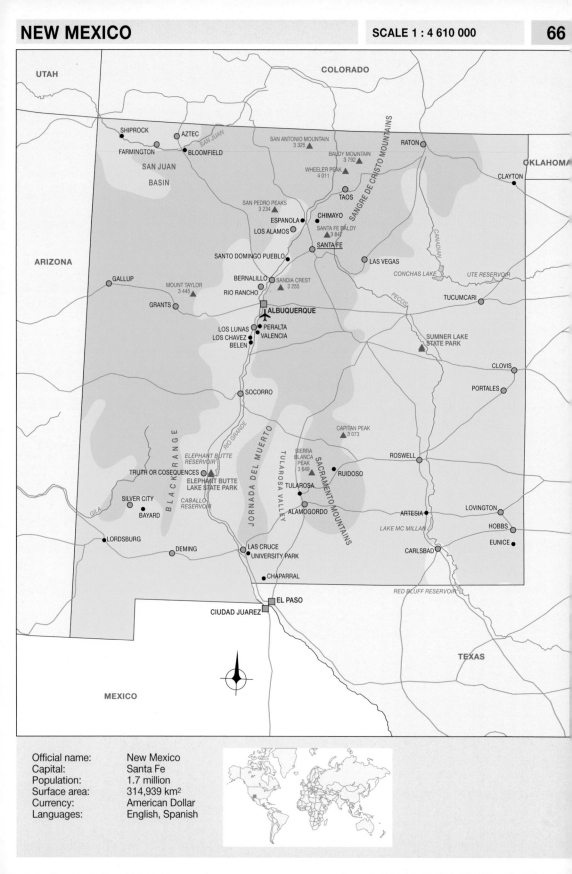

UTAH

COLORADO

OKLAHOMA

ARIZONA

TEXAS

MEXICO

SHIPROCK
AZTEC
FARMINGTON
BLOOMFIELD
SAN JUAN

SAN JUAN
BASIN

SAN ANTONIO MOUNTAIN
3 325 ▲

RATON

BALDY MOUNTAIN
3 792 ▲

WHEELER PEAK
4 011 ▲

CLAYTON

SANGRE DE CRISTO MOUNTAINS

SAN PEDRO PEAKS
3 234 ▲

TAOS

CHIMAYO

ESPANOLA
LOS ALAMOS

SANTA FE BALDY
3 847 ▲

SANTA FE

LAS VEGAS

SANTO DOMINGO PUEBLO

CONCHAS LAKE

UTE RESERVOIR

CANADIAN

GALLUP

MOUNT TAYLOR
3 445 ▲

BERNALILLO
RIO RANCHO

SANDIA CREST
3 255 ▲

PECOS

TUCUMCARI

GRANTS

ALBUQUERQUE

LOS LUNAS
LOS CHAVEZ
BELEN

PERALTA
VALENCIA

SUMNER LAKE
STATE PARK

CLOVIS

PORTALES

SOCORRO

RIO GRANDE

BLACK RANGE

JORNADA DEL MUERTO

TULAROSA VALLEY

CAPITAN PEAK
3 073 ▲

SIERRA
BLANCA
PEAK
3 649 ▲

SACRAMENTO MOUNTAINS

ROSWELL

RUIDOSO

ELEPHANT BUTTE
RESERVOIR

TRUTH OR COSEQUENCES

ELEPHANT BUTTE
LAKE STATE PARK

CABALLO
RESERVOIR

TULAROSA

ALAMOGORDO

ARTESIA

LOVINGTON

HOBBS

GILA

SILVER CITY
BAYARD

LAKE MC MILLAN

EUNICE

LORDSBURG

DEMING

LAS CRUCE
UNIVERSITY PARK

CARLSBAD

CHAPARRAL

RED BLUFF RESERVOIR

EL PASO
CIUDAD JUAREZ

Official name:	New Mexico
Capital:	Santa Fe
Population:	1.7 million
Surface area:	314,939 km²
Currency:	American Dollar
Languages:	English, Spanish

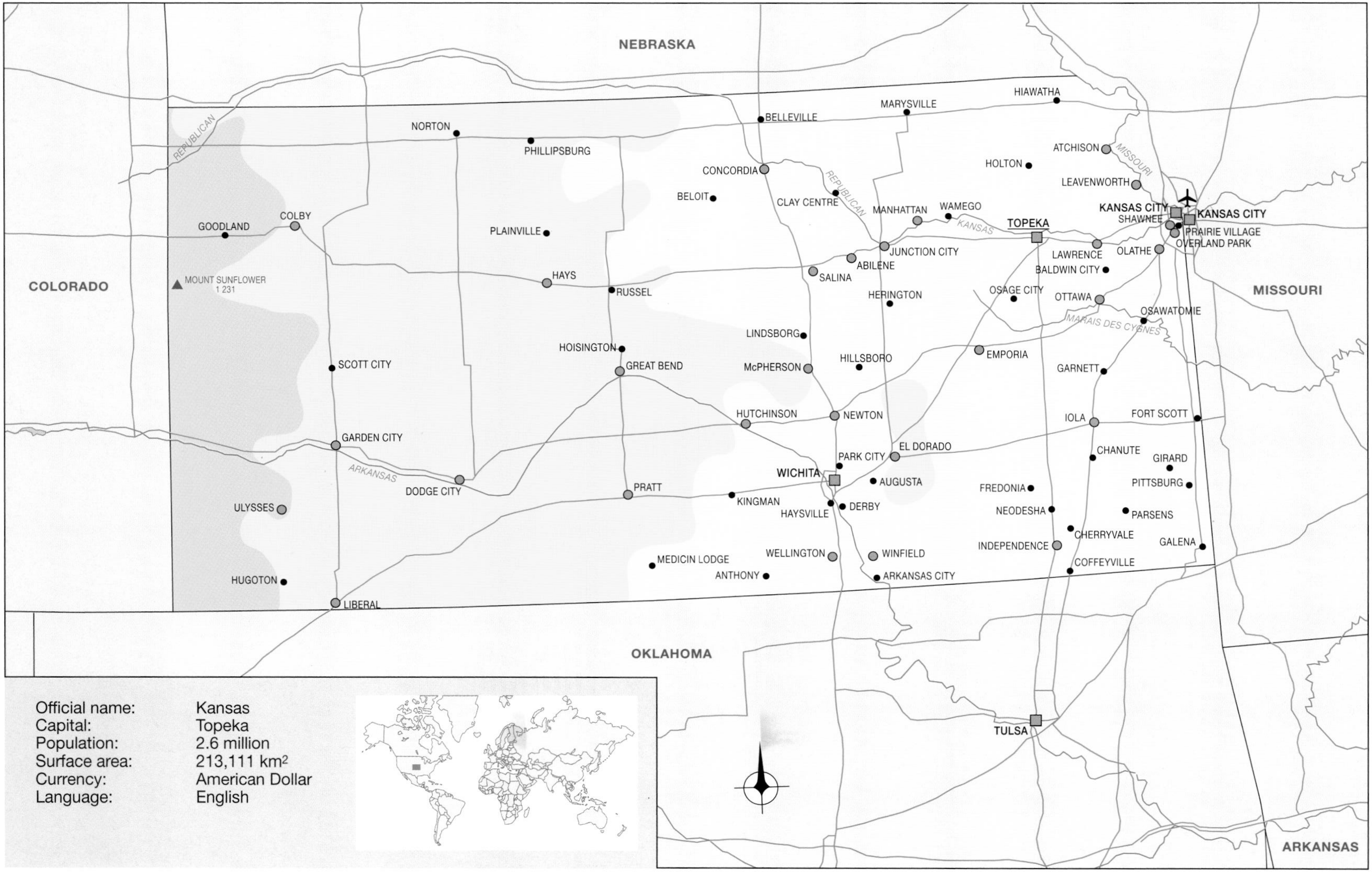

KANSAS

SCALE 1 : 3 850 000

MISSOURI

ARKANSAS

NEBRASKA

COLORADO

OKLAHOMA

KANSAS CITY
PRAIRIE VILLAGE
OVERLAND PARK
SHAWNEE
KANSAS CITY
OLATHE
OSAWATOMIE
LEAVENWORTH
ATCHISON
HIAWATHA
HOLTON
LAWRENCE
BALDWIN CITY
OTTAWA
TOPEKA
OSAGE CITY
MISSOURI
MARAIS DES CYGNES
FORT SCOTT
GIRARD
PITTSBURG
PARSENS
GALENA
CHANUTE
CHERRYVALE
COFFEYVILLE
GARNETT
IOLA
EMPORIA
FREDONIA
NEODESHA
INDEPENDENCE
TULSA
KANSAS
MARYSVILLE
WAMEGO
MANHATTAN
JUNCTION CITY
ABILENE
HERINGTON
SALINA
HILLSBORO
NEWTON
EL DORADO
AUGUSTA
PARK CITY
DERBY
WINFIELD
ARKANSAS CITY
REPUBLICAN
BELLEVILLE
CLAY CENTRE
CONCORDIA
BELOIT
LINDSBORG
McPHERSON
HUTCHINSON
WICHITA
HAYSVILLE
KINGMAN
WELLINGTON
ANTHONY
MEDICIN LODGE
RUSSEL
GREAT BEND
HOISINGTON
PRATT
PHILLIPSBURG
HAYS
PLAINVILLE
NORTON
DODGE CITY
ARKANSAS
SCOTT CITY
GARDEN CITY
LIBERAL
COLBY
GOODLAND
MOUNT SUNFLOWER 1 231
ULYSSES
HUGOTON
REPUBLICAN

Official name:	Kansas
Capital:	Topeka
Population:	2.6 million
Surface area:	213,111 km²
Currency:	American Dollar
Language:	English

OKLAHOMA

SCALE 1 : 4 240 000

COLORADO

NEW MEXICO

KANSAS

MISSOURI

SPRINGFIELD

ARKANSAS

TEXAS

WICHITA

BLACKWELL

ALVA

WOODWARD

GUYMON

AMARILLO

GYPSUM HILLS

ELK CITY

ALTUS

CANADIAN

WEATHERFORD
CLINTON

WICHITA MOUNTAINS

MOUNT SCOTT
751

LAWTON

FREDERICK

WICHITA FALLS

ENID

GUTHRIE

EL RENO

MUSTANG

ANADARKO

CHICKASHA

DUNCAN

EDMOND
VILLAGE
BETHANY

YUKON

OKLAHOMA CITY

MIDWEST CITY
DEL CITY
MOORE
NORMAN

SHAWNEE

PAULS VALLEY

ADA

ARDMORE

LAKE MURRAY
STATE PARK

RED

DALLAS

FORT WORTH

PONCA CITY

STILLWATER

ARKANSAS

BARTLESVILLE

TULSA
SAPULPA

CLAREMONT

MIAMI

VINTA

PRYOR

BROKEN ARROW
WAGONER

TAHLEQUAH

SALLISAW

MUSKOGEE

HENRYETTA

OKMULGEE

CANADIAN

McALESTER

ROBERTS CAVE
STATE PARK

SUGAR LOAF MOUNTAIN
783

POTEAU

OUACHITA MOUNTAINS

WILLIAMS MOUNTAIN
451

BEAVERS BEND
STATE PARK

HUGO

DURANT

LAKE TEXOMA

RED

IDABEL

Official name:	Oklahoma
Capital:	Oklahoma City
Population:	3.3 million
Surface area:	181,048 km²
Currency:	American Dollar
Language:	English

TEXAS

MISSISSIPPI

JACKSON

METAIRIE
NEW ORLEANS
BATON ROUGE

LOUISIANA

ARKANSAS

SHREVEPORT

GULF OF MEXICO

OKLAHOMA

TULSA

OKLAHOMA CITY

TEXARKANA
MOUNT PLEASANT
PARIS
MARSHALL
DENISON
SHERMAN
GREENVILLE
McKINNEY
GARLAND
PLANO
RICHARDSON
MESQUITE
TERRELL
LANCASTER
WAXAHACHIE
GAINESVILLE
FORT WORTH
DALLAS
ARLINGTON

NACOGDOCHES
LUFKIN
HENDERSON
LONGVIEW
TYLER
JACKSONVILLE
PALESTINE

BEAUMONT
PORT ARTHUR
ORANGE
BRIDGE CITY
BAYTOWN
CHANNELVIEW
PASADENA
TEXAS CITY
GALVESTON
HOUSTON
BELLAIRE
SOUTH HOUSTON
ROSENBERG
FREEPORT
LAKE JACKSON

SABINE PASS
GALVESTON BAY

BURKBURNETT
WICHITA FALLS
VERNON
STEPHENVILLE
WACO

HUNTSVILLE
COLLEGE STATION
BRYAN
BRENHAM
MEXIA
MARLIN
TEMPLE
BELTON
KILLEEN
COPPERAS COVE
BROWNWOOD
AUSTIN
SAN MARCOS
NEW BRAUNFELS
SEGUIN

MATAGORDA BAY
BAY CITY
EDNA
VICTORIA
PORT LAVACA
SAN ANTONIO BAY

CHILDRESS
PLAINVIEW
LUBBOCK
SLATON
AMARILLO
CANYON
HEREFORD
LITTLE FIELD
BROWNFIELD
SEMINOLE
LAMESA
BIG SPRING
SNYDER
SWEETWATER
ABILENE
COLEMAN
SAN ANGELO

PALO DURO CAYON
STATE PARK
LAKE MEREDITH
PERRYTON
DUMAS
BORGER
PAMPA
CANADIAN

MIDLAND
ODESSA
MONAHANS
MONAHANS STATE PARK
KERMIT
PECOS
FORT STOCKTON
ALPINE

STOCKTON
PLATEAU
EDWARD
PLATEAU

KERRVILLE
UVALDE
DEL RIO
EAGLE PASS
LAREDO

BALCONES ESCARPMENT

SAN ANTONIO

NUECES
PLAINS
BEEVILLE
PORTLAND
ROBSTOWN
ALICE
KINGSVILLE
CORPUS CHRISTI

ARANSAS PASS
CORPUS CRISTI BAY
PADRE ISLAND
LAGUNA MADRE

EDINBURG
McALLEN
MISSION
PHARR
HARLINGEN
SAN BENITO
BROWNSVILLE
REYNOSA
MATAMOROS

MONTERREY

NEW MEXICO

ALBUQUERQUE

EL PASO
CUIDA JUAREZ
FABENS
GUADALUPE PEAK
2 667
SHEEP PEAK
1 848
GUADALUPE
NATIONAL PARK
RED BLUFF
RESERVOIR

BIG BEND
NATIONAL PARK

MEXICO

CHIHUAHUA

AMSTAD RESERVOIR
FALCON RESERVOIR

PECOS
COLORADO
BRAZOS
RED
CANADIAN
SABINE
RED
NECHES
LAKE TEXOMA
LAKE J.B. THOMAS
LAKE BUCHANAN
LONGHORN CAVERN
FEDERAL FALLS
STATE PARK
LAKE LIVINGSTON
BEND RESERVOIR

Official name:	Texas
Capital:	Austin
Population:	19,1 million
Surface area:	695,676 km²
Currency:	American Dollar
Languages:	English, Spanish

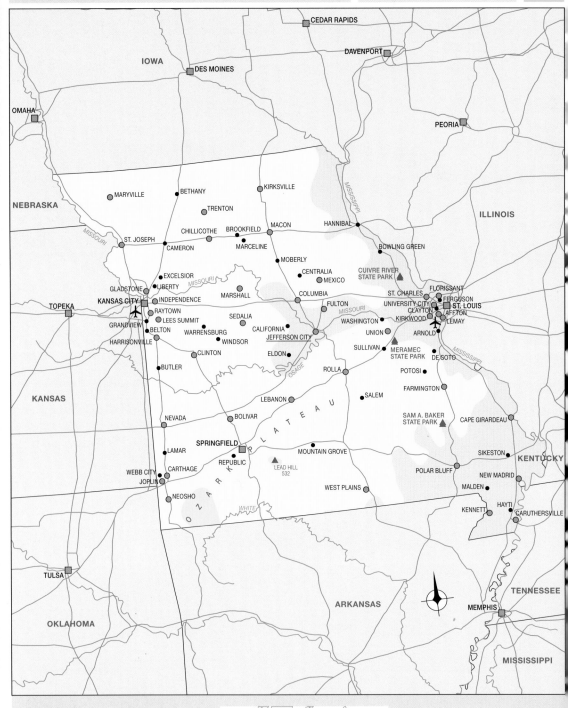

IOWA

CEDAR RAPIDS

DAVENPORT

DES MOINES

OMAHA

PEORIA

NEBRASKA

MARYVILLE

BETHANY

KIRKSVILLE

MISSISSIPPI

TRENTON

ILLINOIS

CHILLICOTHE

BROOKFIELD

MACON

HANNIBAL

ST. JOSEPH

CAMERON

MARCELINE

MOBERLY

BOWLING GREEN

EXCELSIOR

CENTRALIA

CUIVRE RIVER STATE PARK

GLADSTONE

LIBERTY

MISSOURI

MEXICO

ST. CHARLES

FLORISSANT

KANSAS CITY

INDEPENDENCE

MARSHALL

COLUMBIA

FULTON

UNIVERSITY CITY

FERGUSON

TOPEKA

RAYTOWN

MISSOURI

CLAYTON

ST. LOUIS

LEES SUMMIT

SEDALIA

WASHINGTON

KIRKWOOD

AFFTON

GRANDVIEW

BELTON

WARRENSBURG

CALIFORNIA

UNION

LEMAY

HARRISONVILLE

WINDSOR

JEFFERSON CITY

ARNOLD

ELDON

SULLIVAN

MERAMEC STATE PARK

DE SOTO

CLINTON

MISSISSIPPI

BUTLER

ROLLA

POTOSI

OSAGE

FARMINGTON

KANSAS

LEBANON

SALEM

NEVADA

BOLIVAR

P L A T E A U

SAM A. BAKER STATE PARK

CAPE GIRARDEAU

LAMAR

SPRINGFIELD

MOUNTAIN GROVE

SIKESTON

REPUBLIC

KENTUCKY

WEBB CITY

CARTHAGE

LEAD HILL 532

POLAR BLUFF

NEW MADRID

JOPLIN

MALDEN

NEOSHO

WEST PLAINS

HAYTI

O Z A R K

WHITE

KENNETT

CARUTHERSVILLE

TULSA

TENNESSEE

ARKANSAS

MEMPHIS

OKLAHOMA

MISSISSIPPI

Official name:	Missouri
Capital:	Jefferson City
Population:	5.4 million
Surface area:	180,546 km²
Currency:	American Dollar
Language:	English

MISSOURI

SPRINGFIELD

KANSAS

BELLA VISTA
BENTONVILLE
ROGERS
SPRINGDALE
FAYETTEVILLE
SILOAM SPRINGS

POCAHONTAS
PARAGOULD
BLYTHEVILLE
MOUNTAIN HOME
JONESBORO
OSCEOLA
HARRISON
BATESVILLE
TRUMANN
NEWPORT

B O S T O N   M O U N T A I N S

DEVIL'S DEN
STATE PARK

TENNESSEE

WYNNE
MEMPHIS
CLARKSVILLE
SEARCY
WEST MEMPHIS
VAN BUREN
RUSSELLVILLE
FOREST CITY
FORT SMITH
MORRILTON
CONWAY
PETIT JEAN
STATE PARK

O U A C H I T A   M O U N T A I N S

MARIANNA
SHERWOOD
JACKSONVILLE
NORTH LITTLE ROCK
WEST HELENA
LITTLE ROCK
HELENA
BRYANT
HOT SPRINGS
BENTON
STUTTGART
OKLAHOMA
MENA
MALVERN
ARKADELPHIA
PINE BLUFF
DUMAS
MONTICELLO

MISSISSIPPI
ASHDOWN
HOPE
CAMDEN
TEXARKANA
CROSSETT
MAGNOLIA
EL DORADO

RED

WHITE

ARKANSAS

TEXAS

JACKSON

LOUISIANA

SHREVEPORT

Official name:	Arkansas
Capital:	Little Rock
Population:	2.5 million
Surface area:	137,742 km^2
Currency:	American Dollar
Language:	English

ARKANSAS

MISSISSIPPI

LAKE PROVIDENCE

HAYNESVILLE
SPRINGHILL
HOMER
FARMERVILLE
BASTROP
MONROE
RAYVILLE
DELHI
MINDEN
GRAMBLING
RUSTON
WEST MONROE
TALLULAH
COOPER ROAD
SHREVEPORT
BOSSIER CITY
JONESBORO
WINNSBORO
JACKSON

MANSFIELD

WINNFIELD

RED

NATCHITOCHES

FERRIDAY

MISSISSIPPI

MANY

TEXAS

TOLEDO BEND
RESERVOIR
PINEVILLE
SAMTOWN
ALEXANDRIA
KENT
BOGALUSA
MARKSVILLE
AMITE
LEESVILLE
BUNKIE
COVINGTON
OAKDALE
CHICOT
STATE PARK
ZACHARY
HAMMOND
DE RIDDER
NEW ROADS
BAKER
SLIDELL
VILLE PLATTE
BATON ROUGE
SABINE
OPELOUSAS
LAKE MAUREPAS
LAKE
PONTCHARTRAIN
LAKE BORGNE
DE QUINCY
EUNICE
PLAQUEMINE
CHANDELEUR SOUND
CHANDLER ISLANDS
CARENCRO
LA PLACE
METAIRIE
MOSS BLUFF
CROWLEY
BREAUX BRIDGE
KENNER
CHALMETTE
WEST LAKE
LA FAYETTE
DONALDSONVILLE
NEW ORLEANS
SULPHUR
JENNINGS
RAYNE
MARRERO
LAKE CHARLES
KAPLAN
NEW IBERIA
THIBODAUX
BEAUMONT
ABEVILLE
CANE
RACELAND
SABINE LAKE
CALCASIEU LAKE
GRAND LAKE
MORGAN
CITY
HOUMA
LAROSE
CUT OFF
MISSISSIPPI DELTA
WHITE LAKE
GRAND ISLE
PASADENA
BARATARIA BAY
TIMBALIER BAY
TERREBONNE BAY
FER ISLAND
MARSH ISLAND
ATCHAFALAYA BAY

GULF OF MEXICO

Official name:	Louisiana
Capital:	Baton Rouge
Population:	4.4 million
Surface area:	134,275 km²
Currency:	American Dollar
Language:	English

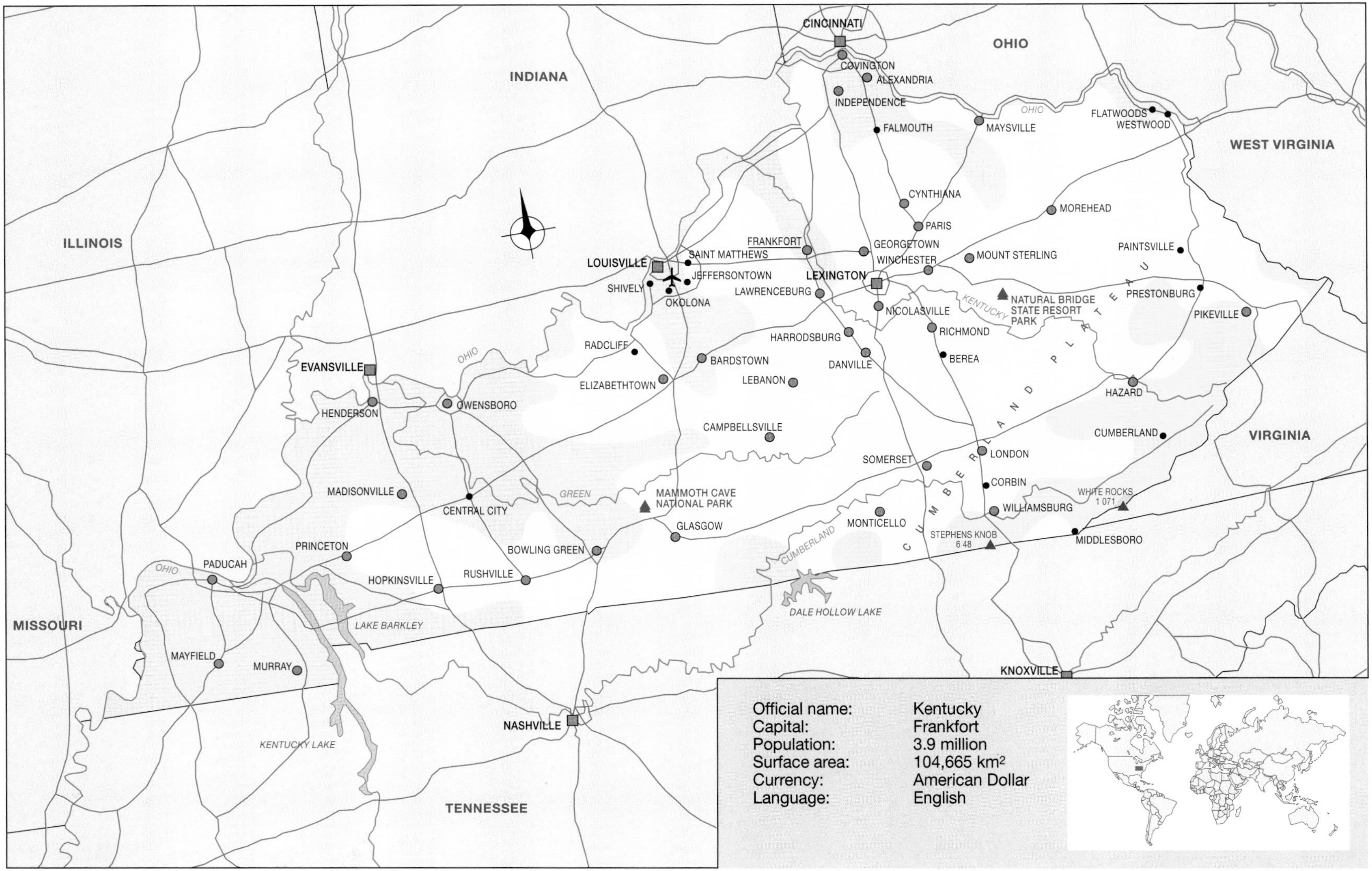

WEST VIRGINIA

OHIO

VIRGINIA

INDIANA

ILLINOIS

MISSOURI

TENNESSEE

CINCINNATI

COVINGTON
ALEXANDRIA
INDEPENDENCE
FALMOUTH
MAYSVILLE
CYNTHIANA
PARIS
GEORGETOWN
WINCHESTER
FRANKFORT
LEXINGTON
LAWRENCEBURG
NICOLASVILLE
RICHMOND
BEREA
MOUNT STERLING
MOREHEAD
FLATWOODS
WESTWOOD
PAINTSVILLE
PRESTONBURG
PIKEVILLE
HAZARD
CUMBERLAND
WHITE ROCKS 1 071
MIDDLESBORO
KNOXVILLE
WILLIAMSBURG
CORBIN
LONDON
STEPHENS KNOB 648
SOMERSET
MONTICELLO
HARRODSBURG
DANVILLE
LEBANON
BARDSTOWN
CAMPBELLSVILLE
SAINT MATTHEWS
JEFFERSONTOWN
OKOLONA
SHIVELY
LOUISVILLE
RADCLIFF
ELIZABETHTOWN
GLASGOW
MAMMOTH CAVE NATIONAL PARK
NATURAL BRIDGE STATE RESORT PARK
OWENSBORO
CENTRAL CITY
RUSSELLVILLE
BOWLING GREEN
HOPKINSVILLE
MADISONVILLE
HENDERSON
EVANSVILLE
PRINCETON
PADUCAH
MURRAY
MAYFIELD
NASHVILLE

OHIO
KENTUCKY R.
GREEN
CUMBERLAND
DALE HOLLOW LAKE
LAKE BARKLEY
KENTUCKY LAKE
OHIO

Official name:	Kentucky
Capital:	Frankfort
Population:	3.9 million
Surface area:	104,665 km²
Currency:	American Dollar
Language:	English

VIRGINIA

Official name: Virginia
Capital: Richmond
Population: 6.7 million
Surface area: 110,792 km²
Currency: American Dollar
Language: English

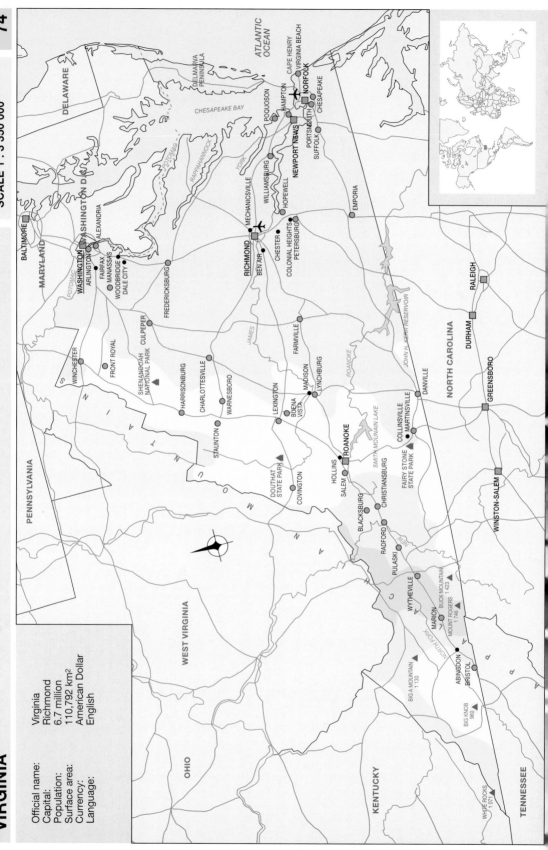

PENNSYLVANIA

OHIO

WEST VIRGINIA

KENTUCKY

TENNESSEE

NORTH CAROLINA

MARYLAND

DELAWARE

ATLANTIC OCEAN

CHESAPEAKE BAY

DELMARVA PENINSULA

BALTIMORE

WASHINGTON D.C.
ARLINGTON
ALEXANDRIA
FAIRFAX
MANASSAS
WOODBRIDGE
DALE CITY

WINCHESTER

FRONT ROYAL

SHENANDOAH NATIONAL PARK

HARRISONBURG

CHARLOTTESVILLE

WARNESBORO

STAUNTON

LEXINGTON

BUENA VISTA

COVINGTON

DOUTHAT STATE PARK

HOLLINS
SALEM
ROANOKE

BLACKSBURG

CHRISTIANSBURG

RADFORD

PULASKI

WYTHEVILLE

MARION

ABINGDON
BRISTOL

BIG A MOUNTAIN 1 130

BIG KNOB 960

WHITE ROCKS 1 071

NORTH FORK

BUCK MOUNTAIN 1 423
MOUNT ROGERS 1 746

FAIRY STONE STATE PARK

SMITH MOUNAIN LAKE

COLLINSVILLE
MARTINSVILLE

DANVILLE

WINSTON-SALEM

GREENSBORO

DURHAM

RALEIGH

JOHN H. KERR RESERVOIR

EMPORIA

ROANOKE

NEW

JAMES

FARMVILLE

MADISON
LYNCHBURG

CULPEPER

FREDERICKSBURG

RAPPAHANNOCK

POTOMAC

YORK

RICHMOND
MECHANICSVILLE
BEN AIR
CHESTER
COLONIAL HEIGHTS
PETERSBURG

HOPEWELL

WILLIAMSBURG

POQUOSON

HAMPTON
NEWPORT NEWS
NORFOLK
PORTSMOUTH
CHESAPEAKE
SUFFOLK

CAPE HENRY
VIRGINIA BEACH

TENNESSEE

VIRGINIA

NORTH CAROLINA

SOUTH CAROLINA

KENTUCKY

GEORGIA

MACON

ATLANTA

ILLINOIS

MISSOURI

ARKANSAS

MISSISSIPPI

ALABAMA

HUNTSVILLE

BRISTOL
KINGSPORT
ELIZABETHTON
JOHNSON CITY
ERWIN
GREENEVILLE
MORRISTOWN
JEFFERSON CITY
MOUNT GYOT 2018
GREAT SMOKEY MOUNTAINS
APPALACHIAN
LA FOLLETTE
NORRIS DAM STATE PARK
KNOXVILLE
MARYVILLE
CLINGMANS DOME 2 025
HAW KNOB 1 666
OAK RIDGE
FARRAGUT
SWEET WATER
ATHENS
CLEVELAND
DALE HOLLOW LAKE
FALL CREEK STATE PARK
COOKEVILLE
DAYTON
SODDY-DAISY
RED
CHATTANOOGA
CUMBERLAND PLATEAU
TENNESSEE
MCMINNVILLE
MURFREESBORO
SHELBYVILLE
TULLAHOMA
LEWISBURG
FAYETTEVILLE
PORTLAND
GALLATIN
LEBANON
NASHVILLE
BRENTWOOD
SPRINGFIELD
JASPER
FRANKLIN
COLUMBIA
TUSCALOOSA
PULASKI
LAWRENCEBURG
CLARKSVILLE
DICKSON
CUMBERLAND
KENTUCKY LAKE
LAKE BARKLEY
SAVANNAH
TENNESSEE
LEXINGTON
MCKENZIE
PARIS
MARTIN
UNION CITY
MILAN
JACKSON
BOLIVAR
DYERSBURG
HUMBOLDT
COVINGTON
MILLINGTON
BARTLETT
GERMANTOWN
COLLIERVILLE
MEMPHIS
SOUTHAVEN
MISSISSIPPI
HOLSTON

Official name:	Tennessee
Capital:	Nashville
Population:	5.3 million
Surface area:	109,158 km²
Currency:	American Dollar
Language:	English

NORTH CAROLINA

Official name:	North Carolina
Capital:	Raleigh
Population:	7.3 million
Surface area:	139,397 km²
Currency:	American Dollar
Language:	English

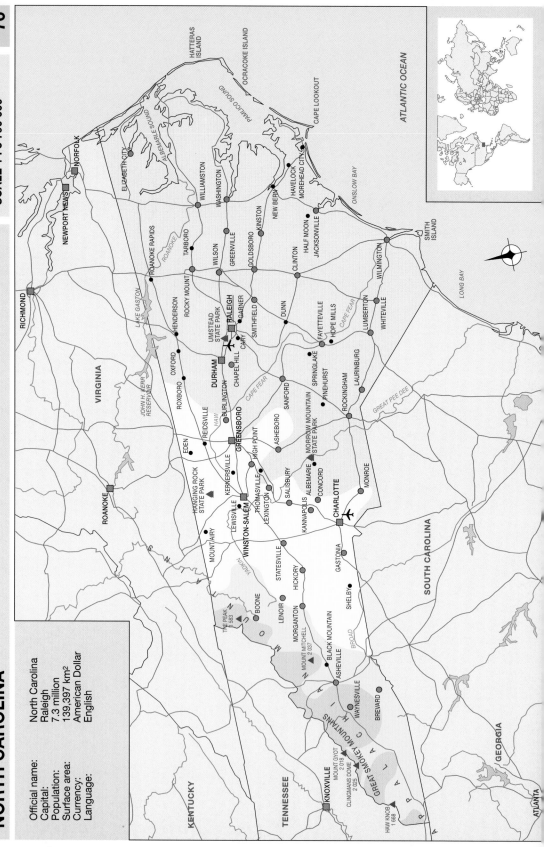

SOUTH CAROLINA

ATLANTIC OCEAN

NORTH CAROLINA

GEORGIA

KNOXVILLE

CHARLOTTE

ATLANTA

Official name: South Carolina
Capital: Columbia
Population: 3.7 million
Surface area: 82,902 km²
Currency: American Dollar
Language: English

NORTH MYRTLE BEACH
MYRTLE BEACH
GARDEN CITY
LONG BAY
SOCASTEE
CONWAY
GREAT PEE DEE
DILLON
MULLENS
MARION
BENNETTSVILLE
LAKE CITY
KINGSTREE
GEORGE TOWN
SANTEE
BULLS BAY
MONCKS CORNER
GOOSE CREEK
HANAHAN
NORTH CHARLESTON
MOUNT PLEASANT
JAMES ISLAND
CHARLESTON
SAINT ANDREWS
LADSON
SUMMERVILLE
SAINT HELENA SOUND
HUNTING ISLAND STATE PARK
HILTON HEAD ISLAND
BEAUFORT
BURTON
WALTERBORO
LAKE MOULTRIE
LAKE MARION
MANNING
SHANNONTOWN
SUMTER
CAMDEN
CHERAW
CHERAW STATE PARK
HARTSVILLE
DARLINGTON
BISHOPVILLE
FLORENCE
LANCASTER
COLUMBIA
CAYCE VIEW
WEST COLUMBIA
BROAD
LAKE MURRAY
ORANGEBURG
SAVANNAH
BARNWELL
AIKEN
NORTH AUGUSTA
BATESBURG
NEWBERRY
GREENWOOD
CLARKS HILL LAKE
ABEVILLE
LAURENS
HONEA PATH
CLINTON
UNION
CROFT STATE PARK
WOODRUFF
SPARTANBURG
GAFFNEY
EAST GAFFNEY
YORK
ROCK HILL
CHESTER
HOGBACK MOUNTAIN 994
GREER
TAYLORS
GREENVILLE
EASLEY
SENECA
ANDERSON
CLEMSON
HARTWELL LAKE
SASSAFRAS MOUNTAIN 1 085

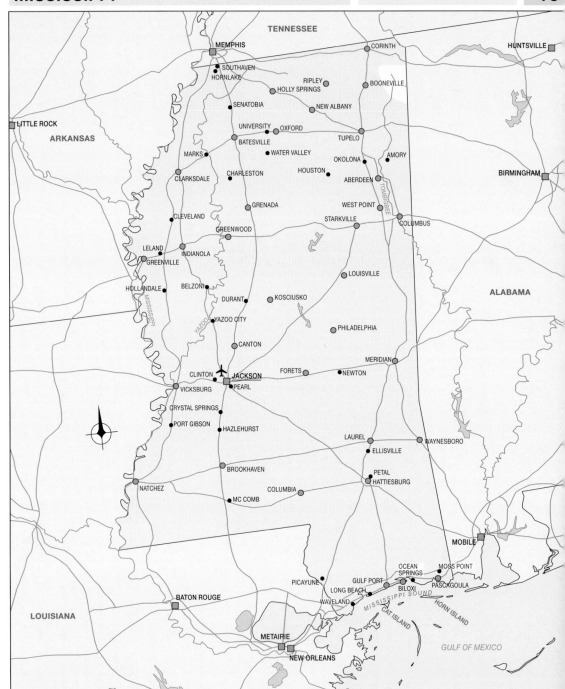

TENNESSEE

MEMPHIS
SOUTHAVEN
HORNLAKE
RIPLEY
HOLLY SPRINGS
BOONEVILLE
CORINTH
HUNTSVILLE

LITTLE ROCK
ARKANSAS
SENATOBIA
NEW ALBANY

UNIVERSITY OXFORD
BATESVILLE
WATER VALLEY
TUPELO

MARKS
CHARLESTON
HOUSTON
OKOLONA
AMORY
ABERDEEN
BIRMINGHAM

CLARKSDALE
GRENADA
WEST POINT

CLEVELAND
GREENWOOD
STARKVILLE
COLUMBUS
TOMBIGBEE

LELAND
INDIANOLA
GREENVILLE
LOUISVILLE
ALABAMA

HOLLANDALE
BELZONI
DURANT
KOSCIUSKO

MISSISSIPPI
YAZOO CITY
YAZOO
PHILADELPHIA

CANTON

CLINTON JACKSON FORETS
MERIDIAN
NEWTON

VICKSBURG
PEARL

CRYSTAL SPRINGS
PORT GIBSON
HAZLEHURST

LAUREL
WAYNESBORO
ELLISVILLE

BROOKHAVEN
PETAL
HATTIESBURG

NATCHEZ
COLUMBIA
MC COMB

MOBILE

OCEAN SPRINGS
MOSS POINT
PICAYUNE
GULF PORT
PASCAGOULA
LONG BEACH
BILOXI
BATON ROUGE
WAVELAND
MISSISSIPPI SOUND
CAT ISLAND
HORN ISLAND

LOUISIANA
METAIRIE
GULF OF MEXICO
NEW ORLEANS

Official name:	Mississippi
Capital:	Jackson
Population:	2.7 million
Surface area:	125,443 km²
Currency:	American Dollar
Language:	English

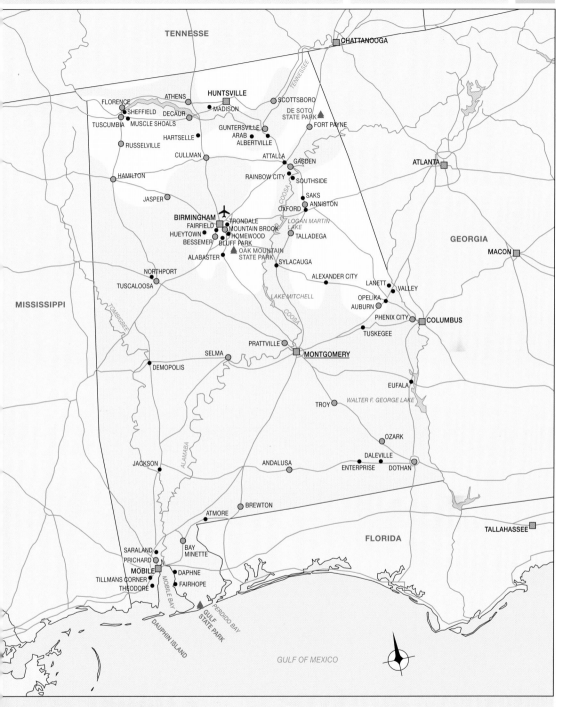

TENNESSE

CHATTANOOGA

HUNTSVILLE
ATHENS
FLORENCE
SHEFFIELD
DECAUR
TUSCUMBIA
MUSCLE SHOALS
RUSSELLVILLE
HARTSELLE
MADISON
SCOTTSBORO
DE SOTO
STATE PARK
FORT PAYNE
GUNTERSVILLE
ARAB
ALBERTVILLE

HAMILTON

CULLMAN
ATTALLA
GADSDEN
RAINBOW CITY
SOUTHSIDE
SAKS
ANNISTON
OXFORD

JASPER

ATLANTA

GEORGIA

MACON

BIRMINGHAM
IRONDALE
FAIRFIELD
MOUNTAIN BROOK
HUEYTOWN
HOMEWOOD
BESSEMER
BLUFF PARK
ALABASTER
OAK MOUNTAIN
STATE PARK
LOGAN MARTIN
LAKE
TALLADEGA
SYLACAUGA

NORTHPORT
TUSCALOOSA

ALEXANDER CITY
LANETT
VALLEY
OPELIKA
AUBURN
PHENIX CITY
COLUMBUS

MISSISSIPPI

LAKE MITCHELL

TOMBIGBEE

COOSA

PRATTVILLE
SELMA
MONTGOMERY
TUSKEGEE

DEMOPOLIS

EUFALA
TROY
WALTER F. GEORGE LAKE

ALABAMA

OZARK
JACKSON
ANDALUSA
DALEVILLE
ENTERPRISE
DOTHAN

BREWTON
ATMORE

FLORIDA

TALLAHASSEE

SARALAND
BAY
MINETTE
PRICHARD
MOBILE
TILLMANS CORNER
DAPHNE
THEODORE
FAIRHOPE
MOBILE BAY
PERDIDO BAY
GULF
STATE PARK
DAUPHIN ISLAND

GULF OF MEXICO

Official name:	Alabama
Capital:	Montgomery
Population:	4.3 million
Surface area:	135,775 km²
Currency:	American Dollar
Language:	English

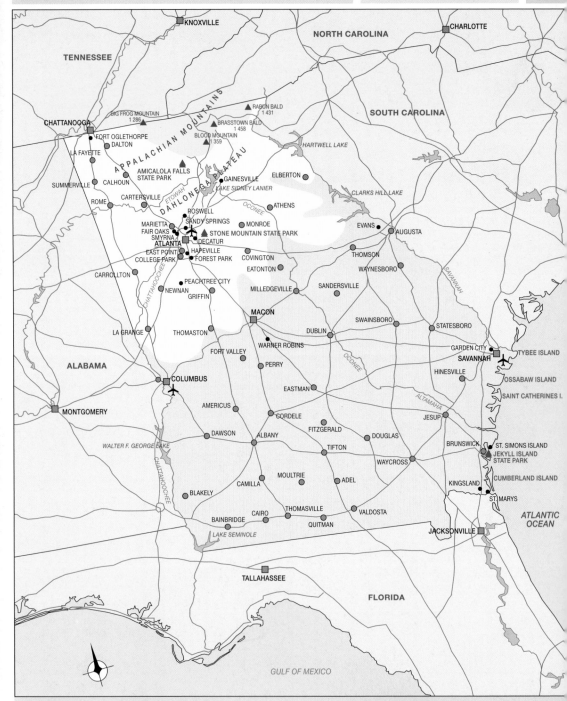

TENNESSEE

KNOXVILLE

NORTH CAROLINA

CHARLOTTE

CHATTANOOGA

BIG FROG MOUNTAIN
1 286

RABUN BALD
1 431

SOUTH CAROLINA

FORT OGLETHORPE
DALTON

BRASSTOWN BALD
1 458
BLOOD MOUNTAIN
1 359

APPALACHIAN MOUNTAINS

LA FAYETTE

HARTWELL LAKE

SUMMERVILLE

CALHOUN

AMICALOLA FALLS
STATE PARK

DAHLONEGA PLATEAU

GAINESVILLE

ELBERTON

CARTERSVILLE

ETOWAH

Lake Sidney Lanier

CLARKS HILL LAKE

ROME

OCONEE

ROSWELL

ATHENS

MARIETTA
FAIR OAKS
SMYRNA
ATLANTA
EAST POINT
COLLEGE PARK

SANDY SPRINGS

DECATUR

MONROE

STONE MOUNTAIN STATE PARK

EVANS

AUGUSTA

HAPEVILLE
FOREST PARK

COVINGTON

THOMSON

CARROLLTON

CHATTAHOOCHEE

PEACHTREE CITY

EATONTON

WAYNESBORO

NEWNAN
GRIFFIN

MILLEDGEVILLE

SANDERSVILLE

SAVANNAH

LA GRANGE

THOMASTON

MACON

DUBLIN

SWAINSBORO

STATESBORO

ALABAMA

FORT VALLEY

WARNER ROBINS

OCONEE

GARDEN CITY

SAVANNAH

TYBEE ISLAND

COLUMBUS

PERRY

HINESVILLE

OSSABAW ISLAND

MONTGOMERY

AMERICUS

EASTMAN

ALTAMAHA

SAINT CATHERINES I.

WALTER F. GEORGE LAKE

DAWSON

CORDELE

ALBANY

FITZGERALD

TIFTON

DOUGLAS

WAYCROSS

JESUP

BRUNSWICK

ST. SIMONS ISLAND
JEKYLL ISLAND
STATE PARK

CHATTAHOOCHEE

CAMILLA

MOULTRIE

ADEL

KINGSLAND

CUMBERLAND ISLAND

BLAKELY

ST. MARYS

BAINBRIDGE

CAIRO

THOMASVILLE

VALDOSTA

ATLANTIC
OCEAN

LAKE SEMINOLE

QUITMAN

JACKSONVILLE

TALLAHASSEE

FLORIDA

GULF OF MEXICO

Official name:	Georgia
Capital:	Atlanta
Population:	7.4 million
Surface area:	153,952 km²
Currency:	American Dollar
Language:	English

FLORIDA

SCALE 1 : 6 030 000

ATLANTIC OCEAN

GULF OF MEXICO

BAHAMA'S

NASSAU

MISSISSIPPI
LOUISIANA
ALABAMA
GEORGIA

MOBILE
WEST PENSACOLA
PENSACOLA
PENSACOLA BAY
CRESTVIEW
FORT WALTON BEACH
CHOCTAWHATCHEE BAY
DE FUNIAK SPRINGS
PANAMA CITY
WEST BAY
EAST BAY
PANAMA BAY
SAINT JOSEPH BAY
CAPE SAN BLAS
MARIANNA
FLORIDA CAVERNS STATE PARK
APALACHICOLA
QUINCY
TALLAHASSEE
LAKE SEMINOLE
APALACHEE BAY
PERRY
LIVE OAK
LAKE CITY
FERNANDINA BEACH
JACKSONVILLE
JACKSONVILLE BEACH
SAINT JOHNS
ST. AUGUSTINE
PALM COAST
PALATKA
STARKE
GAINESVILLE
SILVER SPRINGS
OCALA
LAKE GEORGE
ORMOND BEACH
DAYTONA BEACH
LEESBURG
SANFORD
LAKE APOPKA
ORLANDO
WACCASASSA BAY
BROOKSVILLE
SPRINGHILL
WINTER HAVEN
LAKE LAND
PLANT CITY
LAKE KISSIMMEE
LAKE ISTOKPOGA
TITUSVILLE
CAPE CANAVERAL
MERRIT ISLAND
COCOA ISLAND
COCOA
MELBOURNE
PALM BAY
VERO BEACH
FORT PIERCE
FORT SAINT LUCIE
DUNEDIN
CLEARWATER
LARGO
PINELLAS PARK
TAMPA
BRANDON
TAMPA BAY
ST. PETERSBURG
BRADENTON
SARASOTA
VENICE
MYAKKA RIVER STATE PARK
PORT CHARLOTTE
CHARLOTTE HARBOR
FORT MYERS
CAPE CORAL
LAKE OKEECHOBEE
BELLE GLADE
PALM BEACH
WEST PALM BEACH
BOYTON BEACH
DELRAY BEACH
DEERFIELD BEACH
POMPANO BEACH
BOCA RATON
FORT LAUDERDALE
HOLLYWOOD
DAVIE
MARGATE
HIALEAH
MIAMI BEACH
NORTH MIAMI
MIAMI SPRINGS
MIAMI
CORAL GABLES
KENDALL
HOMESTEAD
NAPLES
COLIER-SEMINOLE STATE PARK
EVERGLADES NATIONAL PARK
CAPE ROMANO
WHITEWATER BAY
EAST CAPE
FLORIDA BAY
CORAL LARGO
KEY LARGO
KEY WEST
FLORIDA KEYS
STRAITS OF FLORIDA

Official name:	Florida
Capital:	Tallahassee
Population:	14.4 million
Surface area:	170,314 km²
Currency:	American Dollar
Language:	English

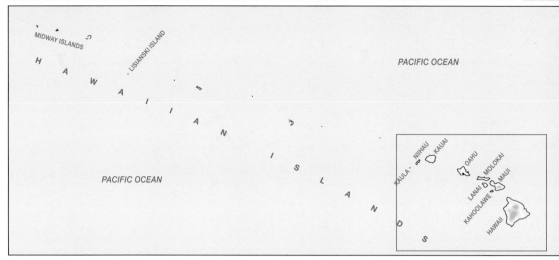

MIDWAY ISLANDS

LISIANSKI ISLAND

PACIFIC OCEAN

H
A
W
A
I
I
A
N

I
S
L
A
N
D
S

PACIFIC OCEAN

KAULA · NIIHAU · KAUAI
OAHU
MOLOKAI
LANAI · MAUI
KAHOOLAWE
HAWAII

SCALE 1 : 4 350 000

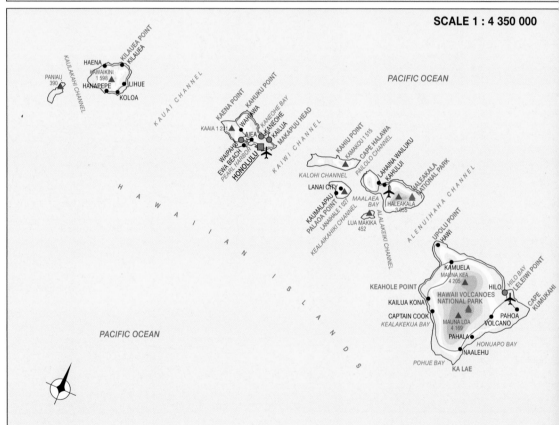

KILAUEA POINT
KILAUEA
HAENA
KAWAIKINI 1 598
HANAPEPE · ILIHUE
KOLOA
KAULAKAHI CHANNEL
PANIAU 390

KAUAI CHANNEL

KAENA POINT
KAHUKU POINT
WAHIAWA
KANEOHE BAY
KAAIA 1 231
AIEA · KANEOHE
KAILUA
MAKAPUU HEAD
WAIPAHU
EWA BEACH
PEARL HARBOR
HONOLULU

PACIFIC OCEAN

KAIWI CHANNEL

KAHIU POINT
KAMAKOU 1 515
CAPE HALAWA
PAILOLO CHANNEL
LAHAINA · WAILUKU
KAHULUI
KALOHI CHANNEL
LANAI CITY

HALEAKALA NATIONAL PARK

KAUMALAPAU
PALAOA POINT
LANAIHALE 1 027
LANAIHIKI CHANNEL
MAALAEA BAY
HALEAKALA 3 055

LUA MAKIKA 452
KEALAIKAHIKI CHANNEL
ALALAKEIKI CHANNEL

ALENUIHAHA CHANNEL

UPOLU POINT
HAWI

H
A
W
A
I
I
A
N

I
S
L
A
N
D
S

KAMUELA
MAUNA KEA 4 205
HILO BAY
LELEIWI POINT
KEAHOLE POINT
HILO
HAWAII VOLCANOES NATIONAL PARK
CAPE KUMUKAHI
KAILUA KONA
CAPTAIN COOK
KEALAKEKUA BAY
MAUNA LOA 4 169
PAHOA
VOLCANO
PAHALA
HONUAPO BAY
NAALEHU
POHUE BAY
KA LAE

PACIFIC OCEAN

Official name:	State of Hawaiian Islands
Capital:	Honolulu
Population:	1.2 million
Surface area:	28,313 km²
Currency:	American Dollar
Language:	English

CENTRAL AMERICA

SCALE 1 : 22 900 000

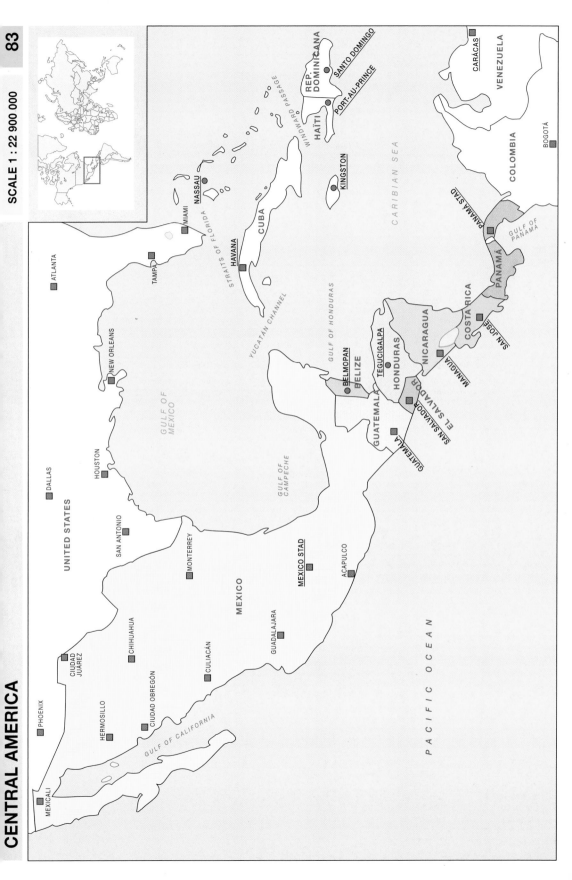

UNITED STATES

PHOENIX
MEXICALI
CIUDAD JUÁREZ
DALLAS
HERMOSILLO
CHIHUAHUA
SAN ANTONIO
ATLANTA
HOUSTON
CIUDAD OBREGÓN
CULIACÁN
MONTERREY
NEW ORLEANS
TAMPA
MIAMI
GUADALAJARA
MEXICO STAD
ACAPULCO
GULF OF CALIFORNIA
MEXICO
GULF OF MEXICO
GULF OF CAMPECHE
STRAITS OF FLORIDA
NASSAU
HAVANA
CUBA
YUCATÁN CHANNEL
GULF OF HONDURAS
BELMOPAN
BELIZE
GUATEMALA
GUATEMALA
SAN SALVADOR
EL SALVADOR
TEGUCIGALPA
HONDURAS
NICARAGUA
MANAGUA
COSTA RICA
SAN JOSE
PANAMÁ
PANAMA STAD
GULF OF PANAMA
KINGSTON
CARIBBEAN SEA
WINDWARD PASSAGE
HAÏTI
PORT-AU-PRINCE
REP. DOMINICANA
SANTO DOMINGO
VENEZUELA
CARACAS
COLOMBIA
BOGOTÁ
PACIFIC OCEAN

MEXICO

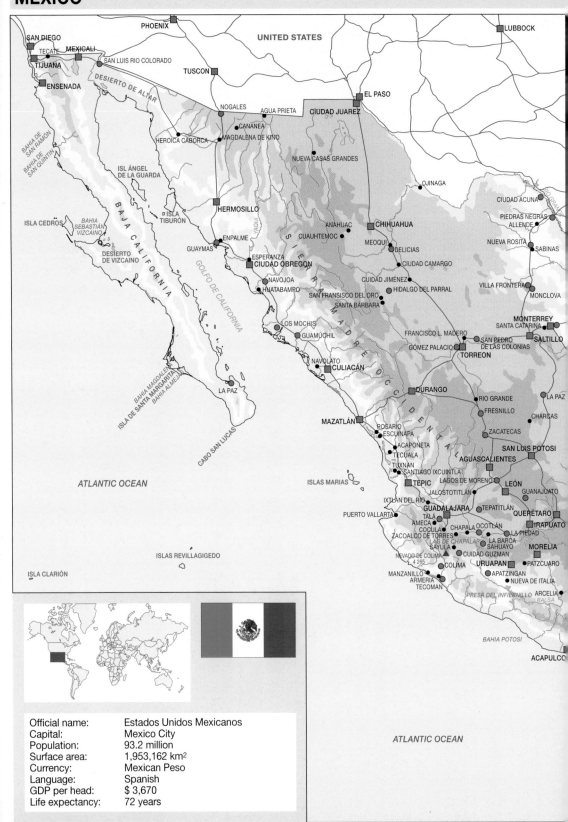

Official name:	Estados Unidos Mexicanos
Capital:	Mexico City
Population:	93.2 million
Surface area:	1,953,162 km²
Currency:	Mexican Peso
Language:	Spanish
GDP per head:	$ 3,670
Life expectancy:	72 years

WICHITA FALLS

FORT WORTH
DALLAS
SHREVEPORT
JACKSON

WACO

UNITED STATES

AUSTIN

SAN ANTONIO
HOUSTON
PASADENA
BATON ROUGE
MOBILE
METAIRIE
NEW ORLEANS

BIRMINGHAM
MACON
COLUMBUS
MONTGOMERY
TALLAHASSEE

LAREDO

CORPUS CHRISTI

FALCON RESERVOIR
SABINAS HIDALGO
REYNOSA
MATAMOROS
GUADELUPE
RIO BRAVO
VALLE HERMOSO
MONTERREY
MONTEMORELOS
LINARES

LAGUNA MADRE

S I E R R A   M A D R E

CIUDAD VICTORIA

CIUDAD MANTE

CIUDAD MADERO
CIUDAD VALLES
TAMPICO

GULF OF MEXICO

LAGUNA DE TAMIAHUA

TAMAZUNCHALE
TANTOYUCA
CERRO AZUL
TUXPAN
QUERÉTARO
POZA RICA DE HIDALGO
SAN JUAN
PAPANTLA
ACTOPAN
PACHUCA
MARTINEZ DE LA TORRE
CIUDAD DE MÉXICO
TEPEJI DEL RIO
TEZUITLAN
IZTACCIHUATL 5286
APIZACO
PEROTE
TOLUCA
JALAPA
CUERNAVACA
PUEBLA
ORIZABA
VERACRUZ
YAUTEPEC
VOLCAN POPOCATEPETL 5452
CORDOBAS
ALVARADO
TAXCO DE ALARCÓN
TIERRA BLANCA
SAN ANDRÉS TUXTLA
IGUALA
TEHUACAN
PRESA MIGUEL ALEMÁN
COATZACOALCOS
ARCELIA
COSAMALOAPAN
ACAYUCAN
MINATITLAN
LAS CHOAPAS
HUAJUAPAN DE LEON
CHILPANCINGO
MATIAS ROMERO
ACAPULCO
OAXACA
CIUDAD IXTEPEC
JUCHITÁN
SALINA CRUZ

BAHIA DE CAMPECHE

LAGUNA DE TÉRMINOS

CAMPECHE
PROGRESSO
TIZIMIN
CANCÚN
MOTUL DE FELIPE
CARRILLO PUERTO
MÉRIDA
TICUL
VALLADOLID
TEKAX DE ALVARO OBREGÓN
CABO CATOCHE
ISLA DE COZUMEL
BAHIA DE LA ASCENSIÓN
BAHIA DEL ESPIRITU SANTO
YUCATAN PENINSULA
CIUDAD CHETUMAL
LAGUNA DE BACALAR

CIUDAD DEL CARMEN
FRONTERA
COMALCALCO
CÁRDENAS
VILLAHERMOSA
MACUSPANA
TENOSIQUE
BELMOPAN
BELIZE
GULF OF HONDURAS

TUXTLA GUTIERREZ
SAN CRISTOBAL DE LAS CASAS
OCOZOCOAUTLA
VENUSTIANO CARRANZA
ARRIAGA
COMITAN
TONALÁ
PRESA DE LA ANGOSTURA
SIERRA MADRE DEL SUR
SIERRA MADRE
PRESA NEZAHUALCÓYOTII

HUIXTLA
TAPACHULA
GUATEMALA
GUATEMALA

SAN PEDRO SULA
HONDURAS
SAN SALVADOR
TEGUCIGALPA
EL SALVADOR
NICARAGUA

GOLFO DE TEHUANTEPEC

PACIFIC OCEAN

MANAGUA

MEXICO

CHETUMAL

CHETUMAL BAY

COROTAL

CALEDONIA

ORANGE WALK

AMBERGRIS CAY

GULF OF MEXICO

INDIAN CHURCH

HILL BANK

SIERRÁ DE AGUA

BELIZE CITY

TURNEFFE ISLANDS

BELMOPAN

BENQUE VIEJO

MIDDLESEX

STAN CREEK

VICTORIA PEAK
▲ 1 122

MAYA MOUNTAINS

GULF OF HONDURAS

PALMAR CAMP

MONKEY RIVER

CASEMERO PALMA

SAN ANTONIO

PUNTA NEGRA

PORT HONDURAS

PUNTA GORDA

GUATEMALA

SARSTOON

BAHIA DE AMATIQUE

HONDURAS

HONDO

BELIZE

BELIZE

Official name:	Belize
Capital:	Belmopan
Population:	0.2 million
Surface area:	22,965 km²
Currency:	Belize Dollar
Language:	English
GDP per head:	$ 2,700
Life expectancy:	75 years

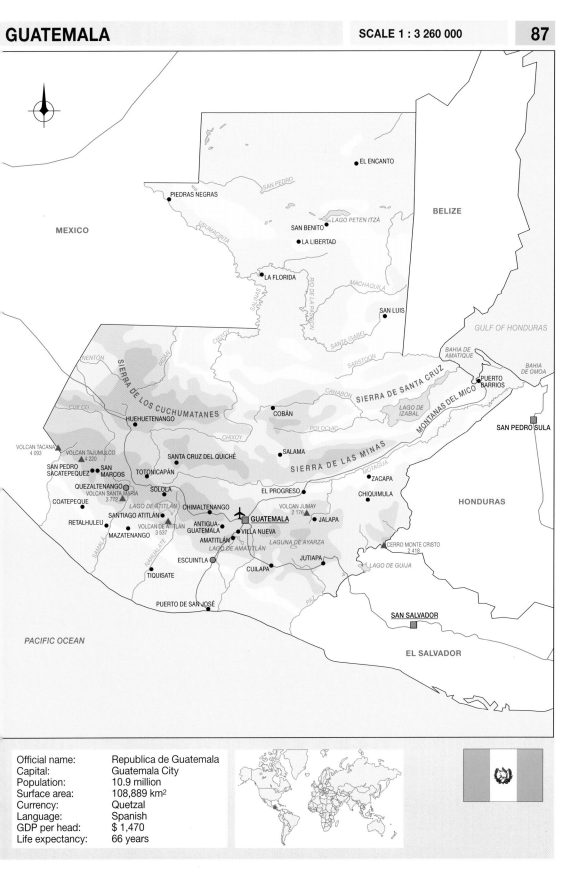

MEXICO

EL ENCANTO

PIEDRAS NEGRAS

SAN PEDRO

LAGO PETEN ITZÀ

BELIZE

SAN BENITO

LA LIBERTAD

USUMACINTA

LA FLORIDA

MACHAQUILA

SAN LUIS

RIO DE LA PASSION

SALINAS

SANTA ISABEL

GULF OF HONDURAS

CHIXOY

NENTÓN

SIERRA DE LOS CUCHUMATANES

CUILCO

IXCAN

SARSTOON

CAHABÓN

SIERRA DE SANTA CRUZ

BAHIA DE AMATIQUE

BAHIA DE OMOA

PUERTO BARRIOS

MONTANAS DEL MICO

HUEHUETENANGO

CHIXOY

COBÁN

POLOCHIC

LAGO DE IZABAL

SAN PEDRO SULA

VOLCAN TACANA 4 093

VOLCAN TAJUMULCO 4 220

SALAMA

SANTA CRUZ DEL QUICHÉ

SIERRA DE LAS MINAS

MOTAGUA

SAN PEDRO SACATEPEQUEZ

SAN MARCOS

TOTONICAPÁN

ZACAPA

QUEZALTENANGO

VOLCAN SANTA MARIA 3 772

SOLOLA

EL PROGRESO

CHIQUIMULA

HONDURAS

COATEPEQUE

LAGO DE ATITLÁN

CHIMALTENANGO

VOLCAN JUMAY 2 176

JALAPA

RETALHULEU

SANTIAGO ATITLÁN

VOLCAN DE ATITLÁN 3 537

ANTIGUA-GUATEMALA

GUATEMALA

MAZATENANGO

VILLA NUEVA

SAMALÁ

NAHUALATE

AMATITLÁN

LAGUNA DE AYARZA

CERRO MONTE CRISTO 2 418

LAGO DE AMATITLÁN

ESCUINTLA

JUTIAPA

CUILAPA

LAGO DE GUIJA

TIQUISATE

PUERTO DE SAN JOSÉ

PAZ

SAN SALVADOR

PACIFIC OCEAN

EL SALVADOR

Official name:	Republica de Guatemala
Capital:	Guatemala City
Population:	10.9 million
Surface area:	108,889 km²
Currency:	Quetzal
Language:	Spanish
GDP per head:	$ 1,470
Life expectancy:	66 years

EL SALVADOR

SCALE 1 : 2 210 000

Official name:	Republica de El Salvador
Capital:	San Salvador
Population:	5.8 million
Surface area:	21,041 km²
Currency:	El Salvador colón
Language:	Spanish
GDP per head:	$ 1,700
Life expectancy:	69 years

HONDURAS

SCALE 1 : 3 500 000

Official name:	Republica de Honduras
Capital:	Tegucigalpa
Population:	6.1 million
Surface area:	112,492 km²
Currency:	Lempira
Language:	Spanish
GDP per head:	$ 660
Life expectancy:	67 years

CARIBBEAN SEA

BELIZE

GUATEMALA

EL SALVADOR

NICARAGUA

PACIFIC OCEAN

GULF OF HONDURAS

GOLFO DE FONSECA

CABO GRACIAS A DIOS

CABO FALSO

LAGUNA DE CARATASCA

PUERTO LEMPIRA

PUNTA PATUCA

LAGUNA DE BRUS

CABO CAMARON

PUNTA CATCHABUTAN

CABO DE HONDURAS

TRUJILLO

PUNTA SAL

BAHIA DE TELA

PUNTA IZOPO

TELA

LA CEIBA

PUERTO CORTES

BAHIA DE OMOA

SAN PEDRO SULA

LA LIMA

EL PROGRESO

CERRO PAYAS 1 128

CERRO PIFLAS 1 035

MONTE LA MORA 470

JUTICALPA

MONTANA DE COLÓN

MONTE MUCUPINA 2 184

CORDILLERA NOMBRE DE DIOS

PICO BONITO 2 435

CERRO SAN FRANCO 2 208

YORO

PICO PUJOL 2 282

MONTANA DE COMAYAGUA

SIGUATEPEQUE

COMAYAGA

LA PAZ

SANTA BARBARA

CORD. DEMONTECILLOS

CERRO CUCHILLA ALPA 1 737

CERRO SAN ILDEFONSO 2 228

LAGO DE YOJOA

CORDILLERA OPALACA

CERRO AZUL 2 225

LA ESPERANZA

SANTA ROSA DE COPAN

GRACIAS

CERRO LAS MINAS 2 849

NUEVA OCOTEPEQUE

CERRO MONTE CRISTO 2 418

TEGUCIGALPA

YUSCARAN

CERRO RINCON DEL OCOTE 1 154

MONTA NA YERBA BUENA 2 243

NACAOME

CHOLUTECA

CERRO GUANACAURE 1 020

PICO MOGOTON 2 107

CORDILLERA ENTRE RIOS

MONTANA VILLA SANTA

GUAYAMBRE

GUAYAPE

JALAN

PATUCA

COCO

SICO

TINTO

AGUAN

VAGUALA

SULACE

HUMUYA

OTORO

JICATUYO

CHABELECON

HIGUITO

MOCAL

PALIALA

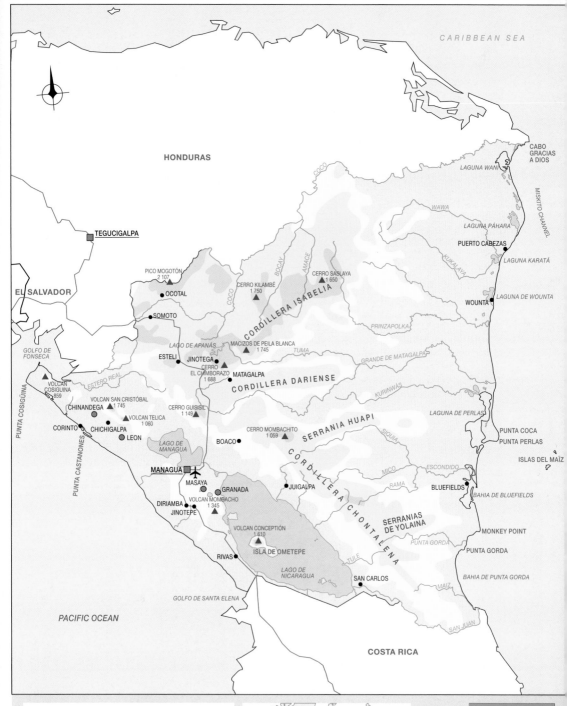

CARIBBEAN SEA

HONDURAS

■ TEGUCIGALPA

EL SALVADOR

CABO GRACIAS A DIOS

LAGUNA WANI

WAWA

LAGUNA PÁHARA

PUERTO CABEZAS

MISKITO CHANNEL

LAGUNA KARATÁ

KUKALAYA

LAGUNA DE WOUNTA

WOUNTA

GOLFO DE FONSECA

PICO MOGOTÓN
2 107
● OCOTAL

● SOMOTO

CERRO KILAMBÉ
1 750 ▲

CERRO SASLAYA
▲ 1 650

COCO

BOCAY

AMICE

CORDILLERA ISABELIA

PRINZAPOLKA

LAGO DE APANÁS

MACIZOS DE PEILA BLANCA
▲ 1 745

TUMA

GRANDE DE MATAGALPA

ESTELI ●   ● JINOTEGA

CERRO
EL CHIMBORAZO
1 688

MATAGALPA
●

CORDILLERA DARIENSE

ESTERO REAL

KURINWÁS

VOLCAN
COSIGÜINA
859 ▲

VOLCAN SAN CRISTÓBAL
CHINANDEGA ▲ 1 745

CERRO GUISISIL
1 149 ▲

LAGUNA DE PERLAS

CORINTO ●   ● CHICHIGALPA
VOLCAN TELICA
1 060 ▲
● LEON

CERRO MOMBACHITO
1 059 ▲

SERRANIA HUAPI

SIQUIA

PUNTA COCA
PUNTA PERLAS

BOACO ●

PUNTA CASTAÑONES

PUNTA COSIGÜINA

LAGO DE
MANAGUA

ISLAS DEL MAÍZ

MANAGUA ■ ✈

MASAYA ●
● GRANADA
DIRIAMBA ●   VOLCAN MOMBACHO
JINOTEPE ●   1 345 ▲

MICO

ESCONDIDO

BLUEFIELDS

BAHIA DE BLUEFIELDS

C
O
R
D
I
L
L
E
R
A
C
H
O
N
T
A
L
E
N
A

JUIGALPA ●

RAMA

SERRANIAS
DE YOLAINA

MONKEY POINT

VOLCAN CONCEPTIÓN
1 610 ▲

RIVAS ●

ISLA DE OMETEPE

PUNTA GORDA

PUNTA GORDA

PACIFIC OCEAN

LAGO DE
NICARAGUA

TULE

SAN CARLOS ●

BAHIA DE PUNTA GORDA

MAIZ

SAN JUAN

GOLFO DE SANTA ELENA

COSTA RICA

Official name:	Republica de Nicaragua
Capital:	Managua
Population:	4.5 million
Surface area:	120,254 km²
Currency:	Cordoba
Language:	Spanish
GDP per head:	$ 380
Life expectancy:	68 years

COSTA RICA

SCALE 1 : 2 740 000

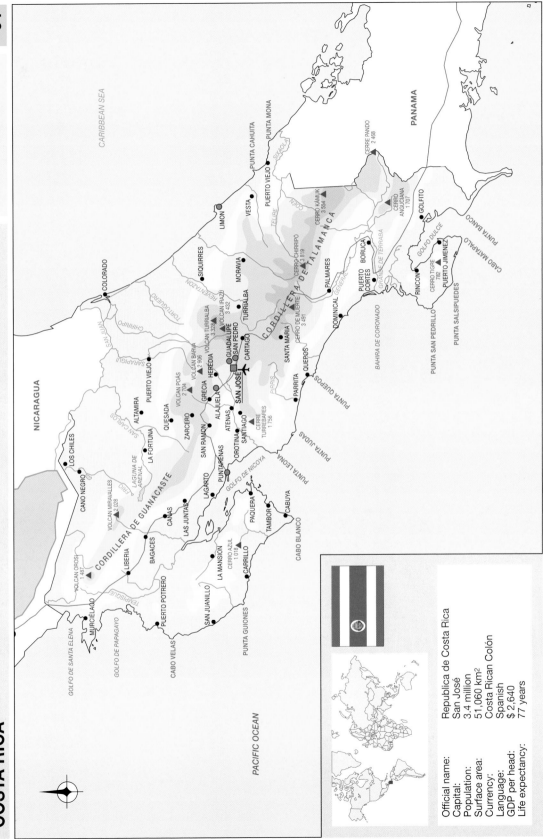

CARIBBEAN SEA

PACIFIC OCEAN

NICARAGUA

PANAMA

GOLFO DE SANTA ELENA
GOLFO DE PAPAGAYO
GOLFO DE NICOYA
CABO VELAS
PUNTA GUIONES
CABO BLANCO
CABUYA
TAMBOR
PAQUERA
PUNTA LEONA
PUNTA JUDAS
PUNTA QUEPOS
BAHIA DE CORONADO
GOLFO DULCE
PUNTA SAN PEDRILLO
PUNTA SALSIPUEDES
CABO MATAPALO
PUNTA BANCO

MURCIELAGO
PUERTO POTRERO
SAN JUANILLO
LA MANSIÓN
CARRILLO
CERRO AZUL 1 018
LIBERIA
BAGACES
CAÑAS
LAS JUNTAS
LAGARTO
PUNTARENAS
VOLCAN OROSÍ 1 487
VOLCAN MIRAVALLES 2 028
CORDILLERA DE GUANACASTE
LOS CHILES
CANO NEGRO
CANO NEGRO
LA FORTUNA
ALTAMIRA
QUESADA
ZARCERO
SAN RAMÓN
ATENAS
OROTINA
SANTIAGO
LAGUNA DE ARENAL
SARAPIQUÍ
PUERTO VIEJO
VOLCAN POÁS 2 704
GRECIA
ALAJUELA
HEREDIA
VOLCAN BARVA 2 906
VOLCAN TURRIALBA 3 328
GUADALUPE
SAN PEDRO
SAN JOSÉ
VOLCAN IRAZÚ 3 432
CARTAGO
TURRIALBA
CERRO TURREBARES 1 756
SANTA MARÍA
CERRO DE MUERTE 3 491
CERRO CHIRRIPÓ 3 819
PARRITA
QUEPOS
PALMARES
DOMINICAL
PUERTO CORTÉS
BORUCA
GRANDE DE TERRABA
RINCON
CERRO TIGRE 782
PUERTO JIMENEZ
GOLFITO
CERRO ANGUCIANA 1 707
CERRO KAMUK 3 554
CERRE PANDO 2 468
SIQUIRRES
MORAVIA
LIMON
VESTA
PUERTO VIEJO
PUNTA CAHUITA
PUNTA MONA

COLORADO

C O R D I L L E R A   D E   T A L A M A N C A

REVENTAZÓN
TORTUGUERO
CHIRRIPÓ
SAN JUAN
SAN CARLOS
TEMPISQUE
BEBEDERO
RIO GRANDE
PIRRIS
COTO
TELIRE
SIXAOLA
COEN

Official name:	Republica de Costa Rica
Capital:	San José
Population:	3.4 million
Surface area:	51,060 km²
Currency:	Costa Rican Colón
Language:	Spanish
GDP per head:	$ 2,640
Life expectancy:	77 years

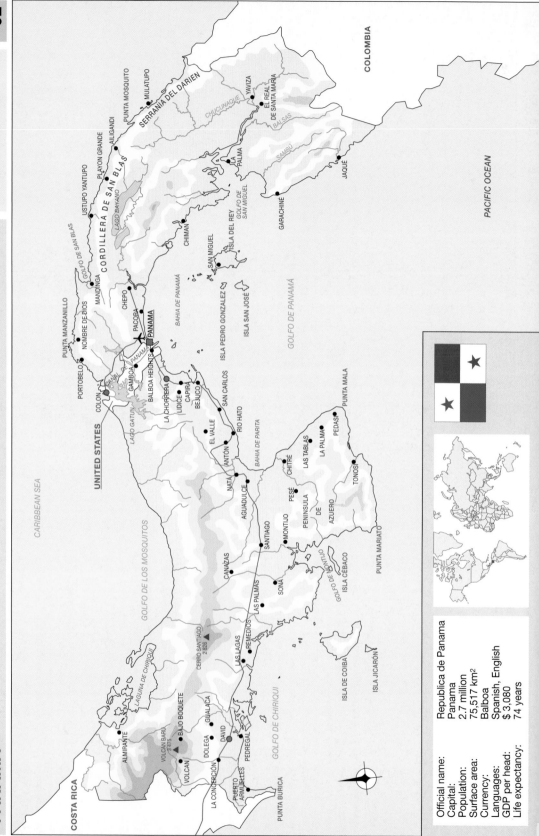

Official name:	Republica de Panama
Capital:	Panama
Population:	2.7 million
Surface area:	75,517 km²
Currency:	Balboa
Languages:	Spanish, English
GDP per head:	$ 3,080
Life expectancy:	74 years

CUBA

SCALE 1 : 5 760 000

ATLANTIC OCEAN

BAHAMAS

GULF OF MEXICO

TONGUE OF THE OCEAN

CROOKED ISLAND PASSAGE

MAYAGUANA PASSAGE

WINDWARD PASSAGE

HAITI

JAMAICA CHANNEL

CARIBBEAN SEA

NICHOLAS CHANNEL

ARCHIPIÉLAGO DE CAMAGUEY

ARCHIPIÉLAGO DE SABANA

BAHÍA DE CÁRDENAS

BAHÍA DE MATANZAS

BAHÍA DE HONDO

ARCHIPIÉLAGO DE LOS COLORADOS

GOLFO DE GUANAHACABIBES

ENSENADA DE LA SIGUANEA

ENSENADA DE CORRIENTES

CABO CORRIENTES

CABO SAN ANTONIO

GOLFO DE BATABANÓ

ENSENADA DE LA BROA

ISLAS DE LA JUVENTUD

CAYO LARGO

GOLFO DE ANA MARIA

ARCH. DE LOS JARDINES DE LA REINA

GOLFO DE GUACANAYABO

BAHÍA DE NUEVITAS

BAHÍA DE MANATÍ

BAHÍA DE CHAPARRA

BAHIA DE NIPE

SANTA DEL CRITSEL 1 143

PICA TURQUINO 1 974

CAUTO

CABO CRUZ

CAYMAN ISKANDS (U.K.)

JAMAICA

KINGSTON

HAVANA
MARIANAO
GUANABACAO
SAN ANTONIO
GUINES
MATANZAS
CARDENAS
JOVELLANOS
COLON
GUANAJAY
ARTEMISA
SAN JUAN Y MARTINEZ
LOS PALACIOS
CONSOLACIÓN DEL SUR
PINAR DEL RIO
DE LOS BAÑOS
NUEVA GERONA
SANTA CLARA
SAGUA LA GRANDE
CIENFUEGOS
MANICARAGUA
PICA SAN JUAN 1 156
TRINIDAD
CAIBARIÉN
PLACETAS
CABAIGUAN
FOMENTO
SANCTI-SPIRITUS
CIEGO DE AVILA
MORÓN
CAMAGUEY
VERTIENTES
NUEVITAS
MINAS
SANTA CRUZ DEL SUR
VICTORIA DE LAS TUNAS
PUERTO PADRE
GIBARA
BANES
PUNTA DE MULAS
HOLGUIN
SAN GERMAN
BAYAMO
MANZANILLO
NIQUERO
JIGUANI
PALMA SORIANO
MAYAN
SAGUA DE TANAMO
BARACOA
PUNTA DEL QUEMADO
GUANTÁNAMO
SANTA DEL CRITSEL
SAN LUIS
SANTIAGO DE CUBA

Official name:	Republica de Cuba
Capital:	Havana
Population:	11 million
Surface area:	110,860 km^2
Currency:	Cuban Peso
Language:	Spanish
GDP per head:	$ 3,115
Life expectancy:	76 years

CARIBBEAN

UNITED STATES

FORT LAUNDERS

MIAMI

GULF OF MEXICO

CAPE SABLE
FLORIDA BAY

FLORIDA KEYS

STRAITS OF FLORIDA

GRAND
BAHAMA

GREAT ABACO ISLAND

BAHAMA'S

NASSAU

ELEUTHERA ISLAND

CAT ISLAND

ANDROS ISLAND

EXUMA SOUND

SAN SALVADOR

DOLLY CAYS

GREAT BAHAMA BANK

LONG ISLAND

CROOKED ISLAND PASSAGE

ATLANTIC OCEAN

MAYAGUANA PASSAGE

MAYAGUANA

CAICOS PASSAGE

YUCATAN CHANNEL

CABO SAN
ANTONIO

HAVANA

GOLFO DE
BATANO

SANTA CLARA

CUBA

ISLA DE LA JUVENTUD

ACKLINS
ISLANDS

GRAND TURK

HOLGUÍN

GOLFO DE
GUACANAYABO

SANTIAGO
DE CUBA

GUANTANAMO

CABO CRUZ

WINDWARD PASSAGE

HAÏTI

CAYMAN ISLANDS (U.K.)

GEORGETOWN

G R E A T E R   A N T I L L E S

JAMAICA CHANNEL

PORT-AU-PRINCE

MONTEGO BAY

JAMAICA

KINGSTON

HONDURAS

CARIBBEAN SEA

PUERTO CABEZAS

NICARAGUA

MANAGUA

LAGO DE
NICARAGUA

COSTA RICA

LIMÓN

SAN JOSÉ

PANAMA CANAL

UNITED STATES

COLÓN

PANAMÁ

PANAMA

GOLFO DE
PANAMÁ

SANTA MARTA

BARRANQUILL

CARTAGENA

MARACAIBO

MONTERIA

CAUCA

CÚCUTA

BUCARAMANGA

MAGDALENA

COLOMBIA

BARRANCABERMAJA

PACIFIC OCEAN

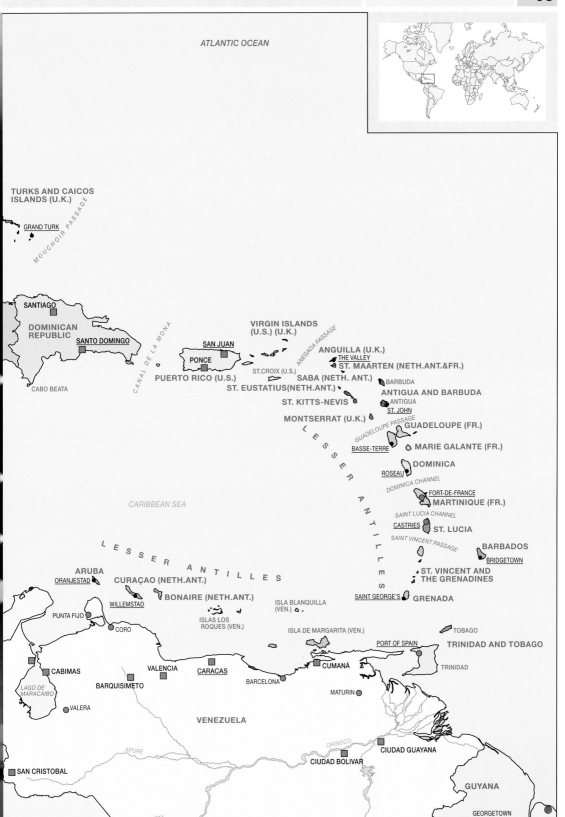

ATLANTIC OCEAN

TURKS AND CAICOS
ISLANDS (U.K.)

GRAND TURK

MOUCHOIR PASSAGE

SANTIAGO

DOMINICAN
REPUBLIC

SANTO DOMINGO

CABO BEATA

CANAL DE LA MONA

VIRGIN ISLANDS
(U.S.) (U.K.)

SAN JUAN

PONCE

PUERTO RICO (U.S.)

ST. CROIX (U.S.)

ANEGADA PASSAGE

ANGUILLA (U.K.)
THE VALLEY
ST. MAARTEN (NETH.ANT.&FR.)

SABA (NETH. ANT.)
ST. EUSTATIUS(NETH.ANT.)

ST. KITTS-NEVIS

MONTSERRAT (U.K.)

BARBUDA

ANTIGUA AND BARBUDA

ANTIGUA
ST. JOHN

GUADELOUPE PASSAGE

GUADELOUPE (FR.)

BASSE-TERRE

MARIE GALANTE (FR.)

DOMINICA

ROSEAU

DOMINICA CHANNEL

L E S S E R   A N T I L L E S

FORT-DE-FRANCE
MARTINIQUE (FR.)

SAINT LUCIA CHANNEL

CASTRIES

ST. LUCIA

SAINT VINCENT PASSAGE

BARBADOS

BRIDGETOWN

CARIBBEAN SEA

L E S S E R   A N T I L L E S

ST. VINCENT AND
THE GRENADINES

SAINT GEORGE'S

GRENADA

ARUBA

ORANJESTAD

CURAÇAO (NETH.ANT.)

BONAIRE (NETH.ANT.)

WILLEMSTAD

PUNTA FIJO

CORO

ISLAS LOS
ROQUES (VEN.)

ISLA BLANQUILLA
(VEN.)

ISLA DE MARGARITA (VEN.)

TOBAGO

PORT OF SPAIN

TRINIDAD AND TOBAGO

TRINIDAD

CABIMAS

VALENCIA

CARACAS

BARCELONA

CUMANÁ

BARQUISIMETO

LAGO DE
MARACAIBO

VALERA

MATURIN

VENEZUELA

APURE

ORINOCO

CIUDAD GUAYANA

CIUDAD BOLIVAR

SAN CRISTOBAL

META

GUYANA

GEORGETOWN

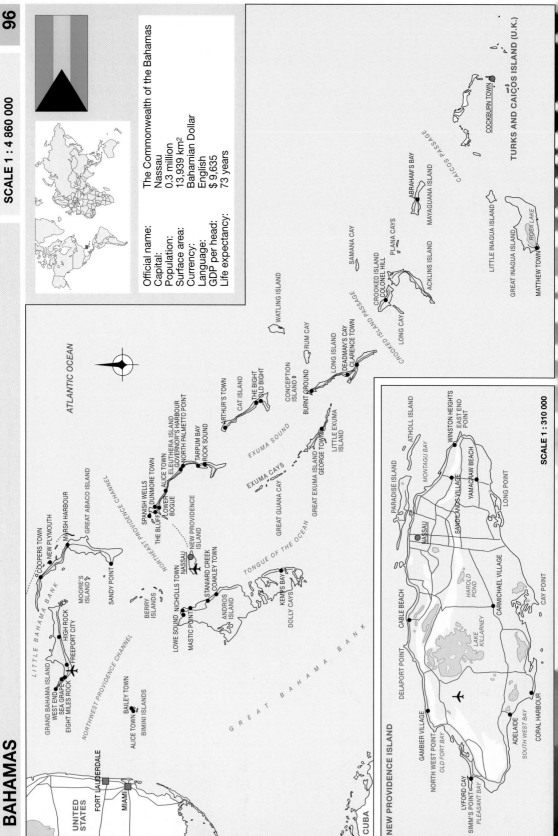

Official name: The Commonwealth of the Bahamas
Capital: Nassau
Population: 0.3 million
Surface area: 13,939 km²
Currency: Bahamian Dollar
Language: English
GDP per head: $ 9,635
Life expectancy: 73 years

UNITED STATES
FORT LAUDERDALE
MIAMI
CUBA

ATLANTIC OCEAN

LITTLE BAHAMA BANK
GRAND BAHAMA ISLAND
WEST END
SEA GRAPE
EIGHT MILES ROCK
HIGH ROCK
FREEPORT CITY
COOPERS TOWN
NEW PLYMOUTH
MARSH HARBOUR
GREAT ABACO ISLAND
MOORE'S ISLAND
SANDY POINT
BAILEY TOWN
ALICE TOWN
BIMINI ISLANDS
BERRY ISLANDS

NORTHWEST PROVIDENCE CHANNEL
NORTHEAST PROVIDENCE CHANNEL

SPANISH WELLS
THE BLUFF
DUNMORE TOWN
LOWER
BOGUE
ELEUTHERA ISLAND
ALICE TOWN
GOVERNOR'S HARBOUR
NORTH PALMETTO POINT
TARPUM BAY
ROCK SOUND
NEW PROVIDENCE ISLAND
NASSAU
STANIARD CREEK
COAKLEY TOWN
NICHOLLS TOWN
LOWE SOUND
MASTIC POINT
ANDROS ISLAND
DOLLY CAYS
KEMPS BAY

TONGUE OF THE OCEAN

GREAT GUANA CAY
EXUMA CAYS
EXUMA SOUND
GREAT EXUMA ISLAND
GEORGE TOWN
LITTLE EXUMA ISLAND

GREAT BAHAMA BANK

ARTHUR'S TOWN
CAT ISLAND
THE BIGHT
OLD BIGHT

WATLING ISLAND

CONCEPTION ISLAND
RUM CAY
BURNT GROUND
LONG ISLAND
DEADMAN'S CAY
CLARENCE TOWN

SAMANA CAY

CROOKED ISLAND
COLONEL HILL
PLANA CAYS
ACKLINS ISLAND
LONG CAY
CROOKED ISLAND PASSAGE

ABRAHAM'S BAY
MAYAGUANA ISLAND

LITTLE INAGUA ISLAND
GREAT INAGUA ISLAND
MATTHEW TOWN
ROSA LAKE

CAICOS PASSAGE

COCKBURN TOWN
TURKS AND CAICOS ISLAND (U.K.)

NEW PROVIDENCE ISLAND

SCALE 1 : 310 000

PARADISE ISLAND
ATHOLL ISLAND
WINSTON HEIGHTS
EAST END POINT
MONTAGU BAY
YAMACRAW BEACH
SANDILANDS VILLAGE
NASSAU
LONG POINT
CABLE BEACH
DELAPORT POINT
HAROLD POND
LAKE KILLARNEY
CARMICHAEL VILLAGE
CAY POINT
GAMBIER VILLAGE
NORTH WEST POINT
OLD FORT BAY
LYFORD CAY
SIMM'S POINT
PLEASANT BAY
SOUTH WEST BAY
ADELAIDE
CORAL HARBOUR

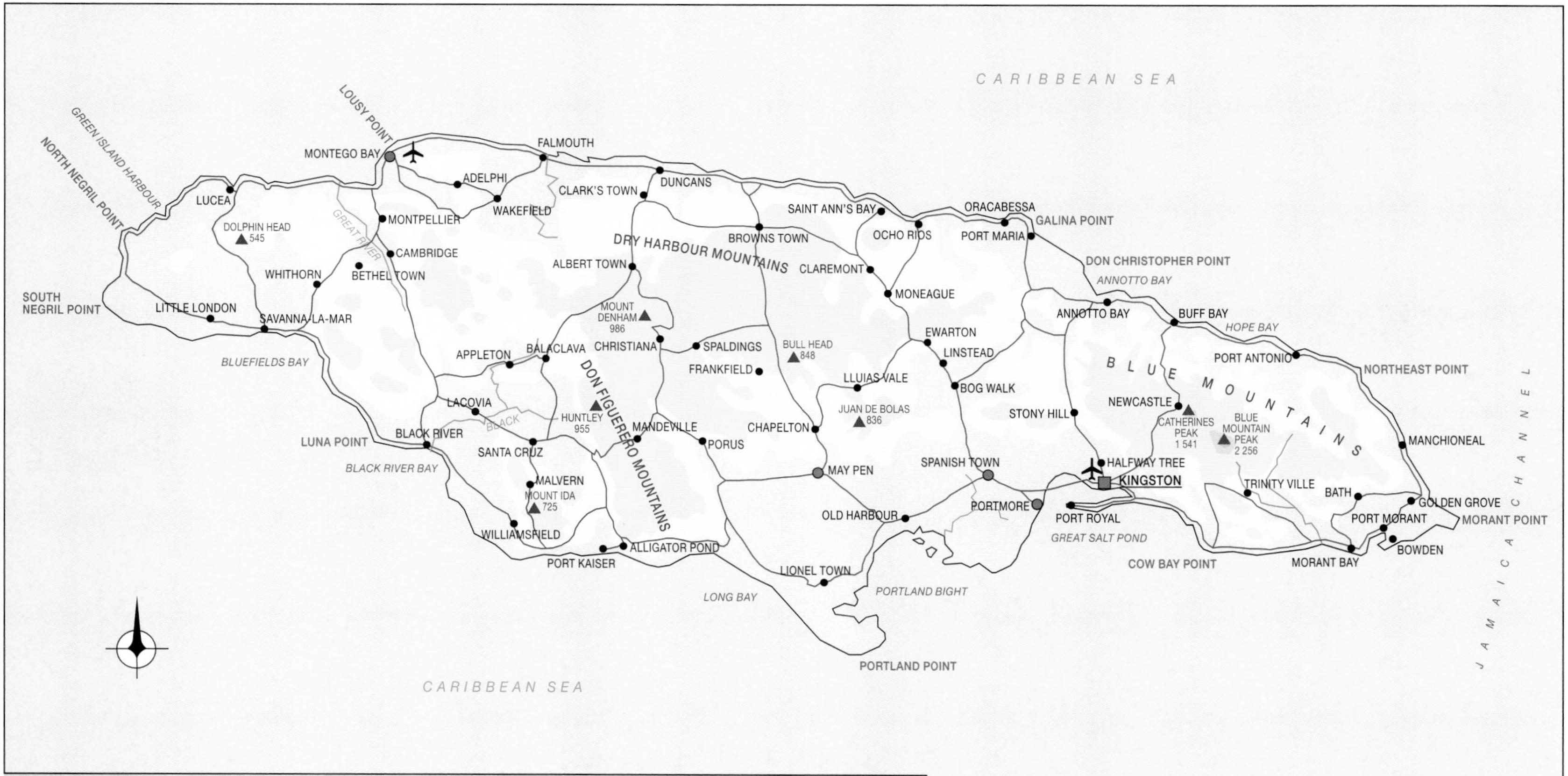

JAMAICA

SCALE 1 : 1 220 000

CARIBBEAN SEA

JAMAICA CHANNEL

BLUE MOUNTAINS

Official name: Jamaica
Capital: Kingston
Population: 2.5 million
Surface area: 10,991 km²
Currency: Jamaican Dollar
Language: English
GDP per head: $ 1,600
Life expectancy: 74 years

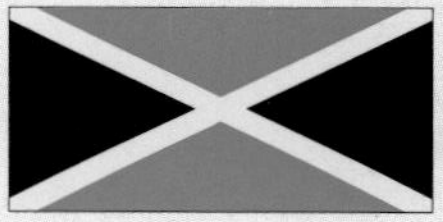

HAITI

SCALE 1 : 2 370 000

ATLANTIC OCEAN

DOMINICAN REPUBLIC

MANZANILLO BAY

ÎLE DE LA TORTUE

CAP-HAÏTIEN

DERAC

TROU-DU-NORD

ST. RAPHAËL

MASSIF DU NORD

PLATEAU CENTRAL

HINCHE

LASCAHOBAS

MORNE BONNONMME
1 788

DESSALINES

ARTIBONITE

MIREBALAIS

GONAÏVES

GROS MORNE

SAINT-MARC

VERRETTES

PORT-DE-PAIX

LE MÔLE ST. NICOLAS

BAIE DE HENNE

CAP DU MÔLE

POINTE DU CHEVAL BLANC

WINDWARD PASSAGE

CUBA

CARIBBEAN SEA

GOLFE DE LA GONÂVE

CANAL DE SAINT-MARC

BAHIA DE PORT-AU-PRINCE

ÎLE DE LA GONÂVE

CANAL DU SUD

PORT-AU-PRINCE

PÉTIONVILLE

CHAÎNE DE LA SELLE
2 674

MASSIF DE LA SELLE

GRAND GOSIER

ANSE-À-PITRE

JACMEL

LÉOGÂNE

PETIT GOAVE

ANSE-À-VEAUX

AQUIN

GRANDE CAYEMITE

MASSIF DE LA HOTTE

PIC DE MACAYA
2 347

LES CAYES

ÎLE À VACHE

POINTE L'ABACOU

JÉRÉMIE

DAME MARIE

ANSE-D'HAINAULT

JAMAICA CHANNEL

CARIBBEAN SEA

Official name:	République d'Haïti
Capital:	Port-au-Prince
Population:	7,3 million
Surface area:	27,750 km²
Currency:	Gourde
Languages:	French, Creole
GDP per head:	$ 310
Life expectancy:	55 years

SCALE 1 : 2 820 000

ATLANTIC OCEAN

CARIBBEAN SEA

PUERTO RICO

CANAL DE LA MONA

HAITI

PORT-AU-PRINCE

MANZANILLO BAY
MONTECRISTI
VILLA-VÁZQUEZ
DAJABÓN
SABENATA
RESTAURACIÓN
ELÍAS PIÑA
JIMENÍ
PEDERNALES
CABO FALSO
ISLA BEATA
CABO BEATA

CABO ISABELA
CABO MARCORIS
CABO FRANCÉS VIEJO

SAN FELIPE DE PUERTO PLATA
PICO DIEGO DE OCAMPO 1 249
SANTIAGO
MOCA
SALCEDO
MAO
YAQUE DEL NORTE

CONCEPCIÓN DE LA VEGA
PICO DUARTE 3 175
CORDILLERA CENTRAL
SAN JUAN
YAQUE DEL SUR
SIERRA DE NEIBA
LAGO ENRIQUILLO
DUVERGE
NEIBA
SIERRA DE BAHORUCO
ENRIQUILLO

SAN FRANCISCO DE MACORÍS
RINCÓN
COTUI
BONA
ALTO BANDERA
YUNA

NAGUA
SÁNCHEZ
BAHIA ESCOCESA
SABANA DE LA MAR
BAHIA DE SAMANÁ
SANTA BÁRBARA DE SAMANÁ
CABO SAMANÁ
MICHES

MONTE PLATA
BAYAGUANA
HATO MAYOR
SANTA CRUZ DE EL SEIBO

ALTAGRACIA
OZAMA
BENEMÉRITA DE SAN CRISTÓBAL
BAJOS DE HAINA
SAINT DOMINGUE
SANTO DOMINGO
ANDRES
PUNTA PALENQUE
BANÍ
SAN JOSÉ DE OCOA
AZUA
BAHIA DE OCEA
BARAHONA
BAHIA DE NEIBA

SAN PEDRO DE MACORIS
LA ROMANA
SALVALEÓN DE HIGÜEY
BAHIA DE YUMA
CABO ENGANO
ISLA SAONA

Official name:	Republica Dominicana
Capital:	Santo Domingo
Population:	8 million
Surface area:	48,422 km²
Currency:	Dominican Peso
Language:	Spanish
GDP per head:	$ 1,600
Life expectancy:	71 years

PUERTO RICO

SCALE 1 : 1 440 000

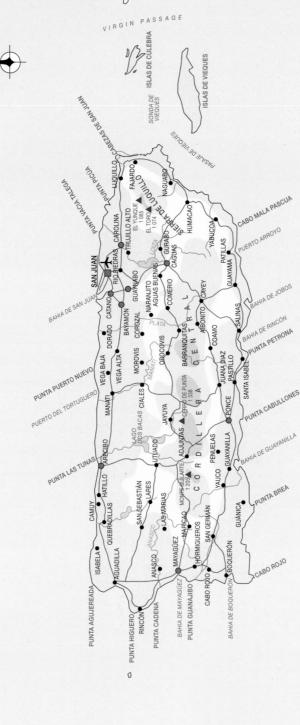

VIRGIN ISLANDS

VIRGIN PASSAGE

ISLAS DE CULEBRA

ISLAS DE VIEQUES

SONDA DE VIEQUES

PASAJE DE VIEQUES

PUNTA TALAVERA
PUNTA NACIA
PUNTA CABEZAS DE SAN JUAN

LUQUILLO
FAJARDO
NAGUABO
TRUJILLO ALTO
CAROLINA
EL YUNQUE 1 065
EL TORO 1 074
SIERRA DE LUQUILLO
HUMACAO
CABO MALA PASCUA

SAN JUAN
RÍO PIEDRAS
GUAYNABO
CATAÑO
BAYAMON
NARANJITO
AGUAS BUENAS
COMERIO
GURABO
CAGUAS
YABUCOA
PATILLAS
CAYEY
AIBONITO
GUAYAMA
PUERTO ARROYO

BAHIA DE SAN JUAN
DORADO
COROZAL
OROCOVIS
BARRANQUITAS
COAMO
SALINAS
BAHIA DE JOBOS
PUNTA PETRONA

VEGA ALTA
VEGA BAJA
MOROVIS
CIALES
CERRO DE PUNTA 1 338
JUANA DIAZ
PASTILLO
SANTA ISABEL
BAHIA DE RINCÓN

MANATI
JAYUYA
ADJUNTAS
PONCE
PUNTA CABULLONES

PUNTA DEL TORTUGUERO
LAGO DOS BOCAS
UTUADO
PEÑUELAS
GUAYANILLA
BAHIA DE GUAYANILLA

ARECIBO
MONTE GUILARTE 1 205
YAUCO
GUANICA
PUNTA BREA

PUNTA LAS TUNAS
HATILLO
LARES
MARICAO
SAN GERMÁN
BOQUERÓN
PUNTA AGUJEREADA

CAMUY
QUEBRADILLAS
SAN SEBASTIÁN
LAS MARIAS
HORMIGUEROS
CABO ROJO

ISABELA
AGUADILLA
AÑASCO
MAYAGÜEZ
PUNTA GUANAJIBO
BAHIA DE BOQUERÓN

PUNTA HIGÜERO
RINCÓN
PUNTA CADENA
BAHIA DE MAYAGÜEZ
CABO ROJO

CORDILLERA CENTRAL
RÍO LOÍZA
RÍO PLATA
RÍO MANATÍ
RÍO AÑASCO

ATLANTIC OCEAN

CARIBBEAN SEA

CANAL DE LA MONA

ISLA DE MONA

PUNTA PUERTO NUEVO

Official name:	Estada Libre Asociado de Puerto Rico
Capital:	San Juan
Population:	3.8 million
Surface area:	8,959 km²
Currency:	American Dollar
Languages:	Spanish, English

VIRGIN ISLANDS

SCALE 1 : 500 000

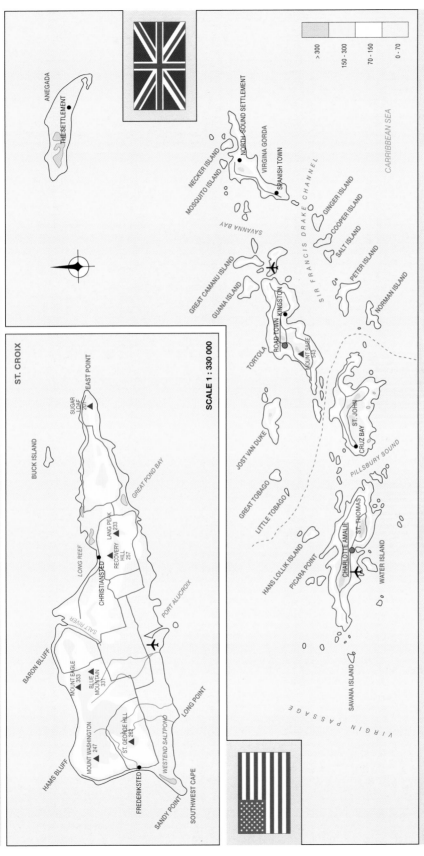

SCALE 1 : 330 000

CARRIBEAN SEA

SIR FRANCIS DRAKE CHANNEL

SAVANNA BAY

VIRGIN PASSAGE

PILLSBURY SOUND

ANEGADA
THE SETTLEMENT
NECKER ISLAND
MOSQUITO ISLAND
NORTH-SOUND SETTLEMENT
VIRGINA GORDA
SPANISH TOWN
GINGER ISLAND
COOPER ISLAND
SALT ISLAND
PETER ISLAND
NORMAN ISLAND
GREAT CAMANU ISLAND
GUANA ISLAND
ROAD TOWN KINGSTON
MOUNT SAGE 543
TORTOLA
JOST VAN DUKE
GREAT TOBAGO
LITTLE TOBAGO
HANS LOLLIK ISLAND
PICARA POINT
ST. JOHN
CRUZ BAY
ST. THOMAS
CHARLOTTE AMALIE
WATER ISLAND
SAVANA ISLAND

ST. CROIX
BUCK ISLAND
EAST POINT
SUGAR LOAF 201
LONG REEF
BARON BLUFF
MOUNT EAGLE 355
BLUE MOUNTAIN 331
LANG PEAK 233
RECOVERY HILL 257
CHRISTIANSTED
GREAT POND BAY
HAMS BLUFF
MOUNT WASHINGTON 247
ST. GEORGE HILL 262
SALT RIVER
PORT ALUCROIX
WESTEND SALTPOND
FREDERIKSTED
SANDY POINT
SOUTHWEST CAPE
LONG POINT

	British Virgin Islands Colony
Official name:	British Virgin Islands Colony
Capital:	Road Town
Population:	18,000
Surface area:	153 km²
Currency:	American Dollar
Language:	English
GDP per head:	$ 1,344
Life expectancy:	72 years

Official name:	Virgin Islands of the United States
Capital:	Charlotte Amalie
Population:	97,120 million
Surface area:	347,1 km²
Currency:	American Dollar
Languages:	English, Creole, Spanish
GDP per head:	$ 1,344
Life expectancy:	72 years

Official name: Département d'Outre-Mer de la Guadeloupe
Capital: Basse-Terre (Guadeloupe)
Population: 28,518
Surface area: 54 km²
Currency: French Franc
Languages: French, Creole

CHANNEL OF ANGUILLA

EASTERN POINT

BELL POINT
ANSE MARCEL
RED ROCK 265

BELL HILL 198
PIGEON PEA HILL 211

ILET PINEL

POINTE MOLLY SMITH
GRAND CASE
CUL-DE-SAC

CAYE VERTE

SAINT MARTIN (FR.)

MONT O' REILLY 381

POINTE DU BLUFF
RAMBAUD

PIC DU PARADIS 424
BAIE DE L'EMBOUCHURE

POINTE PLUM
BAIE ROUGE
COLOMBIER

QUARTIER D'ORLEANS

POINTE BASSE TERRE
TERRES BASSES

FLAG STAFF 380
OYSTER POND

CUPECOYBAAI
SIMPSONBAY LAGOON
GREAT KEY
ST. PETER HILL 316
REWARD
BABIT POINT

MULLET BAY
ST. PETERS
SENTRY HILL 341
WILLIAMS HILL 256
MIDDLE REGION
NAKED BOY 296
GUANA BAY

CARIBBEAN SEA
SIMPSON BAY VILLAGE
SIMPSON BAY
CUL-DE-SAC
COLE BAY
FORT HILL 215
GREAT BAY SALT POND
PHILIPSBURG

CAY BAY HILL 176
LITTLE BAY
GREAT BAY
GENEVA BAY

COLE BAY

POINT BLANCHE
POINT BLANCHE

SINT MAARTEN (NED. ANTILLEN)

CHANNEL DE ST. BARTHÉLEMY

> 300
150 - 300
70 - 150
0 - 70

Official name: De Nederlandse Antillen
Capital: Willemstad (Curaçao)
Population: 32,221
Surface area: 34 km²
Currency: Netherlands Antillean Guilder
Languages: Papiamento, Dutch, English

ANGUILLA

SCALE 1 : 190 000

SNAKE POINT

ISLAND HARBOUR

SHOAL BAY
WHITE HILL

ISLAND HARBOUR
GIBBON POINT

FOUNTAIN HILL 54
MOUNT FORTUNE

FLAT CAP POINT
BETTY HILL

CAULS POND

CROCUS BAY
STONEY GROUND

THE VALLEY
SANDY HILL BAY

CARIBBEAN SEA
ROAD BAY
SHANNON HILL 62
THE QUARTER

NORTH HILLVILLAGE
SANDY GROUNDVILLAGE
ISAAC'S CLIFF 50
SOUTH HILL VILLAGE
FOREST BAY

MEAD'S BAY
LONG BAY

BLOWING POINT
BLOWING POINT

WEST END
COVE POND
RENDEZVOUS BAY
COVE BAY

ANGUILLITA ISLAND

> 50
0 - 50

Official name: Anguilla
Capital: The Valley
Population: 10,302
Surface area: 96 km²
Currency: East Caribbean Dollar
Language: English

SABA

SCALE 1 : 130 000

ST. EUSTATIUS

SCALE 1 : 180 000

SABA (left map)

ATLANTIC OCEAN

FLAT POINT

GREEN ISLAND

GREAT HOLE

COVE BAY

SPRING BAY

CORE GUT BAY

OLD BOOBY HILL
223

CORE GUT

WIBA HOLE

THE LEVEL
500

WINDWARD SIDE

WASH GUT

ABRAHAM'S HOLE

LOWER HELL'S GATE

UPPER HELL'S GATE

PIRATE CLIFF

PETER SIMON'S HILL
554

TOM'S GUT

GREAT POINT

MOUNT SCENERY
870

SAINT JOHN'S HILL

VICTORY GUT

TORRENS POINT

THE BOTTOM

THAIS HILL
339

WELL'S BAY

GREAT HILL
422

BUNKER HILL
377

LADDERBAY

FORTBAY

CARIBBEAN SEA

Official name: De Nederlandse Antillen
Capital: Willemstad (Curaçao)
Population: 1,130
Surface area: 13 km²
Currency: Netherlands Antillean Guilder
Languages: Papiamento, Dutch
GDP per head: $ 5,500
Life expectancy: 74 years

Legend (Saba)
> 800
600 - 800
400 - 600
200 - 400
50 - 200
0 - 50

ST. EUSTATIUS (right map)

ATLANTIC OCEAN

BOVEN BAAI

VENUS BAAI

GREAT BAY

ZEELANDIA BAAI

CONCORDIABAAI

COMPAGNIE BAAI

COCOLUCH BAY

JENKIN'S BAY

BOVEN
289

VENUS

BERGJE
225

TUMBLE DOWN
DICK BAY

SIGNAL
HILL
233

BILLY'S GUT

CONCORDIA

GOLDEN ROCK

ORANJESTAD

GALLOWS
BAY

LOWER
ROUND HILL
154

THE QUILL
277

MAZINGA
601

TONK'S GUT

WHITE
SUGARLOAF

BACK OFF BAY

BUCCANEERS BAY

KAY
BAY

CARIBBEAN SEA

THE CHANNEL OF ST. KITTS

Official name: De Nederlandse Antillen
Capital: Willemstad (Curaçao)
Population: 1,839
Surface area: 21 km²
Currency: Netherlands Antillean Guilder
Languages: Papiamento, Dutch
GDP per head: $ 5,500
Life expectancy: 74 years

Legend (St. Eustatius)
> 200
100 - 200
50 - 100
0 - 50

SCALE 1 : 240 000

SCALE 1 : 210 000

ANTIGUA

BOOM POINT

WEATHERILLS POINT

BEGGARS POINT

LONG ISLAND

GUIANA ISLAND

CRUMP ISLAND

INDIAN TOWN POINT

GREEN ISLAND

NONSUCH BAY

SOLDIER POINT

CEDAR GROVE

NEW WINTHORPES

ST. JOHNSTONE

POTTERS

GUNTHORPES

PARHAM

PARHAM HARBOUR

PARES

SEATONS

WILLIKIES

NEWFIELD

FREETOWN

ST. JOHN'S

GREEN BAY

SEA VIEW FARM

FREEMANSVILLE

ALL SAINTS

BETHESDA

ST. JOHN'S HARBOUR

FIVE ISLANDS

FIVE ISLAND HARBOUR

JENNINGS

BOLANDS

BENDALS

SWETES

LIBERTA

ENGLISH HARBOUR TOWN

NELSON'S DOCKYARD

INDIAN CREEK POINT

WILLOUGHBY BAY

FALMOUTH HARBOUR

ENGLISH HARBOUR

CRAB HILL

JOHNSON'S POINT

URLINGS

BOGGY PEAK 402

SHEKERLEY MOUNTAINS

OLD ROAD

OLD ROAD BLUFF

CARIBISCHE ZEE

> 400

200 - 400

100 - 200

0 - 100

BARBUDA

GOAT POINT

GOAT REEF

GOAT ISLAND

COBB REEF

HOG POINT

PELICAN BAY

SALT PONDS

GRAVENOR BAY

COCOA POINT

CEDAR TREE POINT

CODRINGTON

CODRINGTON LAGOON

DULCINA

PALMETTO POINT

> 20

0 - 20

Official name:	Associated State of Antigua and Barbuda
Capital:	Saint John's
Population:	30,000
Surface area:	441.6 km^2
Currency:	East Caribbean Dollar
Language:	English
GDP per head:	$7,330
Life expectancy:	75 years

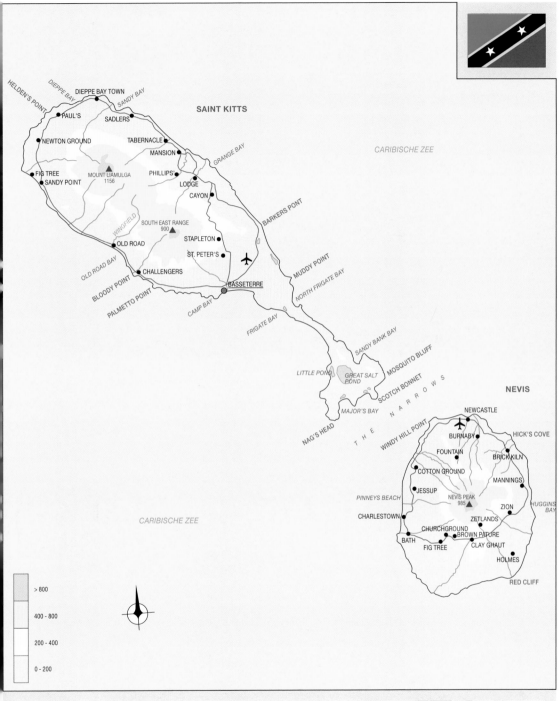

HELDEN'S POINT
DIEPPE BAY
DIEPPE BAY TOWN
SANDY BAY
SANDLERS
PAUL'S
NEWTON GROUND
TABERNACLE
SADLERS
SAINT KITTS
MANSION
GRANGE BAY
FIG TREE
PHILLIPS'
SANDY POINT
MOUNT LIAMULGA 1156
LODGE
CAYON
CARIBISCHE ZEE
BARKERS PONT
WINGFIELD
SOUTH EAST RANGE 900
STAPLETON
OLD ROAD
ST. PETER'S
OLD ROAD BAY
CHALLENGERS
MUDDY POINT
BLOODY POINT
BASSETERRE
NORTH FRIGATE BAY
PALMETTO POINT
CAMP BAY
FRIGATE BAY
SANDY BANK BAY
MOSQUITO BLUFF
LITTLE POND
GREAT SALT POND
SCOTCH BONNET
MAJOR'S BAY
THE NARROWS
NEVIS
NAG'S HEAD
WINDY HILL POINT
NEWCASTLE
BURNABY
HICK'S COVE
FOUNTAIN
BRICK KILN
COTTON GROUND
MANNINGS
JESSUP
NEVIS PEAK 985
ZION
PINNEYS BEACH
HUGGINS BAY
CHARLESTOWN
ZETLANDS
CARIBISCHE ZEE
CHURCHGROUND
BROWN PATURE
BATH
FIG TREE
CLAY GHAUT
HOLMES
RED CLIFF

> 800
400 - 800
200 - 400
0 - 200

Official name:	Federation of St. Christopher (St. Kitts) and Nevis
Capital:	Basseterre
Population:	12,220
Surface area:	261.6 km²
Currency:	East Caribbean Dollar
Language:	English
GDP per head:	$ 5,870
Life expectancy:	70 years

MONTSERRAT

SCALE 1 : 170 000

SAINT BARTHÉELEMY

SCALE 1 : 230 000

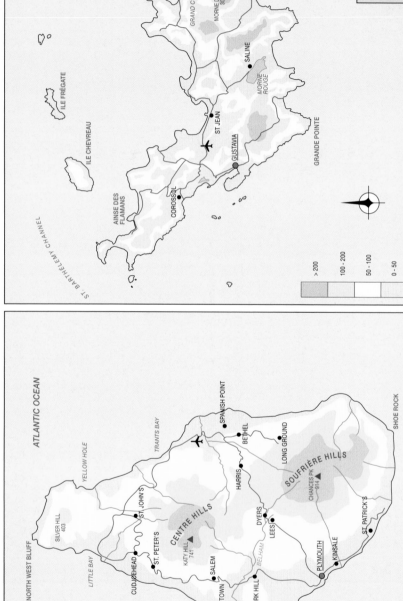

MONTSERRAT (left map)

ATLANTIC OCEAN

NORTH WEST BLUFF

YELLOW HOLE

SILVER HILL
403

LITTLE BAY

ST. JOHN'S

CUDJOEHEAD

ST. PETER'S

CENTRE HILLS

KATY HILL
741

SALEM

OLD TOWN

OLD ROAD BAY

CORK HILL

DYERS

LEES

BELHAM

HARRIS

TRANTS BAY

SPANISH POINT

BETHEL

LONG GROUND

SOUFRIÈRE HILLS

CHANCES PK
914

KINSALE

PLYMOUTH

ST. PATRICK'S

SHOE ROCK

CARIBBEAN SEA

> 600
300 - 600
100 - 300
0 - 100

SAINT BARTHÉELEMY (right map)

ST. BARTHÉLEMY CHANNEL

ILE FRÉGATE

ILE CHEVREAU

AINSE DES FLAMANS

COROSSOL

ST JEAN

GUSTAVIA

GRAND CUL-de-SAC

MORNE DU VITET
309

SALINE

MORNE ROUGE

GRANDE POINTE

> 200
100 - 200
50 - 100
0 - 50

Official name: Colony of Montserrat
Capital: Plymouth
Population: 2,850
Surface area: 102 km²
Currency: East Caribbean Dollar
Language: English
GDP per head: $ 4,780
Life expectancy: 74 years

Official name: Departement d'Outre-Mer de la Guadeloupe
Capital: Gustavia
Surface area: 21 km²
Currency: French Franc
Languages: French, Creole
GDP per head: $ 4,780
Life expectancy: 74 years

GUADELOUPE

SCALE 1 : 470 000

MARIE GALANTE

GROSSE POINTE

CAPESTERRE

ST. LOUIS

BAIE DE ST. LOUIS

GRAND-BOURG

POINTE DES BASSES

SCALE 1 : 350 000

	> 1200
	600 - 1200
	300 - 600
	150 - 300
	0 - 150

ÎLES DES SAINTES

TERRE-DE-HAUT

PETITES ANSES

SCALE 1 : 350 000

ATLANTIC OCEAN

POINTE DE LA GRANDE VIGIE

ANSE BERTRAND

CAMPÊCHE

GROS CAP

PORT LOUIS

PETIT-CANAL

POINTE D'ANTIGUES

GRIPPON

VIEUX BOURG

COURCE

GRANDE TERRE

ABYMES

MORNE L'ESCADE 135

DOUVILLE

MOULE

ST. FRANÇOIS

POINTE DES CHÂTEAUX

STE. ANNE

LE GOSIER

POINTE CANOT

POINTE-A-PITRE

SALÉE

BAIE-MAHAULT

PETIT CUL DE SAC MARIN

GRAND CUL DE SAC MARIN

ÎLET À FAJOU

POINTE ALLÈGRE

STE. ROSE

LAMENTIN

GOYAVES

VERNOU

PETIT BOURG

GOYAVE

ANSE DE SABLE

DUZER

BELLE HOTESSE 777

LA GRANDE ANSE

DESHAIES

POINTE NOIRE

BASSE TERRE

GRAND SANS TOUCHER 1 354

CAPESTERRE

SOUFRIÈRE 1 467

VIEUX HABITANTS

CAPESTERRE

GRANDE POINTE

POINTE À LÉZARD BOUILLANTE

BAILLIF

VIEUX-HABITANTS

ST. CLAUDE

GOURBEYRE

TROIS RIVIÈRES

BASSE TERRE

ANSE TURLET

POINTE DU VIEUX FORT

CARIBBEAN SEA

Official name:	Departement d'Outre-Mer de la Guadeloupe
Capital:	Basse-Terre
Population:	0.4 million
Surface area:	1,705 km²
Currency:	French Franc
Languages:	French, Creole
GDP per head:	$ 3,036
Life expectancy:	74 years

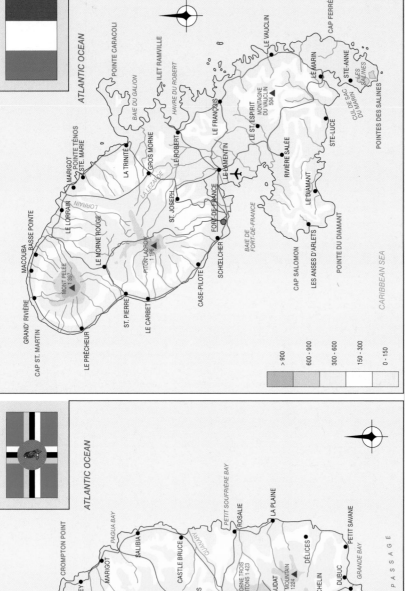

DOMINICA

SCALE 1 : 480 000

ATLANTIC OCEAN

DOMINICA PASSAGE

CAPUAN
POINT JACO
VIEILLE CASE
CROMPTON POINT
DOUGLAS BAY
PRINCE RUPERT BAY
PORTSMOUTH
POINT RONDE
PICARD
DUBLANC
COLIHAUT
HAMPSTEAD
WESLEY
MARIGOT
PAGUA BAY
SALIBIA
CASTLE BRUCE
PETIT SOUFRIÈRE BAY
ROSALIE
LA PLAINE
MORNE DIABLOTINS 1447
MORNE RAQUETTE
SALISBURY
MACOUCHERI
DOUBLSTRI
ST. JOSEPH
LAYOU
LAYOU
BELLS
PONT CASSE
MORNE TROIS PITONS 1423
SPRINGFIELD
LAUDAT
WATT MOUNTAIN 1224
DÉLICES
MAHAUT
MASSACRE
CANEFIELD
PTE. MICHEL
ROSEAU
SOUFRIÈRE
SOUFRIÈRE BAY
SCOTTS HEAD
ROSEAU
PICHELIN
DUBUC
BEREKUA
PETIT SAVANE
GRANDE BAY

CARIBBEAN SEA

MARTINIQUE PASSAGE

> 800
400 - 800
200 - 400
0 - 200

Official name:	Commonwealth of Dominica
Capital:	Roseau
Population:	74,000
Surface area:	751 km²
Language:	English
GDP per head:	$ 3,090
Life expectancy:	74 years

MARTINIQUE

SCALE 1 : 540 000

ATLANTIC OCEAN

POINTE CARACOLI
BAIE DU GALION
ILET RAMVILLE
HAVRE DU ROBERT
POINTE TÉNOS
MARIGOT
STE. MARIE
GRAND' RIVIÈRE
CAP ST. MARTIN
MACOUBA
BASSE POINTE
LE LORRAIN
LE PRÊCHEUR
MONT PELÉE 397
LORRAIN
LE MORNE ROUGE
ST. PIERRE
LE CARBET
PITON LACROIX 1196
CASE-PILOTE
SCHŒLCHER
FORT-DE-FRANCE
LA TRINITÉ
GROS MORNE
ST. JOSEPH
LE ROBERT
LE FRANÇOIS
LE LAMENTIN
LE ST. ESPRIT
MONTAGNE DU VAUCLIN 504
LE VAUCLIN
CAP FERRÉ
STE-ANNE
ILES SALINES
CUL DE SAC DU MARIN
LE MARIN
LA LEZARDE
BAIE DE FORT-DE-FRANCE
RIVIÈRE SALÉE
STE-LUCE
LE DIAMANT
CAP SALOMON
LES ANSES D'ARLETS
POINTE DU DIAMANT
POINTES DES SALINES

CARIBBEAN SEA

> 900
600 - 900
300 - 600
150 - 300
0 - 150

Official name:	Departement d'Outre-Mer de la Martinique
Capital:	Fort-de-France
Population:	0.4 million
Surface area:	1,106 km²
Currency:	French Franc
Languages:	French, Creole
GDP per head:	$ 9,386
Life expectancy:	75 years

ST. LUCIA

SCALE 1 : 430 000

CARIBBEAN SEA

CAP POINT
PIGEON ISLAND
GROS ISLET BAY
CHOC BAY
ESPERANCE HARBOUR
CAPE MARQUIS
MARQUIS BAY
MARQUIS
GROS ISLET
BON AIR
FORESTIÈRE
LA CROIX MAINGOT
CASTRIES
CICERON
ANSE LA RAYE
CANARIES
GRAND CAILLE POINT
SOUFRIÈRE
SOUFRIÈRE BAY
GROS PITON POINT
DERNIÈRE RIVIÈRE
GRANDE RIVIÈRE
DENNERY
FOND D'OR BAY
POINT PRASLIN
TROUGRAS POINT
PRASLIN
FOND
VIERGE POINT
FOND ESTATE
BARRE DE L'ISLE RIDGE
MOUNT GIMIE 950
RAVIN CLARE
MICOUD
FOND DOUX
GROS PITON 796
CHOISEUL
DESRUISSEAUX
SAVANNES BAY
POINTE DES CANELLES
CANELLES
LABORIE
VIEUX FORT
CAPE MOULE A CHIQUE
VIEUX FORT BAY
LABORIE BAY
ROSEAU
CANARIES
TROUMASSE
DOREE

> 800
400 - 400
200 - 400
0 - 200

Official name: The Commonwealth of St. Lucia
Capital: Castries
Population: 0.2 million
Surface area: 616.3 km²
Currency: East Caribbean Dollar
Language: English
GDP per head: $ 3,500
Life expectancy: 70 years

ST. VINCENT / THE GRENADINES

SCALE 1 : 740 000

SCALE 1 : 2 760 000

SAINT VINCENT PASSAGE

SAINT VINCENT
KINGSTOWN

BEQUIA
PORT ELIZABETH
ISLE QUATRE

CANOUAN

T H E   G R E N A D I N E S

GRENADA

CARIBBEAN SEA

PORTER PT.
FANCY
OWIA
ESPAGNOL PT.
NEW SANDY BAY VILLAGE
ORANGE HILL
RABACCA
LA SOUFRIÈRE 1177
CRATER LAKE
RABACCA DRY RIVER
GEORGETOWN
BYERA VILLAGE
BLACK POINT
COLONARIE
RICHMOND PEAK 1074
RICHMOND
ROSE HALL
SPRING VILLAGE
CHATEAUBELAIR
CHATEAUBELAIR BAY
TROUMAKA
CUMBERLAND
WALLILABOU BAY
BARROUALLIE
GRAND BONHOMME 969
PENISTON
LAYOU
VERMONT
CLARE VALLEY
BUCCAMENT
MOUNT ST. ANDREW 735
CAMDEN PARK
EVESHAM
MESOPOTAMIA
NORTH UNION
GREIGGS
YAMBOU HEAD
STUBBS
BRIGHTON
CALLIAQUA
GREATHEAD BAY
YOUNG'S ISLAND
JOHNSON POINT
CANE GARDEN POINT
QUESTELLES BAY
BUCCAMENT BAY
KINGSTOWN
KINGSTOWN BAY

> 800
400 - 800
200 - 400
100 - 200
0 - 100

Official name: Commonwealth of St. Vincent and the Grenadines
Capital: Kingstown
Population: 0.1 million
Surface area: 389.3 km²
Currency: East Caribbean Dollar
Language: English
GDP per head: $ 2,370
Life expectancy: 73 years

BARBADOS (left map)

ATLANTIC OCEAN

NORTH POINT
HARRISON POINT
RIVER BAY
GAY'S COVE
SPRING HALL
GREENIDGE
NESSFIELD
SIX MEN'S BAY
SPEIGHTSTOWN
MOUNT STEPNEY 246
FARLEY HILL 823
SAINT ANDREW
GREENLAND
LONG POND
HILLCREST
NEWCASTLE
BATH
WHITEHAVEN
RAGGED POINT
THE CHAIR
KITRIDGE POINT
BATHSHEBA
BRUCE VALE
BLACKMAN'S
CASTLE GRANT 338
LEMON ARBOUR
TODDS
THREE HOUSES
BAKERS
WESTMORELAND
MOUNT HILLABY 340
WELCHMAN HALL
ELLERTON
KENDAL
ALLEYNES BAY
HOLETOWN
DURANTS
ST. GEORGE
CONSTANT
CARRINGTON
CHARNOCKS
SIX CROSS ROADS
THE CRANE
FOUL BAY
PAYNE'S BAY
JACKSON
BLACK ROCK
ROUEN
BANNATYNE
MAXWELL'S COAST
OISTINS
LONG BAY
SILVERSANDS
SOUTH POINT
FRESHWATER BAY
BRIDGETOWN
CARLISLE BAY
NEEDHAM'S PT.
HASTINGS
WORTHING
SAINT LAWRENCE
OISTINS BAY

Depth/elevation scale:
> 300
200 - 300
100 - 200
0 - 100

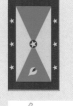

Official name: Barbados
Capital: Bridgetown
Population: 0.3 million
Surface area: 430 km²
Currency: Barbados Dollar
Language: English
GDP per head: $ 9,635
Life expectancy: 76 years

GRENADA (right map)

GREEN ISLAND
SAUTEURS BAY
LEVERA POND
GRENADA BAY
SAUTEURS
DAVID POINT
R. SALLEE
LAKE ANTOINE
TIVOLI
PEARLS
GREAT RIVER BAY
TELESCOPE POINT
GRENVILLE
GRENVILLE BAY
MARQUIS ISLAND
UNION
VICTORIA
MOUNT SAINT CATHERINE 841
CRAYFISH BAY
ANTOINE
SAINT PATRICK
SIMON
GREAT RIVER
HARFORD VILLAGE
BIRCH GROVE
MUNICH
FRANCIS
GREAT BACOLET BAY
SAINT-DAVID'S
ST. DAVID'S PT.
GOUYAVE
GRAND ROY
FEDONS CAMP 764
GRAND ETANG
WILLIS
MOUNT MORITZ
MOUNT LEBANON 715
PROVIDENCE
PERDMONTEMPS
REQUIN BAY
LITTLE MARQUIS
WESTERHALL BAY
BLACK BAY PT.
BLACK BAY
BRIZAN BAY
MOLINIERE PT.
GRAND MAL BAY
BELMONT
WOBURN
CHEMIN
POINT OF FORT JEUDY
CALIVIGNY ISLAND
ST. GEORGE'S
SAINT GEORGE'S HARBOUR
GRANDE ANSE BAY
GOAT POINT
HOG ISLAND
PRICKLY POINT
POINT SALINES

CARIBBEAN SEA

ATLANTIC OCEAN

Elevation scale:
> 800
400 - 800
200 - 400
100 - 200
0 - 100

Official name: Grenada
Capital: St. George's
Population: 0.1 million
Surface area: 344.5 km²
Currency: East Caribbean Dollar
Language: English
GDP per head: $ 2,880
Life expectancy: 72 years

Official name:	Republic of Trinidad and Tobago
Capital:	Port of Spain
Population:	1.3 million
Surface area:	5,128 km²
Currency:	Trinidad and Tobago Dollar
Language:	English
GDP per head:	$ 3,870
Life expectancy:	73 years

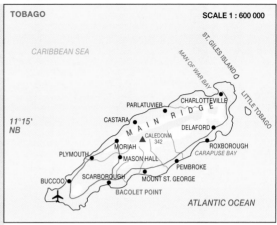

TOBAGO   SCALE 1 : 600 000

CARIBBEAN SEA

ST. GILES ISLAND
MAN OF WAR BAY
LITTLE TOBAGO

11°15' NB

PARLATUVIER
CHARLOTTEVILLE
CASTARA
MAIN RIDGE
DELAFORD
CALEDONIA 342
MORIAH
ROXBOROUGH
CARAPUSE BAY
PLYMOUTH
MASON HALL
PEMBROKE
BUCCOO
SCARBOROUGH
MOUNT ST. GEORGE
BACOLET POINT
ATLANTIC OCEAN

> 800
400 - 800
200 - 400
0 - 200

CARIBBEAN SEA

VENEZUELA

BOCAS DEL DRAGON

CHACACHACARE

MARAVACA ISLAND
MARACAS BAY
LAS CUEVAS BAY
CHUPARA POINT

GREEN HILL
ST. PIERRE
FOUR ROADS
MARAVAL
SAN JUAN
PORT OF SPAIN
TACARIGUA
CARONI
GARONI

NORTHERN RANGE

EL TUCUCHE 936
LA VERONICA
TUNAPUNA
ARIMA
AROUCA

EL CERRO DEL ARIPO 940
VALENCIA

BLANCHISSEUSE
MATELOT
GRANDE RIVIÈRE
SANS SOUCI
TOCO
GALERA POINT
TOMPIRE
REDHEAD

SALIBEA
MATURA
BALANDRA BAY
SALINE BAY

CUMUTO
SANGRE GRANDE
SAN RAFAEL
MATURA BAY

CUNUPIA
CHAGUANAS
LONGDENVILLE
TALPARO
MANZANILLA POINT
MANZANILLA BAY

CAPATO
WATERLOO
COUVA
FREEPORT
MITAN
BICHE
CHARUMA
COCOS BAY

GULF OF PARIA

CALIFORNIA
GRAN COUVA
TORTUGA
FLANNIGAN TOWN
TABAQUITE
NAVET

CLAXTON BAY
MAYO
ECKELL VILLAGE
POINTE-A-PIERRE
BUSY CORNER
TABLELAND
RÍO CLARO
ECCLESVILLE
POINT RADIX
ST. JOSEPH
PIERREVILLE

SAN FERNANDO
PRINCES TOWN
POOLE
ORTOIRE
MAYARO BAY

GUAPO BAY
LA BREA
ST. MARY'S
DÉBÉ
OROPUCHE
PREAU

POINT FORTIN
COCHRANE
PEÑAL
GUAYAGUAYARE
GALEOTA POINT

CAP DE VILLE
SIPARIA
BASSE TERRE
MORUGA

GRANVILLE
BUENOS AYRES
SADHOOWA
LA LUNE
MORUGA

BONASSE
SAN FRANCIQUE
PALO SECO
COORA

ISLOTE BAY
ERIN POINT
ICACOS POINT

ATLANTIC OCEAN

VENEZUELA

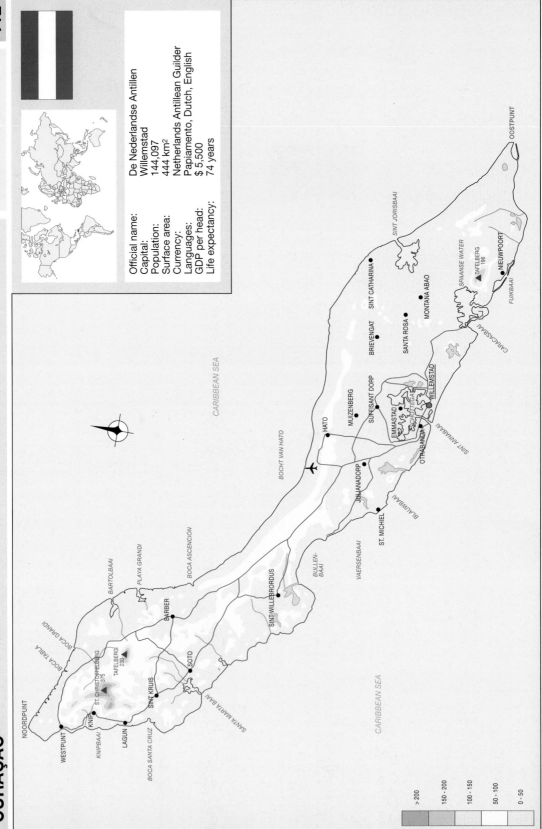

Official name: De Nederlandse Antillen
Capital: Willemstad
Population: 144,097
Surface area: 444 km²
Currency: Netherlands Antillean Guilder
Languages: Papiamento, Dutch, English
GDP per head: $ 5,500
Life expectancy: 74 years

NOORDPUNT

WESTPUNT

KNIP
KNIPBAAI
LAGUN

ST. CHRISTOFFELBERG 375
TAFELBERG 230

SINT KRUIS
SOTO

BOCA TABLA
BOCA GRANDI

BARTOLBAAI
PLAYA GRANDI
BOCA ASCENCIÓN

BOCA SANTA CRUZ
SANTA MARTA BAAI

BARBER

SINT WILLEBRORDUS

BULLEN-BAAI

VAERSENBAAI

ST. MICHIEL

JULIANADORP

BLAUWBAAI

CARIBBEAN SEA

CARIBBEAN SEA

BOCHT VAN HATO

HATO

MUIZENBERG

SUFFISANT DORP

EMMASTAD
SCHOTTEGAT
WILLEMSTAD
OTRABANDA

SINT ANNABAAI

BRIEVENGAT

SANTA ROSA

SINT CATHARINA

MONTANA ABAO

SPAANSE WATER

CARACASBAAI

SINT JORISBAAI

TAFELBERG 196
NIEUWPOORT

FUIKBAAI

OOSTPUNT

> 200
150 - 200
100 - 150
50 - 100
0 - 50

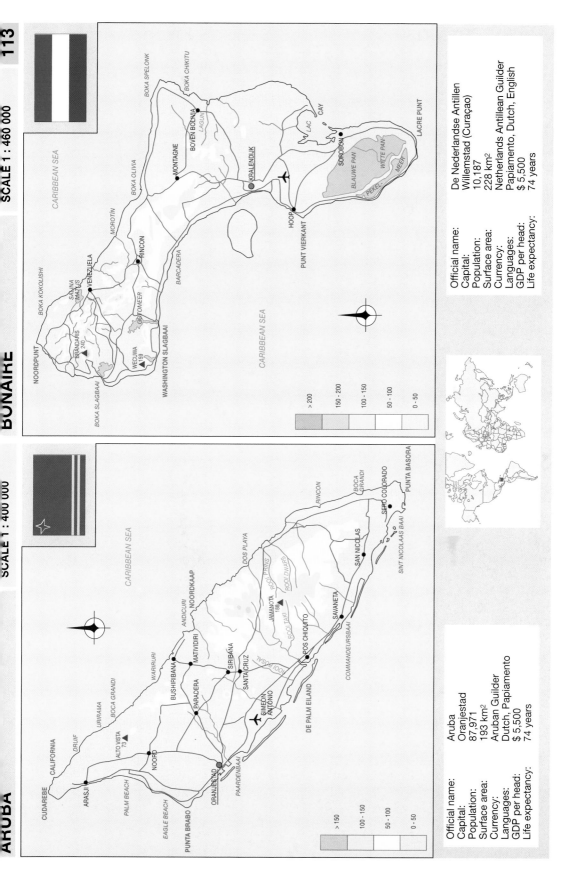

ARUBA — SCALE 1 : 400 000

CARIBBEAN SEA

CUDAREBE
CALIFORNIA
DRUIF
URIRAMA
BOCA GRANDI
WARIRURI
BUSHIRIBANA
PARADERA
MATIVIDIRI
SIRIBANA
SANTA CRUZ
ALTO VISTA 73
NOORD
ARASJI
PALM BEACH
EAGLE BEACH
PUNTA BRABO
ORANJESTAD
PAARDENBAAI
SIMEON ANTONIO
DE PALM EILAND
NOORDKAAP
ANDICURI
DOS PLAYA
ROOI PRINS
ROOI DWARS
JAMANOTA 188
ROOI TAKI
ROOI BOSAL
POS CHIQUITO
SAVANETA
SAN NICOLAS
COMMANDEURSBAAI
SINT NICOLAAS BAAI
RINCON
BOCA GRANDI
SERO COLORADO
PUNTA BASORA

> 150
100 - 150
50 - 100
0 - 50

Official name: Aruba
Capital: Oranjestad
Population: 87,971
Surface area: 193 km²
Currency: Aruban Guilder
Languages: Dutch, Papiamento
GDP per head: $ 5,500
Life expectancy: 74 years

BONAIRE — SCALE 1 : 460 000

CARIBBEAN SEA
CARIBBEAN SEA

NOORDPUNT
BOKA KOKOLISHI
BOKA SPELONK
BOKA CHIKITU
BOKA OLIVIA
MOROTÍN
SABINA MATIJS
VENEZUELA
GOTOMEER
BRANDARIS 240
WECUWA 109
WASHINGTON SLAGBAAI
BOKA SLAGBAAI
RINCON
BARCADERA
MONTAGNE
BOVEN BOLIVIA
LAGUN
KRALENDIJK
HOOP
PUNT VIERKANT
LAC
CAY
SORÓBON
BLAUWE PAN
WITTE PAN
PEKEL-MEER
LACRE PUNT

> 200
150 - 200
100 - 150
50 - 100
0 - 50

Official name: De Nederlandse Antillen
Capital: Willemstad (Curaçao)
Population: 10,187
Surface area: 228 km²
Currency: Netherlands Antillean Guilder
Languages: Papiamento, Dutch, English
GDP per head: $ 5,500
Life expectancy: 74 years

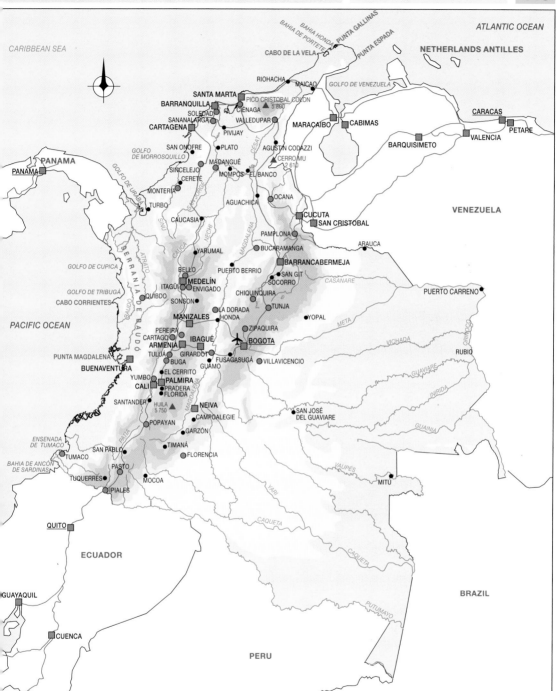

Official name:	Republica de Colombia
Capital:	Bogota
Population:	37.5 million
Surface area:	1,141,748 km²
Currency:	Colombian Peso
Language:	Spanish
GDP per head:	$ 2,140
Life expectancy:	70 years

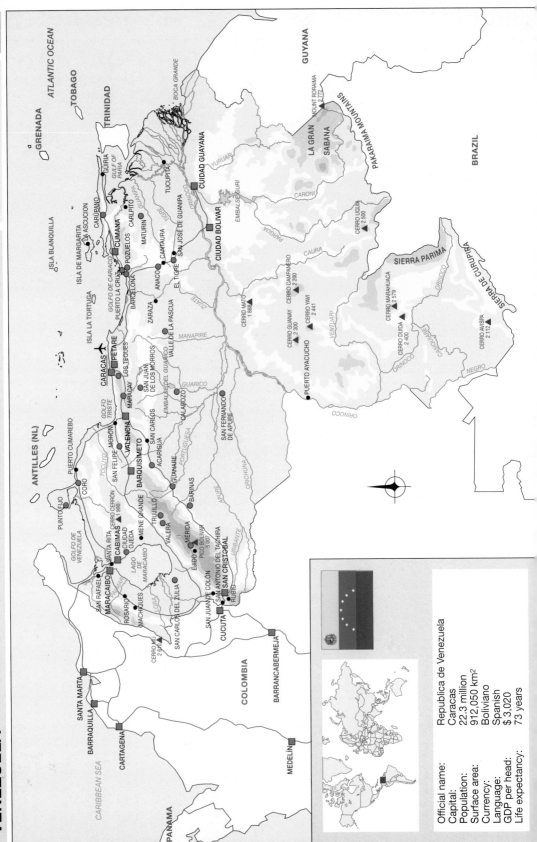

ATLANTIC OCEAN

GRENADA

TOBAGO

TRINIDAD

GUYANA

BRAZIL

COLOMBIA

PANAMA

CARIBBEAN SEA

ANTILLES (NL)

MOUNT RORAIMA
2 772

PAKARAIMA MOUNTAINS

LA GRAN
SABANA

CERRO UDIA
2 500

SIERRA PARIMA

CERRO MARAHUACA
2 579

CERRO DUIDA
2 400

CERRO AVISPA
2 112

SIERRA DE CURUPIRA

ORINOCO

NEGRO

CASIQUIARE

VENTUARI

CERRO YAVI
2 441

CERRO CAMPANERO
2 200

CERRO GUANAY
2 200

PUERTO AYACUCHO

CERRO MATO
1 869

CAURA

PARAGUA

CARONI

EMBALSE GURI

YURUARI

CIUDAD GUAYANA

CIUDAD BOLIVAR

BOCA GRANDE

GULF OF
PARIA

GUIRIA

CARUPANO

CUMANA

PUERTO LA CRUZ

POZUELOS

BARCELONA

CARLPITO

MATURIN

CANTAURA

ANACO

EL TIGRE

SAN JOSE DE GUANIPA

TUCUPITA

GUANIPA

TIGRE

ORINOCO

ISLA BLANQUILLA

ISLA DE MARGARITA
LA ASCUCION

ISLA LA TORTUGA

GOLFO DE CARIACO

GOLFO DE
PARIA

ZARAZA

VALLE DE LA PASCUA

MANAPIRE

GUARICO

SAN JUAN
DE LOS MORROS

EMBALSE DEL GUARICO

CALABOZO

SAN FERNANDO
DE APURE

MANATE

GUARITE

ORICHUNA

APURE

URIBANTE

PORTUGUESA

CARACAS

PETARE

LOS TEQUES

MARACAY

VALENCIA

SAN CARLOS

ACARIGUA

GUANARE

BARINAS

BARINAS

BARQUISIMETO

SAN FELIPE

MORON

CERRO CERRON
1 990

SANTA RITA

CIUDAD
OJEDA

CABIMAS

MENE GRANDE

TRUJILLO

VALERA

MERIDA

PICO BOLIVAR
5 007

EJIDO

SAN CRISTOBAL

RUBIO

SAN ANTONIO DEL TACHIRA

SAN JUAN DE COLON

CUCUTA

SAN CARLOS DEL ZULIA

SAN RAFAEL

MARACAIBO

ROSARIO

MACHIQUES

CERRO MU
2 650

LAGO
DE
MARACAIBO

GOLFO DE
VENEZUELA

CORO

PUNTO FIJO

PUERTO CUMAREBO

GOLFO
TRISTE

TOCUYO

GUAJIRA

SANTA MARTA

BARRANQUILLA

CARTAGENA

BARRANCABERMEJA

MEDELIN

PUERTO FIJO

Official name: Republica de Venezuela
Capital: Caracas
Population: 22.3 million
Surface area: 912,050 km²
Currency: Boliviano
Language: Spanish
GDP per head: $ 3,020
Life expectancy: 73 years

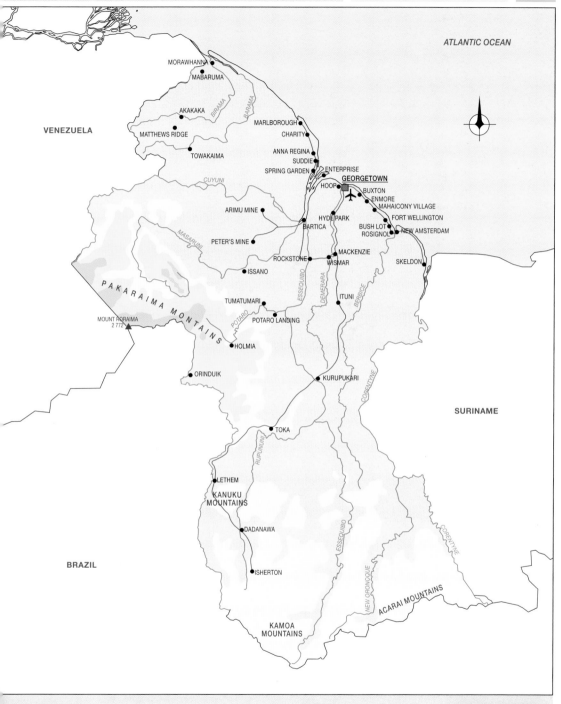

ATLANTIC OCEAN

VENEZUELA

MORAWHANNA
MABARUMA
AKAKAKA
MATTHEWS RIDGE
TOWAKAIMA
BIRAMA
BARAMA
MARLBOROUGH
CHARITY
ANNA REGINA
SUDDIE
SPRING GARDEN
ENTERPRISE
CUYUNI
HOOP
GEORGETOWN
BUXTON
ENMORE
MAHAICONY VILLAGE
ARIMU MINE
HYDE PARK
FORT WELLINGTON
BARTICA
BUSH LOT
ROSIGNOL
NEW AMSTERDAM
MASARUNI
PETER'S MINE
ROCKSTONE
MACKENZIE
WISMAR
SKELDON
ISSANO
ESSEQUIBO
DEMERARA
BERBICE
TUMATUMARI
ITUNI
POTARO
POTARO LANDING
MOUNT RORAIMA
2 772
HOLMIA
COPENTYNE
SURINAME
ORINDUIK
KURUPUKARI
PAKARAIMA MOUNTAINS

TOKA
RUPUNUNI
LETHEM
KANUKU
MOUNTAINS
DADANAWA
ESSEQUIBO
COPENTYNE
BRAZIL
ISHERTON
NEW ORONOQUE
ACARAI MOUNTAINS
KAMOA
MOUNTAINS

Official name:	Cooperative Republic of Guyana
Capital:	Georgetown
Population:	0.8 million
Surface area:	214,969 km²
Currency:	Guyana Dollar
Language:	English
GDP per head:	$ 690
Life expectancy:	64 years

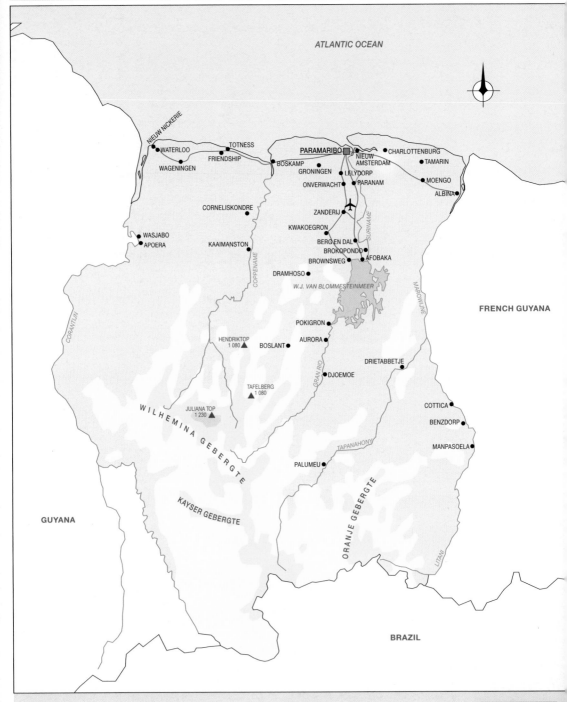

ATLANTIC OCEAN

NIEUW NICKERIE
WATERLOO
TOTNESS
FRIENDSHIP
WAGENINGEN
BOSKAMP
PARAMARIBO
CHARLOTTENBURG
NIEUW AMSTERDAM
TAMARIN
GRONINGEN
LELYDORP
ONVERWACHT
PARANAM
MOENGO
ALBINA
CORNELISKONDRE
ZANDERIJ
WASJABO
APOERA
KAAIMANSTON
KWAKOEGRON
BERG EN DAL
BROKOPONDO
AFOBAKA
BROWNSWEG
DRAMHOSO
W.J. VAN BLOMMESTEINMEER
MAROWIJNE
FRENCH GUYANA
POKIGRON
HENDRIKTOP
1 080
BOSLANT
AURORA
GRAN RIO
DRIETABBETJE
TAFELBERG
1 080
DJOEMOE
COTTICA
JULIANA TOP
1 230
BENZDORP
WILHEMINA GEBERGTE
MANPASOELA
TAPANAHONY
PALUMEU
KAYSER GEBERGTE
ORANJE GEBERGTE
LITANI
GUYANA
CORANTIJN
COPPENAME
SURINAME

BRAZIL

Official name:	Republiek Suriname
Capital:	Paramaribo
Population:	0.4 million
Surface area:	163,265 km²
Currency:	Surinam Guilder
Languages:	Dutch, Spanish, English
GDP per head:	$ 1,000
Life expectancy:	71 years

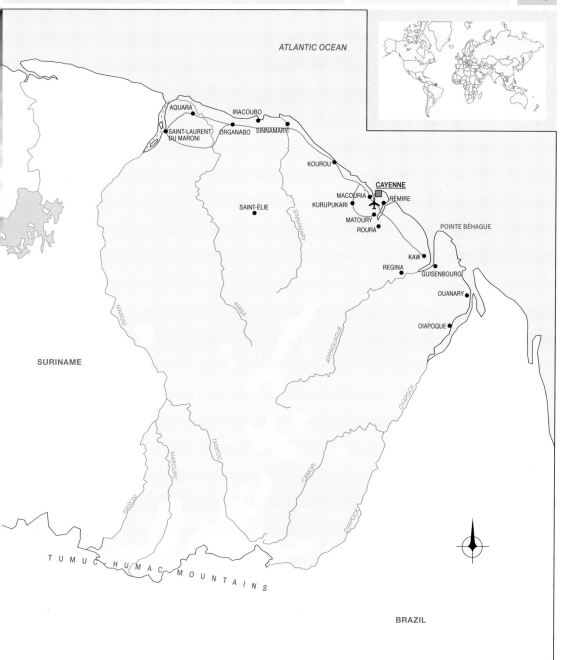

ATLANTIC OCEAN

AQUARA
IRACOUBO
SAINT-LAURENT
DU MARONI
ORGANABO
SINNAMARY
KOUROU
CAYENNE
MACOURIA
RÉMIRE
KURUPUKARI
SAINT-ÉLIE
MATOURY
ROURA
POINTE BÉHAGUE
SINNAMARY
KAW
REGINA
GUISENBOURG
OUANARY
MANA
OIAPOQUE
SURINAME
APPROUAGUE
OYAPOCK
MARONI
TAMPOC
MAROUINI
CAMOPI
MAROUINI
OYAPOCK
TUMUC-HUMAC MOUNTAINS
BRAZIL

Official name:	Département d'Outre-Mer de la Guyane française
Capital:	Cayenne
Population:	153,000
Surface area:	83,534 km²
Currency:	French Franc
Languages:	French, Creole
GDP per head:	$ 9,386
Life expectancy:	78 years

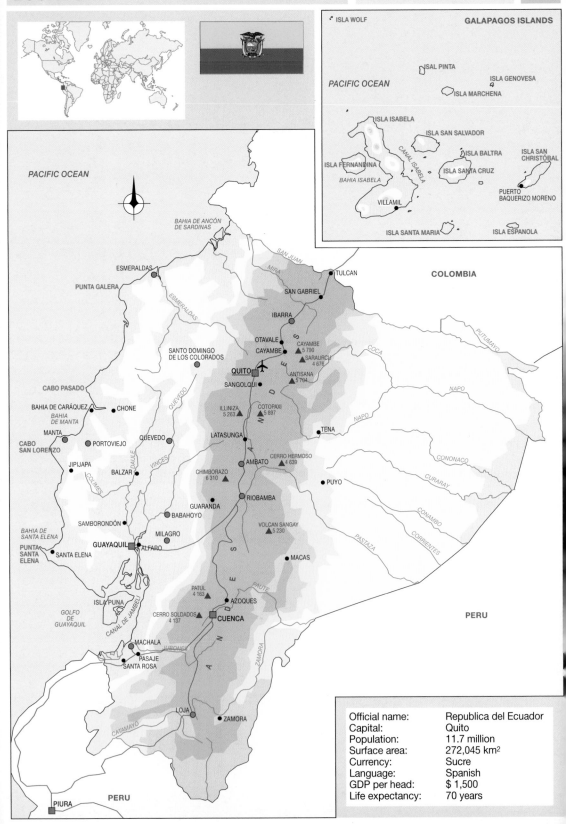

GALAPAGOS ISLANDS

ISLA WOLF

PACIFIC OCEAN

SAL PINTA

ISLA GENOVESA

ISLA MARCHENA

ISLA ISABELA

ISLA SAN SALVADOR

ISLA FERNANDINA

ISLA BALTRA

ISLA SAN CHRISTÓBAL

ISLA SANTA CRUZ

BAHIA ISABELA

CANAL ISABELA

PUERTO BAQUERIZO MORENO

VILLAMIL

ISLA SANTA MARIA

ISLA ESPANOLA

PACIFIC OCEAN

BAHIA DE ANCÓN DE SARDINAS

COLOMBIA

SAN JUAN

MIRA

ESMERALDAS

PUNTA GALERA

TULCAN

SAN GABRIEL

IBARRA

ESMERALDAS

COCA

PUTUMAYO

SANTO DOMINGO DE LOS COLORADOS

OTAVALE

CAYAMBE

CAYAMBE 5 790

SARAURCU 4 676

ANTISANA 5 794

QUITO

SANGOLQUI

CABO PASADO

QUEVEDO

NAPO

NAPO

BAHIA DE CARÁQUEZ

CHONE

ILLINIZA 5 263

COTOPAXI 5 897

BAHIA DE MANTA

TENA

MANTA

PORTOVIEJO

QUEVEDO

LATASUNGA

CONONACO

CABO SAN LORENZO

JIPIJAPA

DAULE

VINCES

AMBATO

CERRO HERMOSO 4 639

BALZAR

CHIMBORAZO 6 310

PUYO

COLIMES

CURARAY

GUARANDA

RIOBAMBA

SAMBORONDÓN

BABAHOYO

CONAMBO

BAHIA DE SANTA ELENA

MILAGRO

VOLCAN SANGAY 5 230

PUNTA SANTA ELENA

GUAYAQUIL

ALFARO

SANTA ELENA

MACAS

CORRIENTES

PASTAZA

ISLA PUNA

PATUL 4 163

GOLFO DE GUAYAQUIL

CERRO SOLDADOS 4 137

AZOQUES

PAUTE

CUENCA

CANAL DE JAMBELI

JUBONES

MACHALA

ZAMORA

PERU

PASAJE

SANTA ROSA

LOJA

ZAMORA

CATAMAYO

PERU

PIURA

Official name:	Republica del Ecuador
Capital:	Quito
Population:	11.7 million
Surface area:	272,045 km²
Currency:	Sucre
Language:	Spanish
GDP per head:	$ 1,500
Life expectancy:	70 years

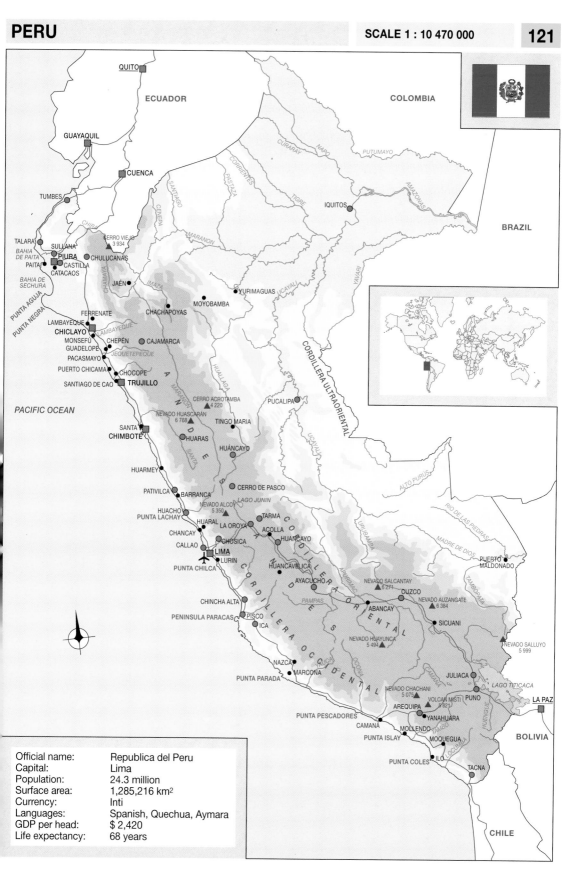

ECUADOR

COLOMBIA

BRAZIL

QUITO

GUAYAQUIL

CUENCA

TUMBES

CURARAY NAPO PUTUMAYO

CORRIENTES

PASTAZA

SANTIAGO

TIGRE

AMAZONAS

YAVARI

IQUITOS

MARAÑON

CENEPA

CHIRA

TALARA
BAHIA DE PAITA
PAITA
SULLANA
PIURA
CASTILLA
CATACAOS
CHULUCANAS
CERRO VIEJO ▲ 3 934

PUNTA AGUJA
BAHIA DE SECHURA
PUNTA NEGRA

JAÉN

YURIMAGUAS

MOYOBAMBA

CHACHAPOYAS

FERRENATE
LAMBAYEQUE
CHICLAYO
LAMBAYEQUE
MONSEFU
GUADELOPE
PACASMAYO
PUERTO CHICAMA
SANTIAGO DE CAO
CHEPÉN
CAJAMARCA
CHOCOPE
TRUJILLO

JEQUETEPEQUE

HUALLAGA

UCAYALI

CORDILLERA ULTRAORIENTAL

PUCALLPA

CERRO ACROTAMBA ▲ 4 220

NEVADO HUASCARAN ▲ 6 768

TINGO MARIA

HUARAS

HUÁNCAYO

MARAÑON

SANTA

PACIFIC OCEAN

HUARMEY

PATIVILCA
BARRANCA

CERRO DE PASCO

LAGO JUNIN

ALTO PURUS

RIO DE LAS PIEDRAS

HUACHO
PUNTA LACHAY
CHANCAY
CALLAO
LIMA
LURIN
PUNTA CHILCA

HUARAL
LA OROYA
CHOSICA

NEVADO ALCOY ▲ 5 350

TARMA
ACOLLA
HUANCAYO

URIBAMBA

MADRE DE DIOS

PUERTO MALDONADO

HUANCAVELICA

AYACUCHO

NEVADO SALCANTAY ▲ 6 271

ABANCAY

CUZCO

NEVADO AUZANGATE ▲ 6 384

SICUANI

CHINCHA ALTA

PAMPAS

APURIMAC

TAMBOPATA

PENINSULA PARACAS
PISCO
ICA

NEVADO HUAYUNCA ▲ 5 494

OCONA

NEVADO SALLUYO ▲ 5 999

NAZCA
MARCONA
PUNTA PARADA

JULIACA

LAGO TITICACA

PUNTA PESCADORES
CAMANA
PUNTA ISLAY

NEVADO CHACHANI ▲ 5 075
AREQUIPA
VOLCAN MISTI ▲ 5 821
YANAHUARA
MOLLENDO
MOQUEGUA

PUNO

LA PAZ

BOLIVIA

CAMANA
TAMBO
LOCUMBA

PUNTA COLES
ILO
TACNA

CHILE

Official name:	Republica del Peru
Capital:	Lima
Population:	24.3 million
Surface area:	1,285,216 km²
Currency:	Inti
Languages:	Spanish, Quechua, Aymara
GDP per head:	$ 2,420
Life expectancy:	68 years

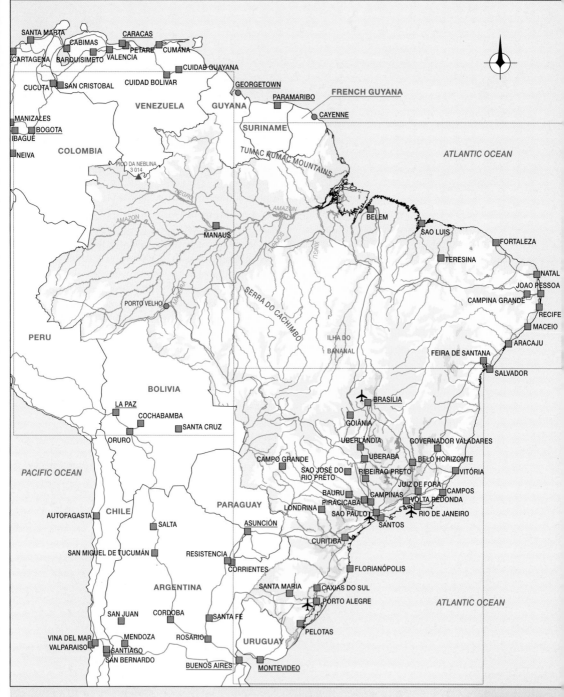

SANTA MARTA

CABIMAS   CARACAS
PETARE   CUMANA
CARTAGENA   BARQUISIMETO   VALENCIA
CUIDAD GUAYANA
CUCUTA   SAN CRISTOBAL   CUIDAD BOLIVAR
GEORGETOWN
PARAMARIBO
MANIZALES
BOGOTA   VENEZUELA   GUYANA   SURINAME   CAYENNE
IBAGUÉ   FRENCH GUYANA
NEIVA   COLOMBIA   ATLANTIC OCEAN

TUMAC HUMAC MOUNTAINS

PICO DA NEBLINA
3 014

NEGRO

AMAZON

BELEM

AMAZON

MANAUS   SAO LUIS

TAPAJOS

XINGU

FORTALEZA

TERESINA

NATAL
JOAO PESSOA
CAMPINA GRANDE
RECIFE
MACEIO

PORTO VELHO

SERRA DO CACHIMBO

PERU

MADEIRA

ILHA DO
BANANAL

FEIRA DE SANTANA   ARACAJU

SALVADOR

BOLIVIA

LA PAZ

COCHABAMBA
ORURO   SANTA CRUZ

BRASÍLIA

GOIÂNIA

UBERLÂNDIA   GOVERNADOR VALADARES

UBERABA

CAMPO GRANDE

SAO JOSÉ DO
RIO PRÉTO   RIBEIRAO PRETO

BELO HORIZONTE
VITÓRIA

JUIZ DE FORA

PACIFIC OCEAN

BAURU   CAMPINAS   CAMPOS
PIRACICABA   VOLTA REDONDA
LONDRINA   SAO PAULO   RIO DE JANEIRO

AUTOFAGASTA   CHILE   PARAGUAY

SALTA

SANTOS

ASUNCIÓN

CURITIBA

SAN MIGUEL DE TUCUMÁN

RESISTENCIA

FLORIANÓPOLIS

CORRIENTES

ARGENTINA

SANTA MARIA   CAXIAS DO SUL

SAN JUAN   CORDOBA   PORTO ALEGRE

ATLANTIC OCEAN

VINA DEL MAR   MENDOZA   SANTA FE   PELOTAS
VALPARAISO   ROSARIO
SANTIAGO   URUGUAY
SAN BERNARDO   BUENOS AIRES   MONTEVIDEO

Official name:	Republica Federativa do Brasil
Capital:	Brasilia
Population:	161.4 million
Surface area:	8,547,404 km²
Currency:	New Cruzado
Languages:	Portuguese, Spanish, English
GDP per head:	$ 4,400
Life expectancy:	67 years

BRAZIL

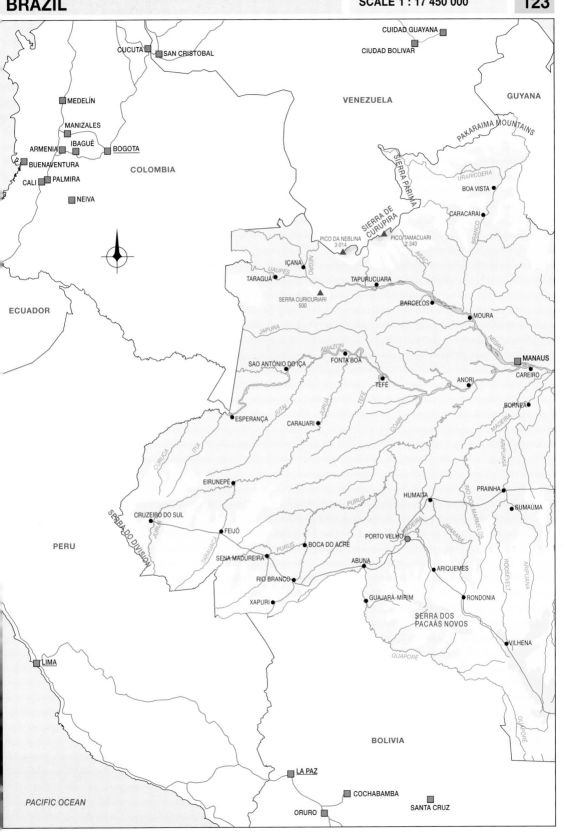

BRAZIL

SCALE 1 : 17 450 000

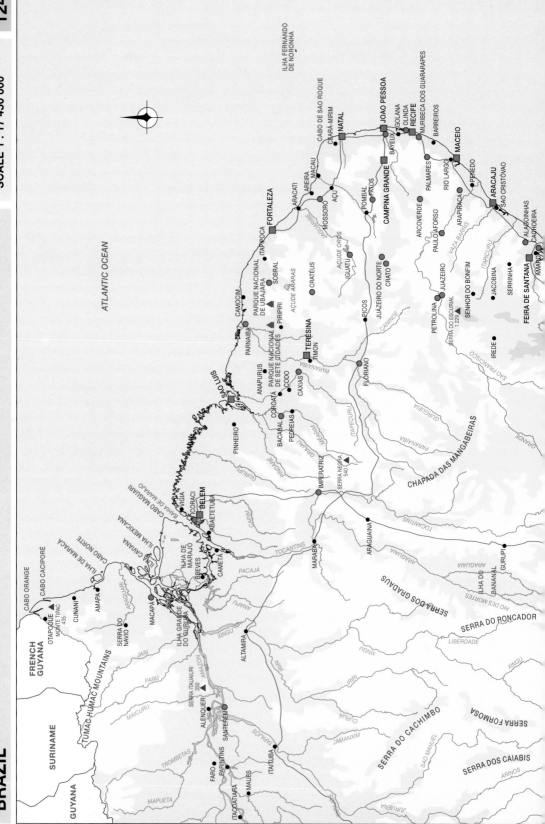

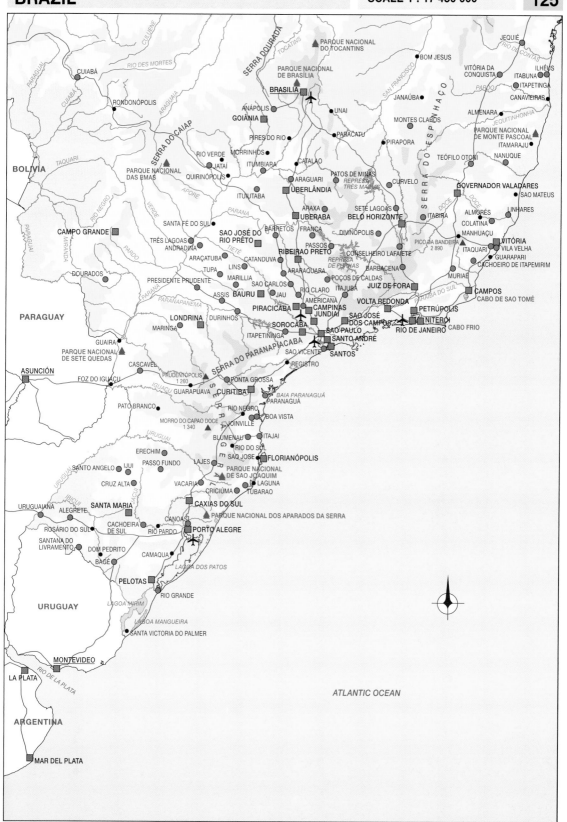

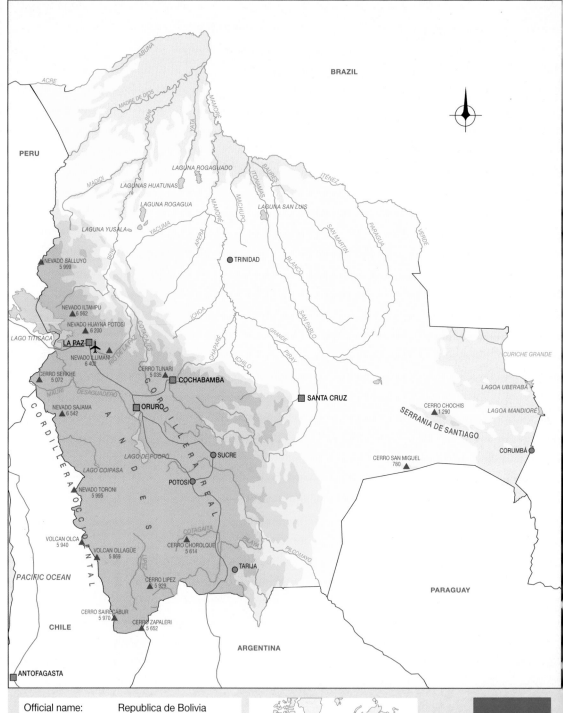

BRAZIL

PERU

ACRE

ABUNA

MADRE DE DIOS

BENI

MADIDI

LAGUNA ROGAGUADO

LAGUNAS HUATUNAS

LAGUNA ROGAGUA

LAGUNA YUSALA

YACUMA

MAMORÉ

APERA

BENI

YATA

MAMORE

MACHUPO

LAGUNA SAN LUIS

ITONAMAS

BAURES

ITENEZ

SAN MARTIN

PARAGUA

VERDE

TRINIDAD

CURICHE GRANDE

NEVADO SALLUYO
5 999

NEVADO ILTAMPU
6 562

NEVADO HUAYNA POTOSI
6 200

LAGO TITICACA

LA PAZ

NEVADO ILLIMANI
6 402

CERRO SERKHE
5 072

MAURI

DESAGUADERO

RIO DE LA PAZ

COTACAJES

CERRO TUNARI
5 035

COCHABAMBA

ICHOA

CHAPARE

ICHILO

GRANDE

PIRAY

SAN PABLO

BLANCO

SANTA CRUZ

LAGOA UBERABÁ

LAGOA MANDIORÉ

NEVADO SAJAMA
6 542

ORURO

CORDILLERA

CERRO CHOCHIS
1 290

SERRANIA DE SANTIAGO

LAGO DE POOPO

LAGO COIPASA

ANDES

REAL

SUCRE

CERRO SAN MIGUEL
780

CORUMBÁ

CORDILLERA

OCCIDENTAL

NEVADO TORONI
5 995

POTOSI

COTAGAITA

VOLCAN OLCA
5 940

VOLCAN OLLAGÜE
5 869

CERRO CHOROLQUE
5 614

LIPEZ

PLAYA

PILCOMAYO

CERRO LIPEZ
5 929

TARIJA

PARAGUAY

PACIFIC OCEAN

CERRO SAIRE CABUR
5 970

CERRO ZAPALERI
5 652

CHILE

ARGENTINA

ANTOFAGASTA

Official name:	Republica de Bolivia
Capital:	Sucre
Population:	7.6 million
Surface area:	1,098,581 km²
Currency:	Boliviano
Languages:	Spanish, Quechua, Aymará
GDP per head:	$ 830
Life expectancy:	61 years

Official name:	Republica de Chile
Capital:	Santiago
Population:	14.4 million
Surface area:	756,626 km^2
Currency:	Chilean Peso
Language:	Spanish
GDP per head:	$ 4,860
Life expectancy:	75 years

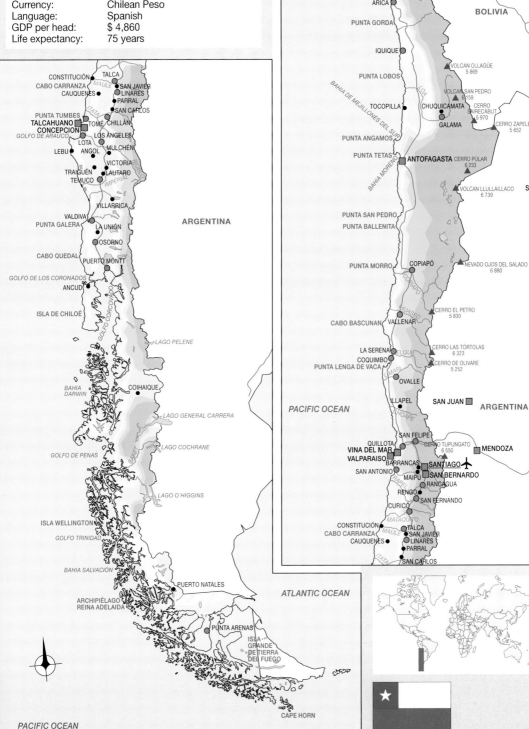

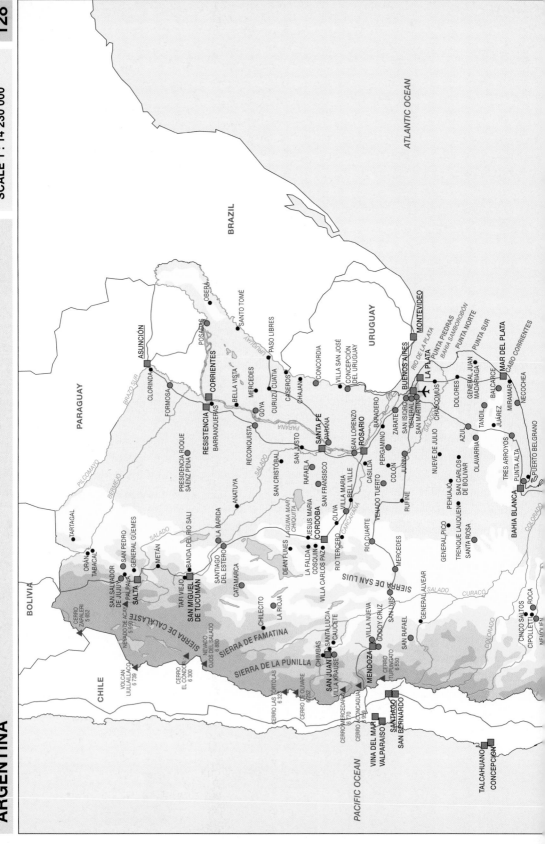

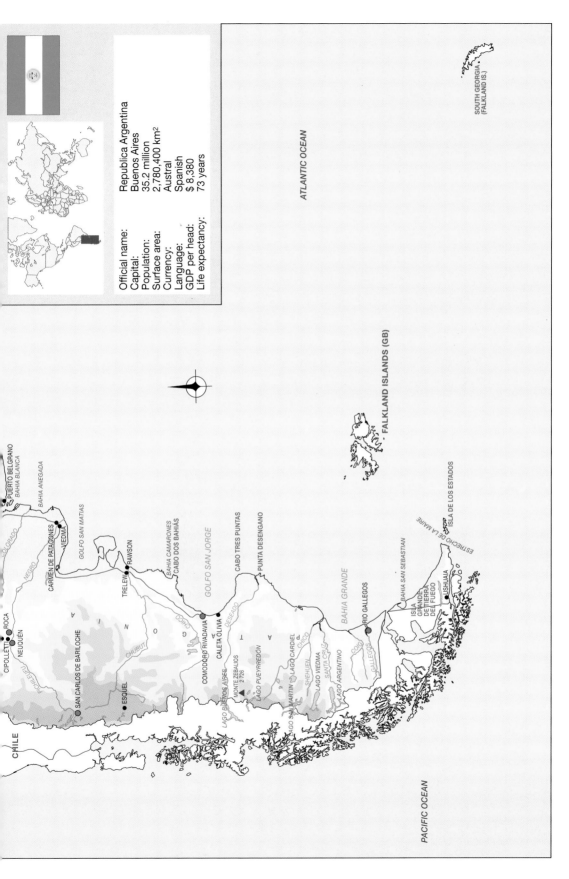

Official name:	Republica Argentina
Capital:	Buenos Aires
Population:	35.2 million
Surface area:	2,780,400 km²
Currency:	Austral
Language:	Spanish
GDP per head:	$ 8,380
Life expectancy:	73 years

ATLANTIC OCEAN

SOUTH GEORGIA.
(FALKLAND IS.)

FALKLAND ISLANDS (GB)

PUERTO BELGRANO
BAHIA BLANCA
BAHIA ANEGADA
CARMEN DE PATAGONES
VIEDMA
GOLFO SAN MATIAS
COLORADO
NEGRO
ROCA
CIPOLLETTI
NEUQUÉN
CHILE
CORDILLERA
N
D
E
S
A
N
D
E
S
SAN CARLOS DE BARILOCHE
ESQUEL
CHUBUT
TRELEW
RAWSON
BAHIA CAMARONES
CABO DOS BAHIAS
GOLFO SAN JORGE
CABO TRES PUNTAS
PUNTA DESENGANO
COMODORO RIVADAVIA
CALETA OLIVIA
DESEADO
CHICO
LAGO BUENOS AIRES
MONTE ZEBALLOS
2726
LAGO PUEYRREDON
LAGO SAN MARTIN
LAGO CARDIEL
LAGO VIEDMA
SHEHUEN
SANTA CRUZ
LAGO ARGENTINO
COIG
GALLEGOS
RIO GALLEGOS
BAHIA GRANDE
BAHIA SAN SEBASTIAN
ISLA
GRANDE
DE TIERRA
DEL FUEGO
ESTRECHO DE LA MAIRE
ISLA DE LOS ESTADOS
USHUAIA

PACIFIC OCEAN

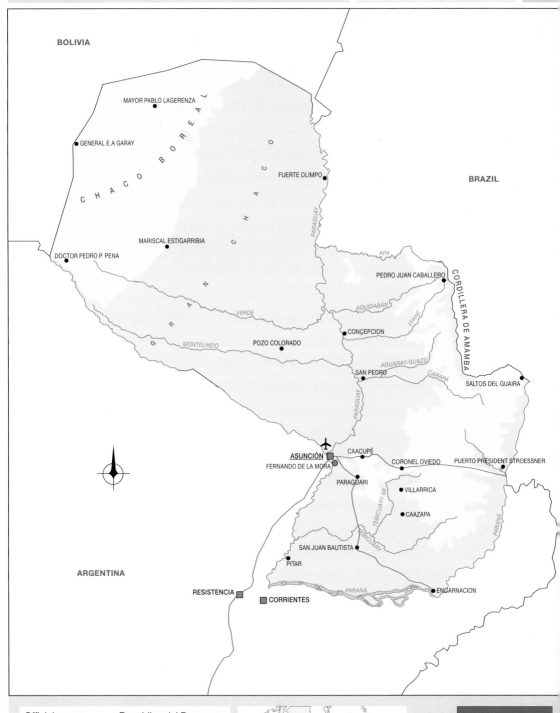

BOLIVIA

MAYOR PABLO LAGERENZA

GENERAL E.A GARAY

FUERTE OLIMPO

BRAZIL

C H A C O   B O R E A L

G R A N   C H A C O

MARISCAL ESTIGARRIBIA

DOCTOR PEDRO P. PENA

PARAGUAY

APA

PEDRO JUAN CABALLERO

CORDILLERA DE AMAMBA

AQUIDABÁN

YPANÉ

VERDE

CONÇEPCION

POZO COLORADO

MONTELINDO

AGUARAY-GUAZÚ

SAN PEDRO

CARAPA

SALTOS DEL GUAIRA

PARAGUAY

ASUNCIÓN ✈

CAACUPÉ

CORONEL OVIEDO

PUERTO PRESIDENT STROESSNER

FERNANDO DE LA MORA

PARAGUARI

TEBICUARY-MI

VILLARRICA

PARANÁ

CAAZAPA

TEBICUARY

SAN JUAN BAUTISTA

PITAR

ARGENTINA

RESISTENCIA

PARANÁ

ENCARNACION

CORRIENTES

Official name:	Republica del Paraguay
Capital:	Asuncion
Population:	5.0 million
Surface area:	406,752 km²
Currency:	Guaraní
Languages:	Spanish, Guaraní
GDP per head:	$ 1,850
Life expectancy:	71 years

ARGENTINA

BRAZIL

GUAREIM

ARTIGAS

RIVERA

SALTO

C O X I L H A   D E   S A N T A N A

TACUAREMBÓ

NEGRO

PAYSANDU

MELO

YAGUARÓN

PASO DE LOS TOROSO

LAGO
ARTIFICIAL RINCÓN
DEL BONETE

LAGUNA MERIN

NEGRO

FRAY BENTOS

MERCEDES

DOLORES

TRINIDAD

DURAZNO

C U C H I L L A   G R A N D E

TREINTA Y TRES

CARMELO

LAGUNA NEGRA

SAN JOSÉ DE MAYO

LAGUNA DE CASTILLOS

JUAN L.LACAZE

SANTA LUCIA

MINAS

CABO POLONIO

COLONIA DEL SACRAMENTO

CANELONES

ROCHA

R I O   D E   L A   P L A T A

LAS PIEDRAS

PANDO

CERRO DE LAS ANIMAS
▲ 501

SAN CARLOS

CABO SANTA MARIA

BUENOS AIRES

LA PAZ

LA PLATA

PUNTA BRAVA

MONTEVIDEO

MALDONADO

PUNTA DEL ESTE

ATLANTIC OCEAN

Official name:	Republica Oriental del Uruguay
Capital:	Montevideo
Population:	3.2 million
Surface area:	176,215 km²
Currency:	Uruguayan Peso
Language:	Spanish
GDP per head:	$ 5,760
Life expectancy:	74 years

FALKLAND ISLANDS (Islas Malvinas)

SCALE 1 : 16 000 000

Official name:	Falkland Islands
Capital:	Port Stanley
Population:	2,564
Surface area:	16,076 km²
Currency:	Falkland Islands Pound
Language:	English
GDP per head:	$ 19,600
Life expectancy:	77 years

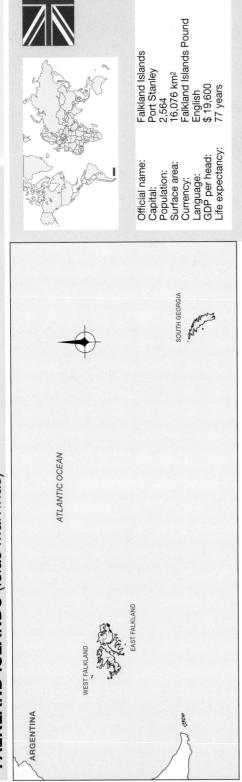

ARGENTINA

ATLANTIC OCEAN

WEST FALKLAND

EAST FALKLAND

SOUTH GEORGIA

FALKLAND ISLANDS (UK)

ATLANTIC OCEAN

JASON ISLANDS

PEBBLE ISLAND

KEPPEL ISLAND

SAUNDERS ISLAND

WESTPOINT ISLAND

BYRON SOUND

KEPPEL SOUND

HILL COVE

ROY COVE

MOUNT ADA 700

CHARTRES

KING GEORGE BAY

DUNNOSE HEAD

SPRING POINT

QUEEN CHARLOTTE BAY

FOX BAY WEST

FOX BAY EAST

WEDDELL ISLAND

BEAVER ISLAND

NEW ISLAND

PORT STEPHENS

PORT HOWARD

CAPE ORFORD

CAPE MEREDITH

MOUNT ALICE 361

FALKLAND SOUND

CAPE DOLPHIN

FOUL BAY

SALVADOR

DOUGLAS

PORT SAN CARLOS

TEAL INLET

MOUNT USBORNE 705

DARWIN

GOOSE GREEN

GLORIOUS HILL 294

CAPE BOUGAINVILLE

PORT LOUIS

BERKLEY SOUND

PORT STANLEY

BLUFF COVE

CAPE CARYSFORT

CHOISEUL SOUND

NORTH EAST LIVELY

LIVELY SOUND

ADVENTURE SOUND

BAY OF HARBOURS

BLEAKER DRIFTWOOD POINT

SEA LION ISLANDS

BARREN ISLAND

GEORGE ISLAND

SPEEDWELL ISLAND

SCALE 1 : 2 890 000

SOUTH GEORGIA

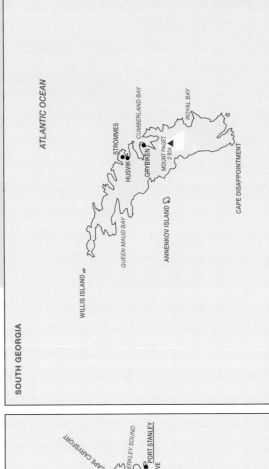

ATLANTIC OCEAN

WILLIS ISLAND

STROMNESS

HUSVIK

GRYTVIKEN

QUEEN MAUD BAY

CUMBERLAND BAY

MOUNT PAGET 2 934

ANNENKOV ISLAND

ROYAL BAY

CAPE DISAPPOINTMENT

SCALE 1 : 2 890 000

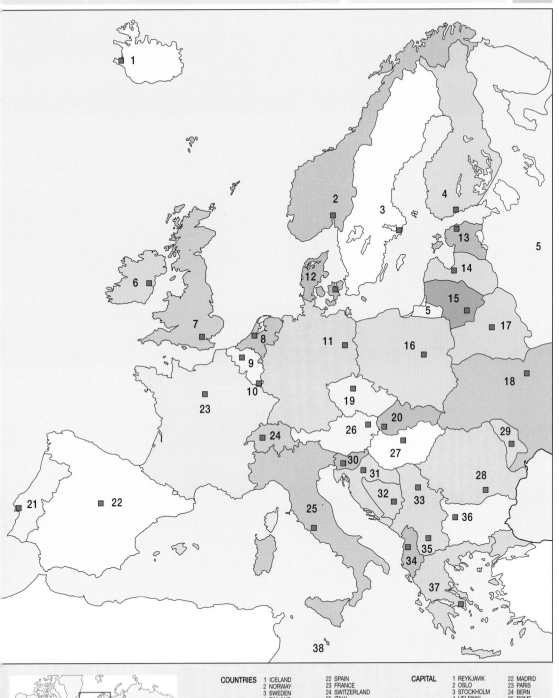

COUNTRIES				CAPITAL			
1	ICELAND	22	SPAIN	1	REYKJAVIK	22	MADRID
2	NORWAY	23	FRANCE	2	OSLO	23	PARIS
3	SWEDEN	24	SWITZERLAND	3	STOCKHOLM	24	BERN
4	FINLAND	25	ITALY	4	HELSINKI	25	ROME
5	RUSSIA	26	AUSTRIA	5	MOSCOW	26	VIENNA
6	IRELAND	27	HUNGARY	6	DUBLIN	27	BUDAPEST
7	UNITED KINGDOM	28	ROMANIA	7	LONDON	28	BUCHAREST
8	THE NETHERLANDS	29	MOLDOVA	8	AMSTERDAM	29	CHISINAU
9	BELGIUM	30	SLOVENIA	9	BRUSSELS	30	LJUBLJANA
10	LUXEMBOURG	31	CROATIA	10	LUXEMBOURG	31	ZAGREB
11	GERMANY	32	BOSNIA-HERZEGOVINA	11	BERLIN	32	SARAJEVO
12	DENMARK	33	SERBIA	12	COPENHAGEN	33	BELGRADE
13	ESTONIA	34	ALBANIA	13	TALLINN	34	TIRANA
14	LATVIA	35	MACEDONIA	14	RIGA	35	SKOPJE
15	LITHUNIA	36	BULGARIA	15	VILNIUS	36	SOFIA
16	POLAND	37	GREECE	16	WARSAW	37	ATHENS
17	BELARUS	38	MALTA	17	MINSK	38	VALLETTA
18	UKRAINE			18	KIEV		
19	CZECH REPUBLIC			19	PRAGUE		
20	SLOVAKIA			20	BRATISLAVA		
21	PORTUGAL			21	LISBON		

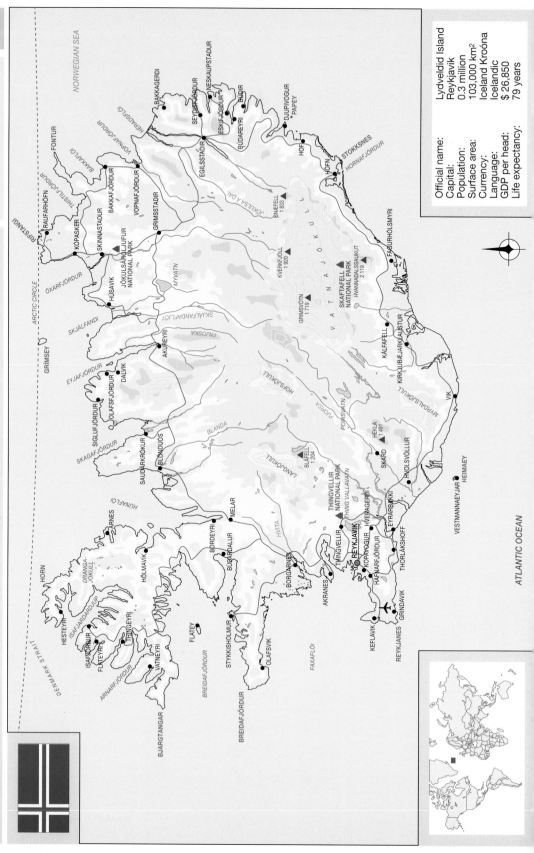

SCALE 1 : 3 420 000

ICELAND

Official name:	Lydveldid Island
Capital:	Reykjavik
Population:	0.3 million
Surface area:	103,000 km²
Currency:	Iceland Króna
Language:	Icelandic
GDP per head:	$ 26,850
Life expectancy:	79 years

NORWEGIAN SEA

ATLANTIC OCEAN

DENMARK STRAIT

ARCTIC CIRCLE

RIFSTANGI

HORN

BJARGTANGAR

BAKKAGERDI
SEYDISFJÖRDUR
NESKAUPSTADUR
ESKIFJÖRDUR
BUDIR
BÚDAREYRI
DJÚPIVOGUR
PAPEY

HÉRADSFLÓI
VOPNAFJÖRDUR
EGILSSTADIR
HÖFN
HÓFN
STOKKSNES
HORNAFJÖRDUR

FAGURHÓLSMYRI

RAUFARHOFN
FONTUR
BAKKAFLÓI
THISTILFJÖRDUR
ÖXARFJÖRDUR
KÓPASKER
SKINNASTADUR
BAKKAFJÖRDUR
VOPNAFJÖRDUR
GRÍMSSTADIR

HÚSAVIK
JÖKULSÁRGLJÚFUR
NATIONAL PARK
MYVATN
SKJÁLFANDAFLJÓT
SKJÁLFANDI
JÖKULSÁ Á DAL

BRÚFELL
1 833

KVERKFJÖLL
1 920

SKAFTAFELL
NATIONAL PARK
HVANNADALSHNÚKUR
2 119

GRÍMSVÖTN
1 719

VATNAJÖKULL

KÁLFAFELL

KIRKJUBÆJARKLAUSTUR

GRIMSEY

EYJAFJÖRDUR
AKUREYRI
DALVIK
FNJÓSKA

ÓLAFSFJÖRDUR
SIGLUFJÖRDUR
SKAGAFJÖRDUR
SAUDÁRKRÓKUR
BLÖNDUÓS
BLANDA

HOFSJÖKULL

THJÓRSÁ
THÓRISVATN

HEKLA
1 491
SKARD

MYRDALSJÖKULL
VIK

HÚNAFLÓI
MELAR
BÖRDEYRI
BÚARDALUR

DRANGA-
JÖKULL

ÍSAFJARDARDJÚP
HÓLMAVIK

HESTEYRI
ÍSAFJÖRDUR
FLATEYRI
THINGEYRI
VATNEYRI
ARNARFJÖRDUR

FLATEY
STYKKISHÓLMUR
ÓLAFSVIK
BREIDAFJÖRDUR

BLÁFELL
1 204
LANGJÖKULL

THINGVELLIR
NATIONAL PARK
THING VALLAVATN
THINGVELLIR
HVERAGERDI
REYKJAVIK
KÓPAVOGUR
HAFNARFJÖRDUR
EYRARBAKKI
THORLÁKSHOFF

HVÍTÁ
BORGARNES
AKRANES

KEFLAVIK
REYKJANES
GRINDAVIK

HVOLSVÖLLUR
VESTMANNAEYJAR
HEIMAEY

FAXAFLÓI

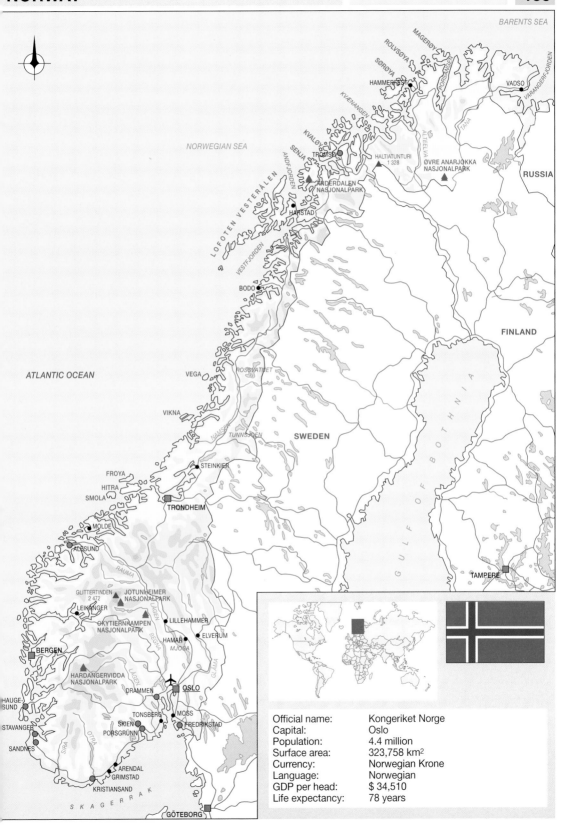

BARENTS SEA

NORWEGIAN SEA

ATLANTIC OCEAN

RUSSIA

FINLAND

SWEDEN

GULF OF BOTHNIA

MAGERØY
ROLVSØYA
SØRØYA
HAMMERFEST
VADSØ
VARANGERFJORDEN
PORSANGEN
KVÆNANGEN
KVALØY
TROMSØ
HALTIATUNTURI 1 328
ØVRE ANARJOKKA NASJONALPARK
ALTEELVA
TANA
SENJA
ANDFJORDEN
ANDERDALEN NASJONALPARK
HARSTAD
LOFOTEN VESTERÅLEN
VESTFJORDEN
BODØ
VEGA
ROSSVATNET
VIKNA
NAMSEN
TUNNSJØEN
FROYA
HITRA
SMOLA
STEINKJER
TRONDHEIM
MOLDE
ÅLESUND
RAUMA
GLITTERTINDEN 2 472
JOTUNHEIMEN NASJONALPARK
LEIKANGER
LÅGEN
LILLEHAMMER
SKYTJERNKAMPEN NASJONALPARK
HAMAR
ELVERUM
MJØSA
BERGEN
HARDANGERVIDDA NASJONALPARK
LÅGEN
BEGNA
OSLO
GLAMA
DRAMMEN
HAUGE-SUND
TONSBERG
MOSS
SKIEN
FREDRIKSTAD
STAVANGER
PORSGRUNN
SANDNES
SIRA
OTRA
ARENDAL
GRIMSTAD
KRISTIANSAND
SKAGERRAK
GÖTEBORG
TAMPERE

Official name:	Kongeriket Norge
Capital:	Oslo
Population:	4.4 million
Surface area:	323,758 km²
Currency:	Norwegian Krone
Language:	Norwegian
GDP per head:	$ 34,510
Life expectancy:	78 years

SKAGERRAK

NORTH SEA

TANNIS BUGT

GRENEN
SKAGEN

GÖTEBORG

HIRTSHALS

HJØRRING

FREDERIKSHAVN

BRONDERSLEV

LÆSØ

SWEDEN

JAMMERBUGTEN

BULBERG
47

ROSHAGE
HANSTHOLM

NORRESUNDBY

ÅLBORG

LINDEN

ÅLBORG BUGT

ANHOLT

HALMSTAD

THISTED

LIMFJORDEN

MORS

NISSUM
BREDNING

SKIVE

SIMESTED

K A T T E G A T

LEMVIG

STRUER

VIBORG

RANDERS

FORNÆS
GRENA

NISSUM FJORD

HOLSTEBRO

GUDENA

AGRI BAVNEHØJ 137

RINGKOBING

HERNING

SILKEBORG

SKANDERBORG

ÅRHUS

STORA

SKJERN

IKAST

YDING SKOVHØJ
173

SAMSØ

SJÆLLANDS
ODDE

FREDERIKSVÆRK

HELSINGOR

HILLERØD

TARM

OMME

HORSENS

SEJERØ

ISE-
FJORD

HØRSHOLM

BIRKERØD

VARDE

GRINDSTED

HEDENSTED
VEJLE

JUELSMINDE

KALUNDBORG

HOLBÆK

KOBENHAVN

MALMÖ

FANØ

ESBJERG

FREDERICIA

KOLDING

MIDDELFART

FYN

SJÆLLAND

ROSKILDE

KØGE BUGT

RINGKOBING
FJORD

FLADSA

RIBE

SKAMLINGSBANKE
118

HADERSLEV

GLAMSBJERG
131

ODENSE

NYBORG

SLAGELSE

SORO

RINGSTED

KØGE

RØMØ

LILLE-
BÆLT

BOJDEN

FABORG

SVENDBORG

STOREBÆLT

KORSØR

NÆSTVED

FAKSE BUGT

ABENRA

SON

ALS
SØNDERBORG

ÆRØ

BADENKOP

LANGELAND

SMÅLANDS-
FARVANDET

VORDINGBORG

MØN

NAKSKOV

LOLLAND

NYKOBING

GEDSER

KIELER BUCHT

FEHMARNBELT

GERMANY

KIEL

SANDVIG

SVANEKE

RONNE

BORNHOLM

Official name:	Kongeriget Danmark
Capital:	Copenhagen
Population:	5.3 million
Surface area:	43,094 km²
Currency:	Danish Krone
Language:	Danish
GDP per head:	$ 32,100
Life expectancy:	75 years

ATLANTIC OCEAN

VADVETJAKKO
NATIONALPARK

ABISKO
NATIONALPARK
TORNETRASK

KEBNEKAISE
2 111
KIRUNA

PADJELANTA
NATIONALPARK

STORA SJÖFALLETS
NATIONALPARK

SULITELNA
1 914
STORA
LULUVATTEN

SAREKS
NATIONALPARK

PIELJEKALSE
NATIONALPARK

HORNAVAN

LULEÄLVEN

KONKAMA

TORNEÄLVEN

NORRA STORFJÄLLET
1 792

STORAVAN

BODEN

LULEA

MARSFJÄLLET
1 590

UMEÄLVEN

SKELLEFTEÄLVEN

BOTTENVIKEN

ÅNGERMANÄLVEN

SKELLEFTEA

TRONDHEIM

HELAGSFJÄLLET
1 796

STORSJÖN ÖSTERSUND

LJUSGAN

UMEÄ

GULF OF BOTHNIA

NORWAY

ORNSKOLDSVIK

TÖFSINGDALENS
NATIONALPARK

SÅNFJÄLLETS
NATIONALPARK

HARNÖSAND

SUNDSVALL

FINLAND

HUDIKSVAL

DALÄLVEN

BOLLNÄS

SÖDERHAMN

MORA

BOTTENHAVET

OSLO

FALUN

BORLÄNGE

GÄVLE

KLARÄLVEN

SANDVIKEN

TAMPERE

ARVIK

KARLSTAD

VÄSTERAS

UPPSALA

TURKU

ÖREBRO

HJELMAREN

ESKILSTUNA

SOLLENTUNA

STOCKHOLM

ESPOO

HELSINKI

SKAGERRAK

UDDEVALLA

VÄNERSBORG

MARIESTAD

SKÖVDE

MOTALA

SÖDERTÄLJE

NORRKÖPING

NYKÖPING

VÄNERN

GULF OF FINLAND

ATINGSÅS
BORAS

LINKÖPING

OXELOSUND

GÖTEBORG
MÖLNDAL

KINNA
JÖNKÖPING

NÄSSJÖ

VÄSTERVIK

GOTSKA SANDÖN

TALLINN

KUNGSBACKA

VARBERG

VÄRNARNO
VETLANDA
BOLMEN
VÄTTERN

OSKARSHAMN

ESTONIA

FALKENBERG

HALMSTAD

LJUNGBY

VÄXJÖ
ÄSNEN

KALMAR

VISBY

GOTLAND

TARTU

KATTEGAT

HELSINGBORG
LANDSKRONA

ÖLAND

KÖBENHAVN

LUND

KRISTIANSTAD

KARLSKRONA

MALMÖ

BALTIC SEA

TRELLEBORG

DANMARK

Official name:	Konungariket Sverige
Capital:	Stockholm
Population:	8.8 million
Surface area:	449,964 km^2
Currency:	Swedish Krona
Language:	Swedish
GDP per head:	$ 25,710
Life expectancy:	79 years

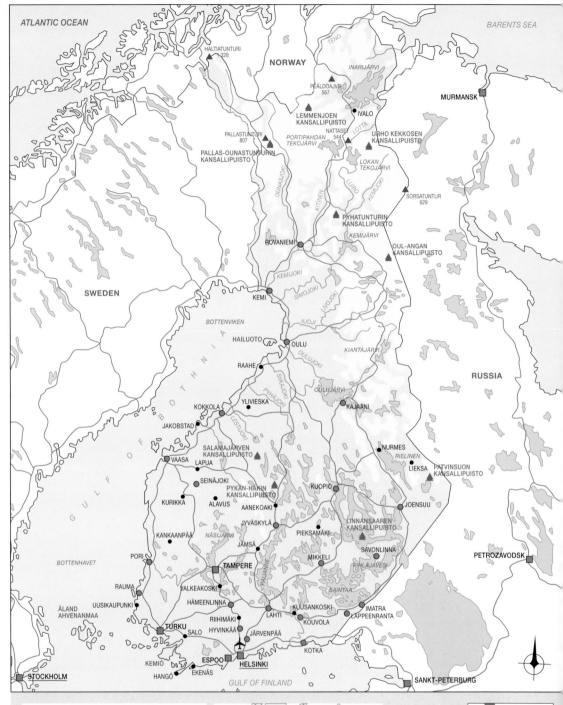

ATLANTIC OCEAN
BARENTS SEA
NORWAY
HÄLTIATUNTURI 1 328
INARIJÄRVI
TENO
MURMANSK
PEÄLDOAJVRI 567
LEMMENJOEN KANSALLIPUISTO
IVALO
PALLASTUNTURI 807
NÄTTASET 544
LOTTA
URHO KEKKOSEN KANSALLIPUISTO
PALLAS-OUNASTUNTURIN KANSALLIPUISTO
PORTIPAHDAN TEKOJÄRVI
LUIRO
KITINEN
OUNASJOKI
LOKAN TEKOJÄRVI
KEMIJOKI
SORSATUNTUR 629
PYHATUNTURIN KANSALLIPUISTO
KEMIJÄRVI
OUL-ANGAN KANSALLIPUISTO
ROVANIEMI
KEMIJOKI
SWEDEN
KEMI
SIMOJOKI
LIVOJOKI
BOTTENVIKEN
HAILUOTO
OULU
IIJOKI
KIANTAJÄRVI
OULUJOKI
RUSSIA
RAAHE
SIIKAJOKI
OULUJÄRVI
PYHÄJOKI
KAJAANI
KOKKOLA
YLIVIESKA
JAKOBSTAD
LESTIJOKI
NURMES
RIELINEN
LIEKSA
PATVINSUON KANSALLIPUISTO
SALAMAJÄRVEN KANSALLIPUISTO
VAASA
LAPUA
SEINÄJOKI
PYKÄN-HÄKIN KANSALLIPUISTO
KUOPIO
KURIKKA
ALAVUS
AANEKOAKI
JOENSUU
G U L F   O F   B O T H N I A
JYVÄSKYLÄ
PIEKSÄMÄKI
LINNANSAAREN KANSALLIPUISTO
KANKAANPÄÄ
NÄSIJÄRVI
JÄMSÄ
SAVONLINNA
PORI
MIKKELI
PETROZAVODSK
BOTTENHAVET
TAMPERE
PÄIJÄNNE
RIHLAJAVESI
RAUMA
VALKEAKOSKI
SAINTAA
UUSIKAUPUNKI
HÄMEENLINNA
KUUSANKOSKI
IMATRA
ÅLAND AHVENANMAA
RIIHIMÄKI
LAHTI
LAPPEENRANTA
KOUVOLA
TURKU
SALO
HYVINKÄÄ
JÄRVENPÄÄ
KEMIÖ
KOTKA
ESPOO
HELSINKI
STOCKHOLM
HANGÖ
EKENÄS
GULF OF FINLAND
SANKT-PETERBURG

Official name:	Suomen Tasavalta
Capital:	Helsinki
Population:	5.1 million
Surface area:	338,144 km²
Currency:	Markka
Language:	Finnish, Swedish
GDP per head:	$ 23,240
Life expectancy:	77 years

ATLANTIC OCEAN

UNITED KINGDOM

MALIN HEAD

RATHLIN ISLAND

NORTH CHANNEL

BLOODY FORELAND

GWEEDORE

COLERAINE

ARAN ISLAND

LOUGH FOLLEY

ERRIGAL MOUNTAIN 752

LONDONDERRY

BALLYMENA

LARNE

GWEEBARRA BAY

LIFFORD

SAWEL MOUNTAIN 678

LOUGHROS MORE BAY

STRABANE

ANTRIM

ROCKY POINT

DONEGAL

NORTHERN IRELAND (U.K.)

BELFAST

NEWTOWNABBEY

BANGOR

NEWTOWNARDS

DONEGAL BAY

OMAGH

LISBURN

LURGAN

STRONGFORD LOUGH

BELMULLET

SLIGO

LOWER LOUGH ERNE

ENNISKILLEN

PORTADOWN

ARMAGH

BLACKSOD BAY

ACHILL HEAD

ACHILL

NEPHIN 806

SWINFORD

LOUGH CONN

UPPER LOUGH ERNE

LOUGH ALLEN

CARRICK ON SHANNON

CAVAN

ANNAGH

DUNDALK

NEWRY

NEWCASTLE

CLEW BAY

CASTLEBAR

WESTPORT

CONNAUGHT

DUNDALK BAY

INISHTURK INISHBOFIN

LOUGH MASK

ROSCOMMON

LONGFORD

MEATH

BOYNE

NAVAN

DROGHEDA

IRISH SEA

CLIFDEN

LOUGH CORRIB

TUAM

LOUGH REE

MULLINGAR

ATHENRY

ATHLONE

GALWAY

SUCK

GALWAY BAY

LOUGHREA

BROSNA

TULLAMORE

DUBLIN

DÚN LAOGHAIRE

ARAN ISLANDS

PORTUMNA

ROSCREA

KILDARE

NAAS

WICKLOW MOUNTAINS

BRAY

HAGS HEAD

LISCANNOR BAY

LOUGH DERG

PORT LAOISE

WICKLOW

WICKLOW HEAD

MILLTOWN MALBAY

ENNIS

NENAGH

CARLOW

LUGNAQUILLIA MOUNTAINS 924

ARKLOW

BALLINA

SLIEVEKIMALTA 694

KILRUSH

LIMERICK

SHANNON

LOOP HEAD

BALLYBUNNION

MAIGUE

KILKENNY

CALLAN

MOUNT LEINSTE 793

CAHORE POINT

KERRY HEAD

FEALE

TIPPERARY

BRANDON MOUNTAIN 953

TRALEE

ABBEYFEALE

GALTY MOUNTAINS

CLONMEL

SUIR

BARROW

SLANEY

WEXFORD

WEXFORD HARBOUR

GREAT BLASKET ISLAND

DINGLE BAY

KILLARNEY

MALLOW

BLACKWATER

DUNGARVAN

WATERFORD

HOOK POINT

GREENORE POINT

CARNSORE POINT

VALENCIA ISLAND

CAHERSIVEEN

CARRAUNTOOHIL 1 038

LEE

CORK

YOUGHAL

DUNGARVAN HARBOUR

ST. GEORGE'S CHANNEL

COBH

BALLINSKELLIGS BAY

CASTLETOWN BEARHAVEN

BANDON

KINSALE

YOUGHAL BAY

DURSEY ISLAND

BEAR ISLAND

BANTRY

BANTRY BAY

CLONAKILTY

CORK HARBOUR

CELTIC SEA

SKULL

MIZEN HEAD

CLEAR ISLAND

OLD HEAD OF KINSALE

CLONAKILTY BAY

ATLANTIC OCEAN

Official name:	Poblacht na h'Éirean
Capital:	Dublin
Population:	3.6 million
Surface area:	70,273 km^2
Currency:	Irish Pound
Languages:	Irish, English
GDP per head:	$ 147,1106
Life expectancy:	76 years

SHETLAND ISLANDS

LERWICK

ATLANTIC OCEAN

NORTH SEA

ORKNEY ISLANDS

KIRKWALL

STORNOWAY

THE MINCH

THE LITTLE MINCH

ISLAND OF SKYE

OUTER HEBRIDES

MORAY FIRTH

INVERNESS

ELGIN

LOCH NESS

SPEY

FORT WILLIAM

BEN NEVIS 1 343

GRAMPIAN MOUNTAIN

DON

DEE

FRASERBURGH

PETERHEAD

ABERDEEN

MONTROSE

ARBROATH

DUNDEE

FORFAR

STIRLING

GLENROTHES

KIRKCALDY

FIRTH OF FORTH

EDINBURGH

GLASGOW

KILMARNOCK

PRESTWICK

AYR

NITH

FIRTH OF CLYDE

GALASHIELS

TWEED

NEWTOWN-ST-BOSWELLS

HAWICK

BERWICK-UPON-TWEED

DUMFRIES

SOLWAY FIRTH

STRANRAER

CARLISLE

MARYPORT

WORKINGTON

WHITEHAVEN

LAKE DISTRICT NATIONAL PARK

BARROW-IN-FURNESS

MORECAMBE

LANCASTER

YORKSHIRE DALES NATIONAL PARK

ISLE OF MAN

DOUGLAS

NORTH CHANNEL

BANGOR

NEWTOWNABBEY

BELFAST

BALLYMENA

COLERAINE

LONDONDERRY

LAKE NEAGH

OMAGH

ENNISKILLEN

NORTHERN IRELAND

DONEGAL BAY

MORPETH

BLYTH

TYNEMOUTH

SOUTH SHIELDS

NEWCASTLE UPON TYNE

GATESHEAD

SUNDERLAND

DURHAM

BISHOP AUCKLAND

HARTLEPOOL

MIDDLESBROUGH

STOCKTON

DARLINGTON

NORTH YORK MOORS NATIONAL PARK

NORTHALLERTON

SCARBOROUGH

FLAMBOROUGH HEAD

BRIDLINGTON

HARROGATE

YORK

OUSE

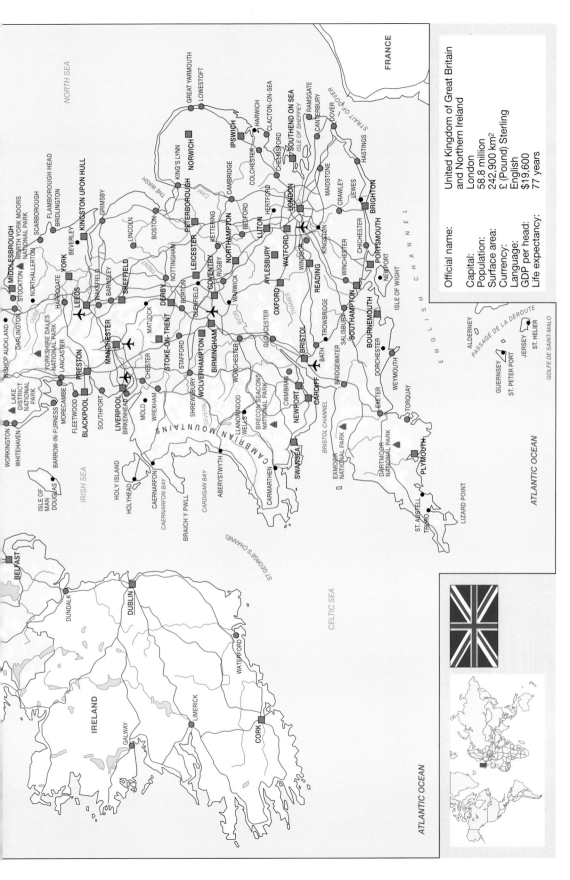

NORTH SEA

FRANCE

Official name:	United Kingdom of Great Britain and Northern Ireland
Capital:	London
Population:	58.8 million
Surface area:	242,900 km^2
Currency:	£ (Pound) Sterling
Language:	English
GDP per head:	$19,600
Life expectancy:	77 years

STRAIT OF DOVER

GREAT YARMOUTH
LOWESTOFT
HARWICH
CLACTON-ON-SEA
ISLE OF SHEPPEY
RAMSGATE
CANTERBURY
DOVER
IPSWICH
NORWICH
KING'S LYNN
COLCHESTER
CHELMSFORD
SOUTHEND ON SEA
HASTINGS
LEWES
MAIDSTONE
HERTFORD
LONDON
BEDFORD
CAMBRIDGE
PETERBOROUGH
BRIGHTON
CAM
KETTERING
LUTON
WATFORD
CRAWLEY
CHICHESTER
WINDSOR
KINGSTON
PORTSMOUTH
NORTHAMPTON
AYLESBURY
READING
WINCHESTER
NEWPORT
ISLE OF WIGHT
RUGBY
COVENTRY
OXFORD
WARWICK
AVON
THAMES
LINCOLN
NOTTINGHAM
DERBY
LEICESTER
SHEFFIELD
BOSTON
GRIMSBY
KINGSTON UPON HULL
BEVERLEY
BRIDLINGTON
SCARBOROUGH
FLAMBOROUGH HEAD
NORTH YORK MOORS NATIONAL PARK
THE WASH
BURTON
CHESTERFIELD
WAKEFIELD
BARNSLEY
LEEDS
HARROGATE
YORK
NORTHALLERTON
STOCKTON
MIDDLESBROUGH
BISHOP AUCKLAND
DARLINGTON
YORKSHIRE DALES NATIONAL PARK
MATLOCK
STOKE-ON-TRENT
STAFFORD
CHESTER
MANCHESTER
PRESTON
LANCASTER
MORECAMBE
FLEETWOOD
BLACKPOOL
SOUTHPORT
LIVERPOOL
BIRKENHEAD
BARROW-IN-FURNESS
LAKE DISTRICT NATIONAL PARK
WORKINGTON
WHITEHAVEN
BISHOP AUCKLAND

ENGLISH CHANNEL

SOUTHAMPTON
BOURNEMOUTH
TROWBRIDGE
SALISBURY
BATH
BRISTOL
GLOUCESTER
WORCESTER
BIRMINGHAM
WOLVERHAMPTON
SHREWSBURY
WREXHAM
MOLD
LLANDRINDOD WELLS
BRECON BEACONS NATIONAL PARK
CWMBRAN
NEWPORT
CARDIFF
SWANSEA
CARMARTHEN
ABERYSTWYTH
CAMBRIAN MOUNTAINS
SEVERN
BRISTOL CHANNEL
BRIDGWATER
EXMOOR NATIONAL PARK
DORCHESTER
WEYMOUTH
EXETER
TORQUAY
DARTMOOR NATIONAL PARK
PLYMOUTH
ST. AUSTELL
TRURO
LIZARD POINT

CARNARFON
HOLYHEAD
HOLY ISLAND
BRAICH Y PWLL
CAERNARFON BAY
CARDIGAN BAY

ST GEORGE'S CHANNEL

ISLE OF MAN
DOUGLAS
IRISH SEA

BELFAST
DUNDALK
DUBLIN
WATERFORD
LIMERICK
GALWAY
CORK
IRELAND
CELTIC SEA
ATLANTIC OCEAN

ALDERNEY
PASSAGE DE LA DÉROUTE
GUERNSEY
ST. PETER PORT
JERSEY
ST. HELIER
GOLFE DE SAINT-MALO

ATLANTIC OCEAN

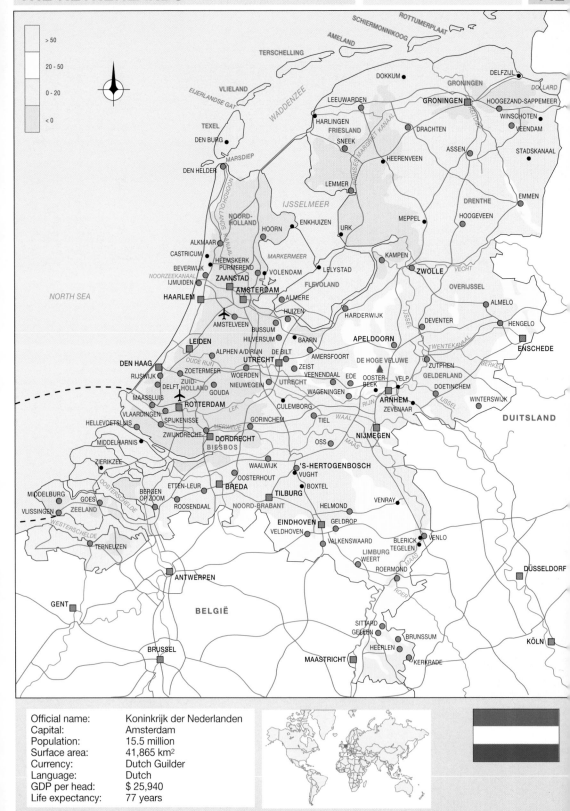

Official name:	Koninkrijk der Nederlanden
Capital:	Amsterdam
Population:	15.5 million
Surface area:	41,865 km²
Currency:	Dutch Guilder
Language:	Dutch
GDP per head:	$ 25,940
Life expectancy:	77 years

BELGIUM

SCALE 1 : 1 670 000

NORTH SEA

THE NETHERLANDS

GERMANY

FRANCE

LUXEMBOURG

Places

GELSENKIRCHEN
ESSEN
OBERHAUSEN
DUISBURG
DÜSSELDORF
KREFELD
MÖNCHENGLADBACH
NEUSS
LEVERKUSEN
KÖLN
TRIER
EINDHOVEN
AACHEN
EUPEN
VERVIERS
MAASTRICHT
MAASMECHELEN
GENK
HASSELT
TONGEREN
HERSTAL
LIÈGE
SPA
SERAING
HUY
LUXEMBOURG
ARLON
VIRTON
NEUFCHÂTEAU
BOUILLON
DINANT
PHILIPPEVILLE
NAMUR
JAMBES
ARDENNE
WAREMME
SINT-TRUIDEN
TIENEN
DIEST
GEEL
MOL
BALEN
LOMMEL
TURNHOUT
BRASSCHAAT
SCHOTEN
ANTWERPEN
MORTSEL
LIER
MECHELEN
AARSCHOT
LEUVEN
GEMBLOUX
NIVELLES
WATERLOO
BRAINE-L'ALLEUD
LA LOUVIÈRE
CHARLEROI
COURCELLES
MONS
BINCHE
BOUSSU
DOUR
SOIGNIES
ATH
TOURNAI
LILLE
ROUBAIX
MOUSCRON
KORTRIJK
IZEGEM
WAREGEM
HARELBEKE
DEINZE
TIELT
TORHOUT
ROESELARE
IEPER
POPERINGE
NIEUWPOORT
DE PANNE
OOSTENDE
BLANKENBERGE
KNOKKE-HEIST
BRUGGE
MALDEGEM
EEKLO
GENT
OUDENAARDE
NINOVE
AALST
ASSE
VILVOORDE
DENDERMONDE
BOOM
SINT-NIKLAAS
LOKEREN
BEVEREN
HALLE
BRUXELLES
SCHAERBEEK
ST-GILLES
EKEREN

Rivers

NETE
SCHELDE
DYLE
DENDER
LEIE
ESCAUT
SENNE
SAMBRE
MEUSE
OURTHE
HAUTES FAGNES

Official name: Koninkrijk België, Royaume de Belgique
Capital: Brussels, Brussel, Bruxelles
Population: 10.2 million
Surface area: 30,528 km²
Currency: Belgian Franc
Languages: Dutch, French, German
GDP per head: $ 26,440
Life expectancy: 77 years

LUXEMBOURG

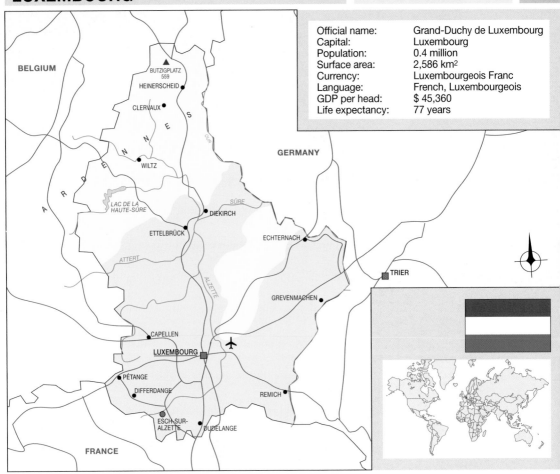

Official name:	Grand-Duchy de Luxembourg
Capital:	Luxembourg
Population:	0.4 million
Surface area:	2,586 km²
Currency:	Luxembourgeois Franc
Language:	French, Luxembourgeois
GDP per head:	$ 45,360
Life expectancy:	77 years

ANDORRA

SCALE 1 : 1 040 000

Official name:	Fürstentum Andorra
Capital:	Andorra la Vella
Population:	71,000
Surface area:	468 km²
Currency:	French Franc
Language:	Catalan, Spanish, French
GDP per head:	$ 9,635
Life expectancy:	77 years

MONACO

SCALE 1 : 98 000

Official name:	Principauté de Monaco
Capital:	Monaco-ville
Population:	32,000
Surface area:	1.9 km²
Currency:	French Franc
Language:	French
GDP per head:	$ 9,635
Life expectancy:	78 years

SCALE 1 : 6 890 000

Official name:	République Française
Capital:	Paris
Population:	56.2 million
Surface area:	551,500 km²
Currency:	French Franc
Language:	French
GDP per head:	$ 20,200
Life expectancy:	77 years

SCALE 1 : 2 860 000

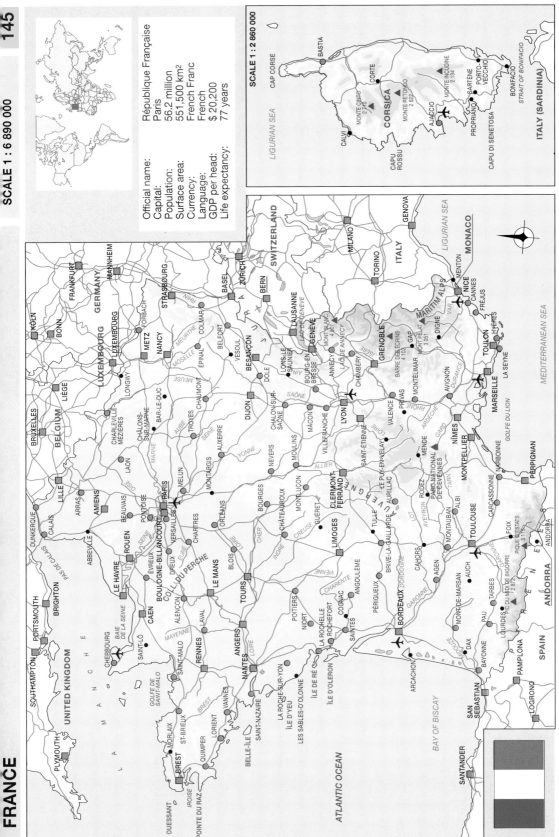

NORTH SEA
DENMARK
BALTIC SEA
KAP ARKONA
SASSNITZ
FLENSBURG
NORDFRIESISCHE INSELN
SCHLESWIG
KIELER BUCHT
DARSSER ORT
HUSUM
KIEL
RÜGEN
POMMERSCHE BUCHT
HEIDE
NEUMÜNSTER
BARTH
STRALSUND
ROSTOCK
WOLGAST
USEDOM
DEUTSCHE BUCHT
ITZEHOE
LÜBECK
WISMAR
GREIFSWALD
DEMMIN
OSTFRIESISCHE INSELN
CUXHAVEN
ELMSHORN
RATZEBURG
GÜSTROW
UECKERMÜNDE
NEUBRANDENBURG
WILLEMS-HAVEN
HAMBURG
SCHWERIN
POLAND
GRONINGEN
EMDEN
BREMERHAVEN
MECKLEN-BURGER BUCHT
WAREN
NEUSTRELITZ
LEER
BREMEN
PARCHIM
SCHWEDT
THE NETHERLANDS
OLDENBURG
DELMENHORST
SOLTAU
MÜRITZ
PRENZLAU
SZCZECIN
AMSTERDAM
EMS
HASE
NIENBURG
CELLE
WITTENBERGE
SALZWEDEL
NEURUPPIN
ANGERMÜNDE
EBERSWALDE
UTRECHT
NORDHORN
LOHNE
ALLER
RATHENOW
GORZÓW WIELKOPOLSKI
RHEINE
OSNABRÜCK
HANNOVER
WOLFSBURG
STENDAL
BERLIN
ARNHEM
HERFORD
BRAUNSCHWEIG
BRANDENBURG
POTSDAM
FÜRSTENWALDE
FRANKFURT AN DER ODER
EINDHOVEN
MÜNSTER
BIELEFELD
HAMELN
DETMOLD
MAGDEBURG
LUCKENWALDE
EISENHÜTTENSTADT
BOCHOLT
AHLEN
WILHELM-PIECK-STADT GUBEN
ZIELONA GÓRA
KLEVE
HAMM
LIPPSTADT
PADERBORN
DESSAU
WITTENBERGE
DUISBURG
ESSEN
DORTMUND
BRILLON
GÖTTINGEN
EISLEBEN
BITTERFELD
COTTBUS
FORST
MÖNCHENGLADBACH
DÜSSELDORF
KASSEL
NORDHAUSEN
HALLE
LEIPZIG
LAUCHHAMMER
HOYERSWERDA
NEUSS
WUPPERTAL
REMSCHEID
KORBACH
MERSEBURG
RIESA
SOLINGEN
LEVERKUSEN
NAUMBURG
MEISSEN
BAUTZEN
KÖLN
MARBURG
EISENACH
ERFURT
DRESDEN
GÖRLITZ
AACHEN
SIEGEN
ROTHAARGEBIRGE
BONN
GIESSEN
GLAUCHAU
FREIBERG
ZITTAU
LIÈGE
FULDA
WASSERKUPPE
ZWICKAU
CHEMNITZ
BELGIUM
KOBLENZ
WETZLAR
VOGELBERG 772
950
THÜRINGERWALD
SUHL
GREIZ
PLAUEN
AUE
FICHTELBERG 1 214
WIESBADEN
FRANKFURT
HOF
EIFEL
ASCHAFFENBURG
SCHWEINFURT
COBURG
SCHNEEBERG 1 051
PRAHA
LUXEMBOURG
BINGEN
MAINZ
BAYREUTH
WEIDEN IN DER OBERPFALZ
LUXEMBOURG
BAD KREUZNACH
WÜRZBURG
BAMBERG
PLZEN
TRIER
HUNSRÜCK
LUDWIGSHAFEN
MANNHEIM
ERLANGEN
AMBERG
CZECH REPUBLIC
METZ
HEIDELBERG
WIESLOCH
FÜRTH
NÜRNBERG
SAARBRÜCKEN
HEILBRONN
PIRMASENS
NANCY
KARLSRUHE
REGENSBURG
BADEN-BADEN
LUDWIGSBURG
STRASBOURG
STUTTGART
ESSLINGEN
INGOLSTADT
STRAUBLING
PASSAU
GÖPPINGEN
TÜBINGEN
REUTLINGEN
ULM
AUGSBURG
DACHAU
LANDSHUT
FRANCE
SIGMARINGEN
FRIESING
LINZ
FREIBURG
MEMMINGEN
KAUFBERGEN
MÜNCHEN
SCHWARZWALD
RAVENSBURG
STARNBERG
ROSENHEIM
SINGEN
KEMPTEN
CHIEMSEE
BASEL
BODENSEE
FRIEDRICHSHAFEN
FÜSSEN
BAD TÖLZ
SALZBURG
AUSTRIA
ZÜRICH
BAYERISCHE ALPEN
SWITZERLAND
ZUGSPITZE 2 963
BERN
VADUZ
INNSBRUCK
LIECHTENSTEIN

Official name:	Bundesrepublik Deutschland
Capital:	Berlin
Population:	81.9 million
Surface area:	357,021 km^2
Currency:	Deutsche Mark
Language:	German
GDP per head:	$ 28,870
Life expectancy:	76 years

SCALE 1 : 2 740 000

Official name:	Ceská Republika
Capital:	Prague
Population:	10.3 million
Surface area:	78,866 km²
Currency:	Koruna
Language:	Czech
GDP per head:	$ 4,740
Life expectancy:	74 years

GERMANY

POLAND

SLOVAKIA

AUSTRIA

HUNGARY

KRAKOW

CZESTOCHOWA

BIELSKOBIALA

KATOWICE

OPOLE

WALBRZYCH

WROCLAW

BRATISLAVA

BUDAPEST

GYOR

DRESDEN

CHEMNITZ

ZWICKAU

REGENSBURG

OSTRAVA

FRÝDEK-MÍSTEK

KRNOV

OPAVA

ŠTERNBERK

BRUNTÁL

HRUBÝ JESENÍKY

PRADĚD
1 432

PŘEROV

KROMĚŘÍŽ

OTROKOVICE

KUNOVICE

VESELÍ NAD

HODONÍN

OLOMOUC

PROSTĚJOV

VYŠKOV

BRNO

ZNOJMO

ŠUMPERK

ČESKÁ

SVITAVY

BLANSKO

MORAVA

TŘEBÍČ

MEZIŘÍČÍ

JIHLAVA

JIHLAVA

NOVÉ MĚSTO

HAVLÍČKŮV BROD

M O R A V S K Á

KRKONOŠE

SNĚŽKA
1 602

TRUTNOV

VRCHLABÍ

HRADEC KRÁLOVÉ

HRONOV

ORLICÍ

PARDUBICE

CHRUDIM

DVŮR KRÁLOVÉ

TURNOV

PODĚBRADY

ČÁSLAV

KOLÍN

KUTNA HORA

PELHŘIMOV

JINDŘICHŮV HRADEC

BRANDÝS NAD LABEM

LIBEREC

JABLONEC NAD NISOU

NOVÝ BOR

ČESKÁ LÍPA

MLADÁ BOLESLAV

MĚLNÍK

LABE

ÚSTÍ NAD LABEM

ROUDNICE

DĚČÍN

TEPLICE

MOST

LOUNY

KLADNO

ROKYCANY

BEROUN

PRAHA

VLTAVA

JAVOROVA SKÁLA
723

BENEŠOV

VLAŠIM

TÁBOR

PÍSEK

ČESKÉ BUDĚJOVICE

ČESKÝ KRUMLOV

ÚDOLNÍ NÁDRŽ
LIPNO

STRAKONICE

KLATOVY

DOMAŽLICE

STŘÍBRO

TACHOV

PLZEŇ

PRAHA
863

PŘÍBRAM

ZATEC

RAKOVNÍK

CHOMUTOV

OSTROV

KLÍNOVEC
1 244

KARLOVY VARY

SOKOLOV

CHEB

MARIÁNSKÉ

KRUŠNÉ HORY

LESNÝ
983

PLECHY
1 378

Š U M A V A

C E S K O M O R A V S K A

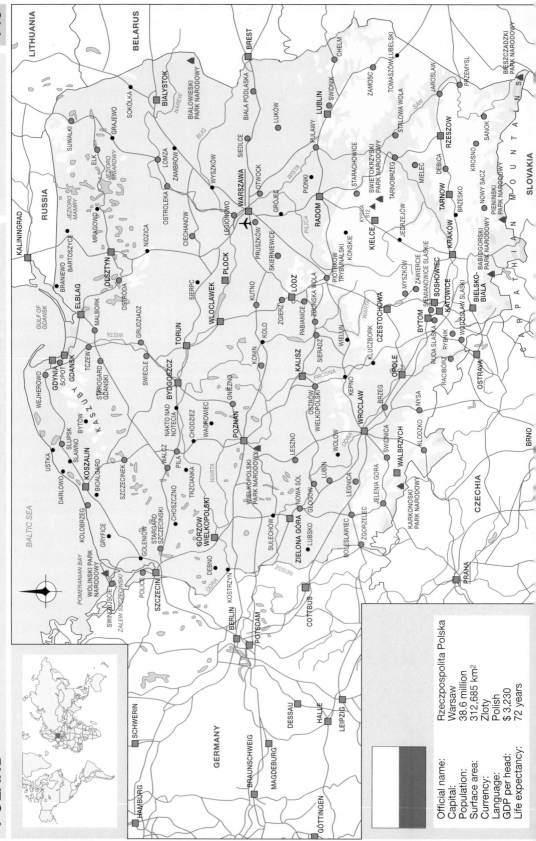

Official name:	Rzeczpospolita Polska
Capital:	Warsaw
Population:	38.6 million
Surface area:	312,685 km²
Currency:	Zloty
Language:	Polish
GDP per head:	$ 3,230
Life expectancy:	72 years

LITHUANIA

BELARUS

RUSSIA

KALININGRAD

BALTIC SEA

GULF OF GDANSK

POMERANIAN BAY

GERMANY

CZECHIA

SLOVAKIA

CARPATHIAN MOUNTAINS

BREST

BIALYSTOK
Bialowieski Park Narodowy
SOKOLKA
SUWALKI
GRAJEWO
ELK
JEZIORO SNIARDWY
JEZIORO MAMRY
MRAGOWO
NIDZICA
OLSZTYN
OSTRODA
BARTOSZYCE
BRANIEWO
ELBLAG
MALBORK
GRUDZIADZ
TCZEW
GDANSK
GDYNIA
SOPOT
WEJHEROWO
KASZUBY
BYTOW
SLUPSK
SLAWNO
USTKA
DARLOWO
KOLOBRZEG
KOSZALIN
BIALOGARD
SZCZECINEK
CHOSZCZNO
GRYFICE
GOLENIOW
STARGARD SZCZECINSKI
SZCZECIN
POLICE
SWINOUJSCIE
WOLINSKI PARK NARODOWY
ZALEW SZCZECINSKI

NAREW
BUG
WISTA

LOMZA
ZAMBROW
BIALA PODLASKA
SIEDLCE
WYSZKOW
OSTROLEKA
CIECHANOW
CHELM
LUKOW
PULAWY
LUBLIN
SWIDNIK
ZAMOSC
TOMASZOW LUBELSKI
STALOWA WOLA
SAN
JAROSLAW
PRZEMYSL
BIESZCZADZKI PARK NARODOWY
RZESZOW
SANOK
KROSNO
NOWY SACZ
PIENINSKI PARK NARODOWY
DEBICA
BRZESKO
MIELEC
TARNOW
KRAKOW
BABIOGORSKI PARK NARODOWY
JEDRZEJOW
KIELCE
SWIETOKRZYSKI PARK NARODOWY
STARACHOWICE
TARNOBRZEG
KONSKIE
RADOM
PIONKI
PILICA
GROJEC
OTWOCK
WARSZAWA
LEGIONOWO
PRUSZKOW
SKIERNIEWICE
PLOCK
SIERPC
WLOCLAWEK
TORUN
BYDGOSZCZ
NAKLO NAD NOTECIA
CHODZIEZ
WAGROWIEC
GNIEZNO
POZNAN
WIELKOPOLSKI PARK NARODOWY
LESZNO
LUBIN
GLOGOW
NOWA SOL
SULECHOW
ZIELONA GORA
LUBSKO
ZGORZELEC
BOLESLAWIEC
JELENIA GORA
KARKONOSKI PARK NARODOWY
LEGNICA
WOLOW
SWIDNICA
WALBRZYCH
KLODZKO
NYSA
OPOLE
BRZEG
WROCLAW
KEPNO
OSTROW WIELKOPOLSKI
KALISZ
PROSNA
SIERADZ
WIELUN
KLUCZBORK
CZESTOCHOWA
MYSZKOW
ZAWIERCIE
SOSNOWIEC
SIEMIANOWICE SLASKIE
KATOWICE
BYTOM
RUDA SLASKA
ZABRZE
GLIWICE
RYBNIK
RACIBORZ
WODZISLAW SLASKI
BIELSKO-BIALA
OSTRAVA
PIOTRKOW TRYBUNALSKI
ZDUNSKA WOLA
PABIANICE
ZGIERZ
LODZ
KOLO
KUTNO
KONIN
KYSZCA 612
STALOWA WOLA

WALCZ
PILA
TRZCIANKA
GORZOW WIELKOPOLSKI
DEBNO
KOSTRZYN
ODRA
NEISSE
WARTA
WARTA
NOTEC

SCHWERIN
MAGDEBURG
BRAUNSCHWEIG
HAMBURG
GOTTINGEN
DESSAU
HALLE
LEIPZIG
COTTBUS
POTSDAM
BERLIN
PRAHA
BRNO

ESTONIA

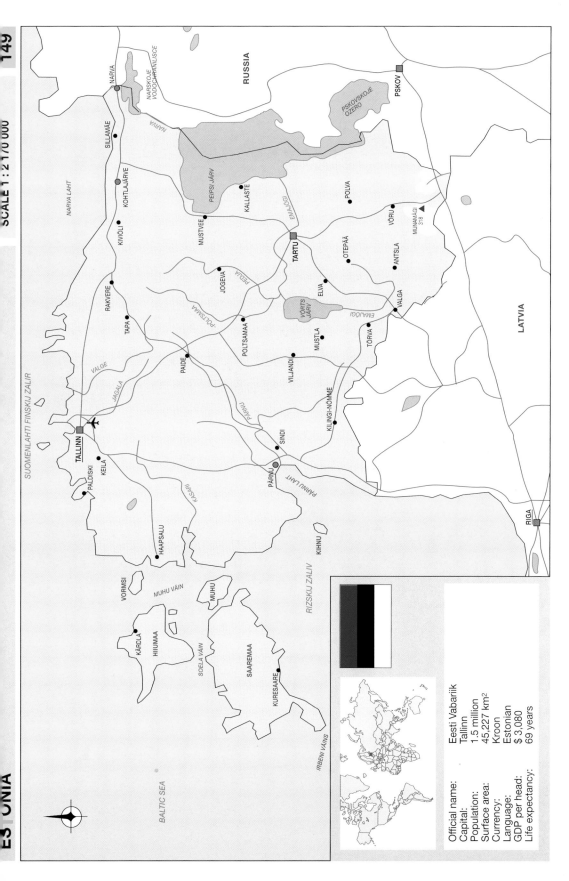

RUSSIA

PSKOV

PSKOVSKOJE OZERO

NARSKOJE VODOCHRANILISCE

NARVA

NARVA

SILLAMÄE

NARVA LAHT

KOHTLA-JÄRVE

KIVIÕLI

PEIPSI JÄRV

MUSTVEE

KALLASTE

EMAJÕGI

PÕLVA

VÕRU

MUNAMÄGI 318

SUOMENLAHTI FINSKIJ ZALIV

RAKVERE

TARTU

OTEPÄÄ

ANTSLA

PEDJA

JÕGEVA

VALGA

TAPA

PÕLTSAMAA

PÕLTSAMAA

ELVA

VÕRTS JÄRV

EMAJÕGI

MUSTLA

TÕRVA

VALGE

PAIDE

VILJANDI

LATVIA

JAGALA

PÄRNU

KILINGI-NÕMME

TALLINN

KEILA

PALDISKI

SINDI

KÄSKA

PÄRNU

PÄRNU LAHT

HAAPSALU

RIGA

VORMSI

MUHU VÄIN

MUHU

KIHNU

RIZSKIJ ZALIV

KÄRDLA

HIIUMAA

SOELA VÄIN

SAAREMAA

KURESAARE

IRBENI VÄINS

BALTIC SEA

Official name:	Eesti Vabariik
Capital:	Tallinn
Population:	1.5 million
Surface area:	45.227 km²
Currency:	Kroon
Language:	Estonian
GDP per head:	$ 3,080
Life expectancy:	69 years

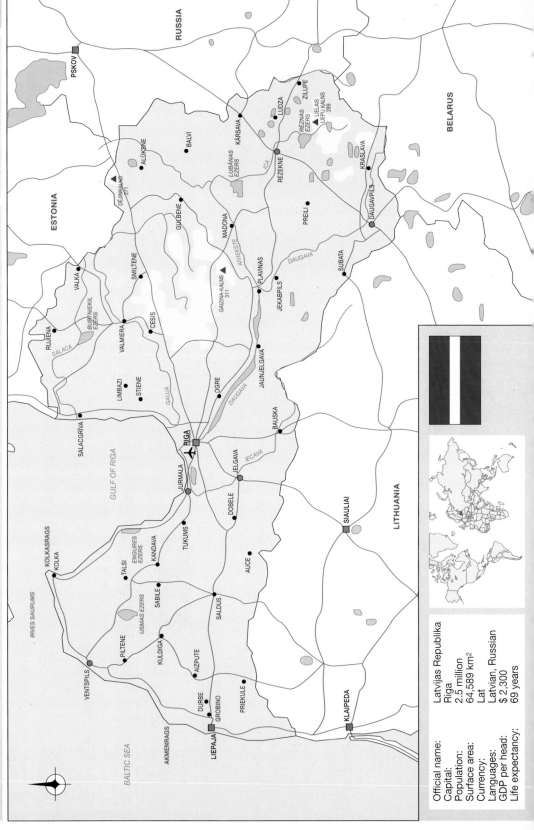

Official name:	Latvijas Republika
Capital:	Riga
Population:	2.5 million
Surface area:	64,589 km²
Currency:	Lat
Languages:	Latvian, Russian
GDP per head:	$ 2,300
Life expectancy:	69 years

LITHUANIA

SCALE 1 : 2 630 000

LATVIA

BELARUS

POLAND

RUSSIA

BALTIC SEA

OZERO DRISVYATY

DYSNU EZERAS

VILNIUS

UTENA

UKMERGE

BIRZAI

PASVALYS

PANEVEZYS

KEDAINIAI

KAUNAS

ALYTUS

DRUSKININKAI

GRODNO

MUSA

STENTOI

NERIS

NEMAN

SAKIAI

KAPSUKAS

RADVILISKIS

SIAULIAI

KURSENAI

NAUJOJI

MEDVIAGALIS ▲ 234

TELSIAI

MAZEIKIAI

PLUNGE

SALANTAI

KRETINGA

KLAIPEDA

SILUTE

TAURAGE

LIEPAJA

KURSKU ZALU

KALININGRAD

Official name:	Lietuvos Respublika
Capital:	Vilnius
Population:	3.7 million
Surface area:	65,301 km²
Currency:	Litas
Language:	Lithuanian
GDP per head:	$ 2,280
Life expectancy:	70 years

SCALE 1 : 4 220 000

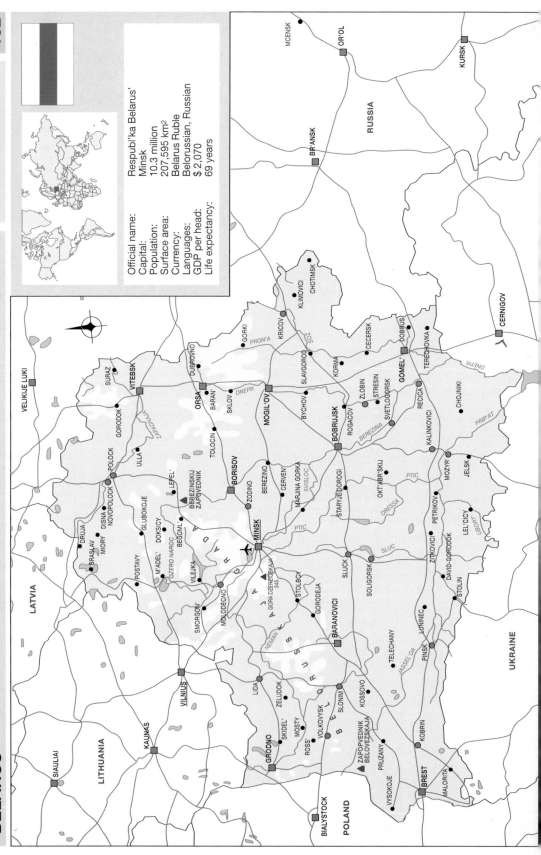

Official name:	Respubl'ka Belarus'
Capital:	Minsk
Population:	10.3 million
Surface area:	207,595 km²
Currency:	Belarus Ruble
Languages:	Belorussian, Russian
GDP per head:	$ 2,070
Life expectancy:	69 years

RUSSIA

LATVIA

LITHUANIA

POLAND

UKRAINE

MCENSK
OR'OL
KURSK
BR'ANSK
CERNIGOV

VELIKIJE LUKI
SURAZ
VITEBSK
GORODOK
POLOCK
NOVOPOLOCK
ULLA
DRUJA
BRASLAV
MIORY
DISNA
GLUBOKOJE
DOKSICY
M'ADEL'
POSTAVY
OZERO NAROC
VILEJKA
SMORGON'
MOLODECNO
VILNIUS
KAUNAS
SIAULIAI
BIALYSTOCK

DUBROVNO
ORSA
BARAN'
SKLOV
TOLOCIN
LEPEL'
BEREZINSKIJ ZAPOVEDNIK
BORISOV
ZODINO
BEREZINO
MINSK
BEGOML'
GORKI
PRON'A
KRICOV
SLAVGOROD
KORMA
SOZ
MOGIL'OV
BYCHOV
ROGACOV
BOBRUJSK
CERVEN'
MARJINA GORKA
SVISLOC
STARYJEDOROGI
BR'ARISKIJ
OKT'ABR'SKIJ
ORESSA
PTIC

CHOTIMSK
KLIMOVICI
CECERSK
DOBRUS
TERECHOVKA
GOMEL'
ZLOBIN
STRESIN
SVETLOGORSK
RECICA
CHOJNIKI
KALINKOVICI
MOZYR
JELSK
PRIP'AT
DNEPR

STRESIN
ZITKOVICI
PETRIKOV
LEL'CICY
UBORT'
DAVID-GORODOK
STOLIN

PTIC

GORA DZERZINSKAJA
345
STOLBCY
GORODEJA
BARANOVICI
SLUCK
SOLIGORSK
SLUC
LUNINEC
TELECHANY
JASSEL DA.
PINSK

LIDA
ZELUDOK
MOSTY
SKIDEL'
GRODNO
ROSS'
VOLKOVYSK
SLONIM
KOSSOVO
ZAPOPVEDNIK BELOVEZSKAJA
PRUZANY
VYSOKOJE
KOBRIN
BREST
MALORITA

NEMAN

ZAPADNAJA

BEREZINA

DNEPR

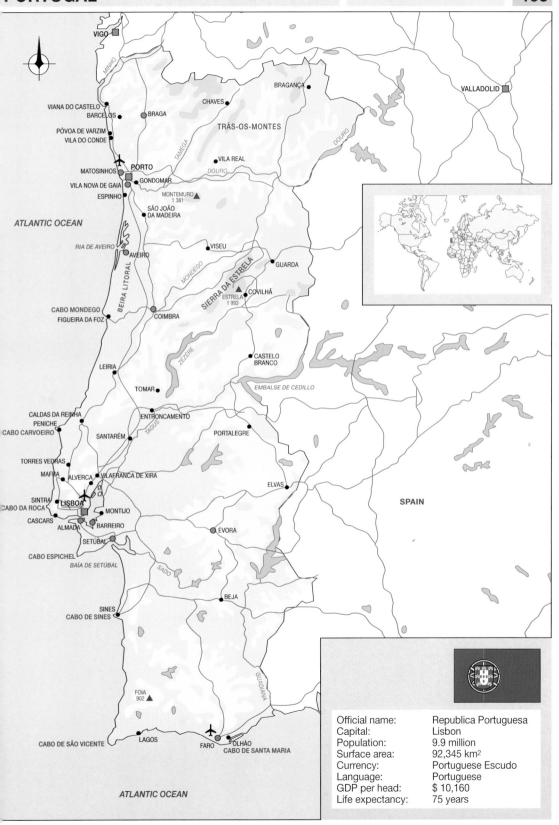

VIGO

VALLADOLID

VIANA DO CASTELO
BARCELOS
BRAGA
BRAGANÇA
CHAVES
TRÁS-OS-MONTES
PÓVOA DE VARZIM
VILA DO CONDE
MINHO
TAMEGA
DOURO
VILA REAL
MATOSINHOS
PORTO
GONDOMAR
DOURO
VILA NOVA DE GAIA
ESPINHO
MONTEMURO
1 381
SÃO JOÃO
DA MADEIRA

ATLANTIC OCEAN

RIA DE AVEIRO
AVEIRO
VISEU
GUARDA
BEIRA LITORAL
MONDEGO
SIERRA DA ESTRELA
ESTRELA
1 993
COVILHÃ
CABO MONDEGO
FIGUEIRA DA FOZ
COIMBRA
ZEZERE
CASTELO
BRANCO
EMBALSE DE CEDILLO
LEIRIA
TOMAR
CALDAS DA REINHA
ENTRONCAMENTO
PENICHE
CABO CARVOEIRO
SANTARÉM
PORTALEGRE
TAGUS
TORRES VEDRAS
MAFRA
ALVERCA
VILAFRANCA DE XIRA
ELVAS
SINTRA
LISBOA
CABO DA ROCA
SPAIN
CASCARS
MONTIJO
ALMADA
BARREIRO
ÉVORA
SETÚBAL
CABO ESPICHEL
BAÍA DE SETÚBAL
SADO
BEJA
SINES
CABO DE SINES
GUADIANA
FOIA
902
CABO DE SÃO VICENTE
LAGOS
FARO
OLHÃO
CABO DE SANTA MARIA

ATLANTIC OCEAN

Official name:	Republica Portuguesa
Capital:	Lisbon
Population:	9.9 million
Surface area:	92,345 km²
Currency:	Portuguese Escudo
Language:	Portuguese
GDP per head:	$ 10,160
Life expectancy:	75 years

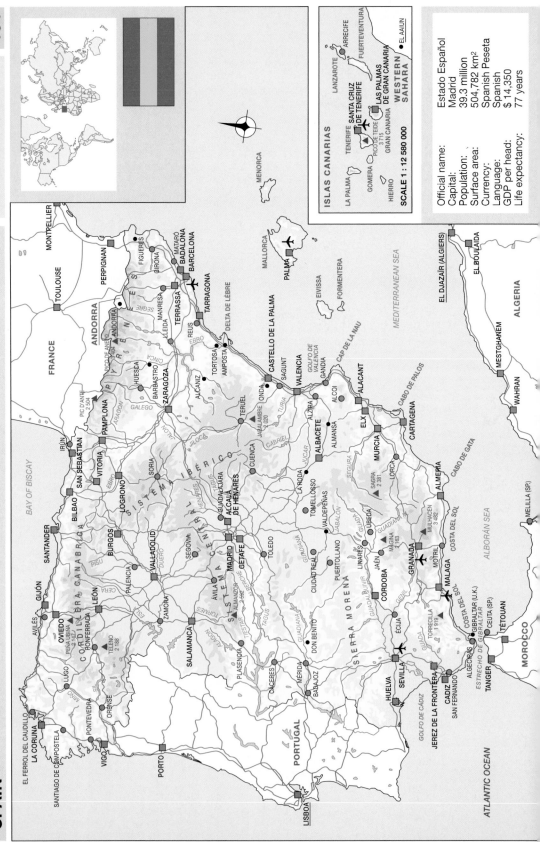

ISLAS CANARIAS

LA PALMA
GOMERA
HIERRO
TENERIFE
SANTA CRUZ DE TENERIFE
PICO DE TEIDE 3715
GRAN CANARIA
LAS PALMAS DE GRAN CANARIA
LANZAROTE
ARRECIFE
FUERTEVENTURA
WESTERN SAHARA
EL AAIUN

SCALE 1 : 12 580 000

Official name:	Estado Español
Capital:	Madrid
Population:	39.3 million
Surface area:	504,782 km²
Currency:	Spanish Peseta
Language:	Spanish
GDP per head:	$ 14,350
Life expectancy:	77 years

SWITZERLAND

Official name:	Schweizerische Eidgenossenschaft
Capital:	Bern
Population:	7.1 million
Surface area:	41,285 km²
Currency:	Swiss Franc
Languages:	German, French, Italian, Romansch
GDP per head:	$ 44,350
Life expectancy:	78 years

GERMANY

AUSTRIA

LIECHTENSTEIN

ITALY

FRANCE

ITALY

BODENSEE
KONSTANZ
SCHAFFHAUSEN
RHEIN
ARBON
RORSCHACH
SANKT GALLEN
FRAUENFELD
WIL
HERISAU
APPENZELL
WINTERTHUR
USTER
ZOLLIKON
JONA
GLARUS
VADUZ
CHUR
RHEIN
SCUOL
INN
DAVOS
SANKT MORITZ
HAEVIANS
ABULA
PIZ BERNINA
4 049

BADEN
ZURICH
ADLISWIL
BAAR
ZUG
SCHWYZ
REUSS
ZUGERSEE
GLARNER ALPS
LEPONTINE ALP

AARAU
OLTEN
WETTINGEN
EMMENBRÜCKE
LUZERN
KRIENS
SARNEN
STANS
VIERWALD-
STÄTTER SEE
ALTDORF
AIROLO
BELLINZONA
LOCARNO
LUGANO

LIESTAL
RIEHEN
BASEL
LANGENTHAL
BURGDORF
LANGNAU
EMME
STEFFISBERG
BRIENZERSEE
INTERLAKEN
WENGEN
AARE
BLINNENHORN
3 374
MONTE LEONE
3 553
RHONE
BRIG
LAGGINHORN
4 010
MONTE ROSA
DUFOURSPITZE
4 634

DELÉMONT
SOLOTHURN
GRENCHEN
BIEL
BIELERSEE
AARE
FRIBOURG
SARINE
KONIZ
BERN
THUN
SIERRE
SION
MATTERHORN
4 478
BERNER ALPEN
ALPES PENNINES

DOUBS
LA CHAUX-DE-FONDS
LE LOCLE
NEUCHÂTEL
LAC DE NEUCHÂTEL
YVERDON
MONTREUX
VEVEY
MARTIGNY
MONTHEY

BESANÇON
MORGES
LAUSANNE
LAC DE GENÈVE
NYON
GENÈVE
VERNIER

AUSTRIA / LIECHTENSTEIN

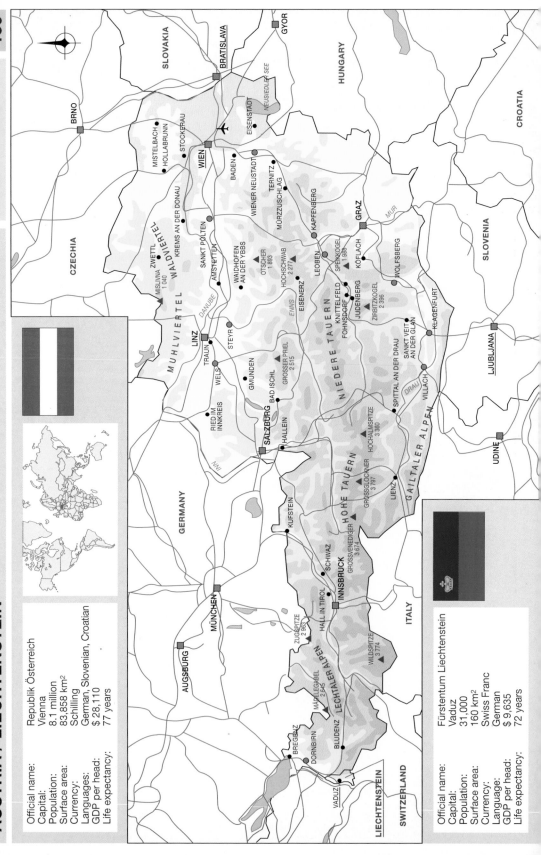

Official name:	Republik Österreich
Capital:	Vienna
Population:	8.1 million
Surface area:	83,858 km²
Currency:	Schilling
Languages:	German, Slovenian, Croatian
GDP per head:	$ 28,110
Life expectancy:	77 years

Official name:	Fürstentum Liechtenstein
Capital:	Vaduz
Population:	31,000
Surface area:	160 km²
Currency:	Swiss Franc
Language:	German
GDP per head:	$ 9,635
Life expectancy:	72 years

SLOVAKIA
BRATISLAVA
GYOR
HUNGARY
CROATIA
BRNO
CZECHIA
NEUSIEDLER SEE
MISTELBACH
HOLLABRUNN
STOCKERAU
WIEN
BADEN
EISENSTADT
WIENER NEUSTADT
TERNITZ
MÜRZZUSCHLAG
KAPFENBERG
GRAZ
MUR
SLOVENIA
ZWETTL
MISLIVNA 1 040
WALDVIERTEL
KREMS AN DER DONAU
SANKT PÖLTEN
AMSTETTEN
WAIDHOFEN AN DER YBBS
ÖTSCHER 1 893
HOCHSCHWAB 2 277
EISENERZ
LEOBEN
SPEIKKOGEL 1 988
KÖFLACH
JUDENBERG
ZIRBITZKOGEL 2 396
WOLFSBERG
KLAGENFURT
LJUBLJANA
MÜHLVIERTEL
DANUBE
LINZ
TRAUN
STEYR
ENNS
GROSSER PRIEL 2 515
KNITTELFELD
FOHNSDORF
NIEDERE TAUERN
SANKT VEIT AN DER GLAN
UDINE
WELS
GMUNDEN
BAD ISCHL
INN
RIED IM INNKREIS
SALZBURG
HALLEIN
SPITAL AN DER DRAU
DRAU
VILLACH
GAILTALER ALPEN
GERMANY
HOCHALMSPITZE 3 360
HOHE TAUERN
GROSSGLOCKNER 3 797
LIENZ
GROSSVENEDIGER 3 674
MÜNCHEN
KUFSTEIN
SCHWAZ
INNSBRUCK
HALL IN TIROL
ITALY
ZUGSPITZE 2 963
WILDSPITZE 3 774
AUGSBURG
LECHTALER ALPEN
MADLEGABEL 2 645
BREGENZ
DORNBIRN
BLUDENZ
VADUZ
LIECHTENSTEIN
SWITZERLAND

Official name: Slovenská Republika
Capital: Bratislava
Population: 5.3 million
Surface area: 49,034 km²
Currency: Koruna
Languages: Slovakian, Czech, Hungarian
GDP per head: $ 3,410
Life expectancy: 73 years

POLAND

UKRAINE

CZECHIA

AUSTRIA

HUNGARY

SLANSKÉ VRCHY

NÍZKE TATRY

SLOVENSKÉ RUDOHORIE

VYSOKÉ TATRY

ŠTIAVNICKÉ VRCHY

MALÉ KARPATY

TATRANSKÝ NARODNÍ PARK

NARODNÍ PARK NÍZKE TATRY

BRATISLAVA

KOŠICE

UZGOROD

BUDAPEST

BRNO

OLOMOUC

NYIREGYHAZA

DEBRECEN

MISKOLC

GYOR

SNINA
HUMENNÉ
VRANOV
MICHALOVCE
TREBIŠOV
NAGY-MILIC 896
BARDEJOV
PREŠOV
MINČOL 1 157
SPIŠSKÁ NOVÁ VES
LEVOCA
KEŽMAROK
POPRAD
GERLACHOVSKÝ ŠTÍT 2 655
RYSY 2 499
DOLNÝ KUBÍN
LIPTOVSKÝ MIKULÁŠ
RUŽOMBEROK
DUMBIER 2 043
BREZNO
BANSKÁ BYSTRICA
MARTIN
ZVOLEN
DETVA
JAVORIE 1 044
LUČENEC
RIMAVSKÁ SOBOTA
FIL'AKOVO
ROŽŇAVA
ČADCA
ŽILINA
POVAŽSKÁ BYSTRICA
BYTČA
PÚCHOV
DUBNICA NAD VÁHOM
PRIEVIDZA
HANDLOVÁ
PARTIZÁNSKE
ŽIAR NAD
TRENČÍN
NOVÉ MESTO NAD VÁHOM
TOPOĽČANY
NITRA
HLOHOVEC
LEVICE
NOVÁ BAŇA
ŠTÚROVO
SERED'
GALANTA
ŠAĽA
NOVÉ ZÁMKY
KOLÁROVO
KOMÁRNO
DUNAJSKÁ STREDA
MYJAVA
PIEŠŤANY
TRNAVA
SKALICA
SENICA
PEZINOK
MALACKY
VÁH
NITRA
DUNAJ

Official name:	Republica Italiana
Capital:	Rome
Population:	57.4 million
Surface area:	301,323 km²
Currency:	Italian Lira
Language:	Italian
GDP per head:	$ 19,880
Life expectancy:	78 years

SLOVENIA

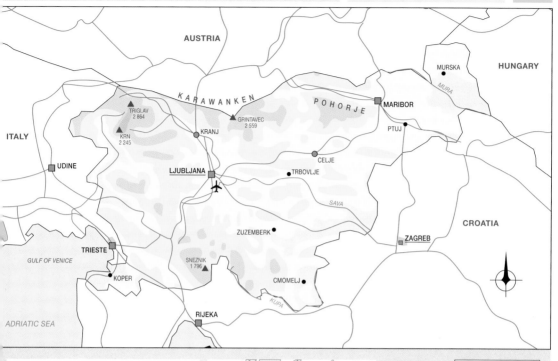

Official name:	Republika Slovenije
Capital:	Ljubljana
Population:	2.0 million
Surface area:	20,253 km²
Currency:	Tolar
Language:	Slovenian, Croatian
GDP per head:	$ 9,240
Life expectancy:	74 years

VATICAN CITY STATE

SCALE 1 : 1 690 000

Official name:	Status Civitatis Vaticane
Population:	1,034
Surface area:	0.44 km²
Currency:	Italian Lira
Languages:	Latin, Italian

SAN MARINO

SCALE 1 : 1 410 000

Official name:	Repubblica di San Marino
Capital:	San Marino
Population:	25,000
Surface area:	60.5 km²
Currency:	Italian Lira
Language:	Italian
GDP per head:	$ 12
Life expectancy:	81 years

SCALE 1 : 2 710 000

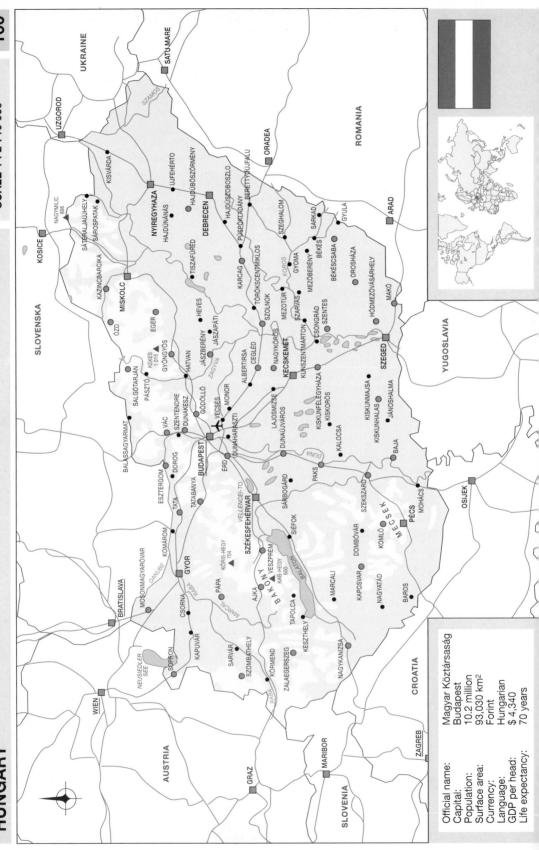

Official name:	Magyar Köztársaság
Capital:	Budapest
Population:	10.2 million
Surface area:	93,030 km²
Currency:	Forint
Language:	Hungarian
GDP per head:	$ 4,340
Life expectancy:	70 years

AUSTRIA

GRAZ

ITALY

MARIBOR

SZÉKESFEHÉRVAR

HUNGARY

UDINE

LJUBLJANA

CAKOVEC

SLOVENIA

VARAZDIN

KOPRIVNICA

PÉCS

BILO GORA

BJELOVAR

TRIESTE

ZAGREB

VIROVITICA

DRAVA

GULF OF
VENICE

RISNJAK
1 528

KUPA

KARLOVAC

SISAK

OSIJEK

DUNA

RIJEKA

ISTRA

RIJECKI
ZALIV

VELIKA KAPELA

PETRINJA

KUTINA

NOVA GRADISKA

SLAVONSKA POZEGA

DAKOVO

VINKOVCI

VUKOVAR

KRK

KVARNER

CRES

PLITVICKA JEZERA
NACIONALNI PARK

SLAVONSKI BROD

PULA

UNIJE

MALI RAJINAC
1 699

SAVA

ZUPANIA

KVARNERIC

PAG

PLJESEVICA

UNA

BANJA LUKA

PREMUDA

VAGANSKI VRH
1 758

MOLAT

PAKLENICA
NACIONALNI PARK

DUGI

ZADAR

BUKOVICA

KNIN

BOSNIA-HERCEGOVINA

SARAJEVO

KORNAT

SIBENIK

DINARA

ZIRJE

SPLIT

BRACKI KANAL

M

SOLTA

BRAC

HVARSKI KANAL

A

ADRIATIC SEA

HVAR

VIS

KORCULANKSI KANAL

PLOCE

YUGOSLAVIA

KORCULA

LASTOVSKI KANAL

PELJESAC

LASTOVO

MILJET
NACIONALNI PARK

PESCARA

MLJET

DUBROVNIK

ITALY

ALBANIA

Official name:	Republika Hrvatska
Capital:	Zagreb
Population:	4.8 million
Surface area:	56,610 km²
Currency:	Kuna
Language:	Serbo-Croat
GDP per head:	$ 3,800
Life expectancy:	72 years

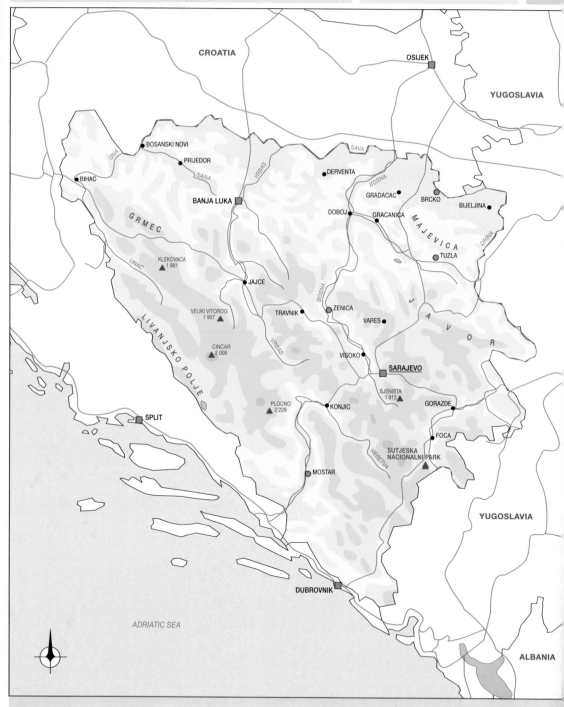

CROATIA

OSIJEK

YUGOSLAVIA

BOSANSKI NOVI

PRIJEDOR

BIHAC

DERVENTA

SAVA

BOSNA

GRADACAC

BRCKO

BIJELJINA

BANJA LUKA

DOBOJ

GRACANICA

M A J E V I C A

DRINA

G R M E C

UNA

SANA

VRBAS

KLEKOVACA
▲ 1 961

UNAC

TUZLA

VELIKI VITOROG
1 907 ▲

JAJCE

TRAVNIK

ZENICA

VARES

J A V O R

BOSNA

CINCAR
▲ 2 006

L I V A N J S K O   P O L J E

VRBAS

VISOKO

PLOCNO
▲ 2 228

KONJIC

SARAJEVO

SJENISTA
1 913 ▲

GORAZDE

SPLIT

FOCA

NERETVA

SUTJESKA
NACIONALNI PARK
▲

MOSTAR

YUGOSLAVIA

DUBROVNIK

ADRIATIC SEA

ALBANIA

Official name: Republika Bosna i Hercegovina
Capital: Sarajevo
Population: 0.4 million
Surface area: 51,129 km²
Currency: B.H. Dinar
Languages: Bosnian, Croatian, Serbo-Croat
GDP per head: $ <785
Life expectancy: 73 years

Official name:	Savezna Republika Jugoslawien
Capital:	Belgrade
Population:	10.6 million
Surface area:	102,173 km²
Currency:	New Yugoslavian Dinar
Languages:	Serbo-Croat, Croatian, Macedonian
GDP per head:	$ 3,115
Life expectancy:	72 years

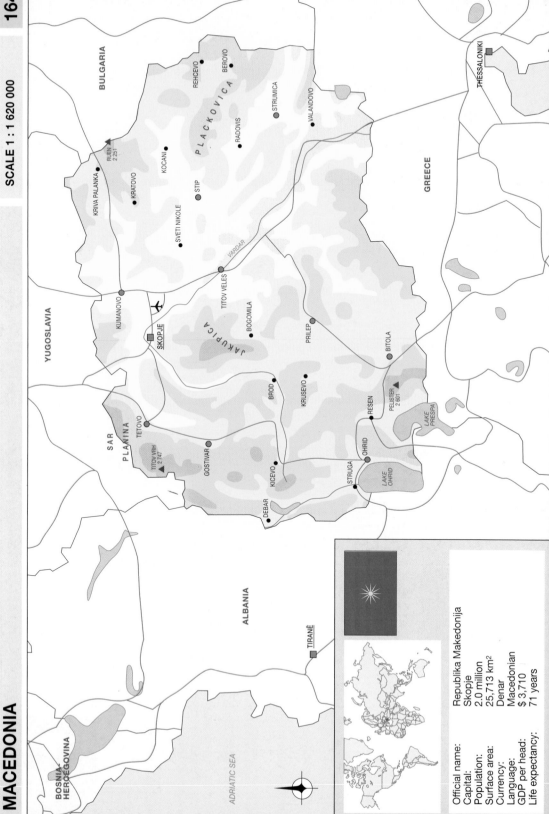

BOSNIA-HERCEGOVINA

YUGOSLAVIA

BULGARIA

KRIVA PALANKA
KRATOVO
RUEN 2 251
KOCANI
REHCEVO
BEROVO
SVETI NIKOLE
STIP
PLACKOVICA
RADOVIS
STRUMICA
VALANDOVO

KUMANOVO
SKOPJE
TITOV VELES
VARDAR
BOGOMILA
PRILEP
BITOLA
GREECE
THESSALONIKI

JAKUPICA

SAR PLANINA
TETOVO
TITOV VRH 2 747
GOSTIVAR
BROD
KRUSEVO
RESEN
PELISTER 2 601
LAKE PRESPA

KICEVO
DEBAR
STRUGA
OHRID
LAKE OHRID

ALBANIA
TIRANË

ADRIATIC SEA

Official name:	Republika Makedonija
Capital:	Skopje
Population:	2.0 million
Surface area:	25,713 km²
Currency:	Denar
Language:	Macedonian
GDP per head:	$ 3,710
Life expectancy:	71 years

YUGOSLAVIA

PRISTINA

JEZERCE
2 693 ▲

BJESHKËT E NEMUNA

TROPOJË

DRIN

LAKE
SCUTARI

KOPLIK

LIQ I FIERZËS

SHKODËR

PUKË

KUKËS

SKOPJE

LEZHË

RRËSHEN

GJIRI I DRINIT

ULZË

PESHKOPI

KEP I RODONIT

LAÇ

BURREL

ADRIATIC SEA

KRUJË

ZERQAN

BISHTI I PALLËS

MACEDONIA

DURRËS

TIRANË

KAVAJË

LIBRAZHD

RROGOZHINË

SHKUMBIN

ELBASAN

PËQIN

CËRRIK

PRENJAS

LAKE
OHRID

LUSHNJE

SEMAN

GRAMSH

DEVOLL

LAKE PRESPA

POGRADEC

FIER

STALIN

BERAT

BALLSH

KORÇË

SELENICË

SAZANIT

VLORË

COROVODË

KEP I GJUHËZËS

GJI I VLORËS

VIJOSE

ERSEKË

STRAIT OF OTRANTO

TEPELENË

PERMET

ITALY

HIMARË

GJIROKASTËR

DELVINË

SARANDE

GREECE

IONIAN SEA

KONISPOL

Official name:	Republika e Shqipërisë
Capital:	Tirana
Population:	3.3 million
Surface area:	28,748 km^2
Currency:	Lek
Language:	Albanian, Greek
GDP per head:	$ 820
Life expectancy:	72 years

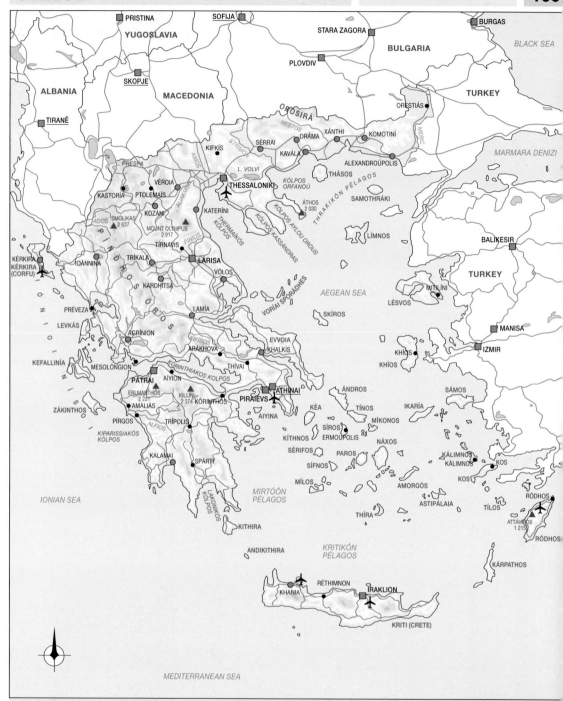

Official name:	Ellinikí Dimokratía
Capital:	Athens
Population:	10.6 million
Surface area:	131,957 km²
Currency:	Drachma
Language:	Greek
GDP per head:	$ 11,460
Life expectancy:	78 years

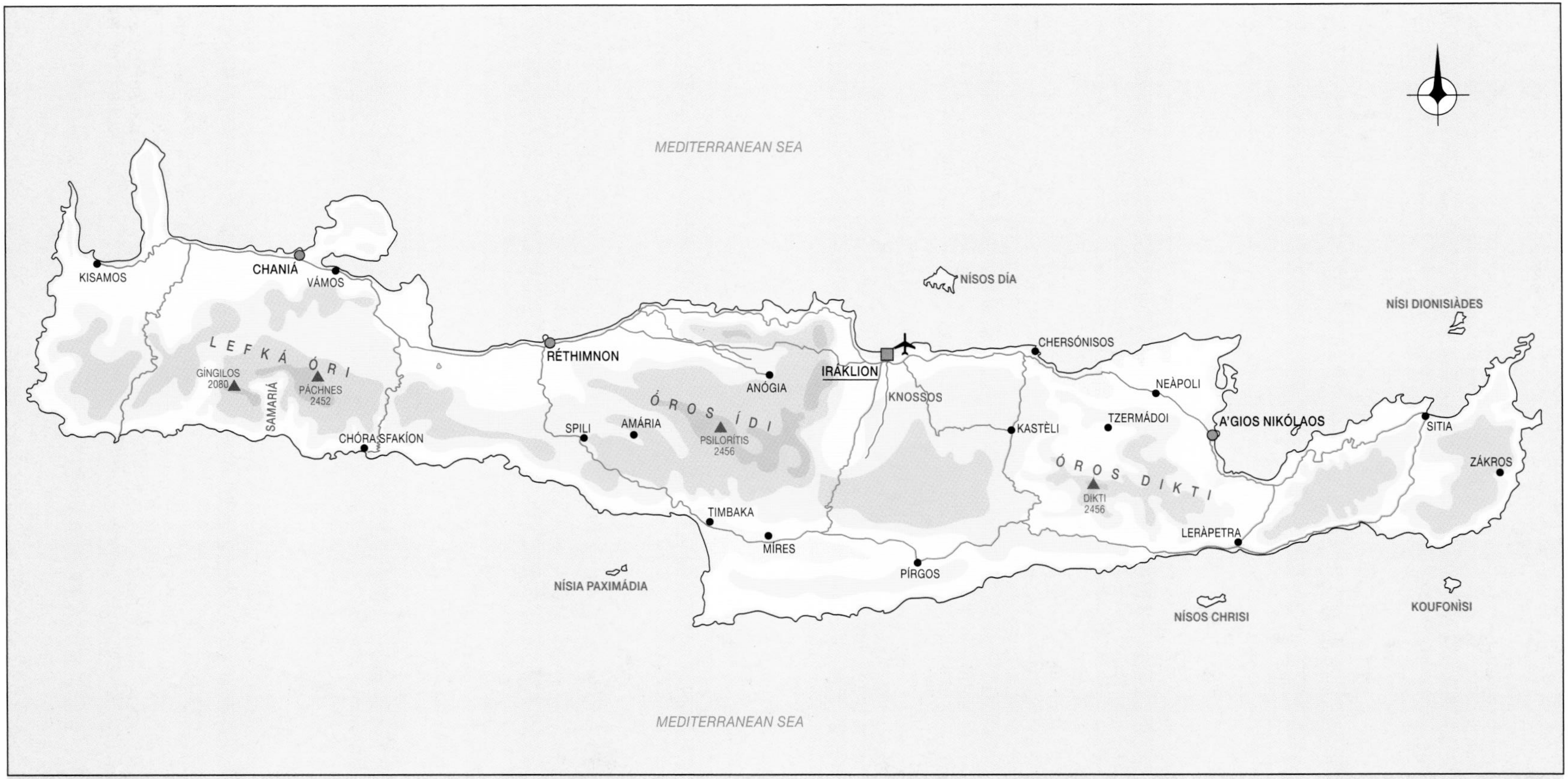

CRETE

MEDITERRANEAN SEA

MEDITERRANEAN SEA

NISI DIONISIÁDES

ZÁKROS

SITÍA

KOUFONÍSI

A'GIOS NIKÓLAOS

NEÁPOLI

LERÁPETRA

NISOS CHRISÍ

TZERMÁDOI

CHERSÓNISOS

KASTÉLI

ÓROS DÍKTI

DÍKTI
2456

NÍSOS DÍA

KNOSSÓS

IRÁKLION

PÍRGOS

ANÓGIA

ÓROS ÍDI

PSILORÍTIS
2456

MÍRES

AMÁRIA

TÍMBAKA

RÉTHIMNON

SPÍLI

NÍSIA PAXIMÁDIA

CHÓRASFAKÍON

VÁMOS

LEFKÁ ÓRI

PÁCHNES
2452

SAMARIÁ

CHANIÁ

GÍNGILOS
2080

KÍSAMOS

Official name:	Kríti
Capital:	Iráklion
Population:	0.5million
Surface area:	8,261 km²
Currency:	Drachma
Language:	Greek
GDP per head:	$ 11,460
Life expectancy:	78 years

MALTA

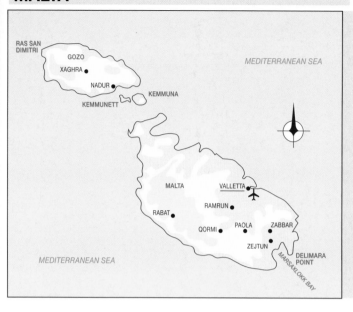

Official name:	Repubblika ta' Malta
Capital:	Valletta
Population:	0.4 million
Surface area:	316 km²
Currency:	Maltese Lira
Languages:	Maltese, English
GDP per head:	$ 9,635
Life expectancy:	77 years

CYPRUS

SCALE 1 : 1 600 000

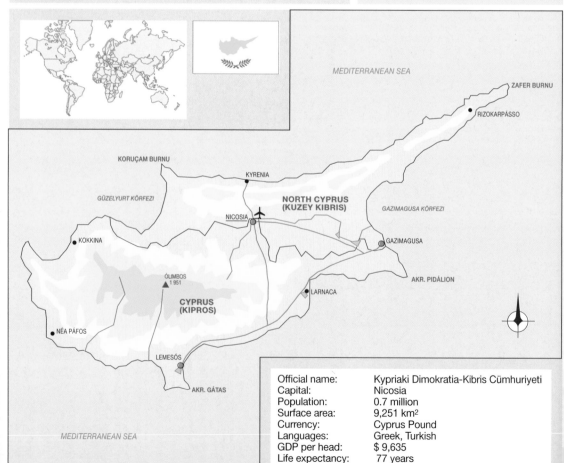

Official name:	Kypriaki Dimokratia-Kibris Cümhuriyeti
Capital:	Nicosia
Population:	0.7 million
Surface area:	9,251 km²
Currency:	Cyprus Pound
Languages:	Greek, Turkish
GDP per head:	$ 9,635
Life expectancy:	77 years

UKRAINE

SCALE 1 : 6 930 000

RUSSIA

RUSSIA

VORONEZ
STARYJ OSKOL
KURSK
KRASNODAR
NOVOROSSIJSK
ROSTOV-NA-DONU
TAGANROG
KERC'
FEDDOSIJA
ALUSTA
JALTA
SEVASTOPOL'
SIMFEROPOL'
KRIMSKIJE GORY
SAKI
BACHCISARAJ
JEVPATORIJA
KALAMITSKIJ ZALIV
DZANKOJ
KARKINITSKIJ ZALIV
GENICESK
SKADOVSK
ASKANIJA-NOVA ZAPOVEDNIK
NOVAJA KACHOVKA
KACHOVKA
BERISLAV
CHERSON
KACHOVSKOJE VODOCHRANILISCE
KAMENNYE MOGILY
CHOMUTOVSKAJA STEP'
ZAPOVEDNIK
ZDANOV
BERD'ANSK
AZOVSKOJE MORE
BLACK SEA

MELITOPOL'
TOKMAK
MARGANEC
NIKOPOL'
ZAPOVEDNIK
VOLNOVACHA
DOKUCAJEVSK
MAKEJEVKA
DONECK
DBAL'CEVO
GORLOVKA
SLAV'ANSK
KRAMATORSK
LISICANSK
SEVERODONECK
STACHANOV
KRASNYJ LUC
VOROSILOVGRAD

KUP'ANSK
IZ'UM
BALAKLEJA
CUGUJEV
CHAR'KOV
DERGACI
BELGOROD
L'UBOTIN
MEREFA
DONEC
ACHTYRKA
TROSTANEC
SUMY
SOSTKA
KONOTOP
NEZIN
CERNIGOV
GOMEL'
DESNA
SEJM
ZAPOVEDNIK MICHAJLOVSKAJA CELINA
LEBEDIN
PRILUKI
ROMNY
SULA
MIRGOROD
PSOL
POLTAVA
VORSKLA
OR'OL
DNEPR
DNEPROPETROVSK
ORDZONIKIDZE
KRIVOJ ROG
DNEPRODZERZINSK
ZAPOROZJE
KACHOVSKOJE

SLUC'
KREMENCUG
KREMENCUGSKOJE VODOCHRANILISCE
SVETLOVODSK
ALEKSANDRIJA
ZNAMENKA
KIROVOGRAD
PERVOMAJSK
VOZNESENSK
JUZNYJ BUG
INGUL
INGULEC
NIKOLAJEV
ZOVTNEVOJE
ODESSA
BELGOROD-DNESTROVSKIJ

KIEV
KIJEVSKOJE VODOCHRANILISCE
IRPEN
BROVARY
DNEPR
ROS
KAN'OV
PEREJASLAV-CHMEL'NICKIJ
ZOLOTONOSA
CERKASSY
LUBNY
SVETLOVODSK
BOJARKA
VASIL'KOV
FASTOV
BELAJA CERKOV
UMAN'
GAJSIN
ZMERINKA
VINNICA
KOTOVSK
MOGL'OV-PODOL'SKIJ
BEL'C
KISIN'OV
MOLDAVIA
DNESTR
TIRASPOL'
BENDERY
RENI
IZMAIL
KILIJA
GALAC
BRAILA
IASI
ROMANIA

KOROSTEN'
TEREBY
UZ
ZITOMIR
NOVOGRAD-VOLYNSKIJ
SEPETOVKA
STAROKONSTANTINOV
CHMEL'NICKIJ
KAMENEC-PODOL'SKIJ
ZBRUC'
CORTKOV
PRUT
CERNOWCY
CARPATHIAN MOUNTAINS
MUKACEVO
CHUST
BEREGOVO
UZGOROD
HUNGARY
DEBRECEN
MISKOLC
KOSICE
SLOVAKIA

ROVNO
DUBNO
KREMENEC
GORYN
STYR
TERNOPOL
IVANO-FRANKOVSK
KALOMYJA
STRYJ
TRUSKAVEC
L'VOV
DRGOBYC
BORISLAV
SAMBOR
DNIESTR

LUCK
VLADIMIR-VOLYNSKIJ
TURJA
BUG
KOVEL'
NOVOVOLYNSK
CERVONOGRAD
LUBLIN
RADOM
POLAND
BREST
GOMEL'
PRIPAT
STIR
SLUC'
SARNY

Official name:	Ukraïna
Capital:	Kiev
Population:	50.7 million
Surface area:	603,700 km^2
Currency:	Hryvnia
Languages:	Ukrainian, Russian,
GDP per head:	$ 1,200
Life expectancy:	67 years

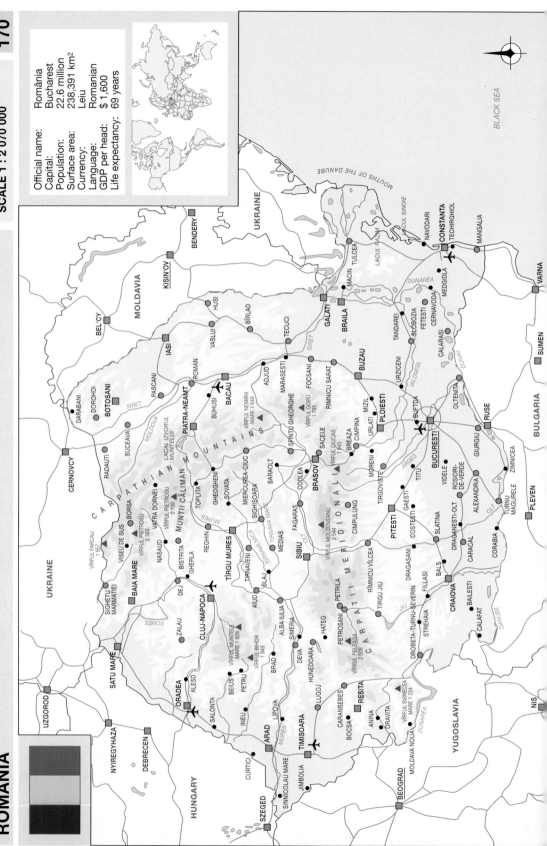

Official name:	România
Capital:	Bucharest
Population:	22.6 million
Surface area:	238,391 km²
Currency:	Leiu
Language:	Romanian
GDP per head:	$ 1,600
Life expectancy:	69 years

BLACK SEA

MOUTHS OF THE DANUBE

UKRAINE

MOLDAVIA

BULGARIA

HUNGARY

YUGOSLAVIA

CARPATHIAN MOUNTAINS

CARPATII MERIDIONALI

MUNTII CALIMAN

BUCURESTI

CONSTANTA

VARNA

RUSE

BEOGRAD

TIMISOARA

ARAD

ORADEA

CLUJ-NAPOCA

SATU MARE

BAIA MARE

IASI

BOTOSANI

SUCEAVA

BRAILA

GALATI

TULCEA

BUZAU

PLOIESTI

BRASOV

SIBIU

TIRGU MURES

PIATRA-NEAMT

BACAU

CRAIOVA

PITESTI

RESITA

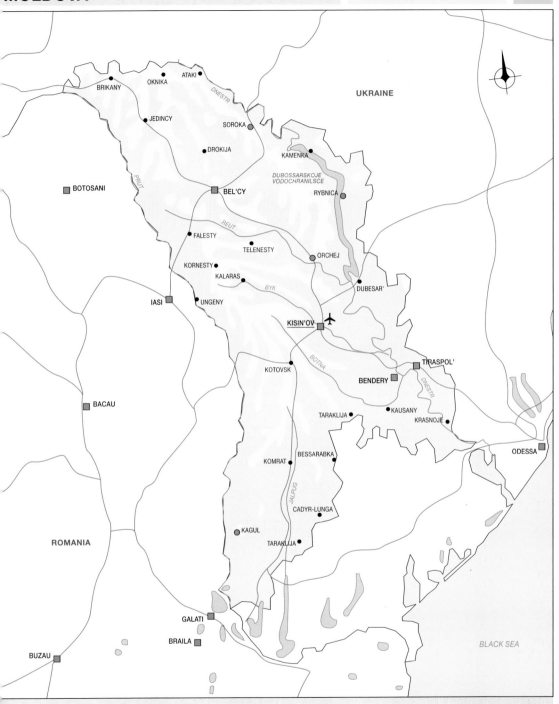

UKRAINE

BRIKANY
OKNIKA
ATAKI
JEDINCY
SOROKA
DROKIJA
KAMENKA
DNESTR
DUBOSSARSKOJE VODOCHRANILSCE
BOTOSANI
BEL'CY
RYBNICA
PRUT
REUT
FALESTY
TELENESTY
ORCHEJ
KORNESTY
KALARAS
BYK
DUBESAR'
IASI
UNGENY
KISIN'OV
KOTOVSK
BOTNA
TIRASPOL'
BENDERY
DNESTR
BACAU
TARAKLIJA
KAUSANY
KRASNOJE
ODESSA
KOMRAT
BESSARABKA
JALPUG
CADYR-LUNGA
ROMANIA
KAGUL
TARAKLIJA
BLACK SEA
GALATI
BRAILA
BUZAU

Official name:	Republica Moldova
Capital:	Chisinâu
Population:	4.3 million
Surface area:	33,700 km^2
Currency:	Leu
Language:	Moldavian
GDP per head:	$ 590
Life expectancy:	67 years

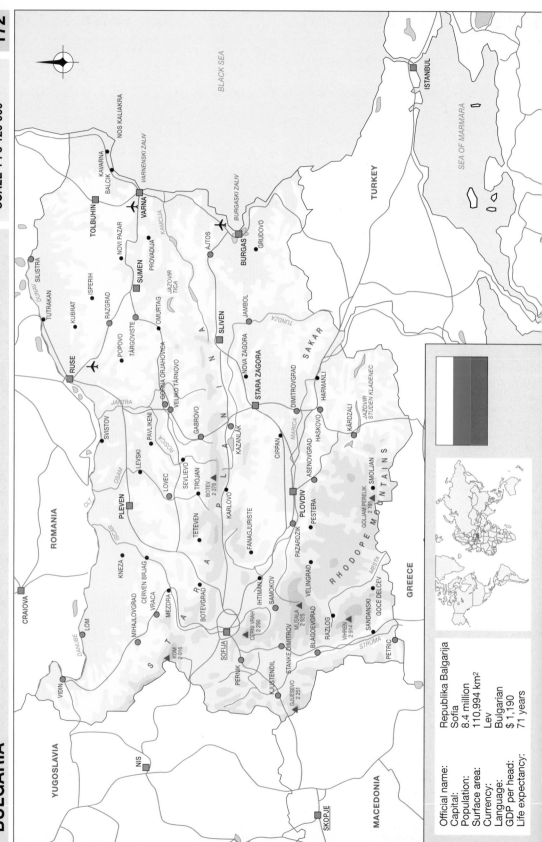

YUGOSLAVIA

MACEDONIA

ROMANIA

TURKEY

GREECE

BLACK SEA

SEA OF MARMARA

NIS

SKOPJE

CRAIOVA

ISTANBUL

VIDIN

LOM

DANUBE

KNEZA

MIHAJLOVGRAD

CERVEN BRJAG

VRACA

MEZDRA

BOTEVGRAD

PERNIK

KJUSTENDIL

GJUESEVO
2 251

STANKE DIMITROV

SOFIJA

CERNI VRAH
2 290

KOM
2 016

SAMOKOV

IHTIMAN

MUSALA
2 925

BLAGOEVGRAD

RAZLOG

VIHREN
2 914

SANDANSKI

GOCE DELCEV

PETRIC

STRUMA

MESTA

VELINGRAD

PAZARDZIK

PESTERA

GOLJAM PERELIK
2 191

SMOLJAN

RHODOPE MOUNTAINS

JAZOVIR
STUDEN KLADENEC

KĂRDŽALI

HASKOVO

ASENOVGRAD

PLOVDIV

KARLOVO

KAZANLĂK

CIRPAN

DIMITROVGRAD

HARMANLI

MARICA

SAKAR

STARA ZAGORA

NOVA ZAGORA

SLIVEN

JAMBOL

TUNDZA

FANAGJURISTE

BOTEV
2 376

TROJAN

TETEVEN

LOVEC

SEVLIEVO

LEVSKI

PAVLIKENI

GABROVO

GORNA ORJAHOVICA

VELIKO TĂRNOVO

JANTRA

ROSICA

OSAM

ISCAR

OLT

PLEVEN

SVISTOV

POPOVO

TĂRGOVISTE

OMURTAG

RAZGRAD

ISPERIH

KUBRAT

TUTRAKAN

SILISTRA

DUNAV

RUSE

SUMEN

NOVI PAZAR

PROVADIJA

JAZOVIR
TICA

TOLBUHIN

BALCIK

KAVARNA

NOS KALIAKRA

VARNA

VARNENSKI ZALIV

KAMCIJA

AJTOS

BURGAS

BURGASKI ZALIV

GRUDOVO

S T A R A   P L A N I N A

STRUMA

Official name:	Republika Balgarija
Capital:	Sofia
Population:	8.4 million
Surface area:	110,994 km²
Currency:	Lev
Language:	Bulgarian
GDP per head:	$ 1,190
Life expectancy:	71 years

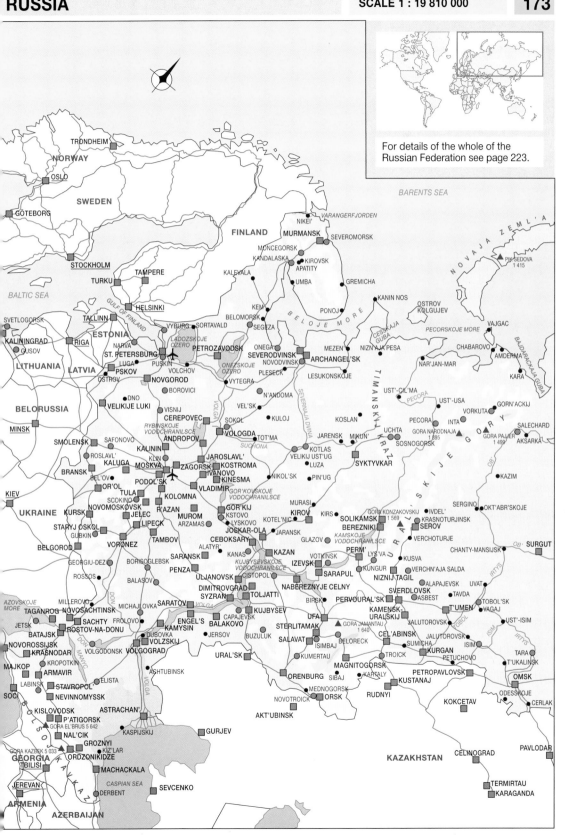

For details of the whole of the
Russian Federation see page 223.

BARENTS SEA

NORWAY
TRONDHEIM
OSLO
SWEDEN
GÖTEBORG
STOCKHOLM
TAMPERE
TURKU
HELSINKI
FINLAND

NOVAJA ZEML'A

PIK SEDOVA 1 415

NIKEL'   VARANGERFJORDEN
MURMANSK
MONCEGORSK   SEVEROMORSK
KANDALAKSA   KIROVSK
APATITY
KALEVALA   UMBA   GREMICHA
KANIN NOS
KEM   PONOJ
KOLGUJEV
BELOMORSK   SEGEZA
OSTROV
KOLGUJEV
VAJGAC

BALTIC SEA
SVETLOGORSK
TALLINN
KALININGRAD   RIGA
GUSOV
LITHUANIA   LATVIA
PSKOV
OSTROV

VYBURG   SORTAVALD
LADOZSKOJE OZERO
ST. PETERSBURG   PUSKIN
LUGA   VOLCHOV
NOVGOROD
BOROVICI
DNO
VELIKIJE LUKI
VISNIJ

PETROZAVODSK
ONEZSKOJE OZERO
ONEGA
SEVERODVINSK
NOVODVINSK
PLESECK
VYTEGRA
N'ANDOMA
VEL'SK
SOKOL

ARCHANGEL'SK
LESUKONSKOJE
MEZEN   NIZN'AJA PESA
KOSLAN

CESSKAJA GUBA
PECORSKOJE MORE
NAR'JAN-MAR
CHABAROVO
AMDERMA
KARA

BALDARACKAJA GUBA

BELORUSSIA
MINSK
SMOLENSK   SAFONOVO
ROSLAVL'
BRANSK
BEL'OV
KALUGA

CEREPOVEC
RYBINSKOJE VODOCHRANILSCE
ANDROPOV
VOLOGDA
TOT'MA
KULOJ
JARENSK   MIKUN'
UST'-CIL'MA
UST'-USA
PECORA   UST'-USA
PECORA   INTA
SOSNOGORSK
UCHTA
GORN'ACKIJ
VORKUTA
SALECHARD
GORA NARODNAJA 1 895
GORA PAJJER 1 499
AKSARKA

KALININ
JAROSLAVL'
MOSKVA
ZAGORSK   KOSTROMA
IVANOVO
KINESMA
VLADIMIR
GOR'KOVSKOJE VODOCHRANILSCE

KLIN
KOTLAS
VELIKIJ UST'UG
LUZA
NIKOL'SK
PIN'UG
SYKTYVKAR

KIEV
UKRAINE
KURSK
STARYJ OSKOL
GUBKIN
BELGOROD

OR'OL
TULA
PODOL'SK
NOVOMOSKOVSK
SCOKINO
KOLOMNA
JELEC
R'AZAN
LIPECK
TAMBOV
MUROM
ARZAMAS
GOR'KIJ
KSTOVO
LYSKOVO
KOTEL'NIC
JARANSK
GLAZOV

JOSKAR-OLA
KIRS
MURASI
KIROV
SOLIKAMSK
BEREZNIKI
GORA KONZAKOVSKIJ 1 569
IVDEL'
KRASNOTURJINSK
SEROV
VERCHOTURJE
OKT'ABR'SKOJE
SERGINO

VORONEZ
SARANSK
CEBOKSARY
ALATYR'
KANAS
KAZAN
VOTKINSK
IZEVSK
PERM'
LYS'VA
KUSVA
VERCHN'AJA SALDA
NIZNIJ TAGIL
ALAPAJEVSK
UVAT
CHANTY-MANSIJSK
SURGUT
OB'

BORISOGLEBSK
PENZA
KUJBYSEVSKOJE VODOCHRANILSCE
KAMSKOJE VODOCHRANILSCE

SARAPUL
KUNGUR
SVERDLOVSK
ASBEST
TAVDA
TOBOL'SK
VAGAJ
UST'-ISIM

BALASOV
ULJANOVSK
DIMITROVGRAD
SYZRAN
TOLJATTI
BIRSK
PERVOURAL'SK
KAMENSK-URALSKIJ
JALUTOROVSK
T'UMEN

AZOVSKOJE MORE
MILLEROVO
TAGANROG   NOVOSACHTINSK
SACHTY
JETSK   FROLOVO
BATAJSK
ROSTOV-NA-DONU
NOVOROSSIJSK
KRASNODAR
VOLGODONSK

MICHAJLOVKA   SARATOV
ENGEL'S
BALAKOVO
KAPEJEVSK
KUJBYSEV
STERLITAMAK
SALAVAT
UFA
GORA JAMANTAU 1 640
BELORECK
ISIMBAJ
KUMERTAU
MAGNITOGORSK
ORENBURG   SIBAJ
CEL'ABINSK
SUMICHA
KURGAN
PETROPAVLOVSK
KUSTANAJ
JALUTOROVSK
ISIM
TROICK
PETUCHOVO
ODESSKOJE
TARA
T'UKALINSK
OMSK
CERLAK

DUBOVKA
KAMYSIN
JERSOV
BUZULUK
VOLGOGRAD

MAJKOP
KROPOTKIN
ARMAVIR
LABINSK
STAVROPOL'
NEVINNOMYSSK
ELISTA
ASTUBINSK
UNAL'SK

SOCI
KISLOVODSK
P'ATIGORSK
GORA EL'BRUS 5 642
NAL'CIK
ASTRACHAN'
GROZNYI
KIZ'LAR
KASPIJSKIJ
GURJEV

GORA KAZBEK 5 033
ORDZONIKIDZE
GEORGIA
TBILISI
MACHACKALA
JEREVAN
ARMENIA   AZERBAIJAN
CASPIAN SEA
DERBENT
SEVCENKO

KAZAKHSTAN
CELINOGRAD
PAVLODAR
TERMIRTAU
KARAGANDA

DON
VOLGA
SUCHONA
SEVERNAJA DVINA
TIMANSKIJ KRIAZ
PECORA
URAL'SKIJE GORY
OB'
IRTYS
TOBOL
ISIM
IRTYS

BELOJE MORE
MEDNOGORSK
NOVOTROICK
ORSK
RUDNYI
KOKCETAV
AKT'UBINSK

GULF OF FINLAND
NARVA
ESTONIA

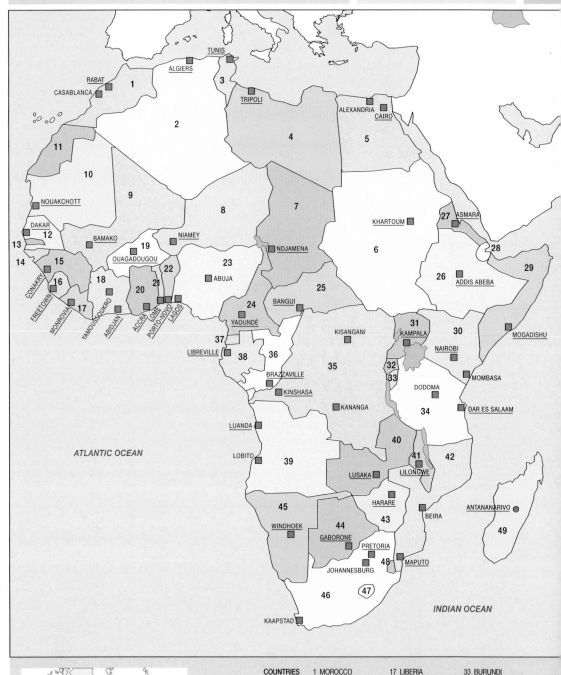

TUNIS

ALGIERS

RABAT

CASABLANCA

1

3

TRIPOLI

ALEXANDRIA

CAIRO

2

4

5

11

10

9

8

7

KHARTOUM

27 ASMARA

NOUAKCHOTT

DAKAR

12

BAMAKO

NIAMEY

28

13

19

NDJAMENA

6

26

29

14

15

OUAGADOUGOU

23

25

ADDIS ABEBA

CONAKRY

16

18

22

ABUJA

FREETOWN

20 21

24

BANGUI

MONROVIA

17

YAMOUSSOUKRO

ABIDJAN

ACCRA

LOME

PORTO-NOVO

LAGOS

YAOUNDÉ

KISANGANI

31

KAMPALA

30

LIBREVILLE

37

38

36

35

NAIROBI

MOGADISHU

BRAZZAVILLE

32

33

DODOMA

MOMBASA

KINSHASA

KANANGA

34

DAR ES SALAAM

LUANDA

40

LOBITO

ATLANTIC OCEAN

39

41

42

LILONGWE

LUSAKA

HARARE

45

44

43

ANTANANARIVO

WINDHOEK

GABORONE

PRETORIA

BEIRA

49

48

MAPUTO

JOHANNESBURG

46

47

KAAPSTAD

INDIAN OCEAN

COUNTRIES		
1 MOROCCO	17 LIBERIA	33 BURUNDI
2 ALGERIA	18 IVORY COAST	34 TANZANIA
3 TUNISIA	19 BURKINA FASO	35 ZAIRE
4 LIBYA	20 GHANA	36 CONGO
5 EGYPT	21 TOGO	37 EQUAT, GUINEA
6 SUDAN	22 BENIN	38 GABON
7 CHAD	23 NIGERIA	39 ANGOLA
8 NIGER	24 CAMEROON	40 ZAMBIA
9 MALI	25 CENTR. AFR. REP.	41 MALAWI
10 MAURITANIA	26 ETHIOPIA	42 MOZAMBIQUE
11 WEST, SAHARA	27 ERITREA	43 ZIMBABWE
12 SENEGAL	28 DJIBOUTI	44 BOTSWANA
13 GAMBIA	29 SOMALIA	45 NAMIBIA
14 GUINEA BISSAU	30 KENYA	46 SOUTH AFRICA
15 GUINEA	31 UGANDA	47 LESOTHO
16 SIERRA LEONE	32 RWANDA	48 SWAZILAND
		49 MADAGASCAR

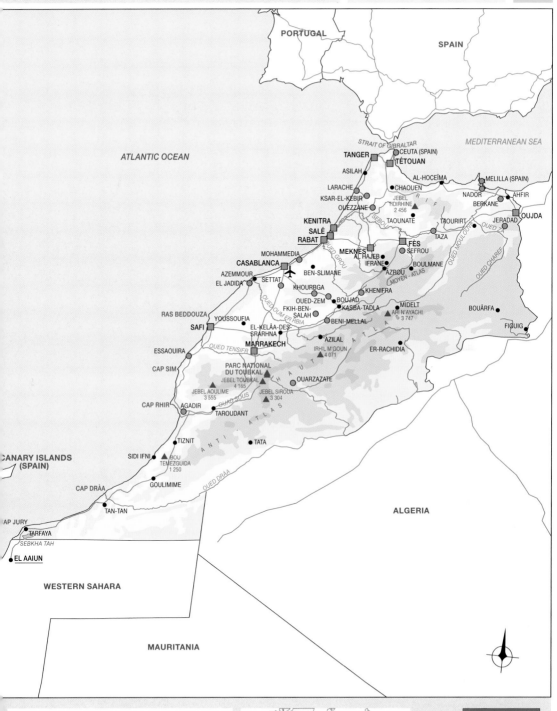

PORTUGAL

SPAIN

ATLANTIC OCEAN

MEDITERRANEAN SEA

STRAIT OF GIBRALTAR

TANGER   CEUTA (SPAIN)
TÉTOUAN

ASILAH

LARACHE   CHAOUEN   AL-HOCEÏMA   MELILLA (SPAIN)
KSAR-EL-KEBIR   NADOR   AHFIR
OUEZZANE   JEBEL   BERKANE
    TIDIRHINE   RIF
    2 456

TAOUNATE   TAOURIRT   JERADAD   OUJDA

KENITRA   TAZA
SALÉ   **FÈS**
RABAT   **MEKNÈS**   SEFROU
MOHAMMEDIA   AL HAJEB
CASABLANCA   IFRANE   BOULMANE
AZEMMOUR   BEN-SLIMANE   AZROU
EL JADIDA   SETTAT   MOYEN - ATLAS
    KHOURBGA   KHENIFRA
    OUED-ZEM   BOUJAD   MIDELT   BOUÂRFA
RAS BEDDOUZA   FKIH-BEN-   KASBA-TADLA   ARI N'AYACHI
    SALAH   S 3 747
YOUSSOUFIA   BENI-MELLAL   FIGUIG
SAFI   EL-KELÂA-DES-
    SRARHNA
ESSAOUIRA   AZILAL   ER-RACHIDIA
    MARRAKECH   IRHIL M'GOUN
CAP SIM   4 071
    OUARZAZATE
    PARC NATIONAL
    DU TOUBKAL
    JEBEL TOUBKAL
CAP RHIR   4 165
AGADIR   JEBEL AOULIME   JEBEL SIROUA
    3 555   3 304
TAROUDANT
    ANTI   ATLAS
TIZNIT   TATA
CANARY ISLANDS   SIDI IFNI   BOU
(SPAIN)   TEMEZGUIDA
    1 250
CAP DRÀA   GOULIMIME   ALGERIA
TAN-TAN   OUED DRAA
AP JURY
TARFAYA
SEBKHA TAH
EL AAIUN

WESTERN SAHARA

MAURITANIA

Official name:	Al Mamlaka al-Maghrebiya
Capital:	Rabat
Population:	27.0 million
Surface area:	458,730 km²
Currency:	Moroccon Dirham
Languages:	Arabic, Berber
GDP per head:	$ 1,290
Life expectancy:	66 years

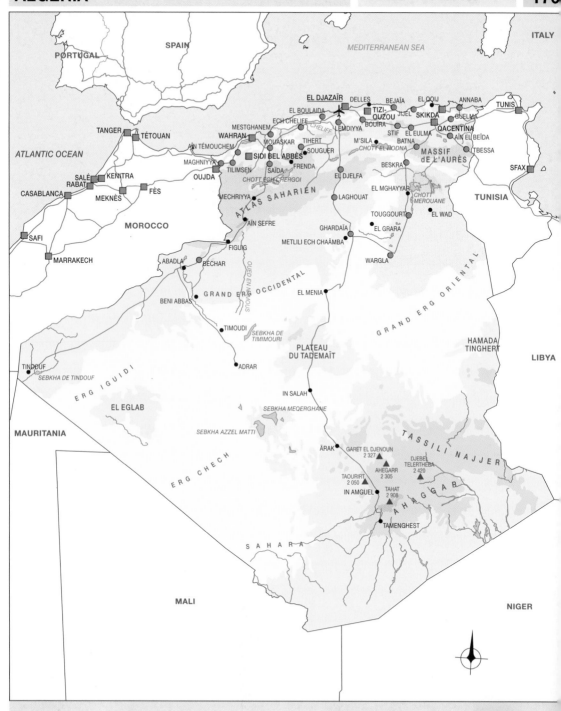

ITALY

SPAIN

MEDITERRANEAN SEA

PORTUGAL

EL DJAZAÏR   DELLES   BEJAÏA   EL QQIJ   ANNABA
EL BOULAIDA   TIZI-   JIJEL   SKIKDA   GUELMA   TUNIS
ECH CHELIFF   OUZOU   BOUIRA   STIF   EL EULMA   QACENTINA
MESTGHANEM   LEMDIYYA   AÏN EL BEÏDA
TANGER   WAHRAN   MOUASKAR   TIHERT   M'SILA   BATNA   TBESSA
TÉTOUAN   AÏN TÉMOUCHEM   SOUGUER   CHOTT EL HODNA   MASSIF
ATLANTIC OCEAN   SIDI BEL ABBÈS   de L'AURÈS
MAGHNIYYA   FRENDA   SFAX
TILIMSEN   SAÏDA   BESKRA
SALÉ   KENITRA   OUJDA   CHOTT ECH CHERGOI   EL DJELFA   EL MGHAYYAR   TUNISIA
RABAT   CHOTT
CASABLANCA   FÈS   MECHRIYYA   LAGHOUAT   MEROUANE
MEKNÈS   ATLAS SAHARIÉN   TOUGGOURT   EL WAD
SAFI   AÏN SEFRE   GHARDAÏA   EL GRARA
MARRAKECH   METLILI ECH CHAÀMBA   MOROCCO
FIGUIG   WARGLA
ABADLA   BÉCHAR   EL MENIA
BENI ABBAS   GRAND ERG OCCIDENTAL   GRAND ERG ORIENTAL   HAMADA
TIMOUDI   SEBKHA DE   TINGHERT
TIMIMOURI   LIBYA
TINDOUF   PLATEAU
SEBKHA DE TINDOUF   DU TADEMAÏT
ADRAR
ERG IGUIDI   IN SALAH
EL EGLAB   SEBKHA MEQERGHANE
MAURITANIA   SEBKHA AZZEL MATTI   TASSILI N AJJER
ÁRAK   GARET EL DJENOUN
2 327   DJEBEL
AHEGARR   TELERTHEBA
TAOURIRT   2 305   2 420
2 050
IN AMGUEL   TAHAT   AHAGGAR
2 908
ERG CHECH   TAMENGHEST
SAHARA
MALI   NIGER

Official name:	Al-Jumjuria al-Jazairia ash-Shaabiya
Capital:	Algiers
Population:	28.7 million
Surface area:	2,381,741 km²
Currency:	Algerian Dinar
Languages:	Arabic, French, Berber
GDP per head:	$ 1,520
Life expectancy:	70 years

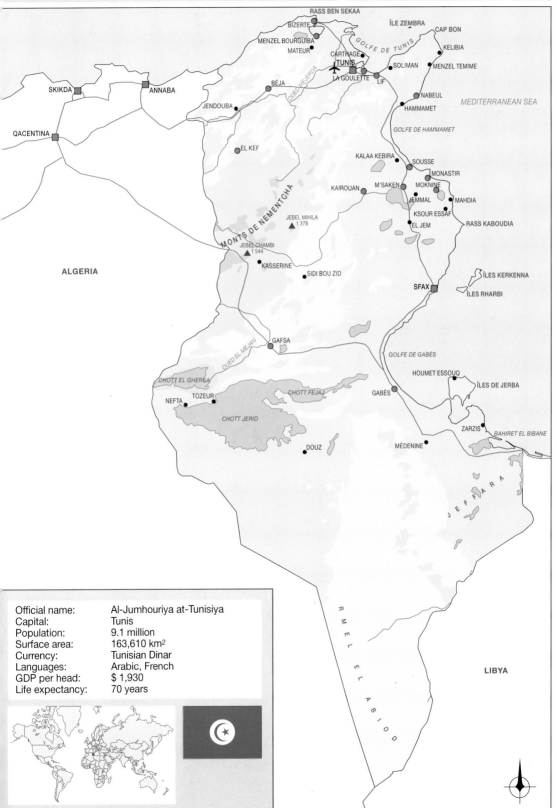

Official name:	Al-Jumhouriya at-Tunisiya
Capital:	Tunis
Population:	9.1 million
Surface area:	163,610 km²
Currency:	Tunisian Dinar
Languages:	Arabic, French
GDP per head:	$ 1,930
Life expectancy:	70 years

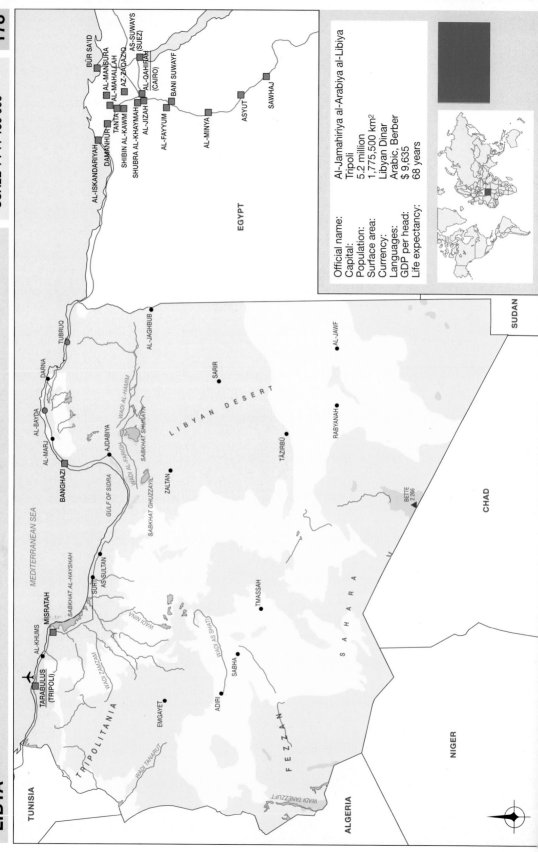

Official name:	Al-Jamahiriya al-Arabiya al-Libiya
Capital:	Tripoli
Population:	5.2 million
Surface area:	1,775,500 km²
Currency:	Libyan Dinar
Languages:	Arabic, Berber
GDP per head:	$ 9,635
Life expectancy:	68 years

EGYPT

SUDAN

CHAD

NIGER

ALGERIA

TUNISIA

MEDITERRANEAN SEA

LIBYAN DESERT

SAHARA

TRIPOLITANIA

FEZZAN

GULF OF SIDRA

BÛR SA'ID
AL-MANSURA
AL-MAHALLAH
AS-SUWAYS
(SUEZ)
AL-QAHIRAH
(CAIRO)
TANTA
AZ-ZAQÂZÎQ
BANI SUWAYF
AL-ISKANDARÎYAH
DAMANHÛR
SHIBIN AL-KAWM
SHUBRA AL-KHAYMAH
AL-JIZAH
AL-FAYYUM
AL-MINYA
ASYUT
SAWHAJ

TUBRUQ
DARNA
AL-BAYDA
AL-MARJ
BANGHAZI
AJDABIYA
AL-JAGHBUB
SARIR
AL-JAWF
RABYANAH
TAZIRBÛ
ZALTAN
BETTE
2 286
AS-SULTAN
SURT
MISRATAH
AL-KHUMS
TARABULUS
(TRIPOLI)
EMGAYET
ADIRI
SABHA
TMASSAH

SABKHAT AL-HAYSHAH
SABKHAT GHUZZAYIL
SABKHAT SHUMAYN
WADI AL-FARIGH
WADI AL-HAMIM
WADI NINA
WADI ZAMZAM
WADI AS-SHATI
WADI TANARUT
WADI TANEZZUFT

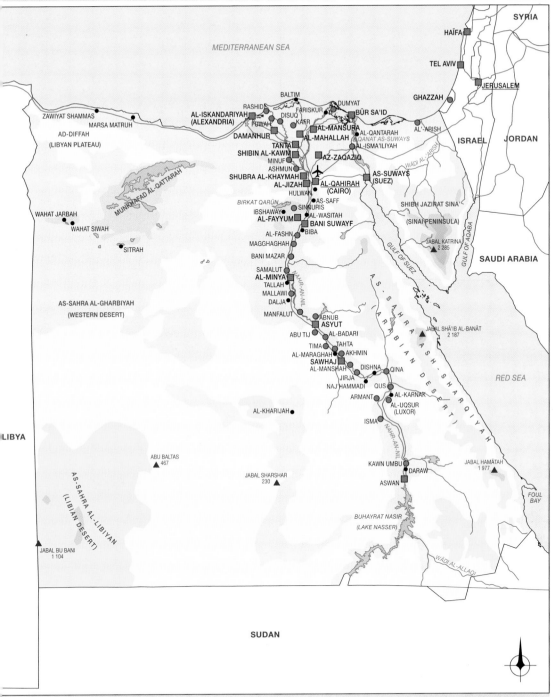

MEDITERRANEAN SEA

SYRIA
HAÏFA
TEL AVIV
JERUSALEM
GHAZZAH
ISRAEL
JORDAN
AL-'ARISH
SAUDI ARABIA
RED SEA
FOUL BAY

ZAWIYAT SHAMMAS
MARSA MATRUH
AD-DIFFAH
(LIBYAN PLATEAU)

RASHID
BALTIM
DUMYAT
BÛR SA'ID
FARISKUR
DISUQ
AL-QANTARAH
AL-ISKANDARIYAH (ALEXANDRIA)
FUWAH
KAFR
AL-MANSURA
(QANAT AS-SUWAYS)
DAMANHUR
AL-MAHALLAH
AL-ISMA'ILIYAH
TANTA
SHIBIN AL-KAWM
AZ-ZAQAZIQ
MINUF
ASHMUN
AS-SUWAYS (SUEZ)
SHUBRA AL-KHAYMAH
AL-JIZAH
AL-QAHIRAH (CAIRO)
HULWAN
AS-SAFF
SHIBH JAZIRAT SINA' (SINAI PENINSULA)
BIRKAT QARÛN
IBSHAWAY
SINNURIS
AL-FAYYUM
AL-WASITAH
BANI SUWAYF
JABAL KATRINA 2 285
AL-FASHN
BIBA
MAGGHAGHAH
BANI MAZAR
SAMALUT
AL-MINYA
TALLAH
MALLAWI
DALJA
MANFALUT
ABNUB
ASYUT
ABU TIJ
AL-BADARI
TIMA
TAHTA
AL-MARAGHAH
AKHMIN
SAWHAJ
DISHNA
AL-MANSHAH
JIRJA
QINA
NAJ HAMMADI
QUS
ARMANT
AL-KARNAK
AL-UQSUR (LUXOR)
ISMA
JABAL SHÂ'IB AL-BANÂT 2 187
KAWN UMBU
DARAW
JABAL HAMÂTAH 1 977
ASWAN
BUHAYRAT NASIR (LAKE NASSER)

WAHAT JARBAH
WAHAT SIWAH
SITRAH
MUNKHAFAD AL-QATTARAH
AS-SAHRA AL-GHARBIYAH (WESTERN DESERT)
AL-KHARIJAH

AS-SAHRA ASH-SHARQIYA (ARABIAN DESERT)

GULF OF SUEZ
GULF OF AQABA

NAHR-AN-NIL

WADI AL-'ARISH

LIBYA
ABU BALTAS 467
JABAL SHARSHAR 230
AS-SAHRA AL-LIBIYAN (LIBIAN DESERT)
JABAL BU BANI 1 104

WADI AL-ALLAQI

SUDAN

Official name:	Al-Jumhuria Misr al-Arabia
Capital:	Cairo
Population:	59.3 million
Surface area:	1,002,000 km²
Currency:	Egyptian Pound
Languages:	Arabic, English, French
GDP per head:	$ 1,080
Life expectancy:	65 years

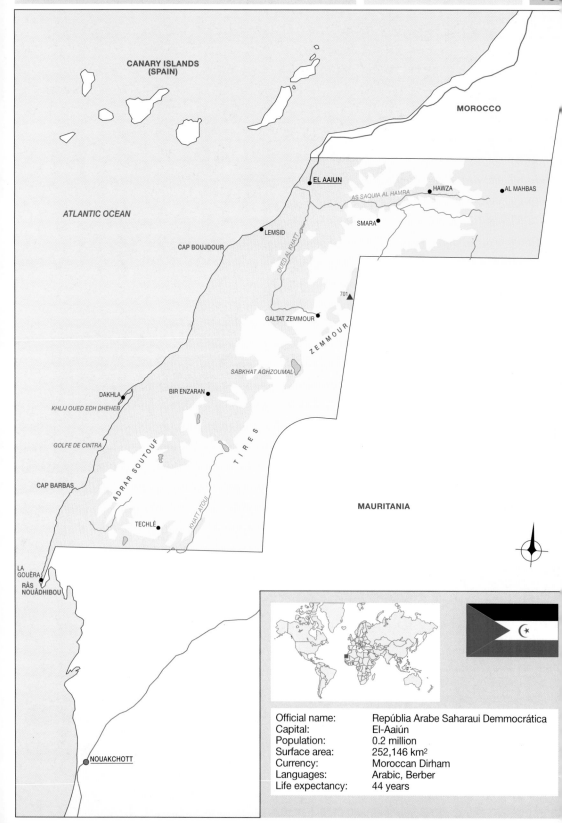

CANARY ISLANDS
(SPAIN)

MOROCCO

EL AAIUN

AS SAQUIA AL HAMRA   HAWZA   AL MAHBAS

ATLANTIC OCEAN

SMARA

LEMSID

CAP BOUJDOUR

OUED AL KHATT

701

GALTAT ZEMMOUR

ZEMMOUR

SABKHAT AGHZOUMAL

DAKHLA   BIR ENZARAN

KHLIJ OUED EDH DHEHEB

GOLFE DE CINTRA

T I R E S

ADRAR SOUTOUF

CAP BARBAS

MAURITANIA

KHATT ATOUI

TECHLÉ

LA GOUÈRA

RÅS NOUÂDHIBOU

NOUAKCHOTT

Official name:	Repúblia Arabe Saharaui Demmocrática
Capital:	El-Aaiún
Population:	0.2 million
Surface area:	252,146 km²
Currency:	Moroccan Dirham
Languages:	Arabic, Berber
Life expectancy:	44 years

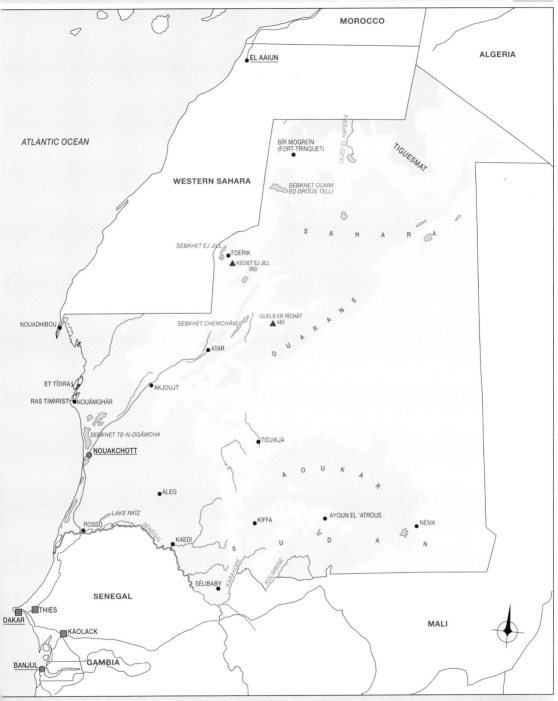

MOROCCO

ALGERIA

EL AAIUN

ATLANTIC OCEAN

BÎR MOGREÍN
(FORT-TRINQUET)

TIGUESMAT

OUED EL HAFEÏRA

WESTERN SAHARA

SEBKHET OUMM
ED DROÛS TELLI

S A H A R A

SEBKHET EJ JILL

FDÉRIK
▲ KEDIET EJ JILL
950

GUELB ER RÎCHÂT
▲ 485

NOUADHIBOU

SEBKHET CHEMCHÂM

O U A R A N E

ATAR

ET TÎDRA

AKJOUJT

RAS TIMIRIST
NOUÂMGHÂR

SEBKHET TE-N-DGÂMCHA

TIDJIKJA

NOUAKCHOTT

A O U K A R

ALEG

LAKE RKÎZ

ROSSO

KIFFA

AYOUN EL 'ATROUS

NÉMA

SENEGAL

KAEDI

S U D A N

KABAKORE

KOLIMBINE

SÉLIBABY

SENEGAL

DAKAR
THIÈS

KAOLACK

MALI

BANJUL
GAMBIA

Official name:	Al-Jumhouriya al-Islamiya al-Muritaniya
Capital:	Nouakchott
Population:	2.3 million
Surface area:	1,030,700 km²
Currency:	Ouguiya
Languages:	Arabic, French
GDP per head:	$ 470
Life expectancy:	53 years

MOROCCO

EL AAIUN

WESTERN SAHARA

ALGERIA

MAURITANIA

S A H A R A

ADRAR
DES
IFOGHAS

VALLÉE DU TILEMSI

VALLÉE DE L'AZAOUAGH

L.FAGUIBINE

TOMBOUCTOU

NIGER

GAO

L. NIANGAY

S
U
D
A
N

HOMBORI TONDO
1 155

NIGER

NIORO DU SAHEL

MOPTI

KAYES

SÉNÉGAL

DJÉNNÉ

CANAL DU SAHEL

BAKOY

BAOULÉ

NIAMEY

BANAMBA

SÉGOU

DOURA

BURKINA FASO

NYAMINA

SAN

KENIÉBA

BAFING

BAKOY

KOULIKORO

DYERO

KOUTIALA

BAGOE

BANI

OUAGADOUGOU

KATI

BAMAKO

FALÉME

FALEA

M
A
N
D
I
N
G

BAOULÉ

BANIFING

SIKASSO

BOBO DIOULASSO

NIGER

GUINEA

IVORY COAST

GHANA

TOGO

BENIN

NIGERIA

Official name:	République du Mali
Capital:	Bamako
Population:	10.0 million
Surface area:	1,240,192 km²
Currency:	CFA Franc Beac
Languages:	French, Bambara
GDP per head:	$ 240
Life expectancy:	50 years

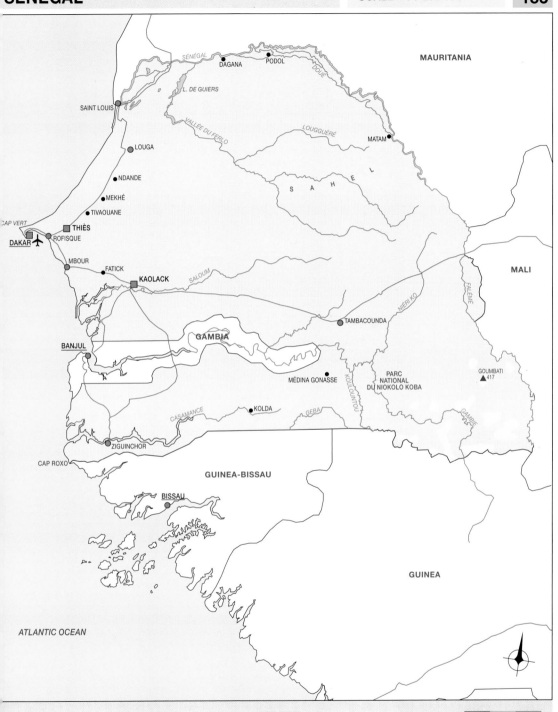

MAURITANIA

SÉNÉGAL
DAGANA • PODOL
L. DE GUIERS
DOUÉ
SAINT LOUIS
VALLÉE DU FERLO
LOUGGUÉRÉ
MATAM
LOUGA
S A H E L
NDANDE
MEKHÉ
TIVAOUANE
CAP VERT
THIÈS
DAKAR ✈
ROFISQUE
MBOUR
FATICK
KAOLACK
SALOUM
TAMBACOUNDA
NIÉRI KO
FALÉMÉ
MALI
GAMBIA
BANJUL
PARC
NATIONAL
DU NIOKOLO KOBA
GOUMBATI
▲ 417
MÉDINA GONASSE
KOULOUNTOU
GAMBIE
CAP ROXO
CASAMANCE
KOLDA
GEBA
ZIGUINCHOR

GUINEA-BISSAU

BISSAU

GUINEA

ATLANTIC OCEAN

Official name:	République du Sénégal
Capital:	Dakar
Population:	8.5 million
Surface area:	196,722 km^2
Currency:	CFA Franc Beac
Languages:	French, Wolof
GDP per head:	$ 570
Life expectancy:	50 years

THE GAMBIA / GUINEA-BISSAU

Official name: Republic of the Gambia
Capital: Banjul
Population: 1.1 million
Surface area: 11,295 km²
Currency: Dalasi
Languages: English, Malinke, Fulani
GDP per head: $ 785
Life expectancy: 53 years

Official name: Republica da Guiné-Bissau
Capital: Bissau
Population: 1.1 million
Surface area: 36,125 km²
Currency: Guinea-Bissau Peso
Language: Portuguese, Portuguese Creole
GDP per head: $ 250
Life expectancy: 44 years

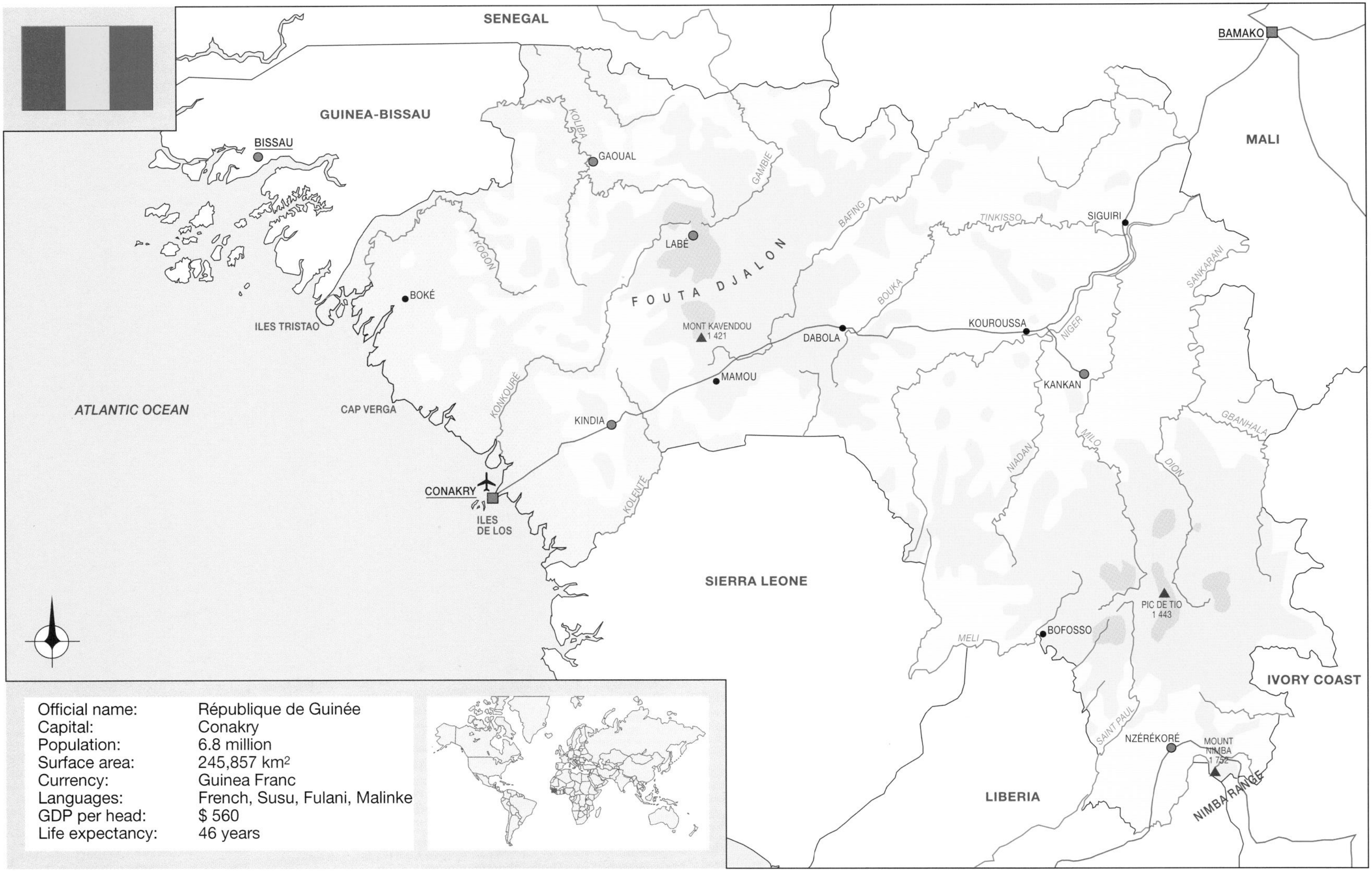

SCALE 1 : 4 550 000

MALI

BAMAKO

SENEGAL

GUINEA-BISSAU

BISSAU

ATLANTIC OCEAN

ILES TRISTAO

CAP VERGA

BOKÉ

KOGON

KOLIBA

GAOUAL

GAMBIE

BAFING

LABÉ

FOUTA DJALON

MONT KAVENDOU 1 421

MAMOU

KINDIA

KOLENTÉ

KONKOURE

CONAKRY

ILES DE LOS

SIGUIRI

KOUROUSSA

DABOLA

BOURA

TINKISSO

SANKARANI

NIGER

KANKAN

NIANDAN

MILO

DION

GBANHALA

PIC DE TIO 1 443

BOFOSSO

SANT PAUL

MELI

SIERRA LEONE

LIBERIA

IVORY COAST

NIMBA RANGE

MOUNT NIMBA

NZÉRÉKORÉ

Official name: République de Guinée
Capital: Conakry
Population: 6.8 million
Surface area: 245,857 km²
Currency: Guinea Franc
Languages: French, Susu, Fulani, Malinke
GDP per head: $ 560
Life expectancy: 46 years

GUINEA

MONGO

LOMA MOUNTAINS

GREAT SCARCIES

LITTLE SCARCIES

▲ BINTIMANI
1 945

PAMPANA

SANKANBIAIWA
1 709 ▲

MAKENI

YENGEMA ●

● KOIDU

PORT LOKO ●

LUNSAR ●

ROKEL

MAGBURAKA ●

MELI

FREETOWN

KOINDU ●

BANANA ISLANDS

BO ●

KENEMA ●

BAGBE

JONG

TURTLE ISLANDS

SHERBO

SHERBO ISLAND

MOA

LIBERIA

ATLANTIC OCEAN

Official name:	Republic of Sierra Leone
Capital:	Freetown
Population:	4.6 million
Surface area:	71,740 km²
Currency:	Leone
Language:	English, Creole
GDP per head:	$ 200
Life expectancy:	37 years

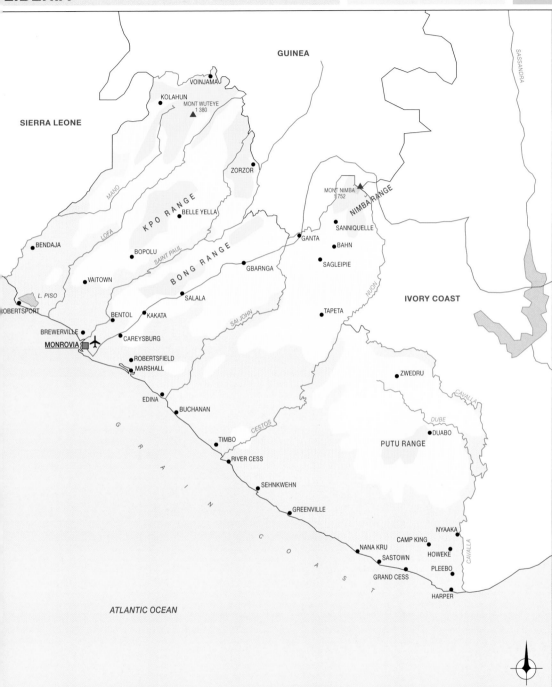

GUINEA

SIERRA LEONE

VOINJAMA

KOLAHUN

MONT WUTEYE
1 380

ZORZOR

KPO RANGE

BELLE YELLA

MONT NIMBA
1 752

NIMBA RANGE

SANNIQUELLE

GANTA

BAHN

SAGLEIPIE

BENDAJA

BOPOLU

SAINT PAUL

BONG RANGE

GBARNGA

MANO

LOFA

VAITOWN

SALALA

L. PISO

ROBERTSPORT

BENTOL KAKATA

BREWERVILLE

MONROVIA

CAREYSBURG

ROBERTSFIELD

MARSHALL

EDINA

BUCHANAN

CESTOS

TIMBO

RIVER CESS

SEHNKWEHN

GREENVILLE

SAI JOHN

TAPETA

NUON

IVORY COAST

ZWEDRU

CAVALLA

DUBE

DUABO

PUTU RANGE

NYAAKA

CAMP KING

NANA KRU

HOWEKE

SASTOWN

PLEEBO

GRAND CESS

HARPER

CAVALLA

G R A I N   C O A S T

ATLANTIC OCEAN

SASSANDRA

Official name: Republic of Liberia
Capital: Monrovia
Population: 2.8 million
Surface area: 97,754 km^2
Currency: Liberian Dollar
Languages: English, Kpelle, Bassa, Gia, Kru
GDP per head: $ 785
Life expectancy: 49 years

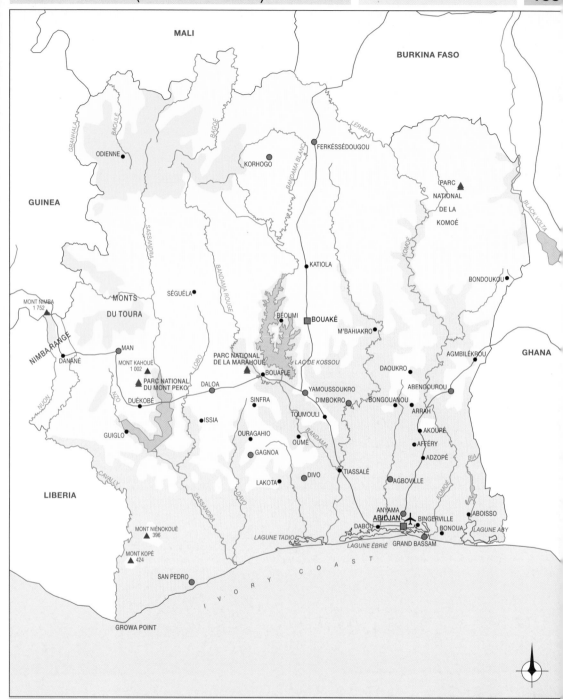

MALI

BURKINA FASO

GUINEA

GHANA

LIBERIA

IVORY COAST

GBANHALA

BAOULE

ODIENNE

KORHOGO

FERKÉSSÉDOUGOU

LÉRABA

BAGOÉ

BANDAMA BLANC

PARC

NATIONAL

DE LA

KOMOÉ

BLACK VOLTA

SASSANDRA

KATIOLA

BONDOUKOU

MONTS
DU TOURA

SÉGUÉLA

BÉOUMI

BOUAKÉ

M'BAHIAKRO

KOMOÉ

MONT NIMBA
1 752

NIMBA RANGE

MAN

MONT KAHOUÉ
1 002

PARC NATIONAL
DE LA MARAHOUÉ

LAC DE KOSSOU

DAOUKRO

AGMBILÉKROU

BANDAMA ROUGE

LOBO

DANANÉ

PARC NATIONAL
DU MONT PEKO

BOUAPLE

DALOA

ABENGOUROU

NZO

DUÉKOBÉ

SINFRA

YAMOUSSOUKRO

DIMBOKRO

BONGOUANOU

ARRAH

NUON

ISSIA

TOUMOULI

AKOUPÉ

GUIGLO

OURAGAHIO

OUMÉ

AFFÉRY

BANDAMA

ADZOPÉ

BIA

GAGNOA

CAVALLY

LAKOTA

DIVO

TIASSALÉ

AGBOVILLE

KOMOÉ

SASSANDRA

DAVO

ANYAMA

ABIDJAN

BINGERVILLE

ABOISSO

MONT NIÉNOKOUÉ
396

DABOU

BONOUA

LAGUNE ABY

LAGUNE TADIO

LAGUNE ÉBRIÉ

GRAND BASSAM

MONT KOPÉ
424

SAN PEDRO

I V O R Y   C O A S T

GROWA POINT

Official name:	République de Côte d'Ivoire
Capital:	Yamoussoukro
Population:	14.3 million
Surface area:	322,462 km²
Currency:	CFA Franc Beac
Language:	French
GDP per head:	$ 660
Life expectancy:	54 years

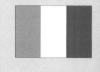

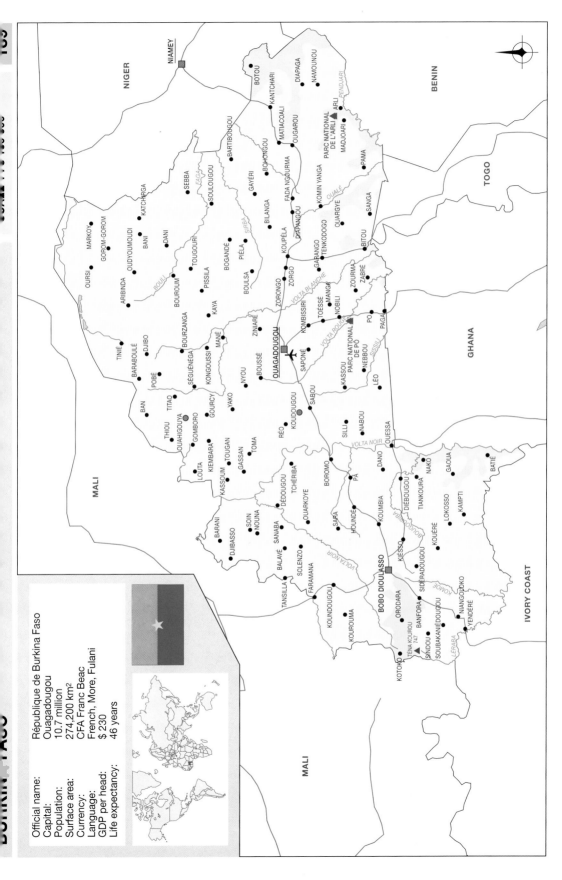

Official name:	République de Burkina Faso
Capital:	Ouagadougou
Population:	10.7 million
Surface area:	274,200 km²
Currency:	CFA Franc Beac
Language:	French, More, Fulani
GDP per head:	$ 230
Life expectancy:	46 years

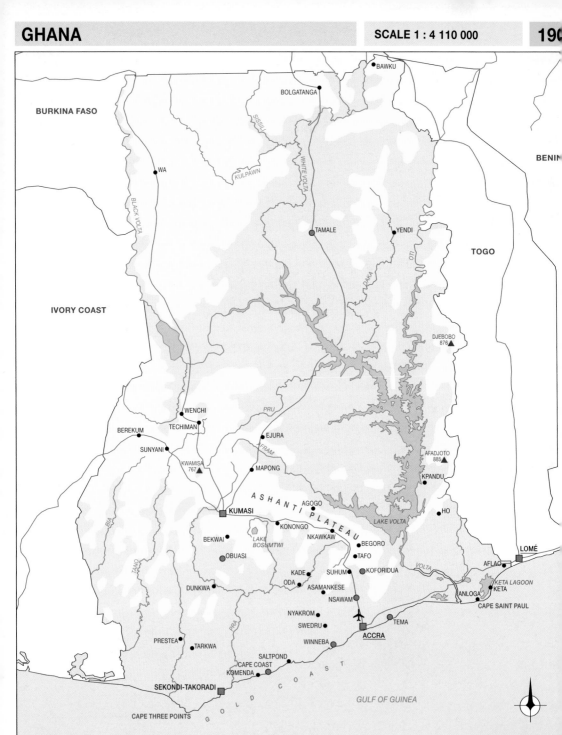

BURKINA FASO

BENIN

TOGO

IVORY COAST

BAWKU

BOLGATANGA

WA

SISSILI

KULPAWN

WHITE VOLTA

BLACK VOLTA

OTI

TAMALE

YENDI

OAKA

DJEBOBO
876▲

WENCHI

PRU

TECHIMAN

BEREKUM

EJURA

SUNYANI

AFRAM

KWAMISA
767▲

MAPONG

AFADJOTO
885▲

KPANDU

ASHANTI PLATEAU

AGOGO

HO

BIA

KUMASI

KONONGO

LAKE VOLTA

BEKWAI

LAKE
BOSUMTWI

NKAWKAW

BEGORO

OBUASI

TAFO

TANO

KADE

SUHUM

KOFORIDUA

VOLTA

LOMÉ

ODA

AFLAO

DUNKWA

ASAMANKESE

KETA LAGOON

NSAWAM

ANLOGA

KETA

PRA

NYAKROM

CAPE SAINT PAUL

SWEDRU

TEMA

PRESTEA

TARKWA

WINNEBA

ACCRA

SALTPOND

CAPE COAST

KOMENDA

SEKONDI-TAKORADI

GOLD COAST

GULF OF GUINEA

CAPE THREE POINTS

Official name:	Republic of Ghana
Capital:	Accra
Population:	17.5 million
Surface area:	238,537 km²
Currency:	Cedi
Languages:	English, Hausa, Akan, Ewe
GDP per head:	$ 360
Life expectancy:	59 years

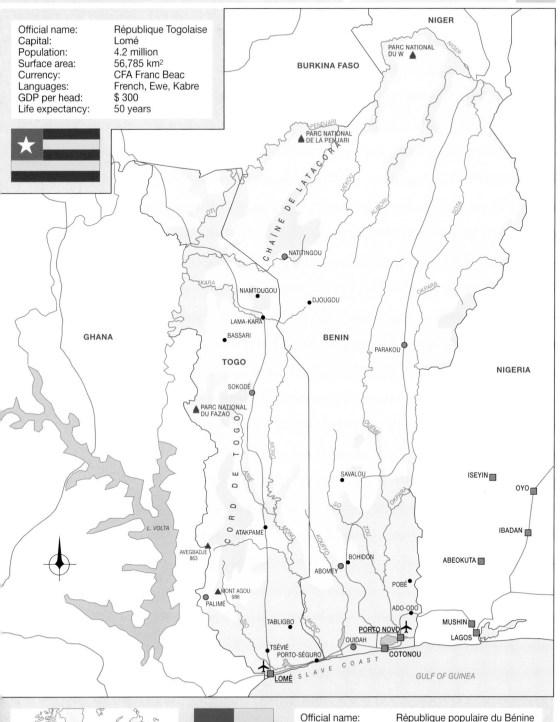

Official name: République Togolaise
Capital: Lomé
Population: 4.2 million
Surface area: 56,785 km²
Currency: CFA Franc Beac
Languages: French, Ewe, Kabre
GDP per head: $ 300
Life expectancy: 50 years

NIGER

BURKINA FASO

PARC NATIONAL
DU W

GHANA

CHAÎNE DE L'ATACORA

PENDJARI
PARC NATIONAL
DE LA PENJARI

OTI

MEKOU

ALIBORI

SOTA

NATITINGOU

KARA

NIAMTOUGOU

DJOUGOU

OKPARA

LAMA-KARA

BASSARI

BENIN

NIGERIA

TOGO

PARAKOU

SOKODÉ

PARC NATIONAL
DU FAZAO

CORD DE TOGO

MONO

OUÉMÉ

SAVALOU

ISEYIN

OYO

IBADAN

L. VOLTA

SO

ZOU

OKPARA

ATAKPAMÉ

ANIÉ

MONO

ABEOKUTA

AVEGBADJE
863

KOUFFO

BOHIDON

ABOMEY

POBÉ

MONT AGOU
986

ADO-ODO

PALIMÉ

SIO

TABLIGBO

MUSHIN

PORTO NOVO

MONO

LAGOS

TSÉVIÉ

OUIDAH

PORTO-SÉGURO

COTONOU

LOMÉ

SLAVE COAST

GULF OF GUINEA

Official name: République populaire du Bénine
Capital: Port Novo
Population: 5.6 million
Surface area: 112,622 km²
Currency: CFA Franc Beac
Languages: French, Fon, Yoruba, Adja
GDP per head: $ 350
Life expectancy: 55 years

NIGER

Official name: République du Niger
Capital: Niamey
Population: 9.3 million
Surface area: 1,267,000 km²
Currency: CFA Franc Beac
Languages: French, Hausa, Fulani
GDP per head: $ 200
Life expectancy: 47 years

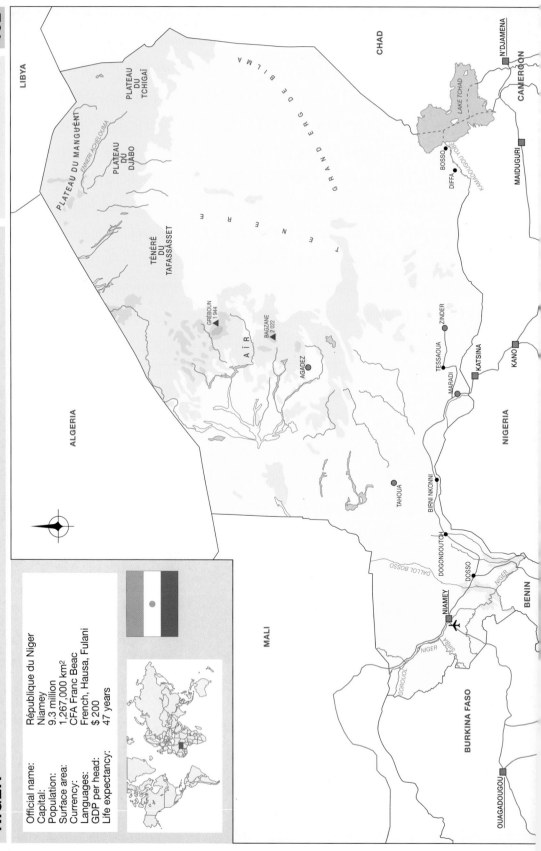

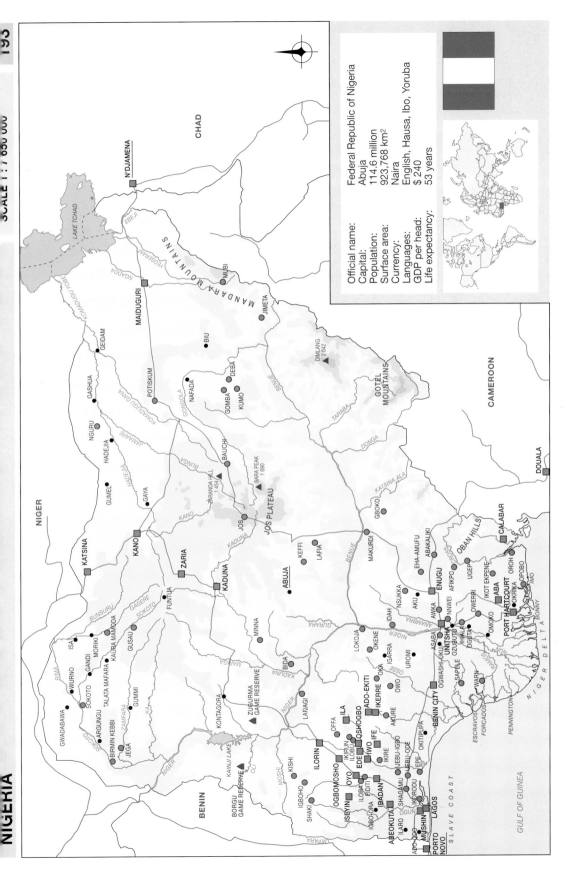

SCALE 1 : 7 650 000

Official name:	Federal Republic of Nigeria
Capital:	Abuja
Population:	114.6 million
Surface area:	923,768 km²
Currency:	Naira
Languages:	English, Hausa, Ibo, Yoruba
GDP per head:	$ 240
Life expectancy:	53 years

NIGER

CHAD

N'DJAMENA

LAKE TCHAD

KOMADOUGOU YOBE
EBEJI
NGADDA
KOMADOUGOU GANA
YEDSERAM
MANDARA MOUNTAINS

MAIDUGURI
MUBI
JIMETA
BIU

GEIDAM
GASHUA
NGURU
HADEJIA
GUMEL
GAYA

POTISKUM
GONGOLA
NAFADA
DEBA
GOMBA
KUMO

DIMLANG
2 042
GOTEL
MOUNTAINS

BENUE
TAPABA
DONGA

KATSINA
KANO
ZARIA
KADUNA

HADEJIA
JAMAARE
BUNGA
KANO
KADUNA

BAUCHI
ZARANDA HILL
1 454
SARA PEAK
1 690
JOS
JOS PLATEAU

KATSINA ALA
GBOKO

KEFFI
LAFIA

MAKURDI

BENUE

OBAN HILLS

CAMEROON

DOUALA

CALABAR

KATSINA ALA
CROSS

EHA-AMUFU
ABAKALIKI

ENUGU
AFIKPO
UGEP
IKOT EKPENE
OROH
OBOPO

NSUKKA
AKU
AWKA
NNWEI
OWERRI
ABA
OMOKO
PORT HARCOURT
OKRIKA
BONNY
IMO

NIGER DELTA

BIRNIN KEBBI
GWADABAWA
SOKOTO
ARGUNGU
VWURNO
ISA
GANDI
MORIKI
KAURA MAMODA
TALATA MAFARA
GUMMI
JEGA

RIMA
SOKOTO
ZAMFARA
GUSAU
GAGERE
GAGERE
BUNSURU
SOKOTO
FUNTUA

KONTAGORA
ZUGURMA
GAME RESERVE
KADUNA
MINNA

KAINJI LAKE
BORGU
GAME RESERVE
OLI
MOSHI

NIGER
KA

LAFIAGI
BIDA

LOKOJA
OKENE
IDAH
NIGER

GURARA

IGARRA
UROMI
OKA
OWO
AKURE

ABUJA

BENIN

PORTO
NOVO
LAGOS
MUSHIN
IKORODU
SHAGAMU
IJEBU-ODE
IJEBU-IGBO
EPE
OKITIPUPA

APA-ODO
OGUN
ILARO
ABEOKUTA
IBORORA
IBADAN
EDE
IWO
IFE
IKIRE
ILESHA
EKITI
OSHOGBO
ADO-EKITI
IKERRE
ILA
OFFA

BENIN CITY
OGWASHI-UKU
ASABA
ONITSHA
SAPELE
OZUBUTU
UGHELLI
WARRI
FORCADOS
ESCRAVOS
PENNINGTON

SHAKI
KISHI
IGBOHO
OYO
OGBOMOSHO
ILORIN
ISEYIN

GULF OF GUINEA

SLAVE COAST

OSSE
OGUN
OSHUN
OKPARA
SOKOTO

UKPARA

Official name:	République du Cameroun
Capital:	Yaoundé
Population:	13.7 million
Surface area:	475,442 km²
Currency:	CFA Franc Beac
Languages:	French, English, Fang, Bamileke
GDP per head:	$ 610
Life expectancy:	56 years

NIGER

LAC TCHAD

CHARI

MAIDUGURI

AFADE

FORT FOUREAU

N'DJAMENA

CHAD

MORA

PARC
NATIONAL
DE WAZA

POUSS

MAROUA

MANDARA MOUNTAINS

LOGONE

KAÉLÉ

DANA

BOULA IBIB

GAROUA

NIGERIA

BÉKA

BOKI

REY BOUBA

GOUNA

PARC NATIONAL
DE BOUBANDJIDAN

HOSÉRÉ VOKRÉ
2 049

PARC NATIONAL
DE LA BÉNOUÉ

BÉNOUÉ

MBÉ

VINA

TOUBORO

DODÉO

TCHABAL MBABO
2 049

N'GAOUNDÉRÉ

MARTAP

ADAMAOUA

BANYO

MONT NGAOUI
1 410

MEIGANGA

NGOL-KEDIU HILL
2 000

BAMENDA

FOUMBAN

BANKIM

TIBATI

DJEREM

BAGODO

CENTRAL AFRICAN REPUBLIC

AJASAO

CROSS

MAMFE

BAFOUSSAM

FOUMBOT

MBAM

DOUMÉ

GAROUA BOULAÏ

BAKEBE

MELONG

BAFANG

BETARÉ OYA

LOM

CALABAR

NKONGSAMBA

TONGA

MANKIM

GARGA SARALI

DENG DENG

KADEÏ

KUMBA

LOUM

BAFIA

MINTA

BERTOUA

BATOURI

MBANGA

WOURI

NTUI

NANGA
EBOKO

BOUMBE II

CAMEROON MOUNTAINS
4 100

BUEA

DOUALA

SANAGA

OBALA

MBONG MBANG

GULF
OF
GUINEA

VICTORIA

BOUMNYEBE

YAOUNDÉ

MALABO

EDÉA

SANAGA

NYONG

MBALMAYO

ZWADIBA

EQUATORIAL
GUINEA

KIRBI

EBOLOWA

MENGONG

SANGMÉLIMA

DJA

BOUMBA

MEYO CENTRE

AMBAM

YEN

KOM

KAMPO

MBALAM

MOLOUNDOU

NGOKO

ATLANTIC OCEAN

EQUATORIAL GUINEA

GABON

CONGO

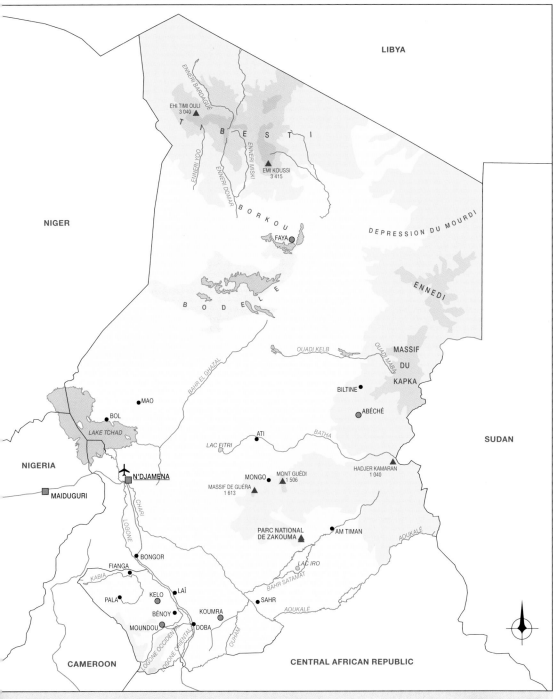

LIBYA

NIGER

ENNERI BARDAGUÉ

EHI TIMI OULI
3 040 ▲

T   I   B   E   S   T   I

ENNERI MISKI

EMI KOUSSI
3 415 ▲

ENNERI YOO

ENNERI DOMAR

B   O   R   K   O   U

DEPRESSION DU MOURDI

FAYA ●

B   O   D   E   L   E

E   N   N   E   D   I

OUADI KELB

OUAD MABA

MASSIF
DU
KAPKA

BILTINE ●

BAHR EL GHAZAL

MAO ●

BOL ●

LAKE TCHAD

ABÉCHÉ ●

ATI ●

LAC FITRI

BATHA

SUDAN

NIGERIA

N'DJAMENA

MAIDUGURI ■

CHARI

LOGONE

MONGO ●

MASSIF DE GUÉRA
1 613 ▲

MONT GUÉDI
1 506 ▲

HADJER KAMARAN
1 040 ▲

PARC NATIONAL
DE ZAKOUMA ▲

AM TIMAN ●

AOUKALÉ

BONGOR ●

FIANGA

KABIA

PALA ●

KELO ●

LAÏ ●

BÉNOY ●

MOUNDOU ●

KOUMRA ●

DOBA ●

SAHR ●

LAC IRO

BAHR SATAMAT

AOUKALÉ

LOGONE OCCIDENTAL

LOGONE ORIENTAL

OUHAM

CAMEROON

CENTRAL AFRICAN REPUBLIC

Official name:	République du Tchad
Capital:	Ndjamena
Population:	6.6 million
Surface area:	1,284,000 km^2
Currency:	CFA Franc Beac
Languages:	French, Arabic
GDP per head:	$ 160
Life expectancy:	48 years

CENTRAL AFRICAN REPUBLIC

Official name:	République Centrafricaine
Capital:	Bangui
Population:	3.3 million
Surface area:	622,984 km²
Currency:	CFA Franc Beac
Languages:	Sango, French, Banda, Baya
GDP per head:	$ 310
Life expectancy:	49 years

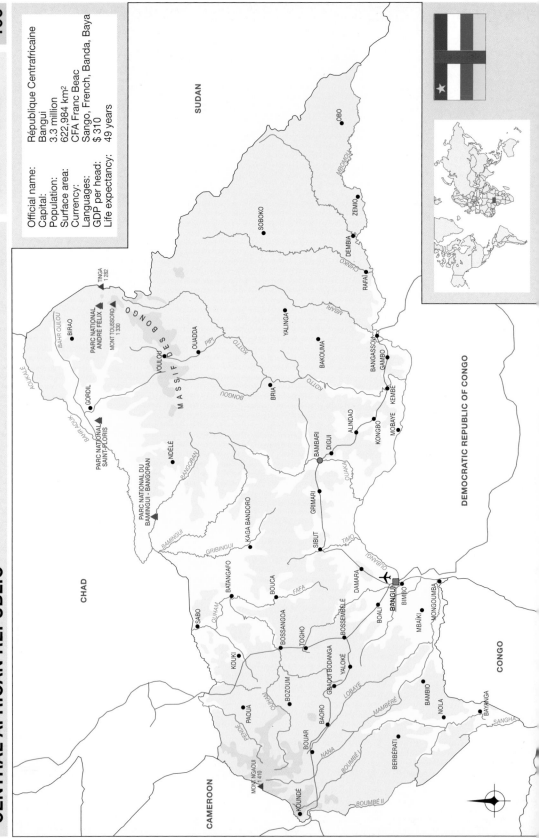

SUDAN

CHAD

CAMEROON

CONGO

DEMOCRATIC REPUBLIC OF CONGO

OBO

ZEMIO

DEMBIA

RAFAÏ

SOBOKO

TINGA 1 282

PARC NATIONAL ANDRÉ FÉLIX

MONT TOUSSORO 1 330

BAHR OULOU

BIRAO

GORDIL

AOUKALÉ

BAHR AOUK

PARC NATIONAL SAINT-FLORIS

MASSIF DES BONGO

YALINGA

OUADDA

PIPI

VOULOU

KOTTO

BAKOUMA

BANGASSOU

GAMBO

KEMBÉ

BRIA

BONGOU

KOTTO

ALINDAO

KONGBO

MOBAYE

NDÉLÉ

BANGORAN

BAMBARI

DIGUI

OUAKA

PARC NATIONAL DU BAMINGUI - BANGORAN

GRIMARI

KAGA BANDORO

BAMINGUI

GRIBINGUI

SIBUT

TIMO

OUBANGUI

BATANGAFO

BOUCA

FAFA

DAMARA

BANGUI

BIMBO

MONGOUMBA

OULHAM

SABO

BOSSANGOA

TOGHO

BOSSEMBÉLÉ

BOALI

MBAÏKI

KOUKI

BOZOUM

GRIMARI BODANGA

YALOKÉ

LOBAYE

BAMBIO

NOLA

BAYANGA

SANGHA

OUHAM

PAOUA

BAORO

MAMBÉRÉ

BERBÉRATI

BOUAR

NANA

MONT NGAOUI 1 410

BOUMBÉ

BOUMBÉ II

BOZOUM

KOUNDÉ

LIBYA

EGYPT

RED SEA

JAZA'IR SIYAL

AL-BAHR AL-AHMAR

(NUBIAN DESERT)

WADI OKO

JABAL ERBA 2 217

RAS AL-HADARIBAH

MUKAWWAR

A S - S A H R A   A L   L I B I Y A N
(L I B Y A N   D E S E R T)

BUR SUDAN
(PORT SOUDAN)

CHAD

JABIL ABYAD PLATEAU

DUNQULAH

NILE

WADI AMUR

JAZIRAT LARBUT

TAWKAR

TOKAR GAME RESERVE

JABAL HAMOYET 2 780

BARBAR

WADI BITIA

ATBARAH

AD-DAMIR

ERITREA

WADI MUQADDAM

NAHR AL-QASH

ATTBARA

SHANDI

SABALUKA GAME RESERVE

TEIGA PLATEAU

WADI AL MALIK

AL-KHARTŪM BAHRĪ

UMM DURMĀN

AL-KHARTUM (KARTOUM)

RUFĀ-AH

KASSALA

KHAZZAN KASHM AL-QIRBAH

AL-HUSAYHISAH

AL-MANĀQIL

WAD MADANI

AL-QADĀRIF

AL-FASHIR

JABAL MARRAH 3 088

S U D A N

AL-JUNAYNAH

ZALINGEI

AL-UBAYYID

AD-DUWAYM

SANNĀR

ES-SUKI

RAHAD GAME RESERVE

AN-NUHŪD

AR-RAHAD

TANDALTI

KUSTI

RABAK

SINJAH

BLUE NILE

DINDER NATIONAL PARC

NYALA

UMM RUWABAH

AR-RUSAYRIS

AD-DU'AYN

BABNŪSAH

AD-DAMAZIN

KHAZZAN AR-RUSAYRIS

KADUQLI

WHITE NILE

BAHR AL-ARAB

BAHR AL-GHAZĀL

MALAKĀL

SOBAT

ETHIOPIA

JUT

AS SUDD

AKUBU

CENTRAL AFRICAN REPUBLIC

KURU

WĀW

RUMBEK

YIROL

BAHR AZ-ZARAF

BAHR AL-JABAL

BOR

KANGEN

BIRE KPATUA GAME RESERVE

ABŪ GATTA HILLS

SUE

BOLI

MBARIZUNGA GAME RESERVE

MONGALLA GAME RESERVE

JUBA

DIDINGA HILLS

YEI

NIMULE NATIONAL PARC

TORIT

KENYA

DEMOCRATIC REPUBLIC OF CONGO

UGANDA

Official name:	Jumhouriyat as-Sudan ad-Dimukratiya
Capital:	Khartoum
Population:	27.3 million
Surface area:	2,505,813 km²
Currency:	Sudanese Dinar
Languages:	Arabic, Dinka, Nubian, Beja, Nuer
GDP per head:	$ 785
Life expectancy:	54 years

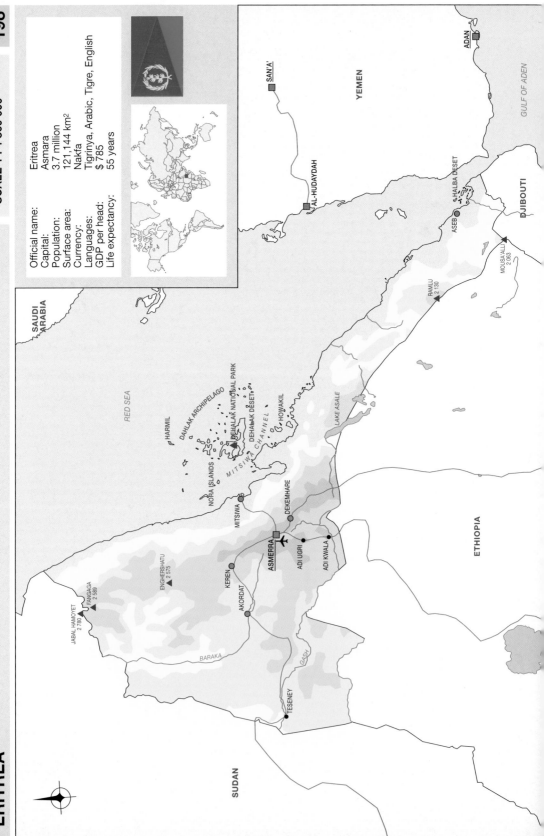

Official name:	Eritrea
Capital:	Asmara
Population:	3.7 million
Surface area:	121,144 km²
Currency:	Nakfa
Languages:	Tigrinya, Arabic, Tigre, English
GDP per head:	$ 785
Life expectancy:	55 years

SAUDI
ARABIA

YEMEN

SAN'A'

AL-HUDAYDAH

GULF OF ADEN

ADAN

DJIBOUTI

SHALBA DESET

ASEB

MOUSA'ALI
2 063

RAMLU
2 130

RED SEA

HARMIL

DAHLAK ARCHIPELAGO

DEHALAK NATIONAL PARK

DEHALAK DESET

HOWAKIL

NORA ISLANDS

MITSIWA CHANNEL

LAKE ASALE

MITSIWA

DEKEMHARE

ASMERRA

ADI UGRI

ADI KWALA

KEREN

ENGHERSHATU
2 575

AKORDAT

FANGAGA
2 569

JABAL HAMOYET
2 780

BARAKA

GASH

TESENEY

SUDAN

ETHIOPIA

Official name:	Itiopia
Capital:	Addis Ababa
Population:	58.2 million
Surface area:	1,133,380 km²
Currency:	Ethiopian Birr
Languages:	Amharic, Oromo, Galla, Tigre
GDP per head:	$ 100
Life expectancy:	49 years

Official name:	République de Djibouti
Capital:	Djibouti
Population:	0.6 million
Surface area:	23,200 km²
Currency:	Djibouti Franc
Languages:	Somali, Arabic, French, Issa
GDP per head:	$ 3,115
Life expectancy:	50 years

INDIAN OCEAN

SOMALIA

YEMEN

GULF OF ADEN

RED SEA

ERITREA

SUDAN

KENYA

UGANDA

MOUSSA ALLI 2 063

DENAKIL

LAKE ASALE

AWASH

AWASH NATIONAL PARK

DANAKIL NATIONAL PARK

MOULHOULÉ
OBOCK
TADJOURA
DJIBOUTI
LAKE GAMARE
LAKE ABE
HOL-HOL
AL-SABIEH
DIKHIL

JIJIGA
DAKETA
HARER
DIRE DAWA

OGADEN

SHEBELE

WABE GESTRO

AUDO RANGE

GENALE

DAWA

MEKELE
ADIGRAT
ADWA
AKSUM
RAS DASHAN 620
SIMEN MOUNTAINS NATIONAL PARK
GONDER
DEBRE TABOR
BAHIR DAR
TALO 4 103
DEBRE MARKOS
BURE
LAKE TANA
LAKE TANA
ATBARA
TAKEZE
BLUE NILE
DINDER
DIDESA

DESE
DEBRE BIRHAN
DEBRE ZEYT
NAZRET
FICHE
ADDIS ABEBA
HAGERE HIYWET
AKAKI-BESEKA
GIYON
LAKE KOKA
LAKE ZIWAY
LAKE ABIYATA
LAKE SHALA
LAKE LANGANO
ASELA
SASHEMENE
AWASA
LAKE AWASA
DILA
LAKE ABAYA
IRGA ALEM
HOSAINA
SODO
LAKE CHAMO
ARBA MINCH
GAGE 4 200
SEGEN
LAKE STEFANIE
LAKE RUDOLF
NEKEMTE
AGARO
JIMA
METU
GORE
BARO
GILO
AKOBO
OMO

GOBA
BATU 4 307
BALE MOUNTAINS NATIONAL PARK
KIBRE MENGIST

A H M A R   M O U N T A I N S

WAD MADANI
ASMERRA
DJIBOUTI

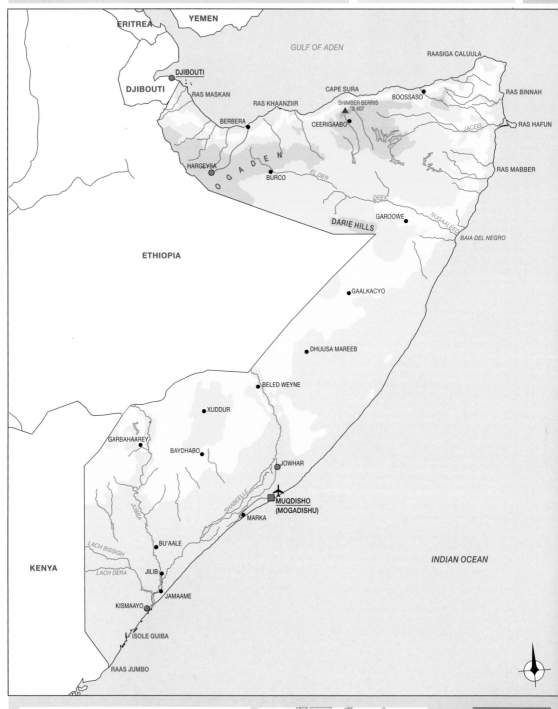

GULF OF ADEN

YEMEN

ERITREA

DJIBOUTI

DJIBOUTI

RAS MASKAN

RAASIGA CALUULA

CAPE SURA

BOOSSASO

RAS BINNAH

RAS KHAANZIIR

SHIMBER BERRIS
2.407

BERBERA

CEERIGAABO

JACEEL

RAS HAFUN

O G A D E N

ELDER

RAS MABBER

HARGEYSA

BURCO

DEEX

GAROOWE

NUGAALEED

DARIE HILLS

BAIA DEL NEGRO

ETHIOPIA

GAALKACYO

DHUUSA MAREEB

BELED WEYNE

XUDDUR

GARBAHAAREY

BAYDHABO

JOWHAR

SHABEELLE

JUBBA

MUQDISHO
(MOGADISHU)

MARKA

LACH BISSIGH

BU'AALE

INDIAN OCEAN

LACH DERA

JILIB

KENYA

JAMAAME

KISMAAYO

ISOLE GUIBA

RAAS JUMBO

Official name:	Jamhuriaydda Soomaliya
Capital:	Mogadishu
Population:	9.8 million
Surface area:	637,657 km²
Currency:	Somali Shilling
Languages:	Somali, Arabic, English
GDP per head:	$ 785
Life expectancy:	49 years

EQUATORIAL GUINEA

Official name:	Republica de Guinea Ecuatorial
Capital:	Malabo
Population:	0.4 million
Surface area:	28,051 km²
Currency:	CFA Franc Beac
Languages:	Spanish, Fang, Bubi., Creole
GDP per head:	$ 530
Life expectancy:	50 years

CAMEROON

EBEBIYIN
OVENG
NSANG
ABAN
MONGOMO
ASOC
NSOC
MBINI
MABELE
ANDOM
MEDOUNEAU
MIKOMESENG
EVANSOC
MVIGA
NOAYONG
NIEFANG
NKIMI
EVINAYONG
ACURENAM
MIDYOBE
NCOATOM
SENYE
MONT MITRA ▲ 1 200
UTONDE
BATA
AYAGFE
ASUABE
COGO
MBINI
BANGÜI
ACALAYONG
ETEMBUE
CABO SAN JUAN
ISLA DE CORISCO
GABON

LIBREVILLE

ATLANTIC OCEAN

MALABO
BASACATO DEL ESTE
PICO DE SANTA ISABEL ▲ 3 008
RIABA
LUBA
BIOKO
BOCOCO

GULF OF GUINEA

PRÍNCIPE

SÃO TOMÉ

SÃO TOME AND PRINCIPE

SANTO ANTÓNIO
PRÍNCIPE
INFANTA DOM HENRIQUE

GULF OF GUINEA

SÃO TOMÉ
BOMBON
CARIDADE
SANTA IRENE
PICO DE SÃO TOMÉ ▲ 2 024
VILA CONCEIÇAO
PORTINHO
N'ZUMBO
ALTO DOURO
PONTA FURADA
ILHA DAS RÔLAS

SCALE 1 : 1 730 000

Official name:	Republica Democrátia de São Tomé e Príncipe
Capital:	São Tomé
Population:	0.1 million
Surface area:	1,001 km²
Currency:	CFA Franc Beac
Languages:	Portuguese, Fang
GDP per head:	$ 330
Life expectancy:	64 years

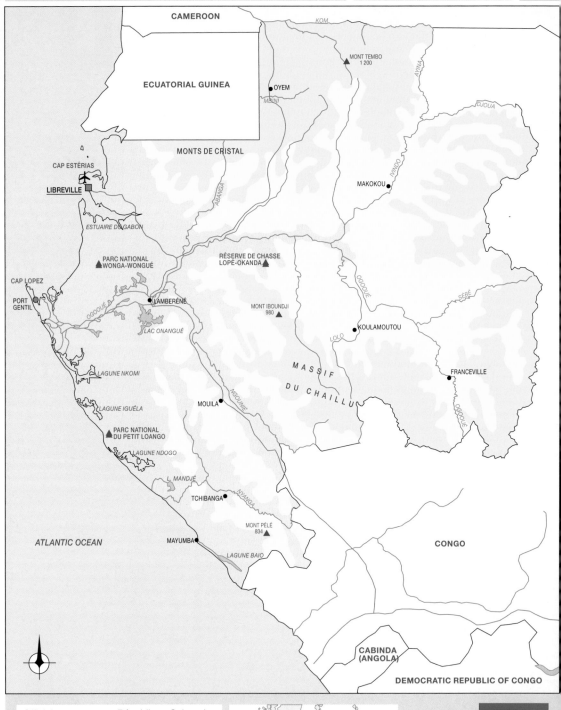

CAMEROON

ECUATORIAL GUINEA

KOM.

MONT TEMBO
1 200

OYEM

MBINI

AYINA

DJOUA

MONTS DE CRISTAL

ABANGA

IVINDO

MAKOKOU

CAP ESTÉRIAS

LIBREVILLE

ESTUAIRE DE GABON

PARC NATIONAL
WONGA-WONGUÉ

RÉSERVE DE CHASSE
LOPÉ-OKANDA

OGOOUÉ

SEBÉ

CAP LOPEZ

PORT
GENTIL

LAMBERÉNÉ

OGOOUÉ

LAC ONANGUÉ

MONT IBOUNDJI
980

LOLO

KOULAMOUTOU

LAGUNE NKOMI

MASSIF

FRANCEVILLE

OGOOUÉ

LAGUNE IGUÉLA

DU CHAILLU

MOUILA

NGOUNIÉ

PARC NATIONAL
DU PETIT LOANGO

LAGUNE NDOGO

L. MANDJÉ

TCHIBANGA

NYANGA

ATLANTIC OCEAN

MONT PÉLÉ
834

CONGO

MAYUMBA

LAGUNE BAIO

CABINDA
(ANGOLA)

DEMOCRATIC REPUBLIC OF CONGO

Official name: République Gabonaise
Capital: Libreville
Population: 1.1 million
Surface area: 267,667 km²
Currency: CFA Franc Beac
Language: French, Fang
GDP per head: $ 3,950
Life expectancy: 55 years

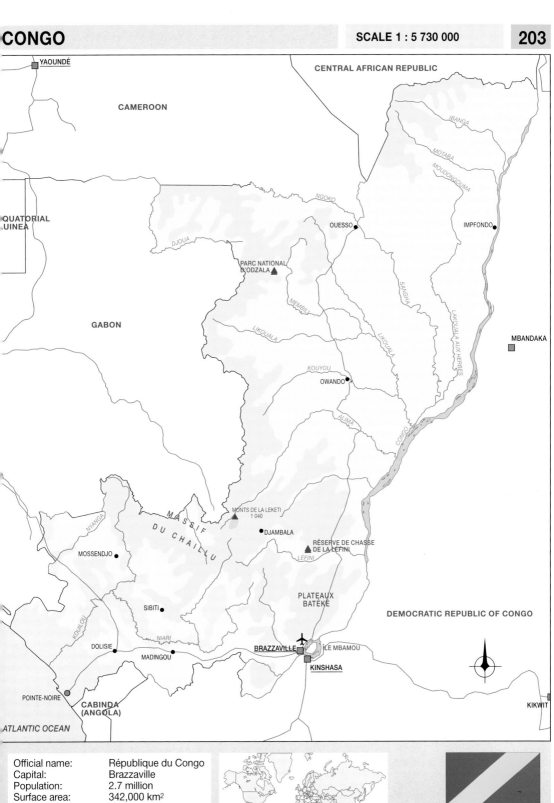

CENTRAL AFRICAN REPUBLIC

CAMEROON

YAOUNDÉ

IBANGA

MOTABA

MOUDONGOUMA

NGOKO

EQUATORIAL GUINEA

OUESSO

IMPFONDO

DJOUA

PARC NATIONAL D'ODZALA

SANGHA

MEMBILI

GABON

LIKOUALA

LIKOUALA

LAKOUALA AUX HERBES

MBANDAKA

KOUYOU

OWANDO

ALIMA

CONGO

MONTS DE LA LEKETI
1 040

MASSIF DU CHAILLU

DJAMBALA

RÉSERVE DE CHASSE DE LA LÉFINI

LÉFINI

NYANGA

MOSSENDJO

PLATEAUX BATÉKÉ

DEMOCRATIC REPUBLIC OF CONGO

SIBITI

KOUILOU

NIARI

DOLISIE

MADINGOU

BRAZZAVILLE

ÎLE MBAMOU

KINSHASA

POINTE-NOIRE

CABINDA
(ANGOLA)

KIKWIT

ATLANTIC OCEAN

Official name:	République du Congo
Capital:	Brazzaville
Population:	2.7 million
Surface area:	342,000 km^2
Currency:	CFA Franc Beac
Language:	French, Kongo
GDP per head:	$ 670
Life expectancy:	51 years

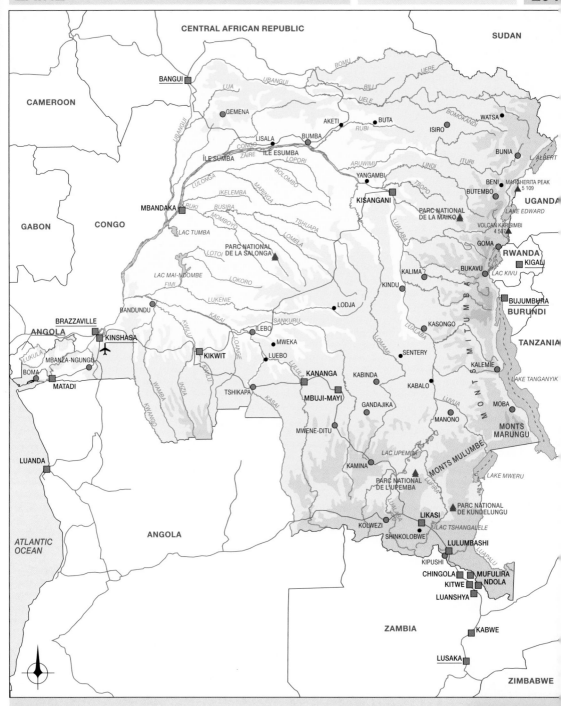

CENTRAL AFRICAN REPUBLIC

SUDAN

CAMEROON

BANGUI

GEMENA

AKETI   BUTA   WATSA

LISALA   BUMBA   ISIRO   BOMOKANDI

ÎLE SUMBA   ÎLE ESUMBA   BUNIA   L. ALBERT

YANGAMBI   BENI   MARGHERITA PEAK 5 109

MBANDAKA   KISANGANI   BUTEMBO   UGANDA

GABON   CONGO   PARC NATIONAL DE LA MAIKO   VOLCAN KARISIMBI 4 507

LAC TUMBA   GOMA   RWANDA

PARC NATIONAL DE LA SALONGA   KALIMA   BUKAVU   KIGALI   LAC KIVU

LAC MAI-NDOMBE   KINDU

BANDUNDU   LODJA   KASONGO   BUJUMBURA   BURUNDI

BRAZZAVILLE   ILEBO   TANZANIA

ANGOLA   KINSHASA   MWEKA   SENTERY   KALEMIE   LAKE TANGANYIKA

KIKWIT   LUEBO   KABINDA   KABALO   MOBA

MBANZA-NGUNGU   KANANGA   GANDAJIKA   MANONO   MONTS MARUNGU

BOMA   TSHIKAPA   MBUJI-MAYI   LAKE MWERU

MATADI   MWENE-DITU   KAMINA   MONTS MULUMBE

LUANDA   LAC UPEMBA

PARC NATIONAL DE L'UPEMBA   PARC NATIONAL DE KUNDELUNGU

ANGOLA   LIKASI   LAC TSHANGALELE

ATLANTIC OCEAN   KOLWEZI   LULUMBASHI

SHINKOLOBWE   KIPUSHI

CHINGOLA   MUFULIRA NDOLA

KITWE

LUANSHYA   KABWE

ZAMBIA

LUSAKA

ZIMBABWE

Official name:	République Démocratique du Congo
Capital:	Kinshasa
Population:	45.2 million
Surface area:	2,344,885 km²
Currency:	Zaire
Languages:	French, Lingala, Swahili, Kongo, Luba
GDP per head:	$ 130
Life expectancy:	53 years

SUDAN

ZULIA
2 149 ▲

KIDEPO
NATIONAL PARK ▲

MORUNGOLE ▲
2 750

●ARUA

ALBERT NILE

PAGET

ACHWA

OKOK

OKERE

MOROTO ▲
3 084

●GULU

MOROTO ●

VICTORIA NILE

KABALEGA FALLS ▲
NATIONAL PARK

DEMOCRATIC REPUBLIC OF CONGO

LAKE KWANIA

SOROTI ●

LAKE BISINA

LAKE ALBERT

KAFO

LAKE KYOGA

MONT ELGON ▲
4 321

MBALE ●

●FORT PORTAL

BOMBO ●

TORORO ●

KENYA

RUWANZORI RA.

KATONGA

JINJA ⊙

KAMPALA ▢ ✈

LAKE GEORGE

ENTEBBE ●

KOME ISLAND

KISUMU ▢

●RUWENZORI
NATIONAL PARK

LAKE EDWARD

MASAKA ●

BUGALA ISLAND

SESE ISLANDS

●MBARARA

LAKE VICTORIA

●KABALE

RWANDA

▢ KIGALI

TANZANIA

BURUNDI

MWANZA ●

Official name:	Republic of Uganda
Capital:	Kampala
Population:	19.7 million
Surface area:	241,139 km^2
Currency:	Uganda Shilling
Languages:	Swahili, English
GDP per head:	$ 300
Life expectancy:	43 years

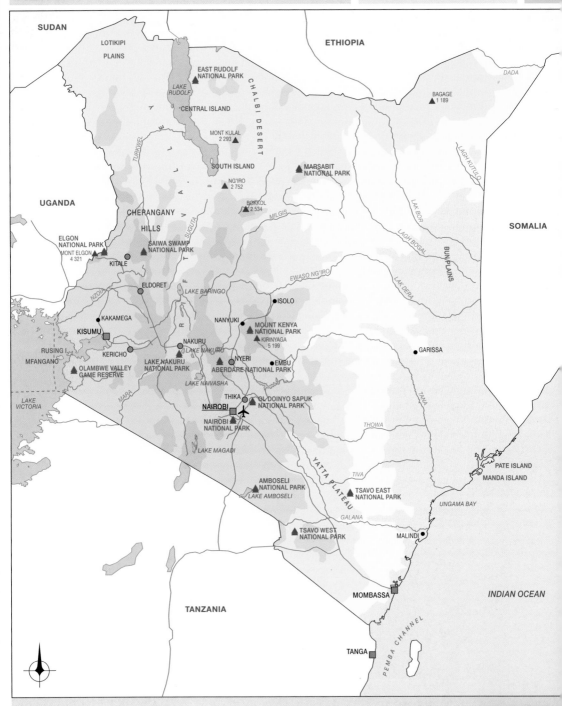

SUDAN

LOTIKIPI PLAINS

ETHIOPIA

EAST RUDOLF NATIONAL PARK

LAKE RUDOLF)

CENTRAL ISLAND

CHALBI DESERT

MONT KULAL 2 293

SOUTH ISLAND

MARSABIT NATIONAL PARK

BAGAGE ▲ 1 189

DADA

TURKWEL

NG'IRO ▲ 2 752

BORKOL ▲ 2 534

MILGIS

LAGH KUTULO

UGANDA

CHERANGANY HILLS

LAK BOR

LAGH BOGAL

SOMALIA

ELGON NATIONAL PARK
MONT ELGON 4 321 ▲

SAIWA SWAMP NATIONAL PARK

KITALE ●

EWASO NG'IRO

LAK DERA

BUN PLAINS

ELDORET ●

NZOIA

LAKE BARINGO

ISOLO ●

KAKAMEGA ●

NANYUKI ●

MOUNT KENYA NATIONAL PARK ▲

GARISSA ●

KISUMU ■

NAKURU ●

KIRINYAGA 5 199 ▲

TANA

RUSING I.
MFANGANO

KERICHO ●

LAKE NAKURU

LAKE NAKURU NATIONAL PARK

NYERI ●

EMBU ●

OLAMBWE VALLEY GAME RESERVE ▲

ABERDARE NATIONAL PARK ▲

LAKE VICTORIA

MARA

LAKE NAIVASHA

THIKA ●

OL DOINYO SAPUK NATIONAL PARK ▲

THOWA

NAIROBI ■ ✈

NAIROBI NATIONAL PARK ▲

LAKE MAGADI

YATTA PLATEAU

TIVA

PATE ISLAND

MANDA ISLAND

AMBOSELI NATIONAL PARK ▲
LAKE AMBOSELI

TSAVO EAST NATIONAL PARK ▲

UNGAMA BAY

GALANA

TSAVO WEST NATIONAL PARK ▲

MALINDI ●

TANZANIA

MOMBASSA ■

INDIAN OCEAN

PEMBA CHANNEL

TANGA ■

Official name:	Jamhuri ya Kenya
Capital:	Nairobi
Population:	27.4 million
Surface area:	580,367 km²
Currency:	Kenyan Shilling
Languages:	Swahili, Kikuyu, English
GDP per head:	$ 320
Life expectancy:	58 years

UGANDA

KAGITUMBA

RUHENGERI

PARC DES BIRUNGU

BYUMBA

PARC NATIONAL DE L'AKAGERA

GISENYI

LAKE KIVU

RWANDA

MURAMBI

KIBUYE

KIGALI

RWAMAGANA

GISHYITA

KIBUNGO

BUNYAMBILI

CYANGUGU

GIKONGORO

BUTARE

NGOZI

MAYINGA

BURUNDI

BUBANZA

MUYAGA

DEMOCRATIC REPUBLIC OF CONGO

MURAMVYA

TANZANIA

BUJUMBURA

GITEGA

KIBUMBU

RUYIGI

KIBUYE

MATANA

BURURI

RUTANA

MAKAMBA

NYANZA-LAC

LAKE TANGANYIKA

LAKE VICTORIA

KAGERA

AKAGERA

RUVUBU

MALAGARASI

Official name: Républika y' uRwanda
Capital: Kigali
Population: 6.7 million
Surface area: 26,338 km²
Currency: Rwanda Franc
Languages: Kinyarwanda, French, English
GDP per head: $ 190
Life expectancy: 41 years

Official name: Républika y' Uburundi
Capital: Bujumbura
Population: 6.4 million
Surface area: 27,834 km²
Currency: Burundi Franc
Languages: Kirundi, French
GDP per head: $ 170
Life expectancy: 47 years

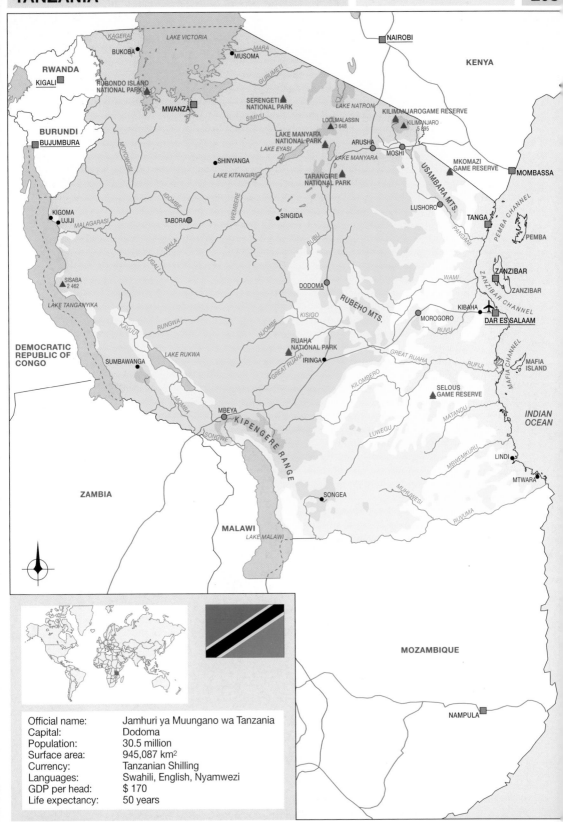

RWANDA
KIGALI

BURUNDI
BUJUMBURA

DEMOCRATIC
REPUBLIC OF
CONGO

ZAMBIA

MALAWI

LAKE VICTORIA
KAGERA
BUKOBA
MUSOMA
MARA
NAIROBI
KENYA

RUBONDO ISLAND
NATIONAL PARK
MWANZA
SERENGETI
NATIONAL PARK
GURUMETI
SIMIYU
LAKE NATRON
KILIMANJAROGAME RESERVE
KILIMANJARO
5 895

LOOLMALASSIN
3 648
LAKE MANYARA
NATIONAL PARK
LAKE EYASI
ARUSHA
MOSHI

SHINYANGA
LAKE MANYARA
MOYOWOSI
LAKE KITANGIRI
MKOMAZI
GAME RESERVE
MOMBASSA

TARANGIRE
NATIONAL PARK
IGOMBE
WEMBERE
USAMBARA MTS.
PEMBA CHANNEL

KIGOMA
UJIJI
MALAGARASI
TABORA
SINGIDA
WALA
BUBU
LUSHORO
PANGANI
TANGA
PEMBA

UGALLA
SISABA
2 462
KAVUU
DODOMA
RUBEHO MTS.
KISIGO
WAMI
ZANZIBAR
ZANZIBAR CHANNEL
ZANZIBAR

LAKE TANGANYIKA
RUNGWA
NJOMBE
MOROGORO
RUVU
KIBAHA
DAR ES SALAAM

SUMBAWANGA
LAKE RUKWA
RUAHA
NATIONAL PARK
GREAT RUAHA
IRINGA
GREAT RUAHA
RUFIJI
MAFIA
CHANNEL
MAFIA
ISLAND

MBEYA
KIPENGERE RANGE
MOMBA
ISONGWE
KILOMBERO
SELOUS
GAME RESERVE
MATANDU
INDIAN
OCEAN

SONGEA
LUWEGU
MBWEMKURU
LINDI
MTWARA

MALAWI
LAKE MALAWI
MUHUWESI
RUVUMA

MOZAMBIQUE

NAMPULA

Official name:	Jamhuri ya Muungano wa Tanzania
Capital:	Dodoma
Population:	30.5 million
Surface area:	945,087 km²
Currency:	Tanzanian Shilling
Languages:	Swahili, English, Nyamwezi
GDP per head:	$ 170
Life expectancy:	50 years

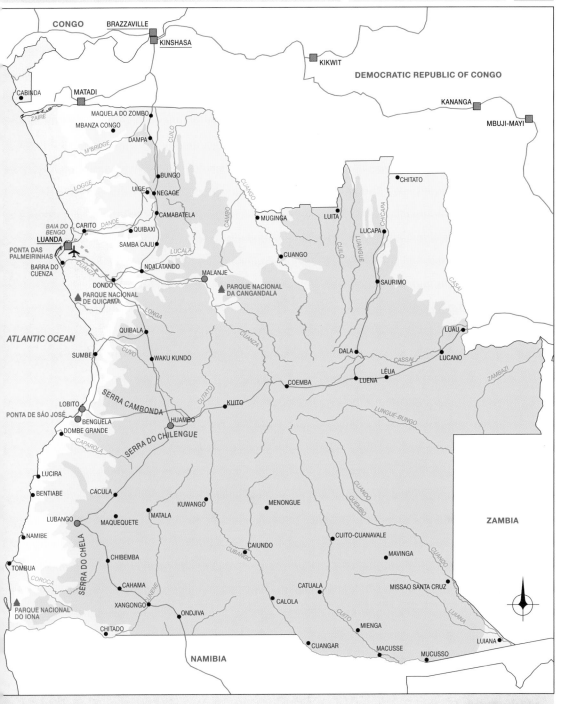

CONGO
BRAZZAVILLE
KINSHASA
KIKWIT
DEMOCRATIC REPUBLIC OF CONGO
KANANGA
MBUJI-MAYI
CABINDA
MATADI
MAQUELA DO ZOMBO
MBANZA CONGO
DAMPA
ZAIRE
CUILO
CHITATO
M'BRIDGE
BUNGO
LOGGE
UIGE
NEGAGE
CAMABATELA
CUANGO
CAMBO
MUGINGA
LUITA
LUCAPA
CHICAPA
CARITO
DANDE
QUIBAXI
BAIA DO BENGO
LUANDA
SAMBA CAJU
LUCALA
CUANGO
LUANGUE
PONTA DAS PALMEIRINHAS
NDALATANDO
CUILO
SAURIMO
CASSAI
BARRA DO CUENZA
MALANJE
DONDO
CUANZA
PARQUE NACIONAL DE QUICAMA
PARQUE NACIONAL DA CANGANDALA
LONGA
LUAU
QUIBALA
CUANZA
DALA
ATLANTIC OCEAN
CUVO
LUCANO
SUMBE
WAKU KUNDO
CASSAI
ZAMBEZI
COEMBA
LÉUA
LUENA
SERRA CAMBONDA
CURATO
KUITO
LOBITO
HUAMBO
LUNGUE-BUNGO
PONTA DE SÃO JOSÉ
BENGUELA
SERRA DO CHILENGUE
DOMBE GRANDE
CAPAROLA
LUCIRA
CACULA
KUWANGO
MENONGUE
CUANDO
BENTIABE
MATALA
QUEMBO
LUBANGO
MAQUEQUETE
CUITO-CUANAVALE
NAMIBE
CAIUNDO
MAVINGA
CUANDO
CHIBEMBA
SERRA DO CHELA
CUBANGO
CATUALA
MISSAO SANTA CRUZ
TOMBUA
CAHAMA
CALOLA
COROCA
CUNENE
XANGONGO
ONDJIVA
CUITO
MIENGA
LUIANA
CHITADO
CUANGAR
MACUSSE
LUIANA
MUCUSSO
NAMIBIA
ZAMBIA

Official name: Republica Popular de Angola
Capital: Luanda
Population: 11.1 million
Surface area: 1,246,700 km²
Currency: Kwanza
Language: Portuguese
GDP per head: $ 270
Life expectancy: 46 years

Official name:	Republic of Zambia
Capital:	Lusaka
Population:	9.2 million
Surface area:	752,614 km²
Currency:	Kwacha
Language:	English, Bemba
GDP per head:	$ 360
Life expectancy:	44 years

TANZANIA

DEMOCRATIC REPUBLIC OF CONGO

MOZAMBIQUE

MALAWI

MOZAMBIQUE

ZIMBABWE

ANGOLA

NAMIBIA

BOTSWANA

LAKE MALAWI

LAKE TANGANYIKA

LAKE MWERU

LAKE BANGWEULU

LAKE KARIBA

LILONGWE

BLANTYRE

CHIPATA

HARARE

CHITUNGWIZA

KASAMA

MANSA

SOLWESI

LIKASI

LULUMBASHI

CHILILABOMBWE

CHINGOLA

MUFULIRA

KITWE

KALULUSHI

NDOLA

LUANSHYA

KABWE

LUSAKA

LIVINGSTONE

MONGU

MWERU WANTIPA NATIONAL PARK

SUMBU NATIONAL PARK

LUSENGA PLAIN NATIONAL PARK

ISANGANG NATIONAL PARK

LAVUSHU MANDA NATIONAL PARK

KASANKA NATIONAL PARK

NORTH LUANGWA NATIONAL PARK

SOUTH LUANGWA NATIONAL PARK

LUKUSUZI NATIONAL PARK

BLUE LAGOON NATIONAL PARK

LOCHINVAR NATIONAL PARK

KAFUE NATIONAL PARK

LIUWA NATIONAL PARK

SIOMA NGWEZE NATIONAL PARK

MUCHINGA MOUNTAINS

MUCHINGA ESCARPMENT

LUANGWA

ZAMBEZE

ZAMBEZE

KAFUE

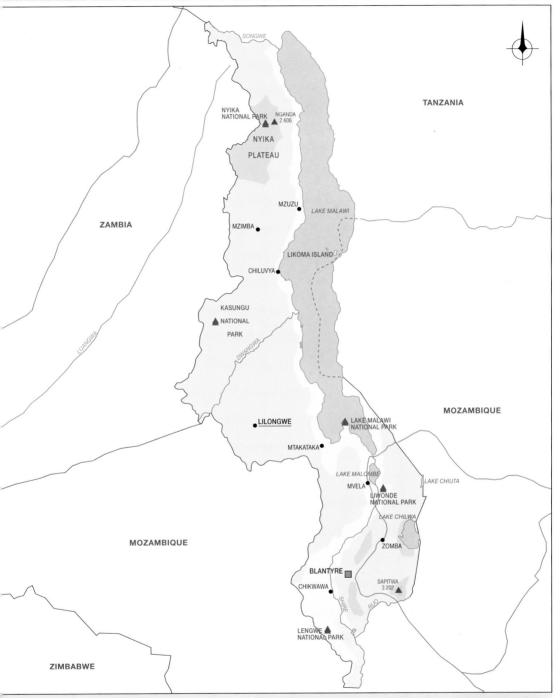

TANZANIA

SONGWE

NYIKA
NATIONAL PARK

NGANDA
2 606

NYIKA
PLATEAU

MZUZU

LAKE MALAWI

ZAMBIA

MZIMBA

LIKOMA ISLAND

CHILUVYA

LUANGWA

KASUNGU
NATIONAL
PARK

DWANGWA

MOZAMBIQUE

LILONGWE

LAKE MALAWI
NATIONAL PARK

MTAKATAKA

LAKE MALOMBE

LAKE CHIUTA

MVELA

LIWONDE
NATIONAL PARK

MOZAMBIQUE

LAKE CHILWA

ZOMBA

BLANTYRE

CHIKWAWA

SAPITWA
3 202

SHIRE RUO

LENGWE
NATIONAL PARK

ZIMBABWE

Official name:	Republic of Malawi
Capital:	Lilongwe
Population:	10.0 million
Surface area:	118,484 km²
Currency:	Kwacha
Languages:	English, Chichewa
GDP per head:	$ 180
Life expectancy:	43 years

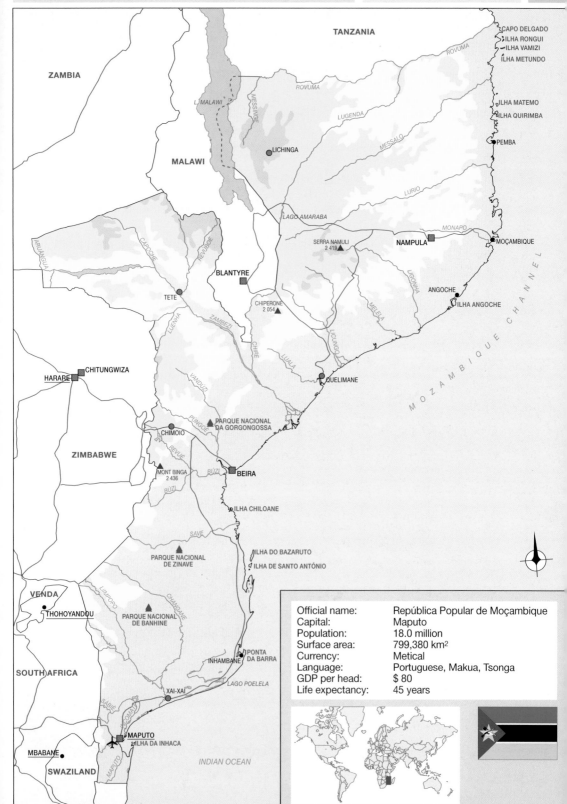

ZAMBIA

TANZANIA

CAPO DELGADO
ILHA RONGUI
ILHA VAMIZI
ÎLHA METUNDO

ROVUMA

ROVUMA

MESSINGE

L. MALAWI

LUGENDA

ILHA MATEMO
ILHA QUIRIMBA

MESSALO

MALAWI

LICHINGA

LURIO

PEMBA

LAGO AMARABA

MONAPO

SERRA NAMULI
2 418

NAMPULA

MOÇAMBIQUE

CAPOCHE

REVUBUE

BLANTYRE

CHIPERONE
2 054

LIGONHA

MELELA

ANGOCHE
ILHA ANGOCHE

TETE

ZAMBEZI

LUGENA

CHIRE

LUALA

LICUNGO

MOZAMBIQUE CHANNEL

VANDUZI

QUELIMANE

HARARE

CHITUNGWIZA

PUNGOE

PARQUE NACIONAL
DA GORGONGOSSA

CHIMOIO

REVUE

ZIMBABWE

MONT BINGA
2 436

BUZI

BEIRA

BUZI

ILHA CHILOANE

SAVE

PARQUE NACIONAL
DE ZINAVE

ILHA DO BAZARUTO
ILHA DE SANTO ANTÓNIO

VENDA

LIMPOPO

CHANGANE

PARQUE NACIONAL
DE BANHINE

THOHOYANDOU

PONTA
DA BARRA

INHAMBANE

SOUTH AFRICA

LAGO POELELA

XAI-XAI

SÁBIE

MAPUTO
ILHA DA INHACA

MBABANE

MAPUTO

SWAZILAND

INDIAN OCEAN

Official name:	República Popular de Moçambique
Capital:	Maputo
Population:	18.0 million
Surface area:	799,380 km²
Currency:	Metical
Language:	Portuguese, Makua, Tsonga
GDP per head:	$ 80
Life expectancy:	45 years

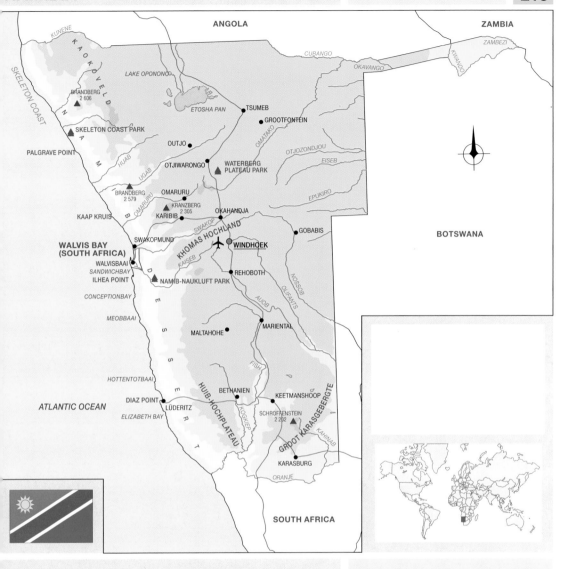

ANGOLA

ZAMBIA

KUNENE

CUBANGO

ZAMBEZI

K A O K O V E L D

OKAVANGO

KWANDO

LAKE OPONONO

SKELETON COAST

BRANDBERG
2 606

ETOSHA PAN

TSUMEB

GROOTFONTEIN

N

SKELETON COAST PARK

OUTJO

OMATAKO

PALGRAVE POINT

A

HUAB

OTJIWARONGO

WATERBERG
PLATEAU PARK

OTJOZONDJOU

EISEB

UGAB

BRANDBERG
2 579

OMARURU

M

OMARURU

KRANZBERG
2 305

OKAHANDJA

EPUKIRO

KAAP KRUIS

B

KARIBIB

SWAKOP

GOBABIS

BOTSWANA

SWAKOPMUND

KHOMAS HOCHLAND

WINDHOEK

WALVIS BAY
(SOUTH AFRICA)

KAISEB

WALVISBAAI

SANDWICHBAY
ILHEA POINT

REHOBOTH

D

NAMIB-NAUKLUFT PARK

NOSSOB

OLIFANTS

CONCEPTIONBAY

E

MEOBBAAI

S

AUOB

MALTAHOHE

MARIENTAL

S

FISH

ATLANTIC OCEAN

E

HOTTENTOTBAAI

HUIB-HOCHPLATEAU

BETHANIEN

KEETMANSHOOP

R

DIAZ POINT

LÜDERITZ

GROOT KARASGEBERGTE

ELIZABETH BAY

KOGKIEP

SCHROFFENSTEIN
2 202

KAHINAB

T

KARASBURG

ORANJE

SOUTH AFRICA

SANTO ANTÃO

POMBAS

ILHAS DE BARLAVENTO

MINDELO

PEDRA LUME

SÃO VICENTE

VILA DA RIBEIRA BRAVA

SAL

SÃO NICOLAU

BOA VISTA

JOÃO BARROSA

ATLANTIC OCEAN

MAIO

TARRAFAL

MAIO

FOGO

SANTIAGO

PRAIA

SÃO FILIPE

ILHAS DE SOTAVENTO

Official name:	Namibia
Capital:	Windhoek
Population:	1.6 million
Surface area:	824,292 km²
Currency:	Rand
Languages:	English, Afrikaans, German
GDP per head:	$ 2,250
Life expectancy:	56 years

ZAMBIA

ANGOLA

ZIMBABWE

KWANDO
LINYATI
CHOBE
KASANE
KASIOKA
KAVIMBA
CHOBE
NATIONAL PARK
PANDAMATENGA

SHAKAWE
DUMA
KAKOAKA
KUMBA PITS

OKAVANGO
SEPOPA

SHALESHANTO
GCOVEREGA

GERUFA

GUMARE
OKAVANGO
NGIGHA
DELTA
KROMBI PITS

NOKAHENG
THAOGE
RANWANALENAUS
MATLAMANYANE
TSEKANYANI

NXAINXAI
MAUN
KANYU
ODIAKWE
MAITENGWE

NHABE
BOTETI
TOTENG
MAKALAMABEDI
GWETA
NATA

SEHITHWA
EISEB
LAKE NGAMI
KHASEBAKE
NTWETWE PAN
MOSETSE
KALAKAMATE

MABELEAPODI
ODANAKUMADONA
SOWA PAN
FRANCISTOWN

NAMIBIA
RAKOPS
XHUMO
MOPIPI
LAKE XAU
TONOTA
OLD TATE
SHASHE

GHANZI
LETIHAKENE
MOTLOUTSE
MMADINARE
MOTIOUTSE

MUMUNGWE
SERULE
SELEBI PHIKWE
BOBONONG

MAMUNO
KALKFONTEIN
SEROWE
PALAPYE
LOTSANE

OKWA
TSHWAANE
TSUKUDU
MAUNATLALA

TAKACHU
LIMPOPO

KULE
KHOMODIMO
MAHALATSWE
SETARE

TIAPENG
MATAPA
QUOXO
MACHANENG

MANYANA
KANG
LEPHEPE
DINOKWE

K A L A H A R I   D E S E R T
METSSEMATLUKU
DIBETE
PHALA

LEHUTUTU
DUTIWE
MOSOMANE

HUKUNTSI
TSHANE
KOKONG
LETIHAKENG
MOCHUDI

MOLEPOLOLE
GABORONE

SEKOMA
MOSOPA

KHAKHEA
RAMOTSWA

MOOKANE
KANYE
OOSTI

WEIRDA
MOSELEBE
LOBATSE

RAMATHLABAMA

GEMSBOK
NATIONAL PARK
PRETORIA

NOSOP
MARALALENG
MOLOPO
MMBATHO

TSHABONG
JOHANNESBURG
BENONI
SPRINGS

SOWETO
GER-
MISTON

KHUIS
MOLOPO
VEREENIGING

SOUTH AFRICA

Official name:	Republic of Botswana
Capital:	Gaborone
Population:	1.5 million
Surface area:	581,730 km²
Currency:	Pula
Language:	English, Setwana
GDP per head:	$ 3,115
Life expectancy:	51 years

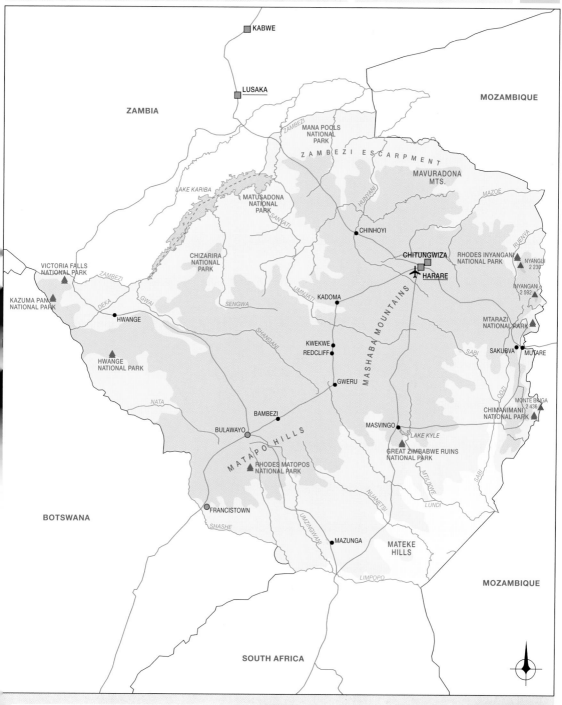

KABWE

LUSAKA

ZAMBIA

MOZAMBIQUE

MANA POOLS
NATIONAL
PARK

Z A M B E Z I   E S C A R P M E N T

ZAMBEZI

MAVURADONA
MTS.

MAZOE

LAKE KARIBA

MATUSADONA
NATIONAL
PARK

SANYATI

HUNYANI

CHINHOYI

RUENYA

CHIZARIRA
NATIONAL
PARK

CHITUNGWIZA
HARARE

RHODES INYANGANI
NATIONAL PARK

NYANGUI
2 230

VICTORIA FALLS
NATIONAL PARK

ZAMBEZI

INYANGANI
2 592

KAZUMA PAN
NATIONAL PARK

DEKA

GWAI

HWANGE

UMNIATI

KADOMA

SENGWA

M
A
S
H
A
B
A

M
O
U
N
T
A
I
N
S

MTARAZI
NATIONAL PARK

HWANGE
NATIONAL PARK

SHANGANI

KWEKWE
REDCLIFF

SABI

SAKUBVA

MUTARE

GWERU

NATA

BAMBEZI

BULAWAYO

QODZI

M
A
T
A
P
O
   H
I
L
L
S

RHODES MATOPOS
NATIONAL PARK

MASVINGO

LAKE KYLE

GREAT ZIMBABWE RUINS
NATIONAL PARK

MONTE BINGA
2 436

CHIMANIMANI
NATIONAL PARK

SABI

BOTSWANA

SHASHE

UMZINGWANI

MAZUNGA

NUANETSI

MTILIKWE

LUNDI

MATEKE
HILLS

FRANCISTOWN

MOZAMBIQUE

LIMPOPO

SOUTH AFRICA

Official name:	Republic of Zimbabwe
Capital:	Harare
Population:	11.2 million
Surface area:	390,757 km²
Currency:	Zimbabwe Dollar
Languages:	English, Shona, Ndebele
GDP per head:	$ 610
Life expectancy:	56 years

SOUTH AFRICA / LESOTHO / SWAZILAND

Official name:	Republic of South Africa
Capital:	Pretoria/Cape Town
Population:	37.6 million
Surface area:	1,219,080 km²
Currency:	Rand
Languages:	Afrikaans, English
GDP per head:	$ 3,520
Life expectancy:	65 years

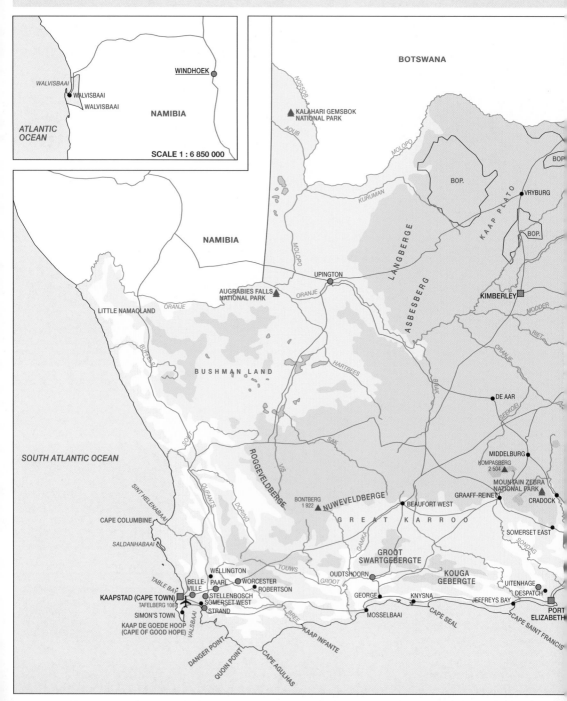

BOTSWANA

WINDHOEK

WALVISBAAI

WALVISBAAI
WALVISBAAI

ATLANTIC
OCEAN

NAMIBIA

SCALE 1 : 6 850 000

NOSSOB

KALAHARI GEMSBOK
NATIONAL PARK

AQUB

MOLOPO

NAMIBIA

BOP.

KAAP PLATO

VRYBURG

BOP.

KURUMAN

LANGBERGE

MOLOPO

UPINGTON

ORANJE

AUGRABIES FALLS
NATIONAL PARK

ASBESBERG

KIMBERLEY

MODDER

LITTLE NAMAQLAND

ORANJE

ORANJE

RIET

BUFFELS

BUSHMAN LAND

HARTBEES

BRAK

SOUTH ATLANTIC OCEAN

SOUT

SAK

VIS

DE AAR

SEEKOEI

ROGGEVELDBERGE

MIDDELBURG

KOMPASBERG
2 504

MOUNTAIN ZEBRA
NATIONAL PARK

OLIFANTS

DORING

BONTBERG
1 922

NUWEVELDBERGE

BEAUFORT WEST

GRAAFF-REINET

CRADOCK

SINT HELENABAAI

CAPE COLUMBINE

GREAT KARROO

SOMERSET EAST

SONDAG

SALDANHABAAI

GAMKA

GROOT
SWARTGEBERGTE

KOUGA
GEBERGTE

UITENHAGE

DESPATCH

WELLINGTON

TOUWS

OUDTSHOORN

PORT
ELIZABETH

TABLE BAAI

BELLE-
VILLE

PAARL

WORCESTER

GROOT

GEORGE

KNYSNA

JEFFREYS BAY

CAPE SAINT FRANCIS

KAAPSTAD (CAPE TOWN)

ROBERTSON

STELLENBOSCH

SOMERSET WEST

MOSSELBAAI

CAPE SEAL

TAFELBERG 1087

SIMON'S TOWN

STRAND

BREE

KAAP DE GOEDE HOOP
(CAPE OF GOOD HOPE)

VALSBAAI

DANGER POINT

KAAP INFANTE

QUOIN POINT

CAPE AGULHAS

ZIMBABWE

BOTSWANA

MOZAMBIQUE

MESSINA

VENDA

BLOUBERG
▲ 2 051
THOHOYANDOU

SOUTPANS
BERG

KRUGER
NATIONAL PARK ▲

PIETERSBURG

WATERBERGE

T R A N S V A A L

ABORONE

MARICO

KROKODIL

BOP.

BOPHUTHATSWANA
(BOP.)

BOP.

BOP.

ELANDS

DIE BERG
2 331 ▲

SABIÉ

NELSPRUIT

DRAKENSBERG

OLIFANTS

MMBATHO

RUSTENBURG

BRITS

PRETORIA

MIDDELBURG

KROKODIL

BARBERTON

MAPUTO

BOP.

KRUGERSDORP
CARLETONVILLE
POTCHEFSTROOM
KLERKSDORP

JOHANNESBURG
SOWETO
GER-
MISTON
VEREENIGING
STILFONTEIN

BENONI
SPRINGS
NIGEL
HEIDELBERG
VANDERBIJLPARK

WITBANK

BETHAL

KOMATI

BHUNYA

TSHANENI

MBABANE
MANZINI

SWAZILAND

ERMELO

ORKNEY
PARYS
SASOLBURG

STANDERTON

PIET
RETIEF

NHLANGANO

KOSIMEER

ODENDAALSRUS
WELKOM
VIRGINIA

VALS

KROONSTAD

BETHLEHEM

VOLKSRUST

NEW CASTLE

BUFFALO

VRYHEID

PONGOLO

SIBAYI

WILGE

GLENCOE
DUNDEE

DRAKENSBERG

LAKE SAINT LUCIA

GOLDEN GATE HIGHLANDS
NATIONAL PARK

HARRISMITH

LADYSMITH

Z U L U L A N D

MIOLOZI

CAPE SAINT LUCIA

INDIAN OCEAN

LOEMFONTEIN

BOP.

COLEDON

HLOTSE
TEYATEYANENG
MASERU
MOKHOFLONG

ROYAL NATAL
NATIONAL PARK
E NJESUTHI
3 446
THABANA
NTLENYANA
3482

GIANT'S CASTLE
3 313

ESTCOURT

HOWICK

STANGER

RICHARD'S BAY

TUGELA

TONGAAT

MORIJA
MAFETENG

L E S O T H O

EDENDALE

PIETERMARITZBURG

MOHALES HOEK

PINETOWN
MARIANHILL

DURBAN

ZASTRON

ORANJE

TRANSKEI

TRANSKEI

KOKSTAD

ALIWAL NORTH
STORMBERG ▲
2 099

UMTATA

TRANSKEI

QUEENSTOWN

SUTTERHEIM

D R A K E N S B E R G

W I L D   C O A S T

FORT
BEAUFORT
GROOT VIS
RAHAMSTOWN

BISHO
KING
WILLIAM'S TOWN
CISKEI

EAST LONDON

LGOABAAI

Official name:	Kingdom of Swaziland
Capital:	Mbabane
Population:	0.9 million
Surface area:	17,363 km²
Currency:	Emalangeni
Languages:	Swazi (Siswati), English
GDP per head:	$ 1,210
Life expectancy:	57 years

Official name:	Kingdom of Lesotho
Capital:	Maseru
Population:	2.0 million
Surface area:	30,355 km²
Currency:	Loti
Languages:	Sesotho, English, Zulu
GDP per head:	$ 660
Life expectancy:	58 years

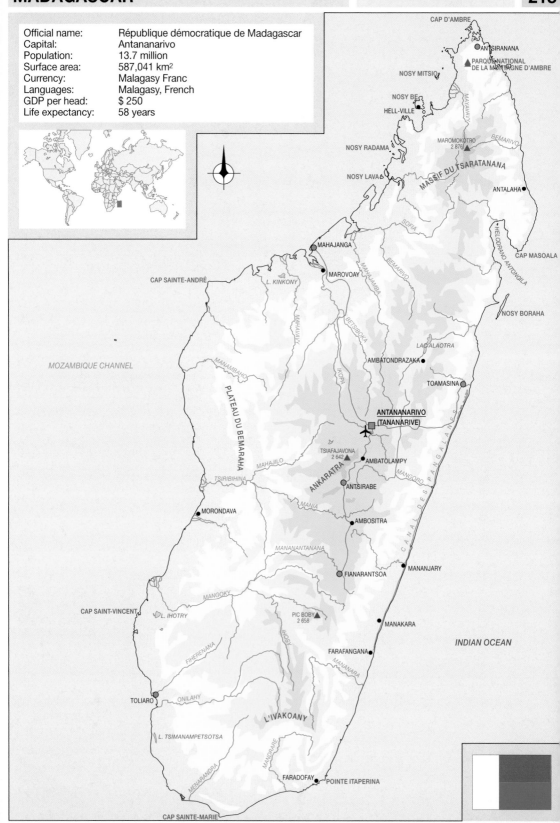

Official name:	République démocratique de Madagascar
Capital:	Antananarivo
Population:	13.7 million
Surface area:	587,041 km²
Currency:	Malagasy Franc
Languages:	Malagasy, French
GDP per head:	$ 250
Life expectancy:	58 years

CAP D'AMBRE

ANTSIRANANA

NOSY MITSIO

PARQUE NATIONAL
DE LA MONTAGNE D'AMBRE

NOSY BE

HELL-VILLE

MAROMOKOTRO
2 876

MASSIF DU TSARATANANA

BEMARIVO

NOSY RADAMA

ANTALAHA

NOSY LAVA

CAP MASOALA

MAHAJANGA

MAROVOAY

L. KINKONY

CAP SAINTE-ANDRÉ

NOSY BORAHA

MOZAMBIQUE CHANNEL

MANAMBAHO

PLATEAU DU BEMARAHA

MAHAVAVY

BETSIBOKA

BEMARIVO

MAHAJAMBA

SOFIA

IKOPA

LAC ALAOTRA

AMBATONDRAZAKA

TOAMASINA

ANTANANARIVO
(TANANARIVE)

TSIAFAJAVONA
2 642

ANKARATRA

AMBATOLAMPY

ANTSIRABE

MAHAJILO

TSIRIBIHINA

MANIA

MORONDAVA

AMBOSITRA

MANANANTANANA

MANGORO

CANAL DES PANGALANES

FIANARANTSOA

MANANJARY

MANGOKY

CAP SAINT-VINCENT

L. IHOTRY

PIC BOBY
2 658

MANAKARA

INDIAN OCEAN

IHOSY

FIHERENANA

FARAFANGANA

MANANARA

TOLIARO

ONILAHY

L'IVAKOANY

L. TSIMANAMPETSOTSA

MENARANDRA

MANDRARE

FARADOFAY

POINTE ITAPERINA

CAP SAINTE-MARIE

COMOROS

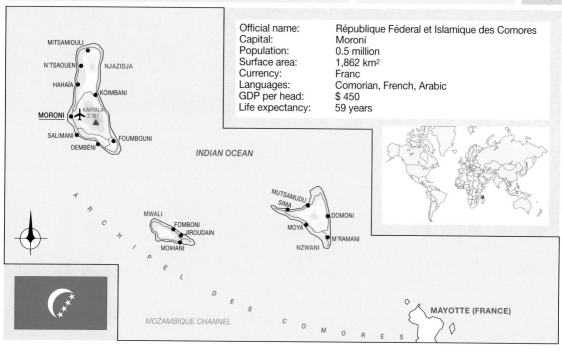

Official name:	République Féderal et Islamique des Comores
Capital:	Moroni
Population:	0.5 million
Surface area:	1,862 km²
Currency:	Franc
Languages:	Comorian, French, Arabic
GDP per head:	$ 450
Life expectancy:	59 years

MITSAMIOULI
N'TSAOUEN   NJAZIDJA
HAHAÏA   KOIMBANI
MORONI   KARTALA 2 361
SALIMANI   FOUMBOUNI
DEMBÉNI

INDIAN OCEAN

ARCHIPEL DES COMORES

MWALI
FOMBONI
JIROUDAIN
MOIHANI

MUTSAMUDU
SIMA
DOMONI
MOYA   M'RAMANI
NZWANI

MOZAMBIQUE CHANNEL

MAYOTTE (FRANCE)

SEYCHELLES

SCALE 1 : 12 000 000

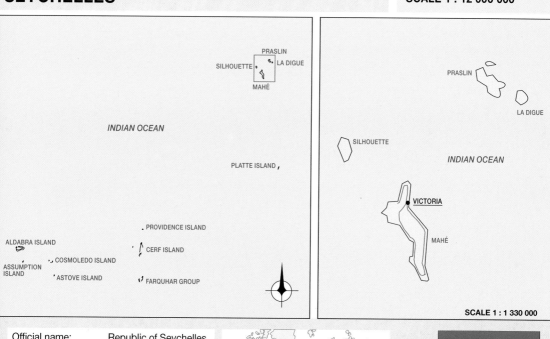

PRASLIN
SILHOUETTE   LA DIGUE
MAHÉ

INDIAN OCEAN

PLATTE ISLAND

PROVIDENCE ISLAND
ALDABRA ISLAND   CERF ISLAND
COSMOLEDO ISLAND
ASSUMPTION ISLAND   ASTOVE ISLAND   FARQUHAR GROUP

PRASLIN
LA DIGUE
SILHOUETTE   INDIAN OCEAN
VICTORIA
MAHÉ

SCALE 1 : 1 330 000

Official name:	Republic of Seychelles
Capital:	Victoria
Population:	77,000
Surface area:	454 km²
Currency:	Seychelle Rupee
Languages:	Creole, English, French
GDP per head:	$ 6,850
Life expectancy:	71 years

REUNION

SCALE 1 : 810 000

MAURITIUS

SCALE 1 : 950 000

REUNION

INDIAN OCEAN

SAINT-DENIS
LA POSSESSION
LE PORT
LE BRÛLÉ
STE-MARIE
STE-SUZANNE
ST-PAUL
GRAND-ÎLET
CÔTE AU VENT
SALAZIE
STE-ANDRÉ
ST-GILLES-LES-BAINS
PITON DES NEIGES 3 069
CILAOS
TROIS-BASSINS
GRAND BÉNARD 2 896
CÔTE SOUS LE VENT
ST-LEU
LES AVIRONS
ENTRE-DEUX
ETANG-SALÉ
ST-LOUIS
ST-PIERRE
TERRE-SAINTE
LE TAMPON
STE-BENOÎT
PITON DE LA FOURNAISE 2 508
STE-ROSE
ST-PHILIPPE
ST. JOSEPH

Official name: Réunion
Capital: Saint-Denis
Population: 0.64 million
Surface area: 2,512 km²
Currency: French Franc
Languages: French, Creole, Gujarati
GDP per head: $ 9,386
Life expectancy: 72 years

MAURITIUS

INDIAN OCEAN

ÎLE D'AMBRE
CAP MALHEUREUX
GRAND BAIE
TRIOLET
MAPOU
PAMPLEMOUSSE
BELLE VUE MAUREL
CENTRE DE FLACQ
PORT LOUIS
QUATIER MILITAIRE
QUATRE BORNES
CUREPIPE
TAMARIN
PITON DE LA PETITE RIVIÈRE NOIRE 828
MAHÉBOURG
RIVIÈRE DES ANGUILLES
CHAMOUNY

Official name: State of Mauritius
Capital: Port Louis
Population: 1.1 million
Surface area: 2,040 km²
Currency: Mauritius Rupee
Languages: English, Creole, Hind
GDP per head: $ 3,710
Life expectancy: 71 years

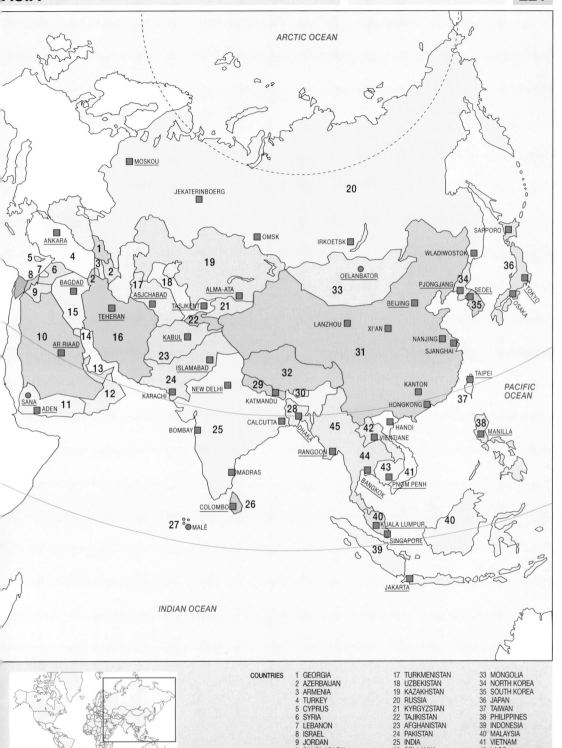

ARCTIC OCEAN

MOSKOU

JEKATERINBOERG

20

OMSK

IRKOETSK

ANKARA

1

4

5

7

6

8

9

BAGDAD

2

17

18

ALMA-ATA

19

ASJCHABAD

TASJKENT

21

15

TEHERAN

22

10

14

16

KABUL

AR RIAAD

23

ISLAMABAD

13

24

NEW DELHI

29

KARACHI

KATMANDU

30

12

28

SANA

ADEN

11

BOMBAY

25

CALCUTTA

DHAKA

RANGOON

MADRAS

COLOMBO

26

27

MALÉ

OELANBATOR

33

WLADIWOSTOK

SAPPORO

36

PJONGJANG

34

SEOEL

TOKYO

35

OSAKA

BEIJING

LANZHOU

XI'AN

NANJING

SJANGHAI

31

KANTON

HONGKONG

TAIPEI

37

PACIFIC OCEAN

32

45

HANOI

42

VIENTIANE

44

43

41

BANGKOK

PNØM PENH

38

MANILLA

40

KUALA LUMPUR

40

SINGAPORE

39

JAKARTA

INDIAN OCEAN

COUNTRIES		
1 GEORGIA	17 TURKMENISTAN	33 MONGOLIA
2 AZERBAIJAN	18 UZBEKISTAN	34 NORTH KOREA
3 ARMENIA	19 KAZAKHSTAN	35 SOUTH KOREA
4 TURKEY	20 RUSSIA	36 JAPAN
5 CYPRUS	21 KYRGYZSTAN	37 TAIWAN
6 SYRIA	22 TAJIKISTAN	38 PHILIPPINES
7 LEBANON	23 AFGHANISTAN	39 INDONESIA
8 ISRAEL	24 PAKISTAN	40 MALAYSIA
9 JORDAN	25 INDIA	41 VIETNAM
10 SAUDI-ARABIA	26 SRI-LANKA	42 LAOS
11 YEMEN	27 MALDIVES	43 CAMBODIA
12 OMAN	28 BANGLADESH	44 THAILAND
13 UNITED ARAB EMIRATES	29 NEPAL	45 MYANAMAR
14 KUWAIT	30 BHUTAN	
15 IRAQ	31 CHINA	
16 IRAN	32 TIBET	

GEORGIA

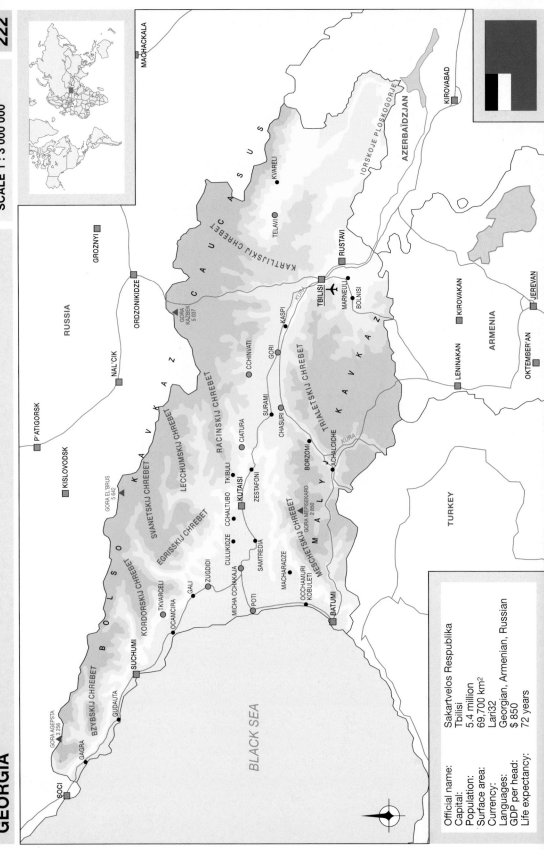

MACHACKALA

KIROVABAD

AZERBAÏDZJAN

IORSKOJE PLOSKOGORJE

KVARELI

TELAVI

KARTLIJSKIJ CHREBET

RUSTAVI

GROZNYJ

RUSSIA

TBILISI

MARNEULI

BOLNISI

KIROVAKAN

ARMENIA

LENINAKAN

OKTEMBER'AN

JEREVAN

ORDZONIKIDZE

GORA KAZBEK
5 037

KASPI

GORI

CCHINVATI

NAL'CIK

KURA

SURAMI

CHASURI

CIATURA

TKIBULI

TRIALE'TSKIJ CHREBET

ACHALCICHE

KURA

BORZOMI

P'ATIGORSK

RACINSKIJ CHREBET

LECCHUMSKIJ CHREBET

KISLOVODSK

GORA EL'BRUS
5 642

K   A   V   K   A   Z

TURKEY

SVANETSKIJ CHREBET

EGRISSKIJ CHREBET

KUTAISI

ZESTAFONI

CCHALTUBO

CULUKIDZE

KORDORSKIJ CHREBET

ZUGDIDI

GORA MEPISEKARO
2 850

M   A   L   Y   J

MESCHETSKIJ CHREBET

SAMTREDIA

MACHARADZE

OCCHAMURI

KOBULETI

BATUMI

B   O   L   S   O   J

TKVARCELI

OCAMCIRA

GALI

MICHA CCHAKAJA

POTI

SUCHUMI

BZYBSKIJ CHREBET

GUDAUTA

GORA AGEPSTA
3 256

GAGRA

SOCI

BLACK SEA

Official name:	Sakartvelos Respublika
Capital:	Tbilisi
Population:	5.4 million
Surface area:	69,700 km^2
Currency:	Lari32
Languages:	Georgian, Armenian, Russian
GDP per head:	$ 850
Life expectancy:	72 years

RUSSIA

Official name:	Rossiyskaya Federatsiya
Capital:	Moscow
Population:	147.8 million
Surface area:	17,075,400 km²
Currency:	Rouble
Language:	Russian, Tatar, Ukrainian
GDP per head:	$ 2,410
Life expectancy:	66 years

SCALE 1 : 37 500 000

1. LITHUANIA
2. LATVIA
3. ESTONIA
4. GEORGIA
5. AZERBAIJAN
6. TURKEY
7. ARMENIA

ARCTIC OCEAN
BERING SEA
ANADYRSKIJ ZALIV
POLUOSTROV KAMCATKA
PETROPAVLOVSK-KAMCATSKIJ
ZALIV SELICHOVA
KORJAKSKOJE NAGORJE
OSREDINNYJ CHREBET
KURIL'SKIJE OSTROVA
JAPAN
SAPPORO
NAGOYA
TOKYO
NORTH KOREA
NACHODKA
VLADIVOSTOK
USSURIJSK
SICHOTE-ALIN
JUZNO-SACHALINSK
OSTROV SACHALIN
TATARSKIJ PROLIV
OCHOTSKOJE MORE
OZERO CHANKA
HARBIN
CHINA
CHABAROVSK
KOMSOMOLSK-NA-AMURE
AMUR
BLAGOVESCENSK
ZEJA
CHREBET DZUGDZUR
STANOVOJ CHREBET
ALDAN
CHREBET CERSKOGO
MAGADAN
KOLYMSKAJA NIZMENNOST
VERCHOJANSKIJ CHREBET
LENA
VILUJ
JAKUTSK
VILUI
CITA
STANOVOJE NAGORJE
ULAN-UDE
IRKUTSK
OZERO BAJKAL
SILKA
ULAANBAATAR
MONGOLIA
VOSTOCNO-SIBIRSKOJE MORE
KOTUJ
NIZNAJA TUNGUSKA
PLATO PUTORANA
SREDNES-SIBIRSKOJE
JENISEJ
BRATSK
KANSK
ACINSK
KRASNOJARSK
ABAKAN
KEMEROVO
NOVOK-UZNECK
BIJSK
BARNAUT
RUBCOVSK
NOVOSIBIRSK
TOMSK
PROKOPJEVSK
UST-KAMENOGORSK
KARAGANDA
OMSK
IRTYS
ISIM
TJUMEN
SURGUT
OB
SEROV
NIZNIJ TAGIL
SVERDLOVSK
CELABINSK
KURGAN
MAGNITOGORSK
ORSK
KAZAKHSTAN
SERVERNAJA ZEML'A
POLUOSTROV TAJMYR
LAPTEV SEA
OSTROVA ANZL
NORIL'SK
OBSKAJA GUBA
KARSKOJE SEA
NOVAJA ZEML'A
BARENTS SEA
OSTROV KOLGUJEV
PECORSKOJE MORE
BELSE MORE
MURMANSK
ARCHANGEL'SK
TIMANSKIJ KRAZ
SYKTYVKAR
KIROV
SOLIKAMSK
PERM
IZEVSK
UFA
URAL'SKIJE GORY
KUJBYSEV
SALAVAT
ORENBURG
NORWAY
SWEDEN
FINLAND
BALTIC SEA
KALININGRAD
ST-PETERSBURG
NOVGOROD
PSKOV
VELIKIJE LUKI
CEREPOVEC
PETROZAVODSK
VOLOGDA
JAROSLAVL
KOSTROMA
IVANOVO
VLADIMIR
GORKIJ
CEBOKSARY
KAZAN
BELORUSSIA
SMOLENSK
KALININ
MOSKVA
TULA
RJAZAN
TAMBOV
SARANSK
PENZAL
ULIANOVSK
BALAKOVO
KAMYSIN
BRANSK
ORJOL
KURSK
LIPECK
VORONEZ
SARATOV
STARYJ OSKOL
BELGOROD
UKRAINE
ROSTOV-NA-DONU
KRASNODAR
SOCI
STAVROPOL'
ARMAVIR
SACHTY
VOLGA
VOLGOGRAD
ASTRACHAN'
CASPIAN SEA
MACHACKALA
GROZNYJ
NAL'CIK
BOLSOJ KAVKAZ
BAKU
AZOVSKOJE MORE
IRAN
UZBEKISTAN

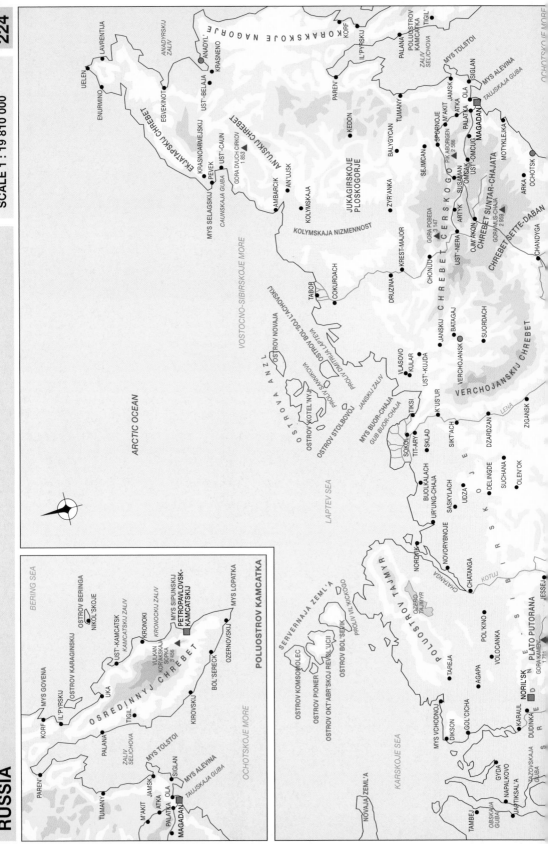

KORJAKSKOJE NAGORJE

KORF

IL'PYRSKIJ

PALANA

POLUOSTROV KAMCATKA

ZALIV SELICHOVA

MYS TOLSTOI

SIGLAN

MYS ALEVINA

TAUJSKAJA GUBA

JAMSK

OLA

ATKA

M'AKIT

PALATKA

MAGADAN

SPORNOJE

USPENSKIJ

MOTYKLEJKA

PIK ABORIGEN 2 586

OMSAK

UST'-OMCUG

OCHOTSK

SUSAMAN

OMGAK

ARKA

ARKAGALA

ANADYL'

ANADYRSKIJ ZALIV

ANADYR

KRASNENO

UST'-BELAJA

PAREN'

TUMANY

BALYGYCAN

SEJMCAN

OJM'AKON

ARTYK

UST'-NERA

GORAMUS-CHAJA 2 959

CHREBET SUNTAR-CHAJATA

CHREBET SETTE-DABAN

CHANDYGA

UELEN

ENURMINO

LAVRENTJA

EGVEKINOT

EKIJTAPSKIJ CHREBET

PEVEK

UST'-CAUN

KRASNOARMEJSKIJ

CAUNSKAJA GUBA

MYS SELAGSKIJ

AMBARCIK

AN'UJSK

GORA DVUCH CIRKOV 1 853

AN'UJSKIJ CHREBET

KOLYMSKAJA

KEDON

ZYR'ANKA

KOLYMSKAJA NIZMENNOST

JUKAGIRSKOJE PLOSKOGORJE

GORA POBEDA 3 147

CHREBET CERSKOGO

KREST-MAJOR

CHONURU

DRUZINA

TABOR

COKURDACH

VOSTOCNO-SIBIRSKOJE MORE

OSTROV NOVAJA

OSTROVA ANZL

OSTROV KOTEL'NYJ

OSTROV DMITRIJA LAPTEVA

PROLIV SANNIKOVA

PROLIV DMITRIJA LAPTEVA

PROLIV BOL'SOJ LJACHOVSKIJ

OSTROV STOLBOVOJ

JANSKIJ ZALIV

MYS BUOR-CHAJA

GUB BUOR-CHAJA

ARCTIC OCEAN

LAPTEV SEA

JANSKIJ

BATAGAJ

VLASOVO

KULAR

UST'-KUJDA

TIKSI

K'USUR

SOKOL

TIT-ARY

SKLAD

SIKT'ACH

VERCHOJANSK

SUORDACH

VERCHOJANSKIJ CHREBET

LENA

DZARDZAN

ZIGANSK

BUOLKALACH

UR'UNG-CHAJA

SASKYLACH

UDZA

DELINGDE

SUCHANA

OLEN'OK

OLEN'OK

NOVORYBNOJE

CHATANGA

CHATANGA

KOTUJ

POLUOSTROV TAJMYR

OZERO TAJMYR

SERVERNAJA ZEML'A

OSTROV KOMSOMOLEC

OSTROV PIONER

OSTROV OKT'ABR'SKOJ REVOL'UCII

OSTROV BOL'SEVIK

PROLIV VIL'KICKOGO

MYS VCHODNOJ

DIKSON

GOLCICHA

KARAUL

DUDINKA

GYDA

NAPALKOVO

JAMTIKSAL'A

OBSKAJA GUBA

TAMBEJ

GAZOVSKOJE

TAREJA

AGAPA

POL'KINO

VOLOCANKA

NORIL'SK

PLATO PUTORANA

GORA KAMEN' 1 701

JESSEJ

NORDVIK

KARSKOJE SEA

NOVAJA ZEML'A

POLUOSTROV KAMCATKA

BERING SEA

OSTROV BERINGA

NIKOL'SKOJE

OSTROV KARAGINSKIJ

UST'-KAMCATK

KAMCATSKIJ ZALIV

KRONOKI

KRONOCKIJ ZALIV

MYS SIPUNSKIJ

PETROPAVLOVSK-KAMCATSKIJ

MYS LOPATKA

OZERNOVSKIJ

KIROVSKIJ

BOL'SERECK

VULKAN KORJAKSKAJA SOPKA 3 456

OSREDINNYJ CHREBET

TIGIL

UKA

PALANA

IL'PYRSKIJ

MYS GOVENA

MYS GOVENA

KORF

PAREN'

TUMANY

M'AKIT

ATKA

PALATA

OLA

SIGLAN

MAGADAN

MYS ALEVINA

TAUJSKAJA GUBA

ZALIV SELICHOVA

MYS TOLSTOI

JAMSK

OCHOTSKOJE MORE

OCHOTSKOJE MORE

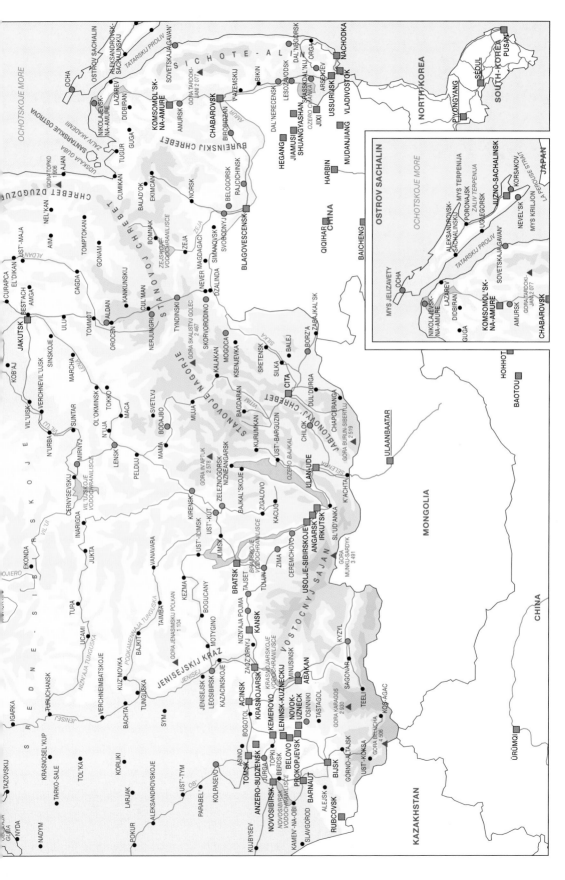

TURKEY

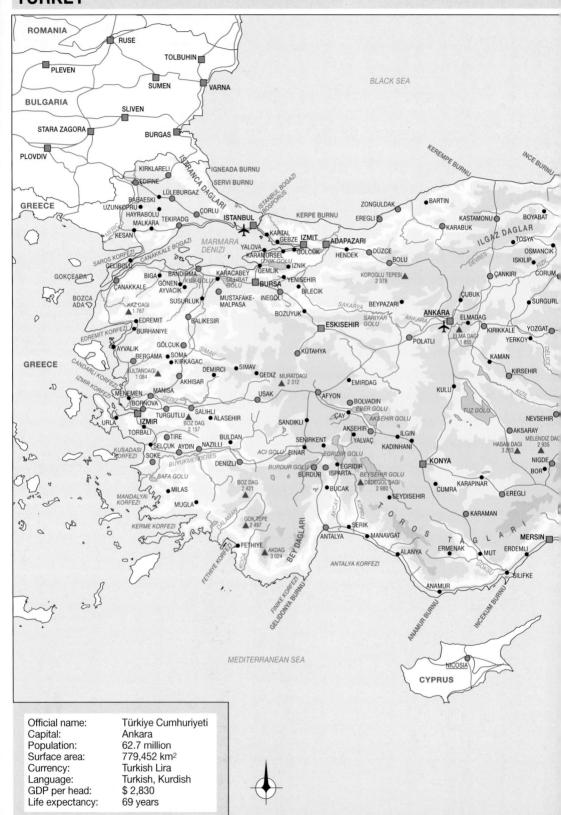

Official name:	Türkiye Cumhuriyeti
Capital:	Ankara
Population:	62.7 million
Surface area:	779,452 km²
Currency:	Turkish Lira
Language:	Turkish, Kurdish
GDP per head:	$ 2,830
Life expectancy:	69 years

RUSSIA

P'ATOGORSK

KISLOVODSK

GROZNYJ

SOCI

NAL'CIK

ORDZONIKIDZE

SUCHUMI

BLACK SEA

KUTAISI

GEORGIA

TBLISI RUSTAVI

BATUMI

AZERBAÏD-ZJAN

SINOP
SINOP BURNU
BAFRA BURNU
SINOP LIMANI

ARSIYAN DAGI
3 165

ÇILDIR GOLU

ARTVIN

KIRSIR DAGI
3 150

KIROVAN

BAFRA

SAMSUN LIMANI

CIVA BURNU

YASUN BURNU

FENER BURNU

RIZE

KARÇKAR DAGI
3 937

DUMANLIDAG
2 699

LENINAKAN

EZIRKOPRU

SAMSUN

TERME

TRABZON

KARS

ARMENIA

ÜMÜSHA-KOY

ÇARSAMBA

UNYE
FATSA

ORDU

TONYA

KIRKLAR DAGI
3 450

DEVE DAGI
3 060

CAMBAR DAGI
2 805

YAGLICA DAGI
2 951

HAVZA

SULUOVA

GIRESUN

HARSIT

ÇAKIRGOL
3 063

MESCIT DAGI
3 255

GÜLLÜ DAGI
2 885

SARIKAMIS
ALADAG
3 138

JEREVAN

MERZIFON

AMASYA

GÜMUSHANE

BAYBURT

AKBABA DAGI
3 069

PASINLER

CORUM

KELKIT

SEBINKARAHISAR

CORUH

ARAS

AGRI DAGI
(MOUNT ARARAT)
5 122

ZILE

TURHAL

TOKAT

YILDIZDAGI
2 537

SUSEHRI

AGRI

IGDIT

AZERBAÏD-ZJAN

ERZINCAN

ERZURUM

KIZIL

KOCBASI
3 510

TENDUREK DAGI
3 533

SIVAS

DIVRIGI

EUPHRATES

SOSAR

SÜPHAN DAGI
4 058

PIRRESIT TEPE
3 195

AKDAGI
2 272

KEBAN GOLU

BINGOL

VAN GOLU

KAYSERI

MURAT

MUS

TATVAN

VAN

IRAN

ELAZIG

BITLIS

ERCIYES DAGI
3 916

HAZAR GOLU

MADEN

DEVELI

MALATYA

ERGANI

BINBOGADAGI
2 856

AFSIN

ELBISTAN

DIYARBAKIR

SIIRT

YAHYALI

ENGIZEK DAGI
2 832

NURHAK DAGI
3090

ADIYAMAN

SIVEREK

BATMAN

MIDYAT

HAKKARI

ORUMIYEH

BUYUKZAB

KOZAN

BESNI

KARACA DAGI
1 919

DERIK

MARDIN

MARAS

KADIRLI

ADANA

CEYHAN

OSMANIYE

URFA

VIRANSEHIR

NUSAYBIN

TARSUS

NIZIP

BIRECIK

KIZILTEPE

GAZIANTEP

DORTYOL

SURUÇ

ISKENDERUN

KILIS

AL-MAWSIL

IRBIL

KIRIKHAN

ISKENDERUN KORFEZI

AMIK GOLU

REYHANLI

ANTAKYA

HALAB

SAMANDÄGI

IRAQ

MEDI-TERRANEAN SEA

AL-LADHIQIYAH

KIRKUK

KARABULUS

SYRIA

HAMAH

LEBANON

HIMS HOMS

BAYRUT

DAMASCUS

TIGRIS DICLE

EUPHRATES

YENICE

ARAS

OTTU

KARS

TBILISI

RUSTAVI

GEORGIA

ALAVERDI

STEPANAGAN

LENINAKAN   SPITAK   KIROVAKAN

GORA TEZLER
▲ 3 101   DILIZAN

KIROVABAD

AZERBAÏDZJAN

ARTIK PEMZASEN

GORA ARAGAC
▲ 4 090

SACHDAGSKIJ CHREBET

P E T I T   C A U C A S E   CARENCAVAN   RAZDAN

OZERO SEVAN

GORA AZDAAK
3 597 ▲

OKTEMBER'AN   ECMIADZIN   JEREVAN

V A R D E N S K I J   C H R E B E T

Araks

TURKEY

Z A N G E Z U P S K I J   C H R E B E T

GORIS

AZERBAÏDZJAN

KAFAN

GORA KAPYLDZUCH
3 904 ▲

IRAN

Official name:	Hayastani Anrapetutiun
Capital:	Yerevan
Population:	3.8 million
Surface area:	29,800 km²
Currency:	Dram
Language:	Armenian, Azeri, Russian
GDP per head:	$ 630
Life expectancy:	73 years

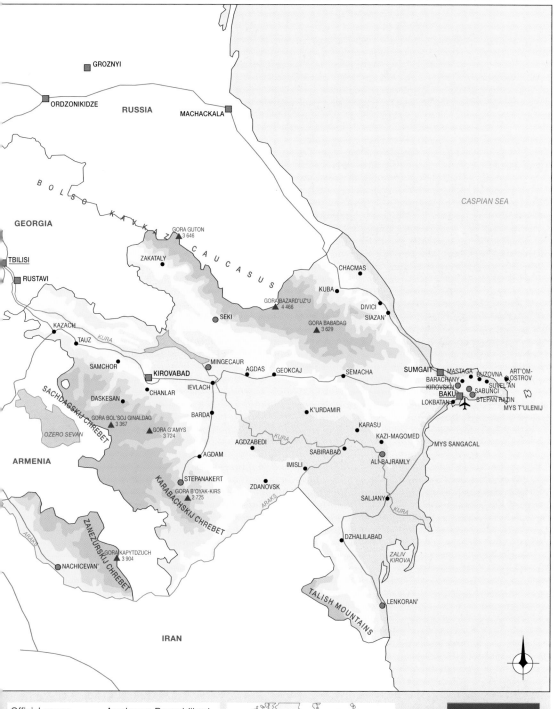

RUSSIA

GROZNYI

ORDZONIKIDZE

MACHACKALA

GEORGIA

CASPIAN SEA

B O L'S O J   K A V K A Z

C A U C A S U S

TBILISI

RUSTAVI

ZAKATALY

GORA GUTON
▲ 3 646

CHACMAS

KUBA

GORA BAZARD'UZ'U
▲ 4 466

DIVICI

SIAZAN'

KAZACH

KURA

SEKI

GORA BABADAG
▲ 3 629

TAUZ

SAMCHOR

MINGECAUR

AGDAS

GEOKCAJ

SEMACHA

SUMGAIT

MASTAGA

BUZOVNA

ART'OM-OSTROV

KIROVABAD

BARACHANY

KIROVSKIJ

SUVEL'AN

SACHDAGSKIJ CHREBET

CHANLAR

IEVLACH

BAKU

SABUNCI

LOKBATAN'

STEPAN RAZIN

DASKESAN

BARDA

K'URDAMIR

MYS T'ULENIJ

GORA BOL'SOJ GINALDAG
▲ 3 367

GORA G'AMYS
▲ 3 724

KARASU

OZERO SEVAN

KAZI-MAGOMED

ARMENIA

AGDAM

AGDZABEDI

SABIRABAD

ALI-BAJRAMLY

MYS SANGACAL

STEPANAKERT

ZDANOVSK

IMISLI

KARABACHSKIJ CHREBET

GORA B'OYAK-KIRS
▲ 2 725

ARAKS

SALJANY

KURA

ZANEZURSKIJ CHREBET

DZHALILABAD

ARAKS

GORA KAPYTDZUCH
▲ 3 904

ZALIV KIROVA

NACHICEVAN'

TALISH MOUNTAINS

LENKORAN'

IRAN

Official name:	Azerbayan Respublikasi
Capital:	Baku
Population:	7.6 million
Surface area:	86,600 km²
Currency:	Manat
Language:	Azeri, Armenian, Russian
GDP per head:	$ 480
Life expectancy:	69 years

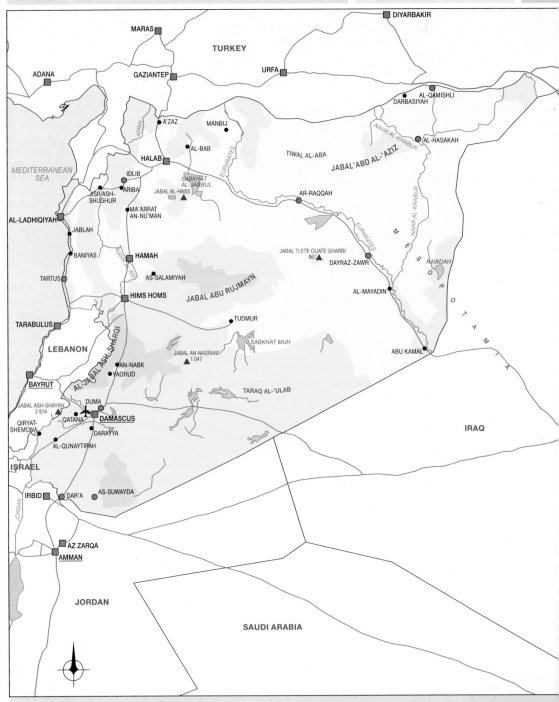

TURKEY

DIYARBAKIR

MARAS

ADANA

GAZIANTEP

URFA

AL-QAMISHLI
DARBASIYAH

A'ZAZ

MANBIJ

AL-BAB

HALAB

NAHR AL-KHABUR

AL-HASAKAH

TIWAL AL-ABA

JABAL 'ABD AL-'AZIZ

*MEDITERRANEAN
SEA*

IDLIB

ARIBA

*SABKHAT
AL-JABBUL*

JISR ASH-
SHUGHUR

JABAL AL-HASS
635 ▲

AR-RAQQAH

NAHR AL-KHABUR

MA'ARRAT
AN-NU'MAN

AL-LADHIQIYAH

JABLAH

NAHR AL-ASI

HAMAH

JABAL TLETE OUATE GHARBI
867 ▲

DAYRAZ-ZAWR

M
E
S
O
P
O
T
A
M
I
A

BANIYAS

AS-SALAMIYAH

RAWDAH

TARTUS

HIMS HOMS

JABAL ABU RUJMAYN

AL-MAYADIN

EUPHRATES

TARABULUS

TUDMUR

SABKHAT MUH

AL-JABAL ASH-SHARQI

LEBANON

JABAL AN-NASRANI
▲ 1 047

ABU KAMAL

AN-NABK
YAORUD

TARAQ AL-'ULAB

BAYRUT

JABAL ASH-SHAYKH
2 814 ▲

DUMA

QATANA

DAMASCUS

QIRYAT-
SHEMONA

DARAYYA

IRAQ

AL-QUNAYTIRAH

ISRAEL

IRBID

DAR'A

AS-SUWAYDA

JORDAN

AZ ZARQA

AMMAN

JORDAN

SAUDI ARABIA

Official name:	Al-Jumhouriya al Arabiya as-Suriya
Capital:	Damascus
Population:	14.5 million
Surface area:	185,180 km²
Currency:	Syrian Pound
Languages:	Arabic, Kurdish, Armenian
GDP per head:	$ 1,160
Life expectancy:	69 years

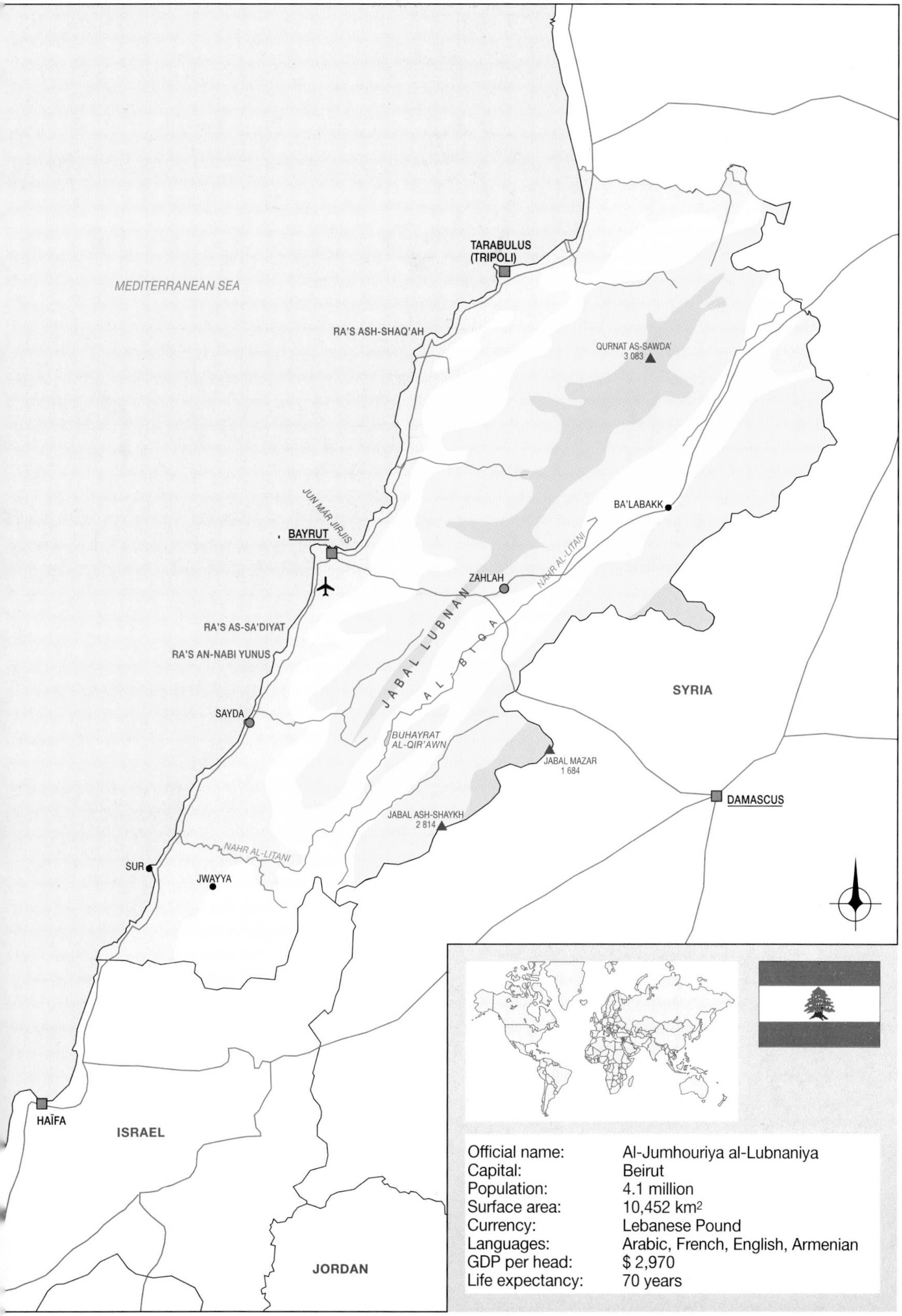

MEDITERRANEAN SEA

TARABULUS
(TRIPOLI)

RA'S ASH-SHAQ'AH

QURNAT AS-SAWDA'
3 083 ▲

BA'LABAKK ●

JUN MAR JIRJIS

BAYRUT

ZAHLAH ●

NAHR AL-LITANI

J A B A L   L U B N A N

A L - B I Q A

RA'S AS-SA'DIYAT

RA'S AN-NABI YUNUS

SYRIA

SAYDA ●

BUHAYRAT
AL-QIR'AWN

JABAL MAZAR
1 684 ▲

JABAL ASH-SHAYKH
2 814 ▲

DAMASCUS ■

NAHR AL-LITANI

SUR ●

JWAYYA ●

HAÏFA ■

ISRAEL

JORDAN

Official name:	Al-Jumhouriya al-Lubnaniya
Capital:	Beirut
Population:	4.1 million
Surface area:	10,452 km²
Currency:	Lebanese Pound
Languages:	Arabic, French, English, Armenian
GDP per head:	$ 2,970
Life expectancy:	70 years

LEBANON

QIRYAT SHEMONA

SYRIA

NAHARIYA

HARE MERON 1 208 ▲ ZEFAT

AKKO

QIRYAT YAM
QIRYAT MOTZKIN — QIRYAT BIALIK
HAÏFA — SHEFAR'ARM
KEFAR ATA
TIRAT KARMEL — NAZERAT'LLIT
NAZARETH — TEVERYA

SEA OF GALILEE

IRBID

MEDITERRANEAN SEA

AFULA

UMM EL FAHM

BET SHE'AN

PARDES HANNA

HADERA

JANIN

NETANYA

TULKARM
ET TAIYIBA

RA'ANANNA
HERZLIYYA — QALQILYAH
RAMAT HASHARON — KEFAR SAVA
RAMAT GAN — BENE BERAQ
TEL AVIV — PETAH TIQWA
— GIVATAYIM
BAT YAM — HOLON
RISHON LEZIYYON — LOD
NES ZIYYONA — RAMLA
REHOVOT
YAVNE

NABULUS

JORDAN

AL-BIRAH
RAM ALLAH
JERICHO

ASHDOD

JERUSALEM

AZ ZARQA

AMMAN

ASHQELON

BET SHEMESH

BAYT LAHM

QIRYAT GAT

JABALYAH
GHAZZAH

AL-KHALIL

SHOMA

DEAD SEA

JORDAN

SAUDI ARABIA

KHAN YUNIS

RAFAH

BE'ER SHEVA

DIMONA

H A N E G E V

MIZPE RAMON

EGYPT

ELAT

GULF OF AQABA

Official name:	Medinat Jisrael
Capital:	Jerusalem
Population:	5.7 million
Surface area:	21,946 km²
Currency:	Shekel
Languages:	Hebrew, Arabic, Yiddish, English
GDP per head:	$ 15,870
Life expectancy:	75 years

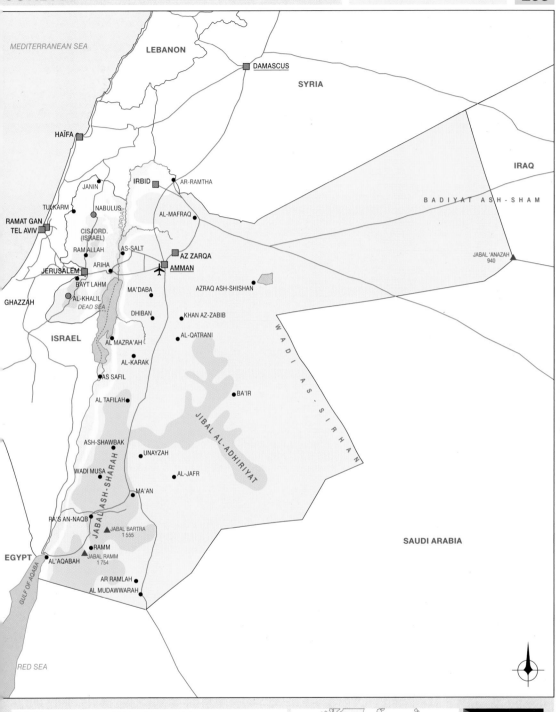

MEDITERRANEAN SEA

LEBANON

DAMASCUS

SYRIA

IRAQ

HAÏFA

BADIYAT ASH-SHAM

JANIN

IRBID

AR-RAMTHA

TULKARM

NABULUS

AL-MAFRAQ

RAMAT GAN
TEL AVIV

CISJORD.
(ISRAEL)

JABAL 'ANAZAH
940

RAM ALLAH

AS-SALT

AZ ZARQA

JERUSALEM

ARIHA

AMMAN

BAYT LAHM

MA'DABA

AZRAQ ASH-SHISHAN

GHAZZAH

AL-KHALIL
DEAD SEA

DHIBAN

KHAN AZ-ZABIB

ISRAEL

AL MAZRA'AH

AL-QATRANI

AL-KARAK

AS SAFIL

BA'IR

AL TAFILAH

WADI AS-SIRHAN

JIBAL AL-ADHIRIYAT

ASH-SHAWBAK

UNAYZAH

WADI MUSA

AL-JAFR

JABAL ASH-SHARAH

MA'AN

RA'S AN-NAQB

JABAL BARTRA
1 555

SAUDI ARABIA

RAMM

EGYPT

JABAL RAMM
1 754

AL'AQABAH

AR RAMLAH

GULF OF AQABA

AL MUDAWWARAH

RED SEA

Official name:	Al-Mamlaka al-Urduniya al-Hashimiya
Capital:	Amman
Population:	4.3 million
Surface area:	89,342 km²
Currency:	Jordanian Dinar
Language:	Arabic
GDP per head:	$ 1,650
Life expectancy:	71 years

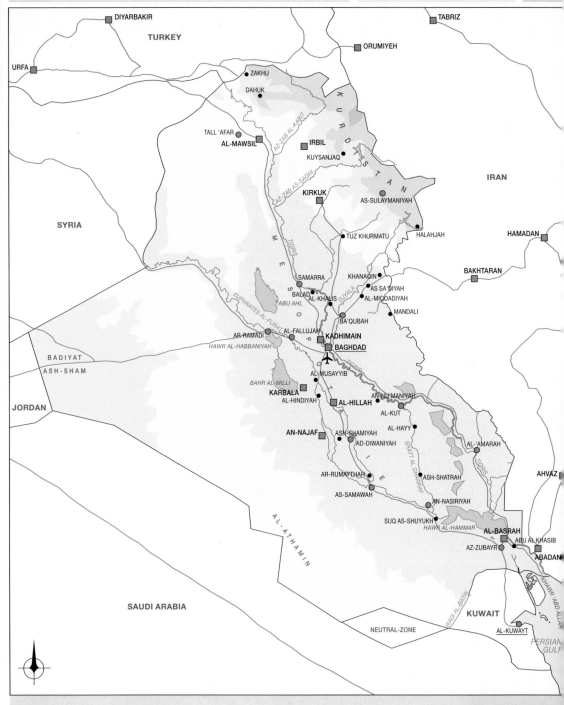

TURKEY

DIYARBAKIR

TABRIZ

ORUMIYEH

URFA

ZAKHU

DAHUK

TALL 'AFAR
AL-MAWSIL

IRBIL

KUYSANJAQ

KURDISTAN

IRAN

KIRKUK

AS-SULAYMANIYAH

TUZ KHURMATU

HALAHJAH

HAMADAN

BAKHTARAN

SYRIA

SAMARRA

KHANAQIN

BALAD
AL-KHALIS

AS SA'DIYAH

AL-MIQDADIYAH

MANDALI

ABU AHL

BA'QUBAH

AR-RAMADI

AL-FALLUJAH

KADHIMAIN

BAGHDAD

HAWR AL-HABBANIYAH

BADIYAT
ASH-SHAM

BAHR AL-MILLI

AL-MUSAYYIB

KARBALA

AL-HINDIYAH

AL-HILLAH

AN NU'MANIYAH

AL-KUT

JORDAN

AN-NAJAF

ASH-SHAMIYAH

AD-DIWANIYAH

AL-HAYY

AL-'AMARAH

AHVAZ

AR-RUMAYTHAH

ASH-SHATRAH

AS-SAMAWAH

AN-NASIRIYAH

SUQ AS-SHUYUKH

HAWR AL-HAMMAR

AL-BASRAH

ABU AL KHASIB

AZ-ZUBAYR

ABADAN

AL-ATHAMIN

SAUDI ARABIA

KUWAIT

NEUTRAL-ZONE

AL-KUWAYT

PERSIAN
GULF

KHAWR ABD ALLAH

EUPHRATES AL-FURAT

TIGRIS

DJYALA

AZ-ZAB AS-SAGHI

AZ-ZAB AL-KABIT

SHATT AL-GHARRAF

TIGRIS

WADI AL-BATIN

Official name:	Al-Jumhouriya al Iraqiya
Capital:	Baghdad
Population:	21.4 million
Surface area:	438,317 km²
Currency:	Iraqi Dinar
Languages:	Arabic, Turkmenish
GDP per head:	$ 3,115
Life expectancy:	62 years

AL-BASRAH

IRAN

IRAQ

ABADAN

KHAWR 'ABD ALLAH

BUBIYAN

KHALIJ AL-KUWAYT

FAYLAKAH

WADI AL-BATIN

AL-JAHRAH

RA'S AL-ARD

AL-KUWAYT

NEUTRAL ZONE

PERSIAN GULF

MINA' AL-AHMADI

RA'S AL-QULAY'AH

WAFRAH

RA'S AZ-ZWAR

SAUDI ARABIA

Official name:	Daulat al Kuwayt
Capital:	Kuwait City
Population:	1.6 million
Surface area:	17,818 km^2
Currency:	Kuwaiti Dinar
Languages:	Arabic, English
GDP per head:	$ 9,635
Life expectancy:	77 years

LEBANON
BAYRÚT
DAMASCUS
ISRAEL
SYRIA
IRAQ
BAGHDAD
ESFAHAN
TEL AVIV
AMMAN
AL-HILLAH
AN-NAJAF
IRAN
JERUSALEM
JORDAN
AHVAZ
AR'AR
SHIRAZ
AL-BASRAH
ABADAN
WADI AS-SIRHAN
AL-HAMAD
SAKAKAH
RAFBA'
KUWAIT
AL-JAWF
NEUTRAL
ZONE
AL-KUWAYT
GULF OF AQABA
JABAL AL-LAWZ 2 580
AN - NAFUD
AD-DIBDIBAH
TABUK
AL-MUWAYLIH
HA'IL
AL-QAYSUMAH
ABU ALI
AL-QATIF
RA'S AT-TANNURAH
AL-WAJH
MADYAN
AD-DAMMAM
BAHREIN
AZ-ZAHRAN
AL-MANAMAH
BURAYDAH
AZ-ZILFI
AL-KHUBAR
QATAR
JABAL RADWA 1 814
'UNAYZAH
AL-MUBARRAZ
PERSIAN GULF
RA'S ABU MADD
ASH-SHAQRA'
AL-HUFUF
AD-DAWHAH
RA'S BARID
YANBU' AL-BAHR
AL-MADINAN
AD-DAWADIMI
AR RIYAD
ABU ZHABY
EGYPT
AS-SULAYMANIYAH
HARAD
UNITED ARAB EMIRATES
RABIGH
AL-HARIQ
AL-HULWAH
RA'S HATIBAH
AR RA'S AL-ASWAD
JIDDAH
MAKKAH (MECCA)
TURABAH
AL-MUBARRAZ
AL-'UBAYLAH
AT TA'IF
AL-LITH
AL-LIDAM
AS-SULAYYIL
RED SEA
QAL'AT BISHAH
BUR SUDAN
AL-QUNFUDHAN
AR RUB' AL KHALI
OMAN
HALT
SUDAN
KHAMIS MUSHAYT
ABHA
JABAL ABU HASAN 2 292
SABYA
ABA AS-SU'UD
RA'S AT-TARFA
ABU ARISH
JIZAN
JAZA'IR FARASAN
ERITREA
YEMEN
ASMERRA
SAN'A'
AL-HUDAYDAH
ARABIAN SEA
ETHIOPIA
ADAN

Official name:	Al-Mamiaka al-Arabiya as-Saudiya
Capital:	Riyadh
Population:	19.4 million
Surface area:	2,240,000 km²
Currency:	Saudi Riyal
Language:	Arabic
GDP per head:	$ 9,635
Life expectancy:	70 years

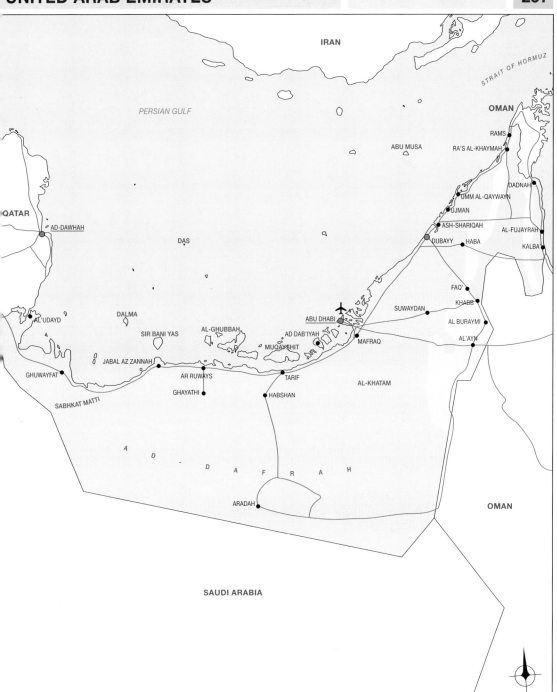

IRAN

STRAIT OF HORMUZ

PERSIAN GULF

OMAN

RAMS

ABU MUSA

RA'S AL-KHAYMAH

DADNAH

UMM AL-QAYWAYN

UJMAN

ASH-SHARIQAH

AL-FUJAYRAH

QATAR

AD-DAWHAH

DAS

DUBAYY

HABA

KALBA

FAQ'

KHABB

DALMA

AL 'UDAYD

SUWAYDAN

AL BURAYMI

SIR BANI YAS

AL-GHUBBAH

ABU DHABI

AD DAB'IYAH

AL'AYN

MUQAYSHIT

JABAL AZ ZANNAH

MAFRAQ

GHUWAYFAT

AR RUWAYS

TARIF

AL-KHATAM

SABHKAT MATTI

GHAYATHI

HABSHAN

A   D   D   A   F   R   A   H

OMAN

ARADAH

SAUDI ARABIA

Official name:	Daulat al-Imarat al-Arabiya al-Muttahida
Capital:	Abu Dhabi
Population:	2.5 million
Surface area:	77,700 km^2
Currency:	Dirham
Languages:	Arabic, English, Hindi, Urdu, Farsi
GDP per head:	$ 9,635
Life expectancy:	75 years

Official name: Daulat al-Bahrayn
Capital: Manama
Population: 0.6 million
Surface area: 707,3 km²
Currency: Bahraini Dinar
Language: Arabic, English
GDP per head: $ 9,635
Life expectancy: 73 years

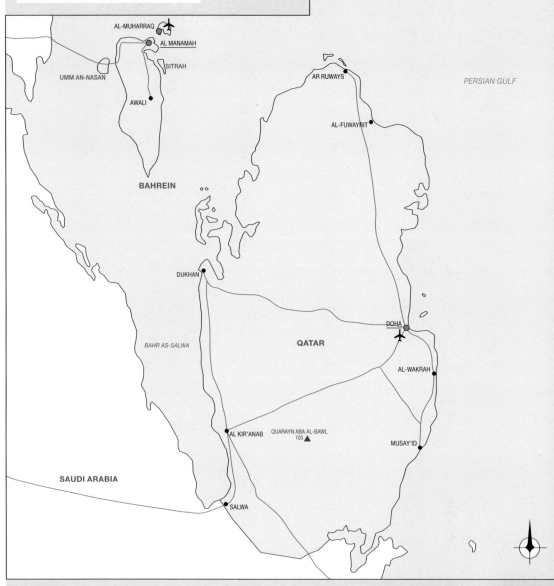

AL-MUHARRAQ

AL MANAMAH

SITRAH

UMM AN-NASAN

AR RUWAYS

PERSIAN GULF

AL-FUWAYRIT

AWALI

BAHREIN

DUKHAN

DOHA

BAHR AS-SALWA

QATAR

AL-WAKRAH

AL KIR'ANAB

QUARAYN ABA AL-BAWL
105 ▲

MUSAY'ID

SAUDI ARABIA

SALWA

Official name: Daulat al-Qatar
Capital: Doha
Population: 0.7 million
Surface area: 11,427 km²
Currency: Quatari Rial
Language: Arabic
GDP per head: $ 9,635
Life expectancy: 72 years

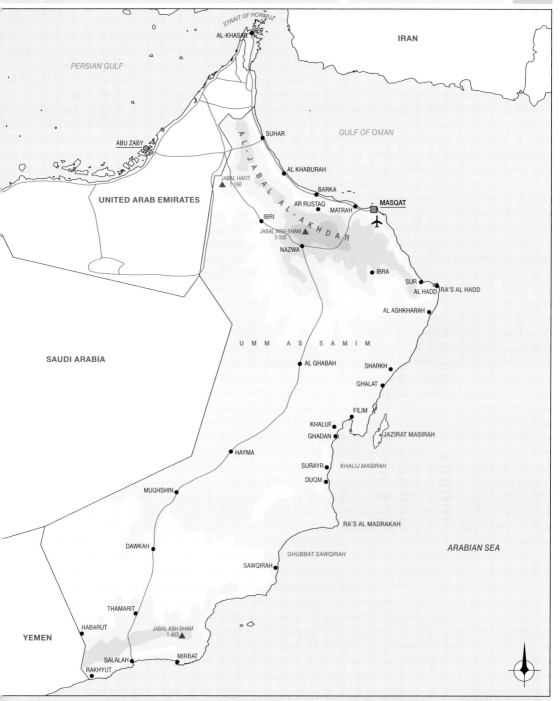

STRAIT OF HORMUZ

AL-KHASAB

IRAN

PERSIAN GULF

GULF OF OMAN

SUHAR

ABU ZABY

AL KHABURAH

BARKA

JABAL HAFIT
1 160

AR RUSTAQ

MATRAH **MASQAT**

UNITED ARAB EMIRATES

IBRI

JABAL ASH-SHAM
3 035

NAZWA

IBRA

SUR
AL HADD RA'S AL HADD

AL ASHKHARAH

AL·JABAL AL·AKHDAR

SAUDI ARABIA

U M M   A S   S A M I M

AL GHABAH

SHARKH

GHALAT

FILIM

KHALUF

GHADAN

JAZIRAT MASIRAH

HAYMA

SURAYR

KHALIJ MASIRAH

DUQM

MUGHSHIN

RA'S AL MADRAKAH

ARABIAN SEA

DAWKAH

GHUBBAT SAWQIRAH

SAWQIRAH

THAMARIT

HABARUT

JABAL ASH SHAM
1 463

YEMEN

SALALAH   MIRBAT

RAKHYUT

Official name:	Sultanatu Oman
Capital:	Muscat
Population:	2.2 million
Surface area:	309,500 km²
Currency:	Rial Omani Rial
Languages:	Arabic, Baluchi
GDP per head:	$ 9,635
Life expectancy:	71 years

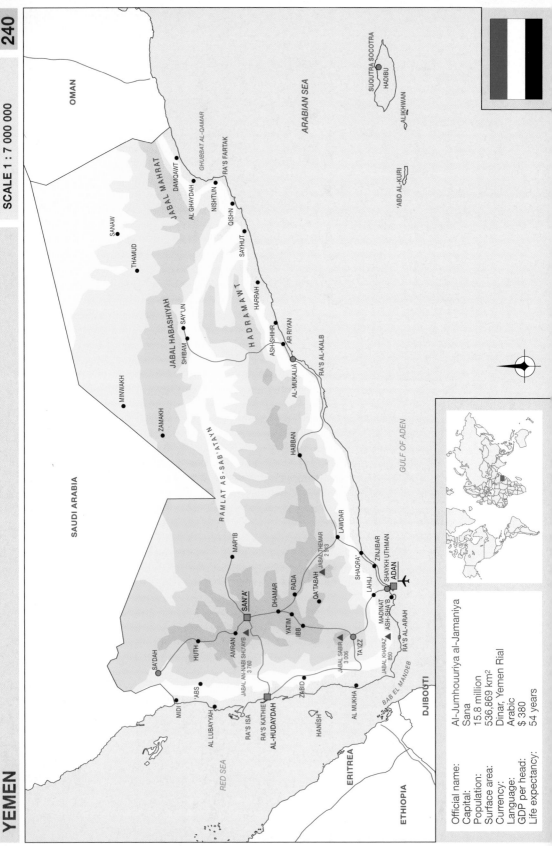

OMAN

SAUDI ARABIA

RAMLAT AS-SAB'ATAYN

MINWAKH

ZAMAKH

SANAW

THAMUD

JABAL MAHRAT

DAMQAWT

AL GHAYDAH

NISHTUN

QISHN

GHUBBAT AL-QAMAR

RA'S FARTAK

SAYHUT

HADRAMAWT

JABAL HABASHIYAH

SHIBAM SAY'UN

HARRAH

ASH-SHIHR

AR RIYAN

AL-MUKALLĀ

RA'S AL-KALB

HABBAN

LAWDAR

ARABIAN SEA

SUQUTRA SOCOTRA

HADIBŪ

'ABD AL-KURI

ALIKHWAN

MA'RIB

JABAL ATHEMAR
2 513

QATABAH

RADA

DHAMAR

SAN'A'

ZINJIBAR

SHAYKH UTHMAN

ADAN

SHAQRA'

LAHIJ

GULF OF ADEN

JABAL AN-NABI SHU'AYB
3 760

AMRAN

HUTH

SA'DAH

YATIM

IBB

MADINAT
ASH-SHA'B

TA'IZZ

JABAL SABIR
3 006

JABAL KHARAZ
850

RA'S AL-ARAH

MIDI

'ABS

AL LUBAYYAH

RA'S ISA

RA'S KATHIB

AL-HUDAYDAH

ZABID

AL MUKHA

BAB EL MANDEB

RED SEA

HANISH

DJIBOUTI

ERITREA

ETHIOPIA

Official name:	Al-Jumhouuriya al-Jamaniya
Capital:	Sana
Population:	15.8 million
Surface area:	536,869 km²
Currency:	Dinar, Yemen Rial
Language:	Arabic
GDP per head:	$ 380
Life expectancy:	54 years

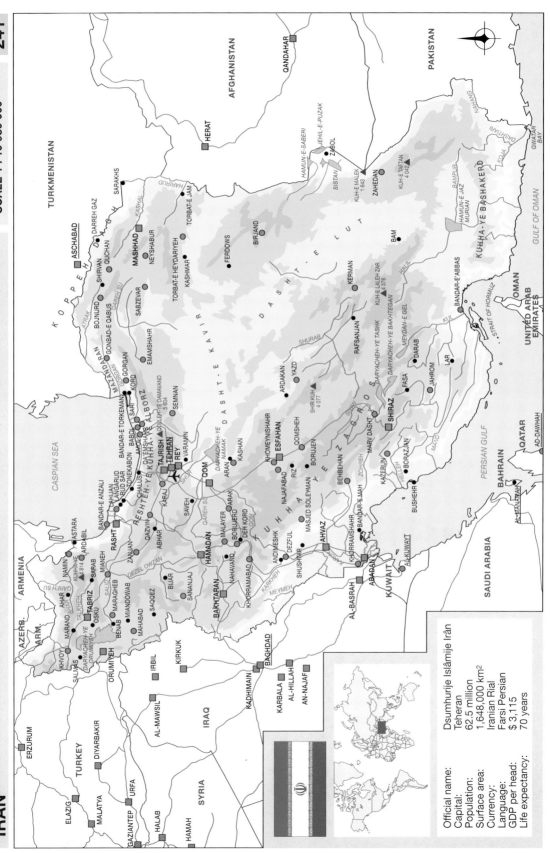

IRAN

TURKMENISTAN

AFGHANISTAN

PAKISTAN

TURKEY

SYRIA

IRAQ

ARMENIA

AZERB.

ARM.

KUWAIT

SAUDI ARABIA

QATAR

BAHRAIN

UNITED ARAB EMIRATES

OMAN

CASPIAN SEA

PERSIAN GULF

GULF OF OMAN

STRAIT OF HORMUZ

GWATAR BAY

QANDAHAR

HERAT

ASCHABAD

SARAKHS

DARREH GAZ

SHIRVAN

QUCHAN

MASHHAD

NEYSHABUR

TORBAT-E JAM

TORBAT-E HEYDARIYEH

KASHMAR

SABZEVAR

BOJNURD

GONBAD-E QABUS

GORGAN

ENAMSHAHR

BIRJAND

FERDOWS

BAM

KERMAN

RAFSANJAN

ZAHEDAN

ZABOL

SISTAN

KUH-E MALEK 1643

KUH-E TAFTAN 4 042

ARDAKAN

YAZD

QOMSHEH

ESFAHAN

NAJAFABAD

KHOMEYNISHAHR

SEMNAN

REY

TEHRAN

TAJRISH

QOLLEH-YE DAMAVAND 5 604

VARAMIN

QOM

KARAJ

SAVEH

QAZVIN

ABHAR

ZANJAN

RASHT

BANDAR-E ANZALI

CHALUS

RUD SAR

LANGARUD

STONEKABON

AMOL

BABOL

SARI

BANDAR-E TORKEMAN

KORD

NOWSHAHR

ASTARA

ARDABIL

NAMIN

AHAR

KHVOY

MARAND

TABRIZ

OSKU

MARAGHEB

MIANDOWAB

MAHABAD

BENAB

MIANEH

BIJAR

SANANDAJ

SAQQEZ

SALMAS

ORUMIYEH

DARYACHEH-YE ORUMIYEH

SARAB

KUH-E SALD 814

TALKHEH

HAMADAN

MALAYER

NAHAVAND

BORUJERD

DEH KORD

ARAK

SAVEH

BORUJEN

RIZ

AHVAZ

DEZFUL

SHUSHTAR

ANDIMESHK

MASJED SOLEMAN

BEHBEHAN

KAZERUN

BORAZJAN

BUSHEHR

BANDAR-E MAH

KHORRAMSHAHR

ABADAN

AL-BASRAH

KUWAIT

AL-KUWAIT

SHIRAZ

FASA

JAHROM

DARAB

LAR

MARV DASHT

KUH-E LALEH ZAR 4 376

DARYACHEH-YE BAKHTEGAN

DARYACHEH-YE TASHK

SHIR KUH 4 077

KASHAN

ARAN NAMAK

DARYACHEH-YE NAMAK

BANDAR-E ABBAS

AD-DAWHAH

AL-MANAMAH

BAKHTARAN

KHORRAMABAD

ERZURUM

DIYARBAKIR

ELAZIG

MALATYA

GAZIANTEP

HALAB

HAMAH

URFA

AL-MAWSIL

IRBIL

KIRKUK

BAGHDAD

KADHIMAIN

KARBALA

AL-HILLAH

AN-NAJAF

KOPPEH

ATRAK

HARIRUD

KASHAF

QAREH SU

SHURAB

SHURAB

HALIL

KUL

MAND

ZOHREH

KARKHEH

KARUN

DEZ

MEYMEH

QEZEL OWZAN

QAREH SU

DASHT-E KAVIR

DASHT-E LUT

RESHTEH-YE KUHHA-YE ALBORZ

KUHHA-YE ZAGROS

KUHHA-YE BASHAKERD

HAMUN-E JAZ MURIAN

HAMUN-E SABERI

SEHIL-E-PUZAK

MAZANDARAN

NAHANG

DASHTIARI

BAMPUR

MANDERUD

Official name:	Dsumhurije Islâmije Irân
Capital:	Teheran
Population:	62.5 million
Surface area:	1,648,000 km²
Currency:	Iranian Rial
Language:	Farsi Persian
GDP per head:	$ 3,115
Life expectancy:	70 years

Official name:	Turkmenostan Respublikasy
Capital:	Ashkhabad
Population:	4.6 million
Surface area:	488,100 km^2
Currency:	Manat
Languages:	Turkmen, Russian
GDP per head:	$ 940
Life expectancy:	66 years

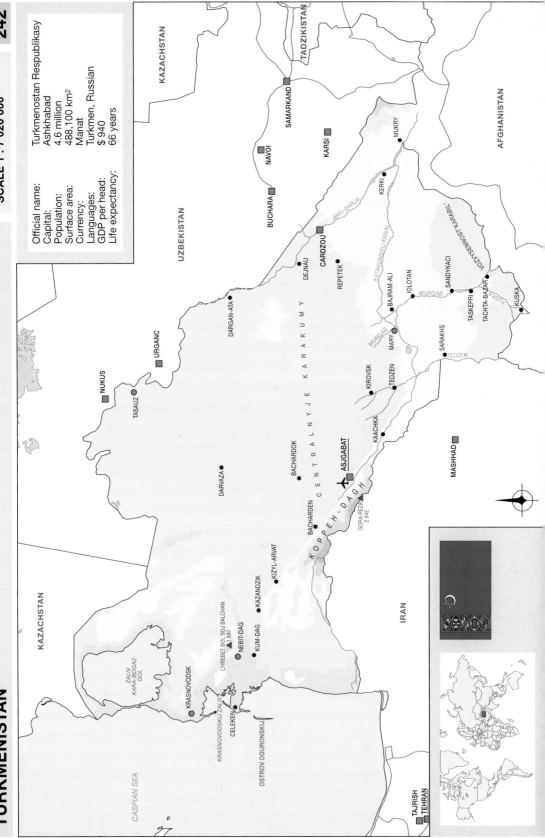

KAZACHSTAN

TADZIKISTAN

KAZACHSTAN

SAMARKAND

NAVOI

KARSI

MUKRY

AFGHANISTAN

UZBEKISTAN

BUCHARA

AMU-DARJA

KERKI

CARDZOU

DEJNAU

REPETEK

KARAKUMSKIJ KANAL

IOLOTAN

BAJRAM-ALI

MURGAB

SANDYKACI

VOZVYSENNOSTI KARABIL'

KUSKA

TASKEPRI

TACHTA-BAZAR

KUSKA

URGANC

DARGAN-ATA

CENTRALNYJE KARAKUMY

MURGAB

MARY

SARACHS

TEDZEN

NUKUS

TASAUZ

BACHARDOK

DARVAZA

KIROVSK

TEDZEN

KAACHKA

ASJGABAT

BACHARDEN

KOPPEH-DAGH

GORA REZA
2 942

MASHHAD

KAZACHSTAN

ZALIV
KARA-BOGAZ-
GOL

KRASNOVODSK

KIZYL-ARVAT

CHREBET BOL SOJ BALCHAN

NEBIT-DAG
1 880

KUM-DAG

KAZANDZIK

KRASNOVODSKIJ ZALIV

CELEKEN

OSTROV OGURONSKIJ

IRAN

CASPIAN SEA

TAJRISH
TEHRAN

03300

SCALE 1 : 7 070 000

Official name:	Uzbekiston Yumjuriati
Capital:	Tashkent
Population:	23,2 million
Surface area:	447,400 km²
Currency:	Som
Languages:	Uzbek, Russian
GDP per head:	$ 1,010
Life expectancy:	69 years

KAZACHSTAN

KIRGIZISTAN

TADZIKISTAN

AFGHANISTAN

TURKMENISTAN

ARALSKOJE MORE

PLATO UST URT

BISHKEK

DZAMBUL

CIMKENT

KZYL-ORDA

GORA MANAS
4 482

NAMANGAN
ANDIZAN
OS
SOVETABAD
LENINSK
KIRGUJ
FERGANA
MARGILAN
CUST
KOKAND
ACHANGARAN
LENINABAD
KRASNOGORSK
ANGREN
PARKENT
ISKANDAR
SKANDAR
CIRQIK
SALAR
TASKENT
JANGIJUL
PSKENT
TOJTEPA
ALMALYK
BEKABAD
CHAVAST
JANGIJER
GULISTAN
SYRDARJA
DZIZAK
KRASNOGVARDEJSK
TURKESTANSKIJ CHREBET
DUSANBE

CHREBET NURATAU
OZERO AJDARKUL'
NUROTA
LANGAR
KARMANA
NAVOI
KATTAKURGAN
KOGON
SAMARKAND
URGUT
KITOB
JAKKABOG
SAHRISABZ
KAMASI
DENAU
SURCI
JARQURGON
TERMEZ
SEROBOD
BOJSUN
GUZOR
KARSI
KOSON
QORAKUL
GIJDUWON
BUCHARA

CARDZOU

ZARAFSON
UCUDUC
IRLIR TOGI
764

MUJNAK
KUNGRAD
CHUJAJLI
CIMBAJ
KEGAJLI
NUKUS
MANGIT
BERUNU
BUSTON
TURTKUL
URGANC
CHIWA
TACHTAKUPIR

TAJIKISTAN

Official name:	Yumhuri Tochikiston
Capital:	Dushanbe
Population:	5.9 million
Surface area:	143,100 km²
Currency:	Rouble
Languages:	Tajik, Uzbek, Russian
GDP per head:	$ 340
Life expectancy:	69 years

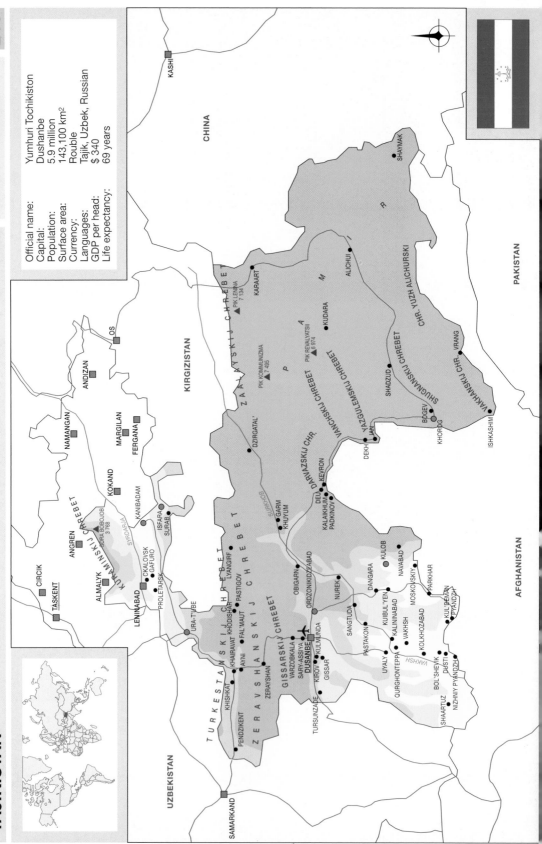

CHINA

KASHI

PAKISTAN

SHAYMAK

PIK LENINA 7 134

KARAART

ALICHUI

KUDARA

CHR. YUZH ALICHURSKI

VRANG

PIK KOMUNIZMA 7 485

PIK REVALYATSII 6 974

SHUGNANSKIJ CHREBET

VAKHANSKIJ CHR.

SHADZUD

BOGEV

KHOROG

ISHKASHIM

VANCHSKIJ CHREBET

YAZGULEMSKIJ CHREBET

DARVAZSKIJ CHR.

DEKH

DZIRGATAL'

KEVRON

DEU

KALAIKHUM

PADKINOV

KULOB

NAVABAD

PARKHAR

GARM

KHUYUM

OBIGARN

ORDZONIKIDZEABAD

DANGARA

MOSKOVSKIY

KUL'DEMEN

PYANDZH

NUREK

KULOB

KALININABAD

OS

ANDIZAN

NAMANGAN

KIRGIZISTAN

MARGILAN

FERGANA

KOKAND

KANIBADAM

ISFARA

SURAB

BABA BOBOJOB 3 768

KURUMINSKIJ CHREBET

ANGREN

ALMALYK

CKALOVSK

GAFURO

PROLETARSK

LENINABAD

CIRCIK

TASKENT

URA-TYBE

SYRDARJA

SURKHOB

TURKESTANSKIJ CHREBET

ZERAVSHANSKIJ CHREBET

GISSARSKIJ CHREBET

KHISHKAT

KHAIRAVAT

KHODISHAR

AYNI

FALMAUT

PASTIGOV

LYANGIRF

VARZOBKALA

SARY-ASSIYA

DUSANBE

KIROV

KULMUNDA

GISSAR

PENDZIKENT

ZERAYSHAN

TURSUNZADE

PASTAKON

SANGTUDA

UYALY

QURGHONTEPPA

VAKHSH

KOLKHOZABAD

BOL'SHEVIK

DUSTI

NIZHNIY PYANDZH

SHAARTUZ

KUIBUL'YEN

VAKHSH

AFGHANISTAN

UZBEKISTAN

SAMARKAND

SAMARKAND

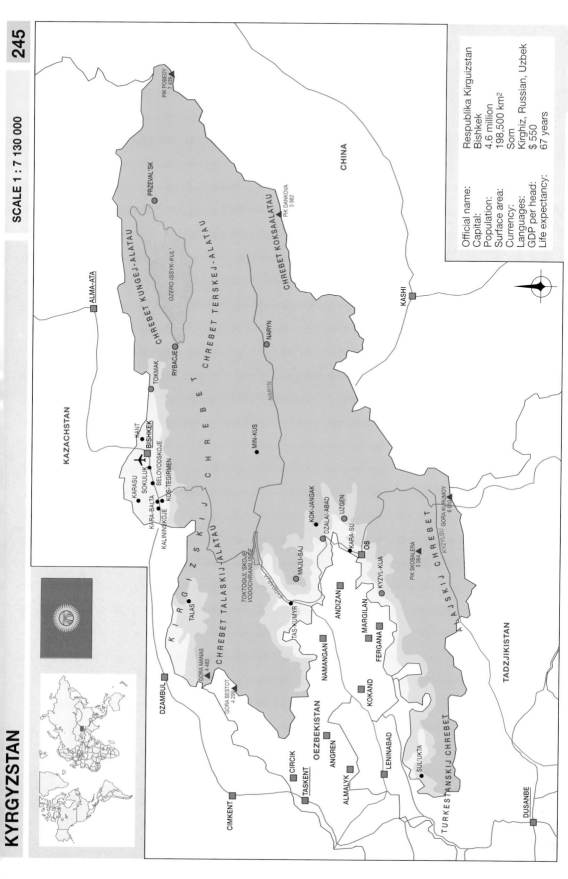

Official name:	Respublika Kirguizstan
Capital:	Bishkek
Population:	4.6 million
Surface area:	198,500 km²
Currency:	Som
Languages:	Kirghiz, Russian, Uzbek
GDP per head:	$ 550
Life expectancy:	67 years

KAZACHSTAN

CHINA

TADZJIKISTAN

OEZBEKISTAN

ALMA-ATA

PIK POBEDY 7 439

PRZEVAL'SK

CHREBET KUNGEJ-ALATAU

OZERO ISSYK-KUL'

PIK DANKOVA 5 982

CHREBET KOKSAALATAU

KASHI

CHREBET TERSKEJ-ALATAU

TOKMAK

RYBAGJE

NARYN

NARYN

MIN-KUS

KANT

BISHKEK

BELOVODSKOJE

KOS-TEGIRMEN

KARASU

SOKULUK

KARA-BALTA

KALININSKOJE

K I R G I Z S K I J   C H R E B E T

KOK-JANGAK

UZGEN

DZALAI-ABAD

KARA-SU

OS

CHREBET TALASKIJ-ALATAU

TOKTOGUL'SKOJE VODOCHRANILISGE

MAJLI-SAJ

KYZYL-KIJA

PIK SKOBALERA 5 064

KYZYLSU GORA KURUMOY 6 010

A L A J S K I J   C H R E B E T

TALAS

GORA MANAS 4 482

GORA BESTOT 4 299

TAS-KUMYR

ANDIZAN

MARGILAN

FERGANA

NAMANGAN

KOKAND

LENINABAD

SUL'UKTA

T U R K E S T A N S K I J   C H R E B E T

DZAMBUL

CIMKENT

CIRCIK

TASKENT

ANGREN

ALMALYK

DUSANBE

KAZAKHSTAN

SCALE 1 : 13 670 000

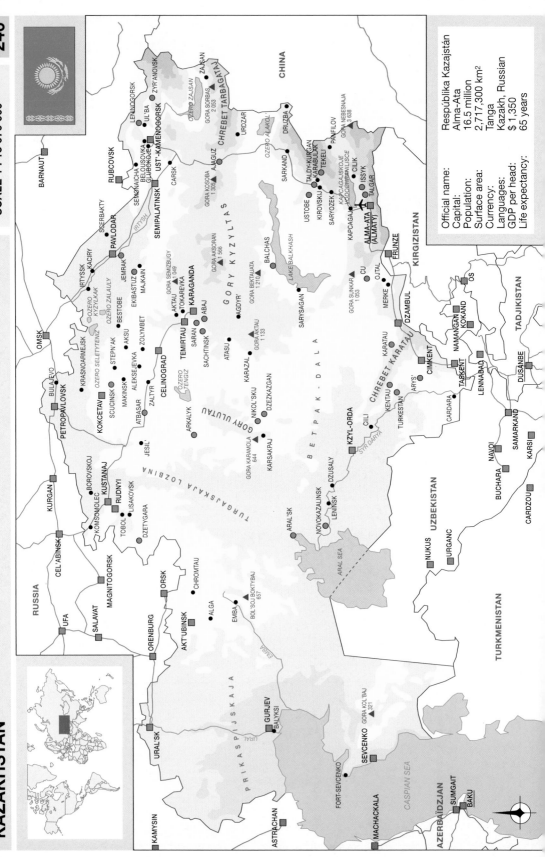

Official name:	Respública Kazajstán
Capital:	Alma-Ata
Population:	16.5 million
Surface area:	2,717,300 km²
Currency:	Tanga
Languages:	Kazakh, Russian
GDP per head:	$ 1,350
Life expectancy:	65 years

CHINA

RUSSIA

KIRGIZISTAN

TADJIKISTAN

UZBEKISTAN

TURKMENISTAN

AZERBAÏDZJAN

CASPIAN SEA

ARAL SEA

LAKE BALKHASH

BETPAK - DALA

GORY KYZYLTAS

GORY ULUTAU

TURGAJSKAJA LOZBINA

PRIKASPIJSKAJA

CHREBET KARATAU

CHREBET TARBAGATAJ

KAMYSIN
BARNAUT
OMSK
KURGAN
CEL'ABINSK
MAGNITOGORSK
UFA
ORENBURG
ORSK
SALAVAT
ASTRACHAN
MACHACKALA
SUMGAIT
BAKU

LENINOGORSK
ZYR'ANOVSK
UL'BA
RUBCOVSK
UST'-KAMENOGORSK
ZAJSAN
OZERO ZAJSAN
GORA SORBAS, 2 053
URDZAR
SEMIJARKA
BELOUSOVKA
GLUBOKOJE
CARSK
SEMIPALATINSK
SSERBAKTY
SEMIONAICHA
KACIRY
PAVLODAR
IRTYSSK
AGUZ
GORA KOSOBA 1 305
SARKAND
DRUZBA
OZERO ALAKOL
PANFILOV
GORA NEBESNAJA 3 638
TALDY-KURGAN
KARABULAK
TEKELI
KIROVSKIJ
USTOBE
SARYOZEK
KAPCAGAJSKOJE VODOCHRANILISCE
KAPCAGAJ
CILIK
ISSYK
TALGAR
ALMA-ATA (ALMATY)
FRUNZE
CU
QJTAL
MERKE
DZAMBUL
KENTAU
CIMKENT
KARATAU
ARYS'
TABKENT
CARDARA
LENNABAD
NAMANGAN
KOKAND
OS
DUSANBE
SAMARKAND
NAVOI
KARSI
CARDZOU
BUCHARA
URGANC
NUKUS

ZVRANOVSK

ZAJSAN

GORA SEMIZBUGY 1 049
AKTAU
STOKAREVKA
KARAGANDA
GORA AKSORAN 1 566
BALCHAS
GORA BEKTAUATA 1 210
GORA SUNKAR 1 053
SARYSAGAN
ABAJ
AGDYR
TEMIRTAU
SARAN
SACHTINSK
ATASU
GORA AKTAU 1 133
KARAZAL
DZEZKAZGAN
NIKOL'SKIJ
CELINOGRAD
OZERO TENGIZ
ARKALYK
GORA KARAMOLA 644
KARSAKPAJ
KRASNOARMEJSK
OZERO SELETYTENIZ
STEPN'AK
MAKINSK
SCUCINSK
KOKCETAV
ATBASAR
ZALTYR
JESIL'
ATAJ
BESTOBE
OZERO ZALAULY
EKIBASTUZ
MAJKAIN
ZOLYMBET
AKSU
ALEKSEJEVKA
OZERO KYZYLKAK
JEMRAK
KACIRY
PETROPAVLOVSK
BOROVSKOJ
KUSTANAJ
RUDNYI
KOMSOMOLEC
TOBOL
LISAKOVSK
DZETYGARA
BULAJEVO
CHROMTAU
ALGA
EMBA
BOL'SOJ BOKTYBAJ 657
AKT'UBINSK
ARAL'SK
NOVOKAZALINSK
LENINSK
DZUSALY
KZYL-ORDA
CIILI
TURKESTAN
SYR DAR'JA
GORA KOLIBAJ 321
SEVCENKO
BALYKSI
GURJEV
URAL'SK
FORT-SEVCENKO
NUKUS
IRTYS

EMBA
URAL

IRTYS

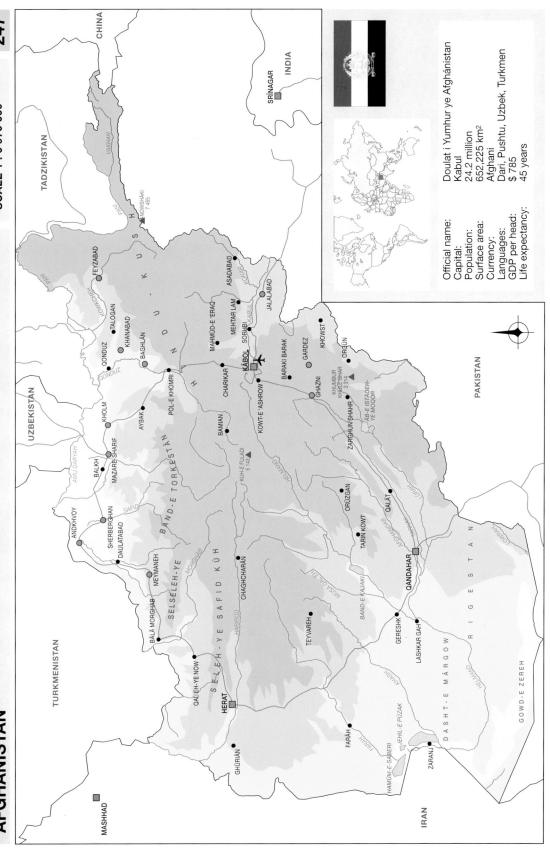

Official name:	Doulat i Yumhur ye Afghánistan
Capital:	Kabul
Population:	24.2 million
Surface area:	652,225 km²
Currency:	Afghani
Languages:	Dari, Pushtu, Uzbek, Turkmen
GDP per head:	$ 785
Life expectancy:	45 years

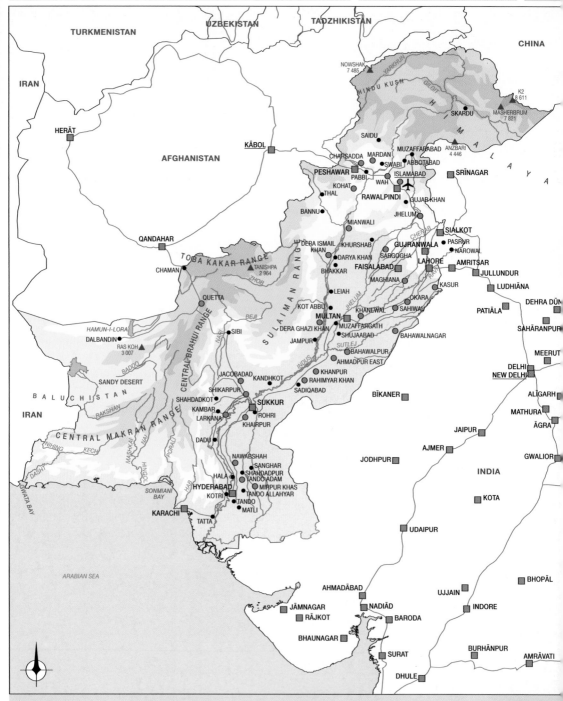

TURKMENISTAN
UZBEKISTAN
TADZHIKISTAN
CHINA
IRAN
NOWSHAK 7 485
YARKHUN
HINDU KUSH
GILGIT
K2 8 611
HIMALAYA
SKARDU
MASHERBRUM 7 821
HERĀT
SAIDU
ANZBARI 4 446
KĀBOL
CHARSADDA MARDAN
MUZAFFARABAD
ABBOTĀBAD
AFGHANISTAN
SWABI
SRĪNAGAR
PESHAWAR
PABBI
ISLAMABAD
WAH
KOHAT
RAWALPINDI
GUJAR KHAN
THAL
JHELUM
BANNU
MIANWALI
QANDAHAR
SIALKOT
DERA ISMAIL KHAN
KHURSHAB
GUJRANWALA
PASRUR
NAROWAL
TOBA KAKAR RANGE
TANISHPA 2 964
DARYA KHAN
SARGOGHA
LAHORE
AMRITSAR
CHAMAN
ZHOB
BHAKKAR
FAISALABAD
JULLUNDUR
QUETTA
LEIAH
MAGHIANA
KASUR
LUDHIĀNA
KOT ABBU
JHELUM
OKARA
DEHRA DŪN
HAMUN-I-LORA
BEJI
MULTAN
KHANEWAL
SAHIWAL
PATIĀLA
DALBANDIN
SIBI
DERA GHAZI KHAN
MUZAFFARGATH
SAHĀRANPUR
RAS KOH 3 007
JAMPUR
SHUJAABAD
BAHAWALNAGAR
MEERUT
SANDY DESERT
SUTLEJ
BAHAWALPUR
BALUCHISTAN
INDUS
AHMADPUR EAST
DELHI NEW DELHI
RAKSHAN
JACOBABAD
KHANPUR
BĪKANER
ALĪGARH
IRAN
KANDHKOT
RAHIMYAR KHAN
SHIKARPUR
SADIQABAD
MATHURA
CENTRAL MAKRAN RANGE
SHAHDADKOT
ĀGRA
KAMBAR
SUKKUR
LARKANA
ROHRI
JAIPUR
GWALIOR
NIHING
KECH
DADU
KHAIRPUR
AJMER
NAWABSHAH
INDIA
SANGHAR
JODHPUR
HALA
SHAHDADPUR
TANDO ADAM
KOTA
HYDERABAD
MIRPUR KHAS
SONMIANI BAY
KOTRI
TANDO ALLAHYAR
TANDO
KARACHI
MATLI
UDAIPUR
TATTA
ARABIAN SEA
AHMADĀBAD
UJJAIN
BHOPĀL
JĀMNAGAR
NADIĀD
INDORE
RĀJKOT
BARODA
BHAUNAGAR
BURHĀNPUR
SURAT
AMRĀVATI
DHULE

Official name:	Islam-i Jamhuriya-e Pakistan
Capital:	Islamabad
Population:	133.5 million
Surface area:	796,095 km²
Currency:	Pakistan Rupee
Languages:	Urdu, Punjabi, Sindi, English
GDP per head:	$ 480
Life expectancy:	63 years

NEPAL

SCALE 1 : 3 950 000

CHINA

KANCHENJUNGA
8 598

ILAM

BIRATNAGAR

MOUNT EVEREST
8 848

RAJBIRAJ

GAURI SANKAR
7 145

RAMECHHAP

SUN KOSI

ARUN

DORJE LAPKA
6 937

BHAKTAPUR

KATHMANDU
LALITPUR
BHIMPHEDI
BIRGANJ

PARDOR
5 928

MANASLU
8 156

POKHARA

KALI GANDAKI

NARAYANI

ANNAPURNA
8 073

BAGLUNG

BHAIRAWA

GORAKHPUR

DARBHANGA

BANGLADESH

H I M A L A Y A

M A H A B H A R A T   R A N G E

C H U R I A   R A N G E

R A N G E

JUMLA

MUGU KARNALI

TILA

SALLYANA

RAPTI

NEPALGANJ

HUMLA KARNALI

KHIURI KHALA
5 990

API
7 132

DANDELDHURA

DHANGARHI

KARNALI

GIRWA

KALI

LUCKNOW

INDIA

SHÂHJAHÂNPUR

KÂNPUR

Official name:	Sri Nepâla Sarkâr
Capital:	Kathmandu
Population:	22.0 million
Surface area:	147,181 km²
Currency:	Nepalese Rupee
Language:	Nepali, English
GDP per head:	$ 210
Life expectancy:	57 years

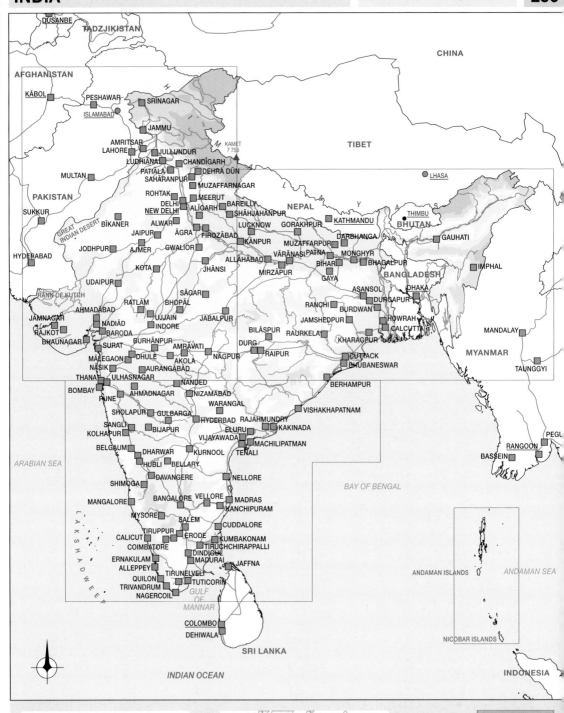

Official name:	Bharat
Capital:	New Delhi
Population:	945.1 million
Surface area:	3,287,263 km²
Currency:	Indian Rupee
Languages:	Hindi, English
GDP per head:	$ 380
Life expectancy:	63 years

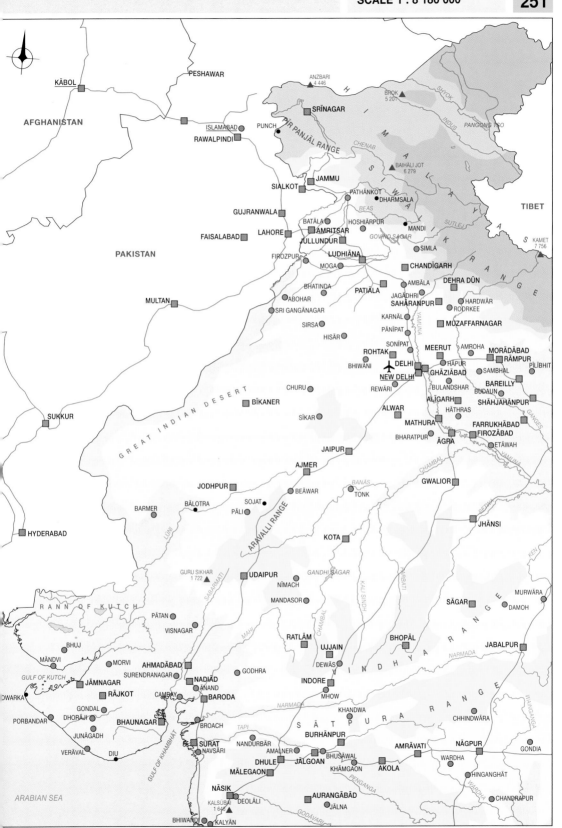

KÄBOL

PESHAWAR

AFGHANISTAN

ANZBARI
▲ 4 446

BROK
▲ 5 201

SHYOK

PANGONG TSO

INDUS

HIMALAYA

SRĪNAGAR

ISLAMABAD   PUNCH

PĪR PANJĀL RANGE

RAWALPINDI

CHENAB

JAMMU

BAIHĀLI JOT
▲ 6 279

TIBET

SIALKOT

PĀTHĀNKOT
DHARMSALA

GUJRANWALA

BEAS

MANDI

FAISALABAD

LAHORE

BATĀLA
HOSHIĀRPUR

AMRITSAR
JULLUNDUR

GOVIND SAGAR

SUTLEJ

KAMET
▲ 7 756

PAKISTAN

FIROZPUR

LUDHIĀNA

SIMLA

S I W A L I K   RANGE

MOGA

CHANDĪGARH

DEHRA DŪN

MULTAN

BHATINDA

ABOHAR

SRI GANGĀNAGAR

SIRSA

HISĀR

AMBĀLA

JAGĀDHRI
SAHĀRANPUR

KARNĀL

PĀNĪPAT

SONĪPAT

ROHTAK

BHIWĀNI

HARDWĀR
ROORKEE

MUZAFFARNAGAR

YAMUNA

MEERUT

AMROHA

MORĀDĀBAD

RĀMPUR

PĪLĪBHIT

DELHI
NEW DELHI

HĀPUR

GHĀZIĀBAD

SAMBHAL

BULANDSHAR

BAREILLY

CHURU

BĪKANER

SĪKAR

REWĀRI

ALĪGARH

HĀTHRAS

BUDAUN

SHĀHJAHĀNPUR

GREAT INDIAN DESERT

ALWAR

MATHURA

BHARATPUR

ĀGRA

FARRUKHĀBAD
FIROZĀBAD

ETĀWAH

GANGES

JAIPUR

YAMUNA

SUKKUR

AJMER

BEĀWAR

TONK

CHAMBAL

BANĀS

GWALIOR

JODHPUR

SOJAT
PĀLI

BARMER

BĀLOTRA

ARAVALLI RANGE

LŪNI

HYDERABAD

KOTA

BETWA

JHĀNSI

GURU SIKHAR
1 722 ▲

UDAIPUR

NĪMACH

GANDHI SAGAR

KALI SINDH

PARBATI

KEN

MURWĀRA

SĀGAR

DAMOH

SABARMATI

MANDASOR

RANN OF KUTCH

PĀTAN

VISNAGAR

RATLĀM

UJJAIN

BHOPĀL

JABALPUR

BHUJ

MĀNDVI

MORVI

AHMADĀBAD

SURENDRANAGAR

GODHRA

DEWĀS

NARMADA

INDHYA

RANGE

WAINGANGA

GULF OF KUTCH

JĀMNAGAR

NADIĀD
ĀNAND

INDORE

MHOW

DWARKA

RĀJKOT

CAMBAY

BARODA

NARMADA

SĀTPURA

RANGE

NĀGPUR

GONDAL

DHORĀJI

BHAUNAGAR

BROACH

KHANDWA

CHHINDWĀRA

PORBANDAR

JUNĀGADH

TAPI

SURAT

NAVSĀRI

NANDURBĀR

AMALNER

BURHĀNPUR

AMRĀVATI

WARDHA

GONDIA

VERĀVAL

DIU

DHULE

JĀLGAON

BHUSĀWAL

KHĀMGAON

AKOLA

HINGANGHĀT

MĀLEGAON

NĀSIK

KALSŪBĀI
1 646 ▲   DEOLĀLI

AURANGĀBAD

JĀLNA

PENGANGA

WARDHA

CHANDRAPUR

ARABIAN SEA

GULF OF KHAMBHĀT

BHIWANDI

KALYĀN

GODĀVARI

SCALE 1 : 8 180 000

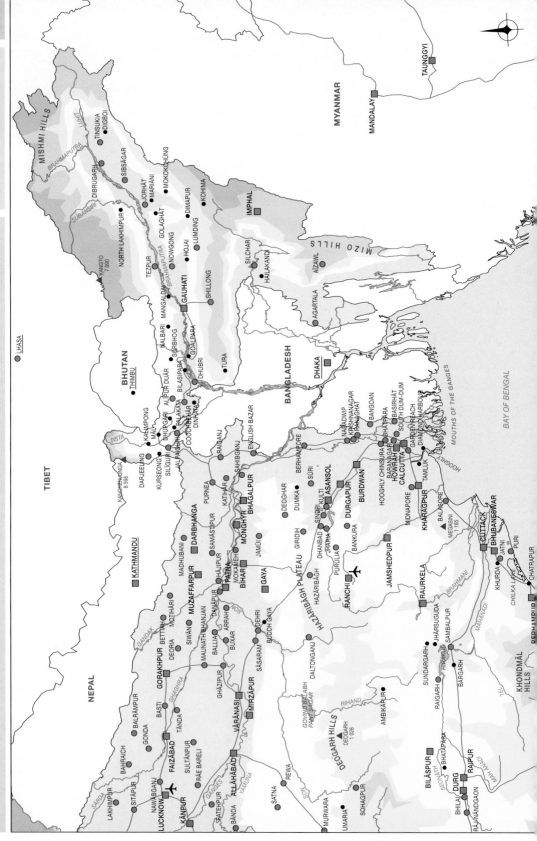

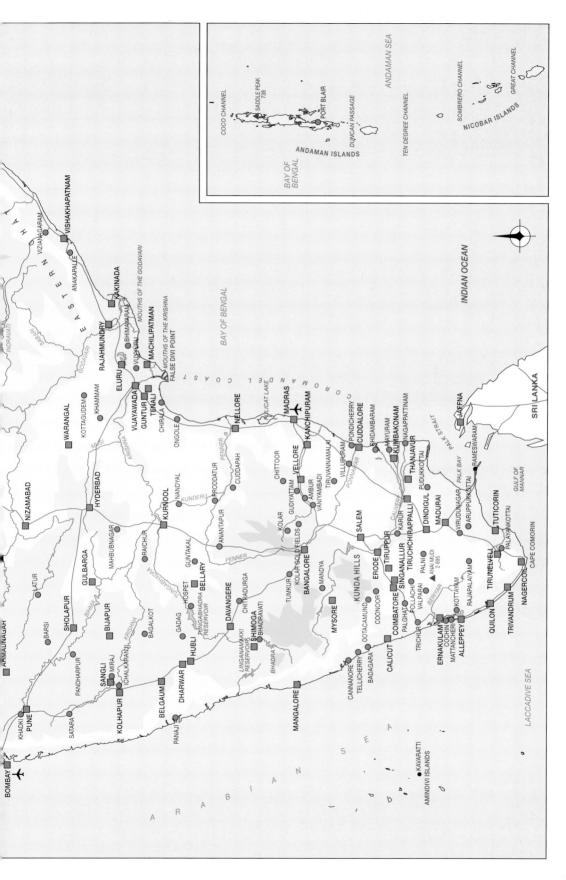

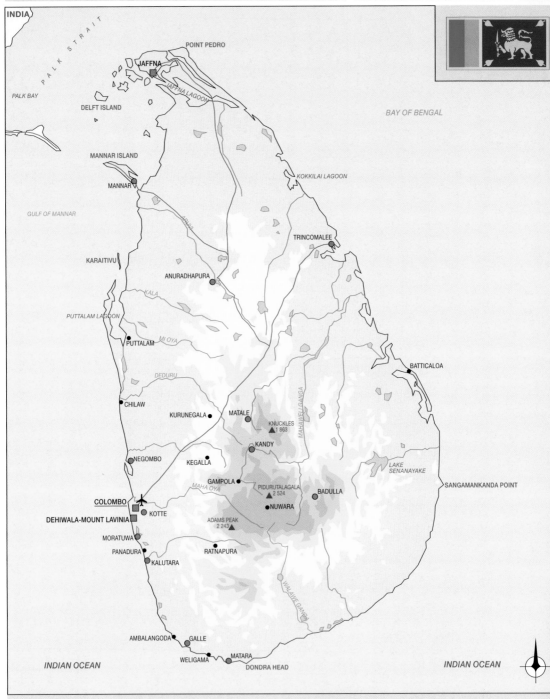

INDIA

PALK STRAIT

POINT PEDRO

JAFFNA

JAFFNA LAGOON

PALK BAY

DELFT ISLAND

BAY OF BENGAL

MANNAR ISLAND

KOKKILAI LAGOON

MANNAR

GULF OF MANNAR

TRINCOMALEE

KARAITIVU

ANURADHAPURA

ARUVI

PUTTALAM LAGOON

KALA

MI OYA

PUTTALAM

DEDURU

BATTICALOA

CHILAW

KURUNEGALA

MATALE

KNUCKLES
▲ 1 863

KANDY

KEGALLA

NEGOMBO

GAMPOLA

MAHA OYA

PIDURUTALAGALA
▲ 2 524

LAKE
SENANAYAKE

BADULLA

SANGAMANKANDA POINT

COLOMBO

NUWARA

KOTTE

DEHIWALA-MOUNT LAVINIA

ADAMS PEAK
2 243 ▲

MORATUWA

PANADURA

RATNAPURA

KALUTARA

MAHAWELI GANGA

WALAWE GANGA

AMBALANGODA

GALLE

WELIGAMA

MATARA

DONDRA HEAD

INDIAN OCEAN

INDIAN OCEAN

Official name:	Democratic Socialist Republic of Sri Lanka
Capital:	Colombo
Population:	18.3 million
Surface area:	65,610 km²
Currency:	Sri Lanka Rupee
Languages:	Sinhalese, Tamil, English
GDP per head:	$ 740
Life expectancy:	73 years

Official name:	Republic of Maldives
Capital:	Malé
Population:	0.3 million
Surface area:	298 km^2
Currency:	Rufiyaa
Language:	Divehi (Maldavian)
GDP per head:	$ 1,080
Life expectancy:	64 years

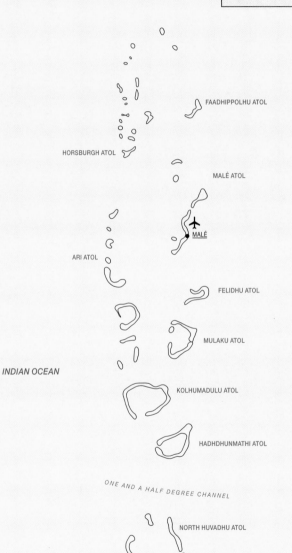

EIGHT DEGREE CHANNEL

IHAVANDIPPOLHU ATOL

FAADHIPPOLHU ATOL

HORSBURGH ATOL

MALÉ ATOL

MALÉ

INDIAN OCEAN

ARI ATOL

FELIDHU ATOL

MULAKU ATOL

INDIAN OCEAN

KOLHUMADULU ATOL

HADHDHUNMATHI ATOL

ONE AND A HALF DEGREE CHANNEL

NORTH HUVADHU ATOL

SOUTH HUVADHU ATOL

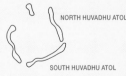

ADDU ATOL GAN

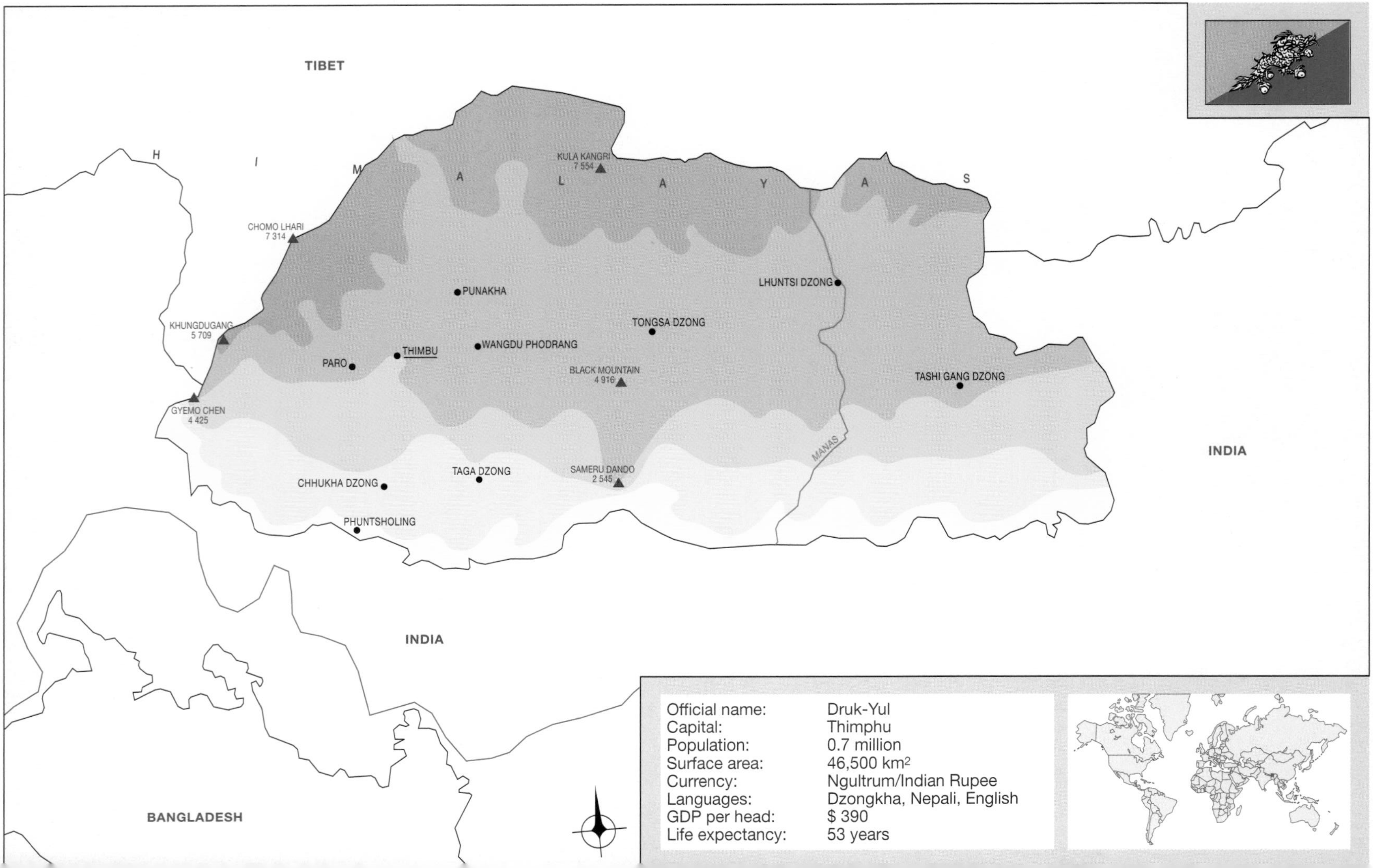

BHUTAN

TIBET

INDIA

INDIA

BANGLADESH

TIBET

H   I   M   A   L   A   Y   A   S

CHOMO LHARI
7 314

KHUNGDUGANG
5 709

GYEMO CHEN
4 425

PARO

THIMBU

PUNAKHA

KULA KANGRI
7 554

WANGDU PHODRANG

BLACK MOUNTAIN
4 916

TONGSA DZONG

LHUNTSI DZONG

TASHI GANG DZONG

SAMERU DANDO
2 545

CHHUKHA DZONG

TAGA DZONG

PHUNTSHOLING

MANAS

Official name:	Druk-Yul
Capital:	Thimphu
Population:	0.7 million
Surface area:	46,500 km²
Currency:	Ngultrum/Indian Rupee
Languages:	Dzongkha, Nepali, English
GDP per head:	$ 390
Life expectancy:	53 years

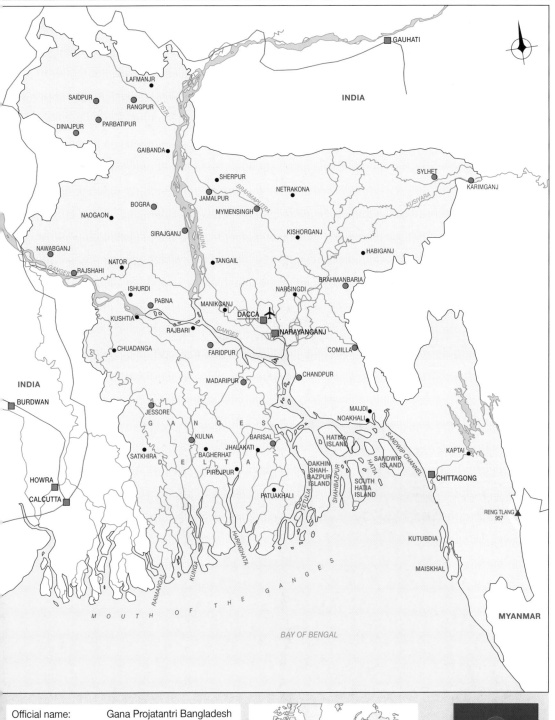

INDIA

LAFMANJR
SAIDPUR
RANGPUR
DINAJPUR
PARBATIPUR
TISTA
GAIBANDA
SHERPUR
NETRAKONA
BRAHMAPUTRA
JAMALPUR
SYLHET
KARIMGANJ
KUSIYARA
BOGRA
MYMENSINGH
NAOGAON
JAMUNA
SIRAJGANJ
KISHORGANJ
NAWABGANJ
NATOR
HABIGANJ
GANGES
RAJSHAHI
TANGAIL
ISHURDI
BRAHMANBARIA
PABNA
NARSINGDI
KUSHTIA
MANIKGANJ
DACCA
RAJBARI
NARAYANGANJ
GANGES
CHUADANGA
FARIDPUR
COMILLA
MADARIPUR
CHANDPUR
INDIA
BURDWAN
MAIJDI
JESSORE
NOAKHALI
G A N G E S
KULNA
BARISAL
SANDWIP CHANNEL
HATIA
ISLAND
SANDWIR
ISLAND
KAPTAI
SATKHIRA
JHALAKATI
BAGHERHAT
DAKHIN
SHAH-
BAZPUR
ISLAND
SOUTH
HATIA
ISLAND
CHITTAGONG
HOWRA
PIROJPUR
D E L T A
CALCUTTA
TETULIA
SHAHBAZPUR
PATUAKHALI
RENG TLANG
957
KUTUBDIA
HARINGHATA
MAISKHAL
KUNGA
RAIMANGAL
M O U T H   O F   T H E   G A N G E S
MYANMAR

BAY OF BENGAL

Official name:	Gana Projatantri Bangladesh
Capital:	Dhaka
Population:	121.7 million
Surface area:	147,570 km²
Currency:	Taka
Languages:	Bengali, Bihari, Hindi, English
GDP per head:	$ 260
Life expectancy:	58 years

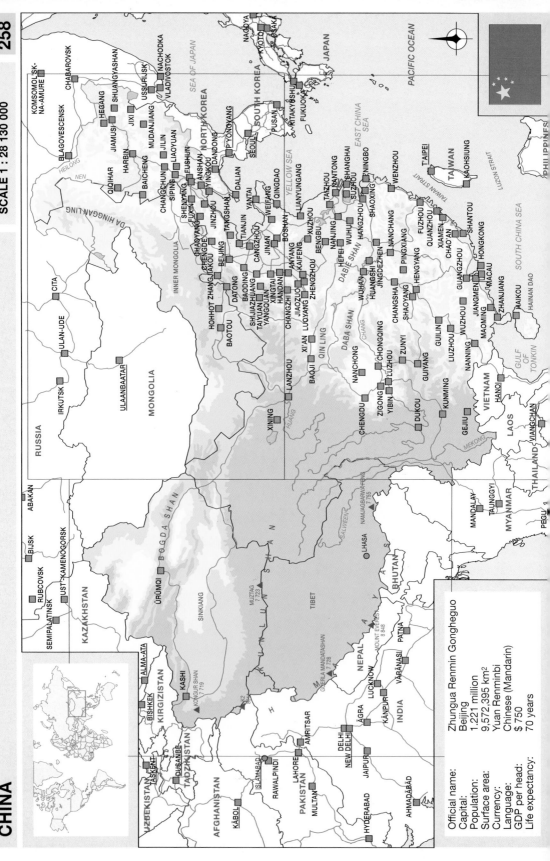

PACIFIC OCEAN

SEA OF JAPAN

JAPAN

NAGOYA
OSAKA
KYOTO
HONSHU
KITAKYUSHU
FUKUOKA

KOMSOMOLSK-NA-AMURE
CHABAROVSK
BLAGOVESCENSK
NACHODKA
USSURIJSK
VLADIVOSTOK
SHUANGYASHAN
HEGANG
JIAMUSI
JIXI
MUDANJIANG
QIQIHAR
HARBIN
BAICHENG
JILIN
LIAOYUAN
CHANGCHUN
SIPING
FUSHUN

NORTH KOREA
SOUTH KOREA
PYONGYANG
SEOUL
PUSAN
DANDONG

ANSHAN
SHENYANG
FUXIN
YINGKOU
DALIAN

HEILONG
NEN

DA HINGGANLING

INNER MONGOLIA

CITA
ULAN-UDE
IRKUTSK

ULAANBAATAR

MONGOLIA

RUSSIA

HOHHOT ZHANGJIAKOU
CHAOYANG
CHENGDE
BEIJING
JINZHOU
TANGSHAN
TIANJIN
BAODING
DATONG
CANGZHOU
YANGQUAN
SHIJIAZHUANG
TAIYUAN
HANDAN
XINGTAI
CHANGZHI
JIAOZUO
ZHENGZHOU
LUOYANG
ANYANG
BOSHAN
JINAN
WEIFANG
YANTAI
QINGDAO
LIANYUNGANG
XUZHOU
KAIFENG
BENGBU

BAOTOU

ABAKAN
BIJSK
RUBCOVSK
SEMIPALATINSK
UST'-KAMENOGORSK

KAZAKHSTAN

ÜRÜMQI

BOGDA SHAN

SINKIANG

KASHI
KONGUR SHAN 7 719

ALMA-ATA
BISHKEK
KIRGIZISTAN
TADZHIKISTAN
DUSANBE

TASKENT
UZBEKISTAN

AFGHANISTAN
KABOL

PAKISTAN
ISLAMABAD
RAWALPINDI
MULTAN
LAHORE
AMRITSAR

MUZTAG 7 723

NAMJAGBARWA FENG 7 755

LHASA

TIBET

KUNLUN SHAN

NANDA DEVI

GURLA MANDATASHAN 7 728

MOUNT EVEREST 8 848

NEPAL

K2

HIMALAYA

SALWEEN
MEKONG

BHUTAN

PATNA
VARANASI
LUCKNOW
KANPUR
AGRA
JAIPUR
DELHI
NEW DELHI

INDIA

AHMADABAD
HYDERABAD

XINING
LANZHOU
BAOJI
XI'AN
QIN LING

HUANG

DABA SHAN

CHENGDU
NANCHONG
CHONGQING
ZIGONG
LUZHOU
YIBIN
DUKOU
ZUNYI
GUIYANG

KUNMING
GEJIU

CHANG

WUHAN
JINGDEZHEN
HUANGSHI
CHANGSHA
SHAOYANG
HENGYANG
PINGXIANG
NANCHANG

DABIE SHAN

HEFEI
NANJING
WUHU
HANGZHOU
SHAOXING
NINGBO
WENZHOU
SUZHOU
SHANGHAI
NANTONG
TAIZHOU

EAST CHINA SEA

YELLOW SEA

GUILIN
LIUZHOU
WUZHOU
NANNING

GUANGZHOU
JIANGMEN
ZHANJIANG
MAOMING
FUZHOU
QUANZHOU
XIAMEN
CHAO'AN
SHANTOU
HONGKONG
MACAU

FOSHAN

TAIPEI
TAIWAN
KAOHSIUNG

TAIWAN STRAIT
LUZON STRAIT

PHILIPPINES

SOUTH CHINA SEA

HAIKOU
HAINAN DAO

GULF OF TONKIN

VIETNAM
HANOI

LAOS
VIANGCHAN

MYANMAR
MANDALAY
TAUNGGYI
PEGU

THAILAND

Official name:	Zhunghua Renmin Gongheguo
Capital:	Beijing
Population:	1.221 million
Surface area:	9,572.395 km²
Currency:	Yuan Renminbi
Language:	Chinese (Mandarin)
GDP per head:	$ 750
Life expectancy:	70 years

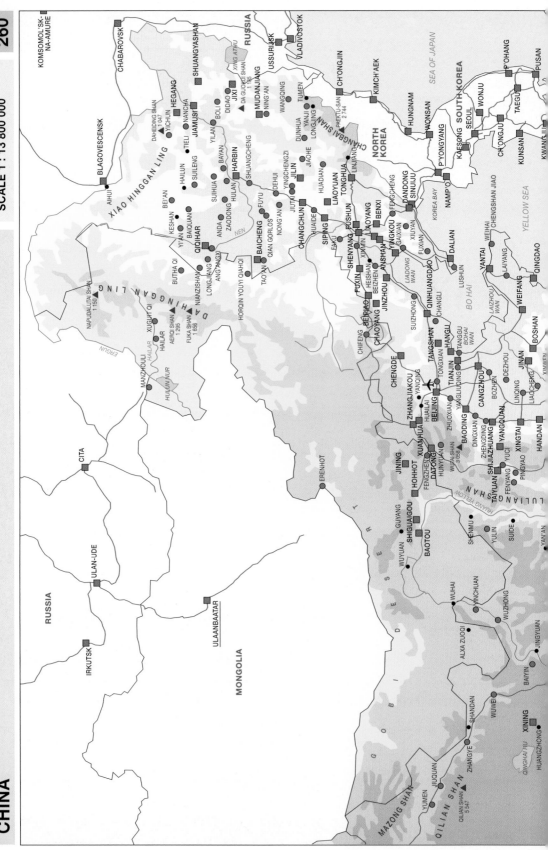

KOMSOMOL'SK-NA-AMURE

CHABAROVSK

BLAGOVESCENSK

AIHUI

XIAO HINGGAN LING

DAHEIDING SHAN
1 047

YICHUN

HEGANG

NANCHA

SHUANGYASHAN

XING'ATHU

RUSSIA

USSURIJSK

VLADIVOSTOK

JIAMUSI

TIELI

BOLI

DIDAO

JIXI

MUDANJIANG

DA GUOKUI SHAN
1 735

NING'AN

WANGQING

CH'ONGJIN

KIMCH'AEK

SEA OF JAPAN

BEI'AN

SUILENG

YILAN

SHUANGCHENG

DUNHUA

YANJI

LONGJING

TUMEN

CHANGBAI SHAN
PAEKTU-SAN
2 744

HUNGNAM

WONSAN

P'OHANG

PUSAN

HAILUN

SUIHUA

BAYAN

HULAN

HARBIN

FUYU

YINGCHENGZI

JILIN

JIAOHE

HUADIAN

TONGHUA

LINJIANG

SINUIJU

NORTH KOREA

PYONGYANG

KAESONG

SEOUL

SOUTH KOREA

WONJU

TAEGU

KESHAN

YI'AN

BAIQUAN

ZAODONG

ANDA

NONG'AN

DEHUI

JIUTAI

CHANGCHUN

HUAIDE

SIPING

LIAOYUAN

FENGCHENG

DANDONG

NAMP'O

KOREA BAY

CHONGJU

KWANGJU

KUNSAN

BUTHA QI

QIQIHAR

LONGJIANG

ANGANGXI

QIAN GORLOS

TAO'AN

BAICHENG

FAKU

SHENYANG

FUSHUN

XIMIN

LIAOYANG

BENXI

XIUYAN

YINGKOU

GAIXIAN

FUXIAN

DALIAN

LUSHUN

YANTAI

WEIHAI

CHENGSHAN JIAO

LAIYANG

QINGDAO

YELLOW SEA

NAPUDLUTAI SHAN
1 150

DA HINGGAN LING

NIANZISHAN

HORQIN YOUYI QIANQI

BEIPIAO

HEISHAN

BEIZHEN

ANSHAN

LIADONG WAN

BO HAI

LAIZHOU WAN

BOHAI WAN

WEIFANG

BOSHAN

HAILAR

XUGUIT QI

AEROI SHAN
1 295

FUKA SHAN
1 656

CHIFENG

CHAOYANG

JINZHOU

SUIZHONG

CHANGLI

QINHUANGDAO

TANGSHAN

HANGU

TANGGU

BOZHOU

DEZHOU

JINAN

LIAOCHENG

MANZHOULI

HULUN NUR

ERGUN

CHENGDE

ZHANGJIAKOU

HUAILAI

BEIJING

YANQING

TIANJIN

YANGLIUQING

CANGZHOU

LINQING

HANDAN

CITA

ERENHOT

GOBI

D E S E R T

HOHHOT

XUANHUA

FENGZHEN

HUNYUAN

DATONG

ZHUOXIAN

BAODING

DINGXIAN

SHIJIAZHUANG

ZHENGDING

YUCI

PINGYAO

XINGTAI

ULAN-UDE

RUSSIA

GUYANG

SHIGUAIGOU

BAOTOU

WUYUAN

WUTAI SHAN
3 058

TAIYUAN

FENYANG

LÜLIANG SHAN

HUANG YELLOW

YANGQUAN

IRKUTSK

ULAANBAATAR

MONGOLIA

WUHAI

SHENMU

YULIN

SUIDE

YAN'AN

YINCHUAN

WUZHONG

ALXA ZUOQI

BAIYIN

JINGYUAN

WUWEI

SHANDAN

XINING

HUANGZHONG

QINGHAI HU

MAZONG SHAN

QILIAN SHAN

QILIAN SHAN
5 547

YUMEN

JIUQUAN

ZHANGYE

TIBET (Xizang)

Official name: Tibet (Xizang)
Capital: Lhasa
Population: 2.2 million
Surface area: 1,228,000 km²
Currency: Yuan Renminbi
Languages: Tibetan, Chinese
GDP per head: $ 750
Life expectancy: 70 years

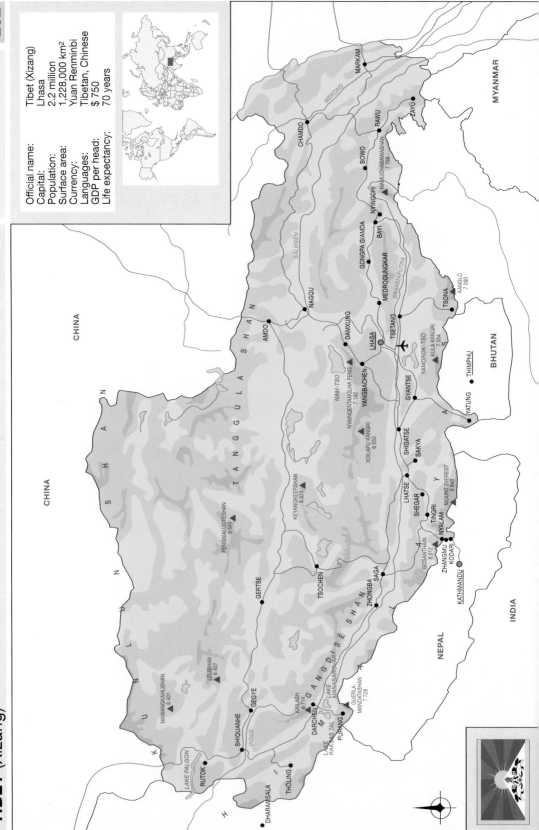

MONGOLIA

CHAOYANG

CHENGDE

CHENGDE

ZHANGJIAKOU

HOHHOT

CHINA

CITA

ULAN-UDE
RUSSIA

ANGARSK

IRKUTSK

COJBALSAN

BARUUN-URT

BUIR NUUR

KERULEN

ONON

ONDORCHAAN

CHENTEJN NURUU

SAJNSAND

NALAJCH

ULAANBAATAR

DARCHAN

SUHBAATAR

MANDALGOV'

SELENGE

ORCHON

TUUL

BULGAN

DALAN DZADGAD

SAND UUL
2 846

EGUIN

CECERLEG

ARVAJCHEER

BAJANCHONGOR

CHANGAJN NURUU

BARUN BOGD UUL
3 957

CHOVSGOL
NUUR

MORON

DELGER

DELGER

IDERLIN

TESIJN

ULIASTAJ

OGON TENGER UUH
4 031

CHANUJN

JUMT UUL
2 076

GOBI

G

ALTAJ

ICH OVOO UUL
3 761

ALTAJN NURUU

DZAVCHAN

CHJARGAS NUUR

ULAANGOM

UVS NUUR

MONGOL

CHAR US
NUUR

CHOVD

ULUNGUR

OLGIJ

Official name:	Bügd Nairamdach Mongol Ard Uls
Capital:	Ulan Bator
Population:	2.5 million
Surface area:	1,566,000 km²
Currency:	Tugrik
Languages:	Khalka (Mongolian), Kazakh
GDP per head:	$ 360
Life expectancy:	65 years

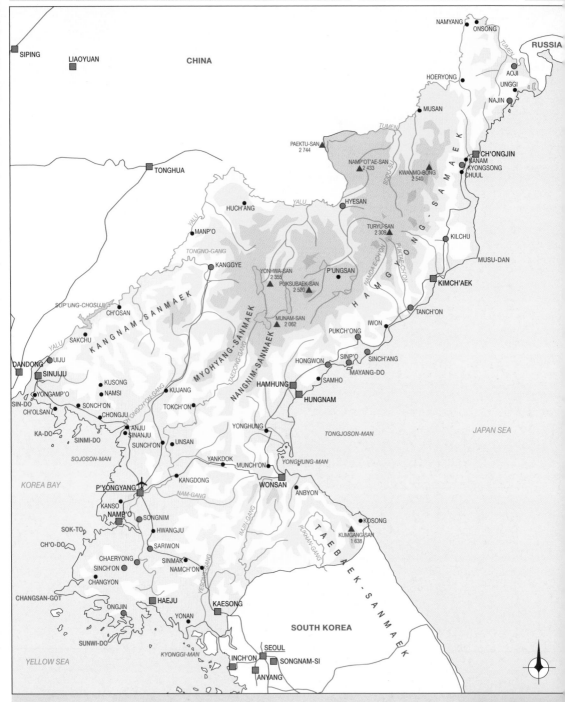

CHINA

SIPING

LIAOYUAN

NAMYANG

ONSONG

RUSSIA

TONGHUA

HOERYONG

AOJI

UNGGI

MUSAN

NAJIN

PAEKTU-SAN
2 744

NAMP'OT'AE-SAN
2 433

KWANMO-BONG
2 540

CH'ONGJIN
NANAM
KYONGSONG
CHUUL

HUCH'ANG

HYESAN

TUMEN

YALU

MANP'O

TONGNO-GANG

TURYU-SAN
2 309

KILCHU

MUSU-DAN

KANGGYE

YONHWA-SAN
2 355

PUKSUBAEK-SAN
2 520

P'UNGSAN

SUP'UNG-CHOSUJI

CH'OSAN

YALU

SAKCHU

MUNAM-SAN
2 062

PUKCH'ONG

IWON

TANCH'ON

KIMCH'AEK

KANGNAM-SANMAEK

MYOHYANG-SANMAEK

NANGNIM-SANMAEK

HONGWON

SINP'O

SINCH'ANG

DANDONG
UIJU

SINUIJU

KUSONG

NAMSI

KUJANG

MAYANG-DO

SAMHO

HAMHUNG

HUNGNAM

JAPAN SEA

SIN-DO
CH'OLSAN

YONGAMP'O

SONCH'ON

CHONGJU

TOKCH'ON

KA-DO

SINMI-DO

ANJU
SINANJU

SUNCH'ON

UNSAN

YONGHUNG

TONGJOSON-MAN

SOJOSON-MAN

YANKDOK

MUNCH'ON

YONGHUNG-MAN

KOREA BAY

P'YONGYANG

KANGDONG

NAM-GANG

WONSAN

ANBYON

KANSO
NAMP'O

SONGNIM

HWANGJU

SOK-TO

KOSONG

CH'O-DO

SARIWON

KUMGANG-SAN
1 638

CHAERYONG

SINMAK

SINCH'ON

NAMCH'ON

CHANGYON

TAEBAEK-SANMAEK

CHANGSAN-GOT

ONGJIN

HAEJU

KAESONG

YONAN

SOUTH KOREA

SUNWI-DO

YELLOW SEA

KYONGGI-MAN

SEOUL

INCH'ON

SONGNAM-SI

ANYANG

Official name: People's Democratic Republic of Korea
Capital: Pyongyang
Population: 22.5 million
Surface area: 122,762 km²
Currency: North Korean Won
Languages: Korean, Chinese
GDP per head: $ 3,115
Life expectancy: 63 years

NORTH KOREA

JAPAN SEA

SOKCH'O

HWACH'ON-CHOSUJI

CH'UNCH'ON

KANGUNG

KYEBANG-SAN
1 577

KAESONG

IMJIN-GANG

KANGHWA-DO

UIJONGBU

SEOUL

SONGNAM-SI

HAN-GANG

PUKHAN-GANG

SAMCH'OK

ANYANG

INCH'ON

SUWON

ICH'ON

YOJU

WONJU

HAMBAEK-SAN
1 573

TAE-SAN
1 549

KYONGGI-MAN

KANGHWA-MAN

OSAN

CHANGHOWON

P'YONGT'AEK

ANSONG

CHECH'ON

CH'UNGJU

YONGJU

YECH'ON

ANDONG-CHOSUJI

TOKCHOK-KUNDO

ASAN-MAN

CH'ONAN

CHINCH'ON

YESAN

CHOCH'IWON

CH'ONGJU

HONGSONG

ANDONG

NAKTONG-GANG

ANMYON-DO

TAECH'ON

KONGJU

KUM-GANG

SANGJU

UISONG

OEYON-DO

TAEJON

YONGDONG

SONSAN

NENSAN

KANGGYONG

KUMSAN

KIMCH'ON

YONGCH'ON

YONGIL-MAN

P'OHANG

CHANGGI-AP

KUNSAN

IRI

SAMNYE

TOGYU-SAN
1 608

KYONGJU

TAEGU

KAMP'O

YELLOW SEA

KIMJE

CHONJU

KOCH'ANG

ULSAN

PUAN

TAEIN

WI-DO

CHONGUP

MIRYANG

NAKTON-GANG

MUJANG-NI CHANGSONG

NAMWON

CHIJ-SAN
1 915

KIMHAE

ANMA-DO

POPSONG

TAMYANG

CHINJU

MASAN

CHINHAE

TONGNAE

PUSAN

IMJA-DO

SONGJONG

HAMP'YONG

NAJU

KWANGJU

HADONG

KOSONG

YONGSAMP'O

KWANGYANG

SAMCH'ONP'O

CHAUN-DO

SUNCH'ON

KOJE-DO

PIGUM-DO

MOKP'O

POLGYO

YOSU

NAMHAE-DO

TAEHUKSAN-DO

CHANGHUNG

UI-DO

KANGJIN

TOLSAN-DO

YOKCHI-DO

CHIN-DO

HAENAM

KUMO-DO

SORI-DO

OERARO-DO

HAJO-DO

WAN-DO

CHO-DO

POGIL-DO

SOAN-DO

CH'ONGSAN-DO

KOMUN-DO

JAPAN

KOREA STRAIT

Official name:	Republic of Korea
Capital:	Seoul
Population:	45.5 million
Surface area:	99,268 km²
Currency:	Won
Language:	Korean
GDP per head:	$ 10,610
Life expectancy:	72 years

CHEJU

HALLA-SAN
1 950

CHEJU-DO

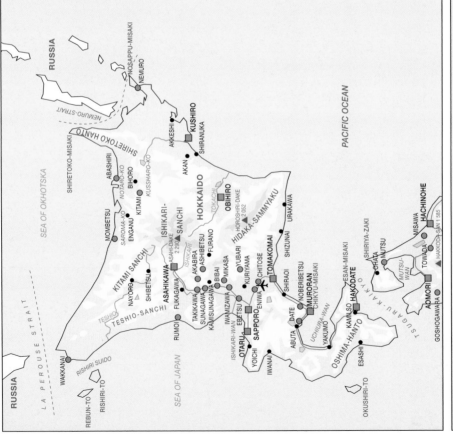

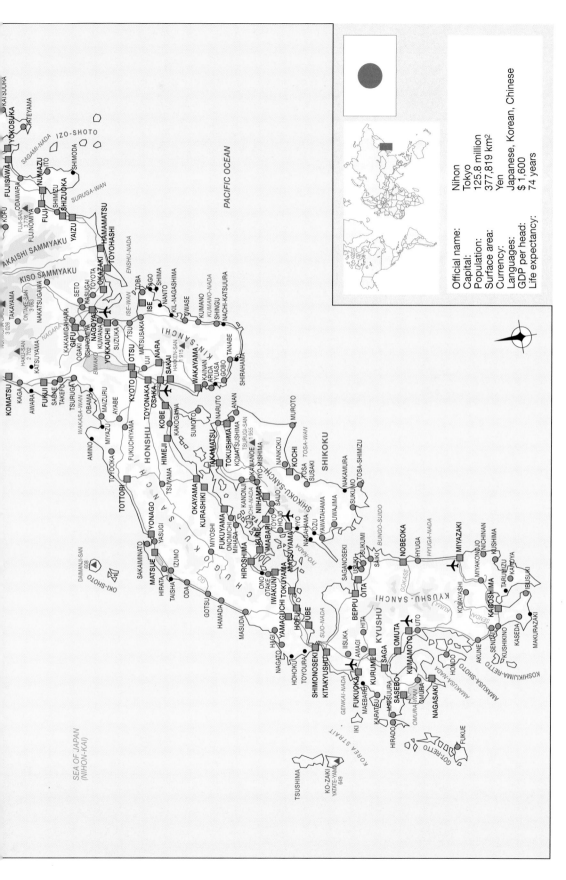

SEA OF JAPAN
(NIHON-KAI)

PACIFIC OCEAN

KOREA STRAIT

TSUSHIMA
KO-ZAKI
YATATE-YAMA
649

OKI-SHOTO
DAMANJI-SAN
608

IZO-SHOTO

SAGAMI-NADA

SURUGA-WAN

ENSHU-NADA

ISE-WAN

KUMANO-NADA

TOSA-WAN

KUMANO

KII-NAGASHIMA

NACHI-KATSUURA

HYUGA-NADA

BUNGO-SUIDO

SUO-NADA

IYO-NADA

AKI-NADA

BINGO-NADA

HARIMA-NADA

WAKASA-WAN

GENKAI-NADA

OMURA-WAN

AMAKUSA-NADA

KOSHIKIJIMA-RETTO

AMAKUSA-SHOTO

GOTO-RETTO

KYUSHU

SHIKOKU

HONSHU

CHU-GOKU-SANCHI

KYUSHU-SANCHI

SHIKOKU-SANCHI

KIN-SANCHI

AKAISHI SAMMYAKU

KISO SAMMYAKU

Cities and places

KAISUUKA
YOKOSUKA
HAYAMA
FUJISAWA
ODAWARA
NUMAZU
ITO
SHIMODA
ATAMI
MISHIMA
FUJI
FUJINOMIYA
FUJI-SAN 3 776
SHIZUOKA
YAIZU
HAMAMATSU
TOYOHASHI
OKAZAKI
TOYOTA
KASUGAI
SETO
NAGOYA
ICHINOMIYA
GIFU
OGAKI
KAKAMIGAHARA
KUWANA
YOKKAICHI
SUZUKA
TSU
MATSUSAKA
TOBA
ISE
UJI-YAMADA
NABARI
NANTO
SHIMA
WASE
SHINGU
TANABE
SHIRAHAMA
GOBO
YUASA
ARIDA
KAINAN
WAKAYAMA
HASHIMOTO
HAIKEN-SAN 1 915
NARA
SAKAI
OSAKA
TOYONAKA
KYOTO
OTSU
BIWAKO
NAGARA
HAKUSAN 2 702
KATSUYAMA
ONTAKESAN 3 063
TAKAYAMA
HOTAKA 3 026
NAKATSUGAWA
KATSUYAMA
KOMATSU
KAGA
AWARA
FUKUI
SABAE
TAKEFU
TSURUGA
OBAMA
MAIZURU
AYABE
MIYAZU
AMINO
TOYOOKA
FUKUCHIYAMA
TSUYAMA
HIMEJI
KOBE
KAKOGAWA
SUMOTO
NARUTO
TOKUSHIMA
KOMATSUSHIMA
TSURUGI-SAN 1 955
ANAN
KOCHI
NANKOKU
SUSAKI
NAKAMURA
SUKUMO
TOSA-SHIMIZU
UWAJIMA
YAWATAHAMA
OZU
IYO
MATSUYAMA
HOJO
TOYO
IYO-MISHIMA
KAWANOE
NIIHAMA
SAIJO
IMABARI
TAKAMATSU
MARUGAME
KANONJI
MIHARA
ONOMICHI
FUKUYAMA
KURASHIKI
OKAYAMA
TOTTORI
YONAGO
YASUGI
MATSUE
IZUMO
HIRATA
TAISHA
ODA
GOTSU
HAMADA
MASUDA
HAGI
NAGATO
HOHOKU
TOYOURA
SHIMONOSEKI
KITAKYUSHU
UBE
YAMAGUCHI
TOKUYAMA
HOFU
IWAKUNI
OTAKE
ONO
HIROSHIMA
KURE
MIYOSHI
YUKI
MYOSHI
SAGANOSEKI
OITA
BEPPU
USUKI
TSUKUMI
SAIKI
NOBEOKA
HYUGA
MIYAZAKI
NICHINAN
KUSHIMA
MIYAKONOJO
KOBAYASHI
KAGOSHIMA
SENDAI
AKUNE
KUSHIKINO
IJUIN
KASEDA
MAKURAZAKI
IBUSUKI
TARUMIZU
KANOYA
HONDO
UTO
KUMAMOTO
OMUTA
SAGA
KURUME
FUKUOKA
AMAGI
IIZUKA
HITA
MAEBARU
KARATSU
IKI
IMARI
MATSUURA
SASEBO
OMURA
NAGASAKI
HIRADO
FUKUE

Data panel

Official name:	Nihon
Capital:	Tokyo
Population:	125.8 million
Surface area:	377,819 km²
Currency:	Yen
Languages:	Japanese, Korean, Chinese
GDP per head:	$ 1,600
Life expectancy:	74 years

FUZHOU

CHINA

EAST CHINA SEA

TAIWAN STRAIT

FUKUEI CHIAO

CH'INSHAN SHAN 1 128
TANSHUI
CHILUNG
SANTIAO CHIAO

HSINCHUANG
T'AIPEI
T'AIPEIHSIEN
HSINTIEN
CHUNGLI

KUEISHAN TAO

HSINCHU
CHUTUNG

HAN
LOTUNG

CHUNAN

MIAOLI

HSUEH SHAN
3 931
NANHUTA SHAN
3 598

TACHIA
TUNGSHIH
FENGYUAN
TACHIA

T'AICHUNG
CHANGHUA

LUKANG
YUANLIN
PULI
HUALIEN

HSIHU
NANT'OU

ERHLIN
CHOSHUI

HSILO
HSINMEN

CHUNGYANG SHANMO

HUWEI
TOULIU
TOUNAN

PEIKANG
CHIAI

HAIAN SHANMO

HUALIEN

P'OTZU
YU SHAN
3 997

YENSHUICHEN

HSUEHCHIA
MATOU
CHIALI

SANHSIENT'AI

KUAN SHAN
3 715

PACIFIC OCEAN

HSINHUA
CH'ISHAN
T'AITUNG
LU TAO

T'AINAN
KANGSHAN

TSOYING
P'INGTUNG
KAOHSIUNGHSIEN
CH'AOCHOU

KAOHSIUNG
TUNGKANG

LIUCH'IU HSU

SOUTH CHINA SEA

LAN YU

CHIPEI TAO

P'ENGHU CH'UNTAO
MAKUNG

P'ENGHU SHUITAO

HSICHI YU

CH'IMEI YU

NAN WAN
OLUAN PI

LUZON STRAIT

Official name:	Ta Chung-hua Min-kuo
Capital:	Taipei
Population:	21.5 million
Surface area:	36,000 km²
Currency:	New Taiwan Dollar
Language:	Chinese (Mandarin)
GDP per head:	$12,838
Life expectancy:	75 years

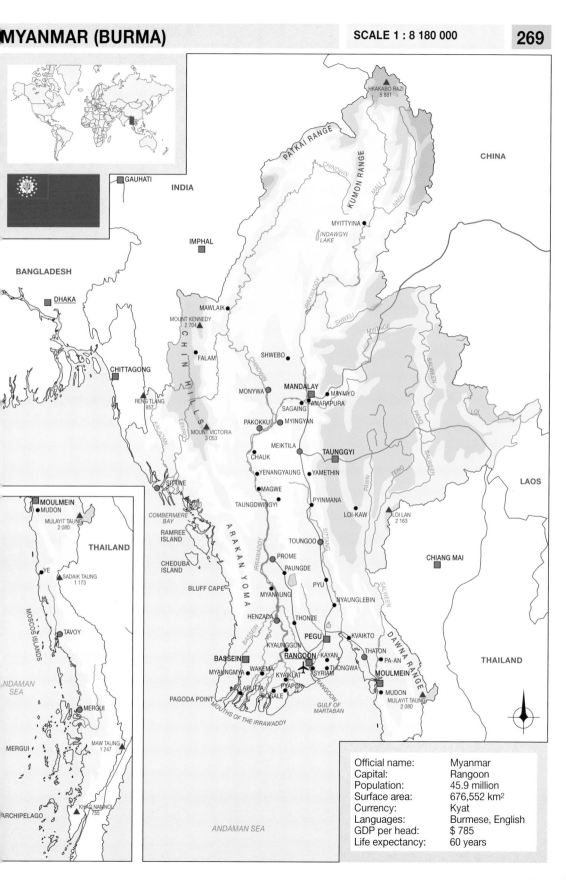

HKAKABO RAZI
5 881

CHINA

PATKAI RANGE

KUMON RANGE

CHINDWIN

MALI

NMAI

GAUHATI

INDIA

MYITTYINA

INDAWGYI
LAKE

IMPHAL

BANGLADESH

DHAKA

MAWLAIK

MOUNT KENNEDY
2 704

CHIN HILLS

IRRAWADDY

SHWELI

MYITNGE

FALAM

SHWEBO

CHITTAGONG

RENG TLANG
957

CHINDWIN

MONYWA

MANDALAY

MAYMYO

SALWEEN

KALADAN

LEMRO

MOUNT VICTORIA
3 053

SAGAING

AMARAPURA

PAKOKKU

MYINGYAN

LOI

PANG

SITTWE

MEIKTILA

CHAUK

TAUNGGYI

YENANGYAUNG

YAMETHIN

LAOS

MAGWE

PYINMANA

TENG

SALWEEN

TAUNGDWINGYI

LOI-KAW

LOI LAN
2 163

COMBERMERE
BAY

RAMREE
ISLAND

TOUNGO

PAWN

CHIANG MAI

MOULMEIN

MUDON

MULAYIT TAUNG
2 080

THAILAND

CHEDUBA
ISLAND

BLUFF CAPE

PROME

PAUNGDE

PYU

SITTANG

ARAKAN YOMA

IRRAWADDY

MYANAUNG

NYAUNGLEBIN

YE

SADAIK TAUNG
1 173

HENZADA

THONZE

SALWEEN

MOSCOS ISLANDS

TAVOY

BASSEIN

KYAUNGGON

PEGU

KVAIKTO

THATON

PA-AN

DAWNA RANGE

THAILAND

MYAUNGMYA

WAKEMA

BASSEIN

RANGOON

KAYAN

THONGWA

MOULMEIN

KYAIKLAT

SYRIAM

PYAPON

LABUTTA

BOGALE

MUDON

MULAYIT TAUNG
2 080

PAGODA POINT

MOUTHS OF THE IRRAWADDY

GULF OF
MARTABAN

RANGOON

NDAMAN
SEA

MERGUI

MERGUI

MAW TAUNG
1 247

ARCHIPELAGO

KHAO NAMNOI
755

ANDAMAN SEA

Official name:	Myanmar
Capital:	Rangoon
Population:	45.9 million
Surface area:	676,552 km²
Currency:	Kyat
Languages:	Burmese, English
GDP per head:	$ 785
Life expectancy:	60 years

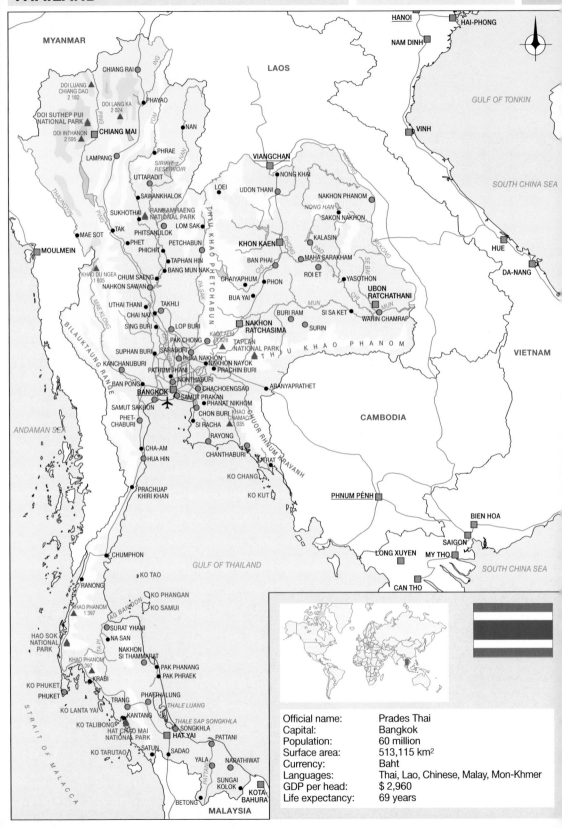

Official name:	Prades Thai
Capital:	Bangkok
Population:	60 million
Surface area:	513,115 km²
Currency:	Baht
Languages:	Thai, Lao, Chinese, Malay, Mon-Khmer
GDP per head:	$ 2,960
Life expectancy:	69 years

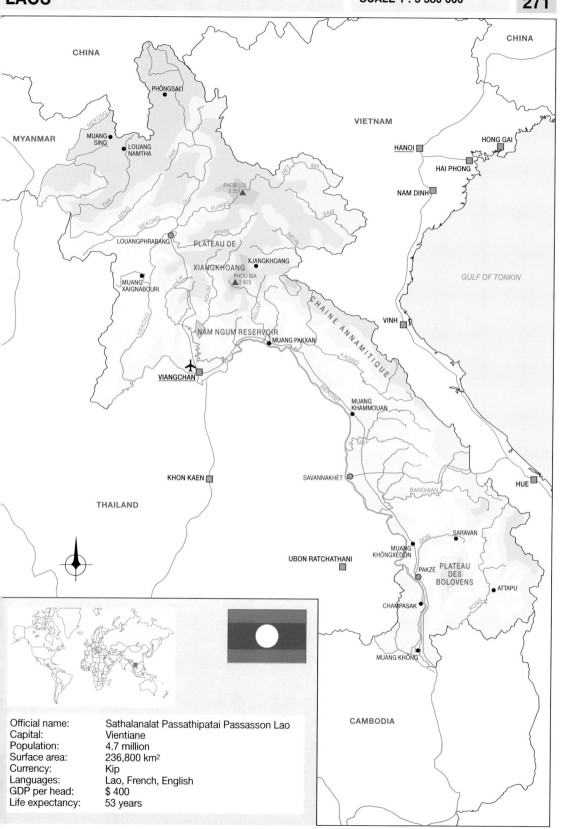

CHINA

CHINA

VIETNAM

MYANMAR

PHÔNGSALI

MUANG
SING

LOUANG
NAMTHA

HONG GAI

HANOI

HAI PHONG

NAM DINH

PHOB LOI
2 257

LOUANGPHRABANG

PLATEAU DE

XIANGKHOANG

XJANGKHOANG

GULF OF TONKIN

MUANG
XAIGNABOURI

PHOU BIA
2 820

VINH

NAM NGUM RESERVOIR

MUANG PAKXAN

CHAINE ANNAMITIQUE

VIANGCHAN

MUANG
KHAMMOUAN

KHON KAEN

SAVANNAKHÈT

HUE

THAILAND

BANGHIAN

SARAVAN

UBON RATCHATHANI

MUANG
KHÔNGXÉDON

PAKZÉ

PLATEAU
DES
BOLOVENS

ATTAPU

CHAMPASAK

MUANG KHÔNG

CAMBODIA

Official name:	Sathalanalat Passathipatai Passasson Lao
Capital:	Vientiane
Population:	4.7 million
Surface area:	236,800 km²
Currency:	Kip
Languages:	Lao, French, English
GDP per head:	$ 400
Life expectancy:	53 years

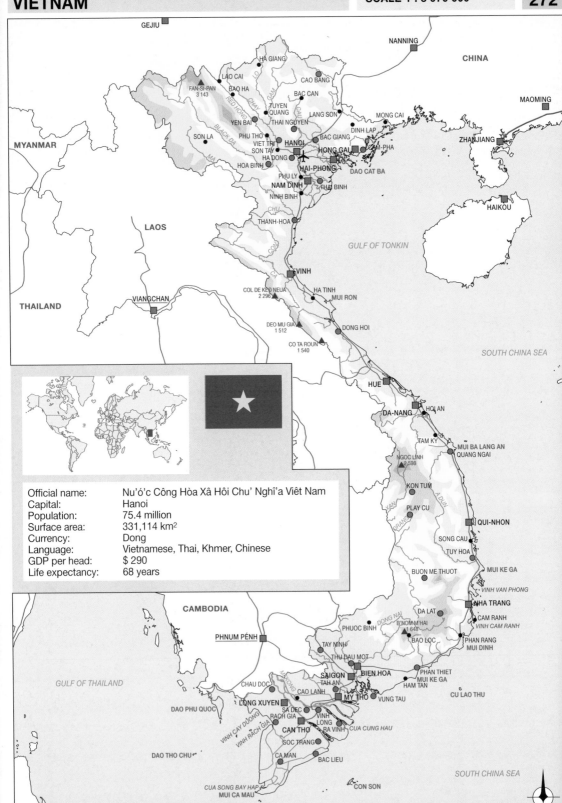

GEJIU

NANNING

CHINA

HA GIANG

LAO CAI

FAN-SI-PAN
3 143

BAO HA

CAO BANG

MAOMING

BAC CAN

TUYEN
QUANG

YEN BAI

LANG SON

MONG CAI

SON LA

THAI NGUYEN

DINH LAP

ZHANJIANG

MYANMAR

PHU THO

BAC GIANG

VIET TRI

HANOI

HONG GAI

CAM-PHA

SON TAY

HA DONG

HOA BINH

HAI-PHONG

DAO CAT BA

PHU LY

NAM DINH

THAI BINH

HAIKOU

NINH BINH

LAOS

THANH-HOA

GULF OF TONKIN

VINH

THAILAND

VIANGCHAN

COL DE KEO NEUA
2 296

HA TINH

MUI RON

DEO MU GIA
1 512

DONG HOI

SOUTH CHINA SEA

CO TA ROUN
1 540

HUE

HOI AN

DA-NANG

TAM KY

MUI BA LANG AN
QUANG NGAI

NGOC LINH
2 598

KON TUM

PLAY CU

QUI-NHON

SONG CAU

TUY HOA

MUI KE GA

BUON ME THUOT

VINH VAN PHONG

Official name: Nu'ó'c Công Hòa Xâ Hôi Chu' Nghî'a Viêt Nam
Capital: Hanoi
Population: 75.4 million
Surface area: 331,114 km²
Currency: Dong
Language: Vietnamese, Thai, Khmer, Chinese
GDP per head: $ 290
Life expectancy: 68 years

NHA TRANG

DA LAT

CAM RANH

CAMBODIA

PHUOC BINH

B'NOM M'HAI
1 648

VINH CAM RANH

BAO LOC

PHAN RANG
MUI DINH

PHNUM PÉNH

TAY NINH

THU DAU MOT

PHAN THIET
MUI KE GA

SAIGON

TAH AN

BIEN HOA

HAM TAN

CU LAO THU

CHAU DOC

CAO LANH

MY THO

VUNG TAU

GULF OF THAILAND

LONG XUYEN

SA DEC

DAO PHU QUOC

RACH GIA

VINH
LONG

RA VINH

CUA CUNG HAU

CAN THO

SOC TRANG

DAO THO CHU

CA MAN

BAC LIEU

SOUTH CHINA SEA

CUA SONG BAY HAP

MUI CA MAU

CON SON

SCALE 1 : 4 210 000

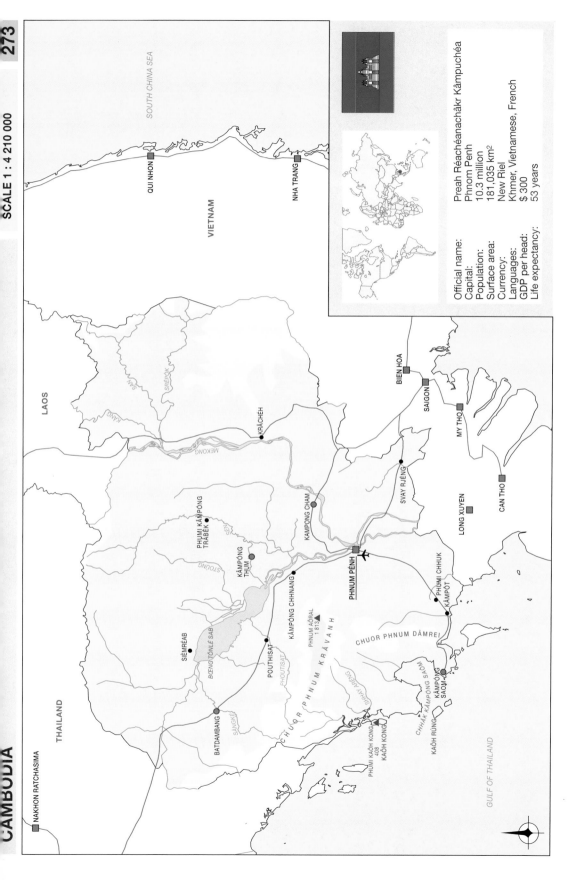

Official name:	Preah Réachéanachâkr Kâmpuchéa
Capital:	Phnom Penh
Population:	10.3 million
Surface area:	181,035 km²
Currency:	New Riel
Languages:	Khmer, Vietnamese, French
GDP per head:	$ 300
Life expectancy:	53 years

THAILAND

NAKHON RATCHASIMA

LAOS

SOUTH CHINA SEA

QUI NHON

VIETNAM

NHA TRANG

SAN

SRÉPÔK

KÂNG

MEKONG

KRÂCHÉH

SIĚMRÉAB

PHUMI KÂMPÓNG
TRÂBÊK

KÂMPÓNG
THUM

STŒNG

SEN

BŒNG TÔNLÉ SAB

POUTHISAT

STŒNG POUTHISAT

BATDAMBANG

SANGKÊ

KÂMPÓNG CHHNANG

KÂMPÓNG CHAM

PHNUM AÔRAL
1 813

CHUOR PHNUM KRÂVANH

PHNUM PÉNH

SVAY RIĔNG

SVAY RIĔNG

SVAY ATÉNG

CHUOR PHNUM DÂMREI

PHUMI CHHUK

KÂMPÔT

KÂMPÓNG
SAÔM

CHHAK KÂMPÓNG SAÔM

PHUMI KAÔH KONG
408

KAÔH KONG

KAÔH RŬNG

GULF OF THAILAND

BIEN HOA

SAIGON

MY THO

LONG XUYEN

CAN THO

MALAYSIA / SINGAPORE

Official name:	Malaysia
Capital:	Kuala Lumpur
Population:	20.6 million
Surface area:	329,758 km²
Currency:	Malaysian Dollar (Ringgit)
Languages:	Malay, English, Chinese, Tamil
GDP per head:	$ 4,370
Life expectancy:	72 years

THAILAND

THALE LUANG

THALE SAP SONGKHLA

HAT YAI

PULAU PERLIS

KANDAR

ALOR SETAR

SUNGAI PETANI

PULAU PINTANG

BUTTERWORTH

GEORGE TOWN

KULIM

TAIPING

KUALA KANGSAR

IPOH

GUNONG BATU BERINCHANG 2 031

BATU GAJAH

KAMPAR

KUALA LIPIS

TELEK ANSON

RAUB

KUALA KUBU BAHARU

BENTONG

SHAH ALAM

KUALA LUMPUR

KELANG

KAJANG

SEREMBAN

KUALA

PORT DICKINSON

SEGAMAT

LABIS

MELAKA

MUAR

BATU PAHAT

KULAI

KOTA TINGGI

JOHOR BAHARU

SINGAPORE

SINGAPORE

SINGAPORE STRAIT

MUDA

PERAK

STRAIT OF MALACCA

BIKIT ULU LAHO 1 202

KELANTAN

PASIR MAS

KOTA BAHURA

PULAU REDANG

GUNONG LAWIT 1 519

KUALA TERENGGANU

TEMBELING

GUNONG TAHAN 2 187

DUNGUN

GUNONG TAPIS 1 512

CHUKAI

KUANTAN

GUNONG BENOM 2 107

PAHANG

MENTAKAB

BAHAU

GUNONG BESAR 1 036

MERSING

KELUANG

PULAU TIOMAN

SOUTH CHINA SEA

INDONESIA

PEKANBARU

STRAIT OF KARIMA

INDONESIA

KALIMANTAN (BORNEO)

PONTIANAK

PADANG

INDONESIA (SUMATERA)

JAMBI

PALEMBANG

Official name:	Republic of Singapore
Capital:	Singapore
Population:	3.0 million
Surface area:	647,5 km²
Currency:	Singapore Dollar
Languages:	Chinese, English, Malay
GDP per head:	$ 30,550
Life expectancy:	76 years

PHILIPPINES

B A L A B E C   S T R A I T

PULAU BALAMBANGAN

PULAU BANGGI

TELUKAN PAITAN

PULAU JAMBONGAN

TELUK LABUK

GUNONG KINABALU
4 101

KOTA KINABALU

BANJARAN CROCKER

KINABALU
NATIONAL PARK

SANDAKAN

SOUTH CHINA SEA

PULAU LABUAN
VICTORIA

TELUK BRUNEI

GUNONG TRUS MADI
2 649

LAHAD DATU

BANDAR SERI BEGAWAN

GUNONG LUMAKU
1 966

GUNONG ANTULAI
1 713

TELUKAN LAHAD DATU

BRUNEI

MIRI

BARAM

GUNONG MULU
2 377

BUKIT PAGON
1 850

TAWAU

PULAU SEBATIK

TELUK SEBUKU

GUNONG MULU
NATIONAL PARK

GUNONG MURUD
2 423

CELEBES SEA

PULAU BRUIT

BUKIT NAONG
1 071

SIBU

SARIKEI

BUKIT BATU
2 028

PEGUNUNGAN KAPUAS HULU

KUCHING

PONTIANAK

INDONESIA
KALIMANTAN
(BORNEO)

SAMARINDA

BALIKPAPAN

INDONESIA
SULAWI
(CELEBES)

BANJARMASIN

Official name:	Islamic Sultanate of Brunei
Capital:	Bandar Seri Begawan
Population:	0.3 million
Surface area:	5,765 km^2
Currency:	Brunei Dollar
Languages:	Malay, English, Chinese
GDP per head:	$ 9,635
Life expectancy:	75 years

PHILIPPEINES

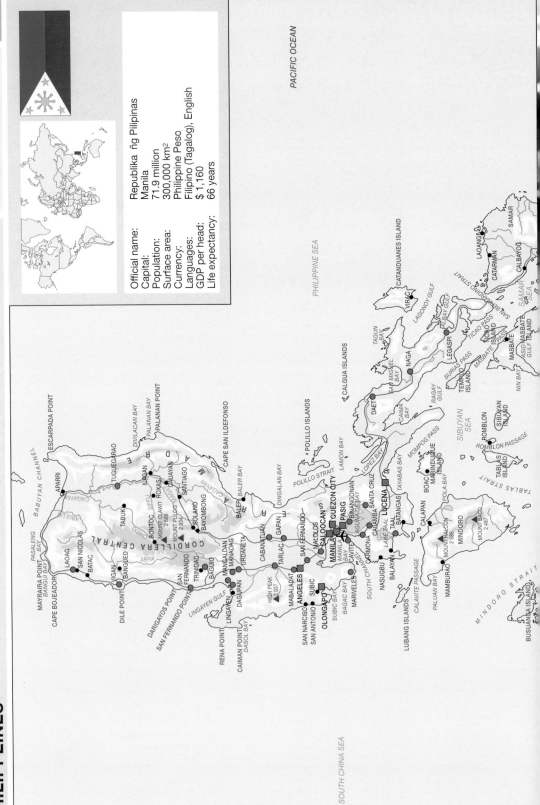

Official name:	Republika ñg Pilipinas
Capital:	Manila
Population:	71.9 million
Surface area:	300,000 km²
Currency:	Philippine Peso
Languages:	Filipino (Tagalog), English
GDP per head:	$ 1,160
Life expectancy:	66 years

PACIFIC OCEAN

PHILIPPINE SEA

SOUTH CHINA SEA

SIBUYAN SEA

MINDORO STRAIT

TABLAS STRAIT

SAMAR SEA

PALANAN POINT

ESCARPADA POINT

DIVILACAN BAY

PALANAN BAY

CAPE SAN ILDEFONSO

BABUYAN CHANNEL

MAYRAIRA POINT
BANGUI BAY
PASALENG BAY

CAPE BOJEADOR

DILE POINT

RENA POINT

CAIMAN POINT
DASOL BAY

DARIGAYOS POINT

SAN FERNANDO POINT

LINGAYEN GULF

SUBIC BAY

BAGAC BAY

SOUTH CHANNEL

MANILA BAY

CAVITE PASSAGE

CALAVITE PASSAGE

PALUAN BAY

LUBANG ISLANDS

BUSUANGA ISLAND

POLA BAY

MARINDUQUE ISLAND

ROMBLON PASSAGE

TABLAS ISLAND

SIBUYAN ISLAND

ROMBLON

MOMPOG PASS

TAYABAS BAY

RAGAY GULF

BURIAS ISLAND

MASBATE ISLAND

TICAO ISLAND

TICAO PASS

TEMPLAS ISLAND
TEMPLAS PASS

NIN BAY

SAN BERNARDINO STRAIT

CALBAYOG

CATARMAN

LAOANG

SAMAR

CATANDUANES ISLAND

VIRAC

LAGONOY GULF

SAN MIGUEL BAY

CAIMA BAY

TAGUN BAY

ALBAY GULF

LEGASPI

NAGA

DAET

CALGUA ISLANDS

POLILLO ISLANDS

POLILLO STRAIT

LAMON BAY

LOPEZ BAY

BALER BAY

DINGALAN BAY

APARRI

CAGAYAN

TUGUEGARAO

ILAGAN

CAUAYAN
ROXAS
CLAVIT
SANTIAGO
SOLANO
BAYOMBONG

BONTOC

MOUNT PULOG 2 934

MOUNT POLO 2 669

TABUK

BANGUED
ABRA

SAN NICOLAS
BATAC
VIGAN
LAOAG

SAN FERNANDO
TRINIDAD
BAGUIO

MANGALDAN
MANAOAG
URDANETA

LINGAYEN
DAGUPAN

SAN NARCISO
SAN ANTONIO
OLONGAPO
SUBIC

ANGELES
MABALACAT

HIGH PEAK 2 037

CABANATUAN
TARLAC
GAPAN
SAN FERNANDO

VALCOLS
CALOOCAN
MANILA
QUEZON CITY
PASIG
BINANGONAN
CARMONA
LAGUNA DE BAY
SANTA CRUZ
CALAMBA
TAAL LAKE
TAAL
LUCENA

BATANGAS

BALAYAN

NASUGBU

MARIVELES

MAMBURAO

MOUNT HALCON 2 586

MINDORO

MOUNT BACO 2 487

BOAC

CALAPAN

CORDILLERA CENTRAL

CAGAYAN

INDONESIA

THAILAND

HAT YAI

KOTA BAHURA

SOUTH CHINA SEA

BANDA ACEN

LHOKSEUMAWE

GUNUNG PEUETSAGOE
2 780

JAMBOAIE

PEG. PUSAI GAYO

GUNUG ABONGABONG
2 985

GUNUG LEUSER
3 381

LANGSA

PINANG

KUALA TERENGGANU

TAIPING

IPOH

MALAYSIA

NATUNA BESAR

BINJAI

KEPULAUAN ANAMBAS

TAPAKTUAN

BINJAI

MEDAN

TEBINGTINGGI

KISARAN

KUATAN

STRAIT OF MALACCA

PEMATANGSIANTAR

TANJUNGBALAI

KUALA LUMPUR

KELANG

SEREMBAN

DANAU TOBA

DOLOKSHABUHABU
2 300

RANTAUPRAPAT

BAGANSIAPIAPI

BATUMUN

PULAU SIMEULUE

SIBOLGA

DUMAI

KEPULAUN TAMBELAN

GUNUNGSITOLI

PADANGSIDEMPUAN

SUMATERA

ROKAN

SIAK

JOHOR BAHARU

SINGAPORE

TANJUNGPINANG

KEPULAUAN RIAU

PULAU NIAS

BANGKINANG

PEKANBARU

TALU

LUBUKSIKAPING

KAMPER

KEPULAUN BATU

BUKITTINGGI

PAYAKUMBUH

BATUSANGKAR

TEMBILAHAN

KEPULAUAN LINGGA

TALUK

RENGAT

PADANGPANJANG
PARIAMAN

PADANG

TELUKBAYUR

SUNGAIDAREH

SELAT BERHALA

PAINAN

PULAU SIBERUT

MUARABUNGO

MUARATEBO

HARI

JAMBI

GUNUNG KERINCI
3 800

MUARATEMBESI

PULAU BANGKA

BANGKO

SAROLANGUN

SELAT MENTAWAI

KEPULAUAN MENTAWAI

SURULANGUN

PANGKALPINANG

GUNUNG MASURAI
2 933

MUKOMUKO

TANJUNGPANDAN

LUBUKLINGGAU

TALANGBETUTU

PALEMBANG

INDIAN OCEAN

LAIS

CURUP

PERABUMULIH

TANJUNGRAJA

KAYUAGUNG

BELITUNG

BENGKULU

LAHAT

MUARAENIM

GUNUNG DEMPO
3 159

BATURAJA

TAIS

MARTAPURA

MANNA

MUARADUA

MENGGALA

LAUT JAWA

BINTUHAN

KOTABUMI

METRO

DANAU RANAU

KRUI

PRINGSEWU

SUKADANA

PULAU ENGGANO

KOTAAGUNG

PANJANG

TANJUNGKARANGTELUKBETUNG

SELAT SUNDA

ANYER

TANGERAN

JAWA
(JAVA)

SERANG

JAKARTA

LABUHAN

DEPOK

KARAWANG

UJUNGKULON
NATIONAL PARK

RANGKASBITUNG

CIBI-
NONG

PUR-
WAKARTA

CICURUG

BOGOR

BANDUNG

PELABUHANRATH

SUKABUMI

JAMPUNG-KULON

GARUT

SINDANGBARANG

TASIKMAL

PAMEUNGPEUK

CIJULANG

Official name:	Indonesia
Capital:	Jakarta
Population:	197.1 million
Surface area:	1,904,443 km²
Currency:	Rupiah
Languages:	Bahasa (Indonesian)
GDP per head:	$ 1,080
Life expectancy:	65 years

PHILIPPINES

SOUTH CHINA SEA

NATUNA BESAR

KEPULAUAN NATUNA SELATAN

SELAT SERASAN

BANDAR SERI BEGAWAN

BRUNEI

MALAYSIA

TARAKAN

CELEBES SEA

KAYAN

TANJUNGREDEP

PEGUNUNGAN KAPUAS HULU

TELUK DONDO

SAMBAS
GUNUNG NIUT
1 701
SINGKAWANG

DANAU LUAR
DANAU SENTARUM
BUKIT BATUBROK
2 240

PEGUNUNGAN MÜLLER

BULU OGOAMAS
2 913

BUKIT MALINO
2 443

SEMITAU

MAHAKAM

TELUK TAMBU

TELUK
TOMINI

PONTIANAK

KAPUAS

SINTANG

NANGAPINOH

BUKIT RAYA
2 278

KENOHAN SEMAYANG

LONGIRAM

SAMARINDA

PALU

PEG. TAKOLEKAJU

SULAWI
(CELEBES)

POSO

GUNUNG SARAN
1 758

PEGUNUNGAN SCHWANER

KENOHAN JEMPANG

TELUK PALU

DANAU POSO

PULAU MAYA

SUKADANA

KALIMANTAN
(BORNEO)

SAMBOJA

BALIKPAPAN

KARAMA

BULU GANDADIWATA
3 074

GUNUNG BALEASE
3 016

DANAU MATENA

KEPULAUAN
KARIMATA

NANGATAYAN

KETAPANG

PALANGKARAYA

PEMBUANG

PEGUNUNGAN MERATUS

BARITO

GUNUNG
BESAR
1 892

SELAT MAKASAR

PALOPO

DANAU TOWUTI

POLEWALI

MAJENE

GUNUNG MEKONGGA
2 799

KENDAWANGAN

SUKARAJA

SAMPIT

KUALAKAPUAS

KANDANGAN

PINRANG

TELUK MANDAR

PAREPARE

SINGKANG

MANGGAR
BELITUNG

BANJARMASIN

MARTAPURA

WATANSOPENG
BULU LAPOSO
1 395

WATAMPONE

TELUK
BONE

PULAU LAUT

PANGKAJENE
MAROS

LAUT JAWA

KEPULAUAN
LAUT KECIL

UJUNGPANDANG

SINJAI

BULUKUMBA

KEPULAUAN KARIMUNJAWA

PULAU BWEAN

TAKALAR

JENEPONTO

BANTAENG

PULAU SELAYAR

INDRAMAYU

KLANGENAN
CIREBON

JEPARA

TAYU

REMBANG

MADURA

AMBUNTENTIMUR

KEPULAUAN KANGEAN

PULAU TANAHJAMPEA

PEKALONGAN

KUDUS

BANGKALAN

SUMENEP

LAUT FLORES

TEGAL

PURWO-
KERTO

SEMARANG

JAWA
(JAVA)

GRESIK

PAMEKASAN

SELAT MADURA

SURABAYA

SURAKARTA

MADIUN

BANGIL

PROBO-
LINGGO

SITUBONDO

LAUT BALI

SUMBAWA

FLORES

CILACAP

PURWOREJO

KEDIRI

PASURUAN

YOGYAKARTA

MALANG

JEMBER

BANYU-
WANGI

SINGARAJA

TEJAKULA

BAYAN

SUMBAWA BESAR

RABA

LABUHANBAJO

RUTENG

PACITAN

TULUNGAGUNG

BLITAR

LUMAJANG

MUNCAR

NEGARA

PENEBEL

TANJUNG

LOMBOK

TALIWANG

PLAMPANG

BAJAWA

ENDE

DENPASAR

MATARAM

KLUNG
KUNG

PRAYA

BALI

LOMBOK

WAIKELO

MEMBORO

LAUT SAWU

WAINGAPU

PAYETI

SUMBA

PULAU
SAWU

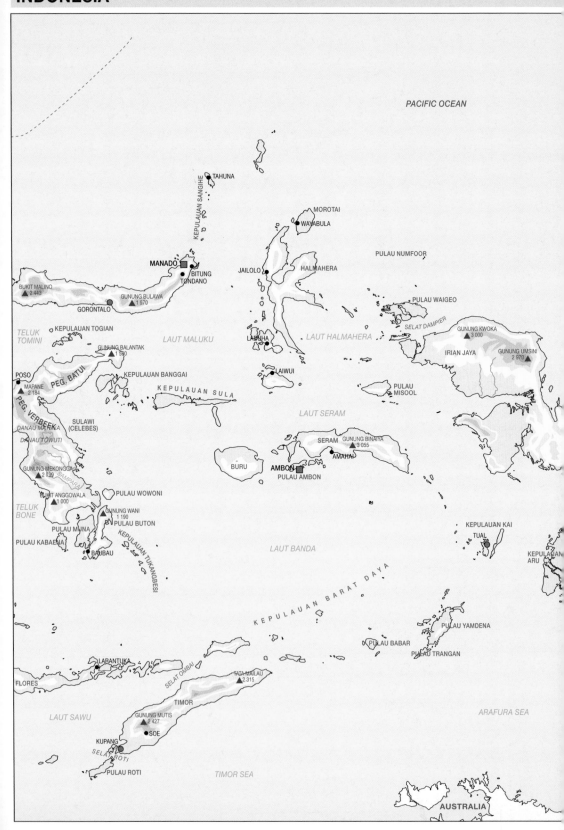

PACIFIC OCEAN

TAHUNA

MOROTAI
WAYABULA

KEPULAUAN SANGIHE

PULAU NUMFOOR

MANADO
BITUNG
TONDANO

JAILOLO
HALMAHERA

PULAU WAIGEO

BUKIT MALINO
2 443

GUNUNG BULAWA
1 970
GORONTALO

LABUHA

SELAT DAMPIER

GUNUNG KWOKA
3 000

IRIAN JAYA
GUNUNG UMSINI
2 970

TELUK
TOMINI

KEPULAUAN TOGIAN

LAUT MALUKU

LAUT HALMAHERA

GUNUNG BALANTAK
1 590

LAIWUI

POSO
MAPANE
2 184

PEG. BATUI

KEPULAUAN BANGGAI

KEPULAUAN SULA

PULAU
MISOOL

PEG. VERBEEK
DANAU MATANA

SULAWI
(CELEBES)

LAUT SERAM

DANAU TOWUTI

SERAM
GUNUNG BINAIYA
3 055

GUNUNG MEKONGGA
2 799

SAMPARA

BURU
AMBON
AMAHAI
PULAU AMBON

BUKIT ANGGOWALA
1 000

PULAU WOWONI

TELUK
BONE

GUNUNG WANI
1 190
PULAU BUTON
PULAU MUNA

KEPULAUAN KAI
TUAL

KEPULAUAN
ARU

KEPULAUAN TUKANGBESI

PULAU KABAENA

LAUT BANDA

BAUBAU

KEPULAUAN BARAT DAYA

PULAU YAMDENA

PULAU BABAR
PULAU TRANGAN

LARANTUKA

FLORES

SELAT OMBAI

TATA MAILAU
2 315

LAUT SAWU

TIMOR

ARAFURA SEA

GUNUNG MUTIS
2 427
SOE

KUPANG

SELAT ROTI

PULAU ROTI

TIMOR SEA

AUSTRALIA

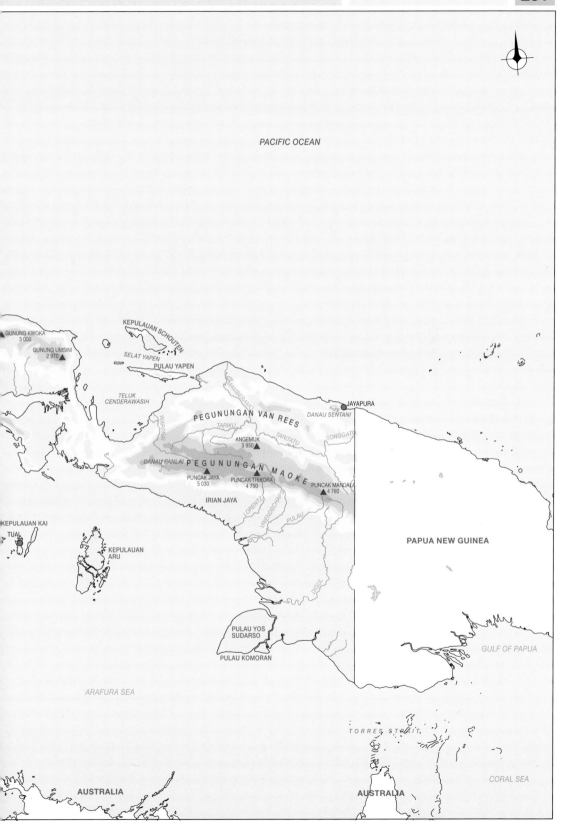

PACIFIC OCEAN

GUNUNG KWOKA
3 000

GUNUNG UMSINI
2 970

KEPULAUAN SCHOUTEN

SELAT YAPEN

PULAU YAPEN

TELUK
CENDERAWASIH

MAMBERAMO

JAYAPURA

DANAU SENTANI

PEGUNUNGAN VAN REES

TARIKU

WARENAI

TARITATU

SONGGATO

ANGEMUK
3 950

DANAU PANLAI

PEGUNUNGAN   MAOKE

PUNCAK JAYA
5 030

PUNCAK TRIKORA
4 750

PUNCAK MANDALA
4 760

IRIAN JAYA

ORENTZ

VRIENDSCHAPS

PULAU

KEPULAUAN KAI

TUAL

KEPULAUAN
ARU

PAPUA NEW GUINEA

DIGUL

PULAU YOS
SUDARSO

GULF OF PAPUA

PULAU KOMORAN

ARAFURA SEA

TORRES STRAIT

AUSTRALIA

AUSTRALIA

CORAL SEA

AUSTRALIA

Official name:	Commonwealth of Australia
Capital:	Canberra
Population:	18.3 million
Surface area:	7,682,300 km²
Currency:	Australian Dollar
Language:	English, Italian, Greek
GDP per head:	$ 20,090
Life expectancy:	78 years

INDONESIA

ARAFURA SEA

TIMOR SEA

CROKER ISLAND

MELVILLE ISLANDS
BATHURST ISLANDS
BEAGLE GULF
VAN DIEMEN GULF
DARWIN
ADELAIDE RIVERS
PINE CREEK
ARNHEMLAND

JOSEPH BONAPARTE GULF
DALY
KATHERINE
ROPER
MATARANKA

COLLIER BAY
DRYSDALE
KEEP RIVER NATIONAL PARK
DALY WATERS
NEWCASTLE WATERS

KING SOUND
DURACK
LAKE ARGYLE
VICTORIA

FITZROY
KIMBERLEY PLATEAU
KING LEOPOLD RANGES
DEBRY
HALLS CREEK
ORD

INDIAN OCEAN

BROOME
FITZROY CROSSING
STURT CREEK
TANAMI DESERT

ROWLEY SHOALS

GREAT SANDY DESERT
LAKE WHITE
LAKE HAZLETT
LAKE MACKAY

PORT HEDLAND
SHAY GAP
DE GREY
MARBLE BAR

MONTE BELLO ISLANDS
BARROW ISLAND
DAMPIER
ROEBOURNE
KARRATHA
CHICHESTER RANGE
OAKOVER

MOUNT LIEBIG 1 524
MOUNT ZEIL 1 511
MACDONNEL RANGES
ALICE SPRINGS

ONSLOW
WITTENOOM
LAKE MACDONALD
LAKE HOPKINS
LAKE NEALE

EXMOUTH GULF
EXMOUTH
HAMERSLEY RANGE
ASHBURTON
FORTESCUE

LAKE DISAPPOINTMENT
LAKE AMADEUS
AYERS ROCK 876

BARLEE RANGE
GIBSON DESERT
MOUNT MORRIS 1 288
MOUNT WOODROFFE 1 440

GASCOYNE
BERNIER ISLAND
DORRE ISLAND
SHARK BAY
DIRK HARTOG ISLAND

PEAK HILL
LAKE CARNEGIE

MEEKATHARRA
WILUNA
GREAT VICTORIA DESERT

MURCHISON

KALBARRI
MOUNT MAGNET
MOUNT REDCLIFFE 562
LAVERTON
LAKE CAREY

MULLEWA
LAKE BARLEE
LEONORA

GERALDTON
MORAWA
MENZIES
GOONGARRIE NATIONAL PARK
EUCLA
CEDUNA

THREE SPRINGS
LAKE MOORE
MOUNT BURGES 554
KALGOORLIE
STRICKY BAY

MOORA
BULLFINCH
LAKE COWAN

WANNEROO
STIRLING
PERTH
FREMANTLE
GOSNELLS
ARMADALE
MANDURAH
SWAN
BOORABBIN NATIONAL PARK
NORSEMAN
POINT CULVER

CAPE BOULEVARD
PEAK CHARLES NATIONAL PARK
ESPERANCE
GREAT AUSTRALIAN BIGHT

GEOGRAPHE BAY
BUNBURY
CAPE NATURALISTE
BLACKWOOD
RAVENSTHORPE
HOPETOUN
CAPE PASLEY

MARGARET RIVER
CRANBOOK
CAPE LEEUWIN
DENMARK
D'ENTRECASTEAUX NATIONAL PARK
ALBANY

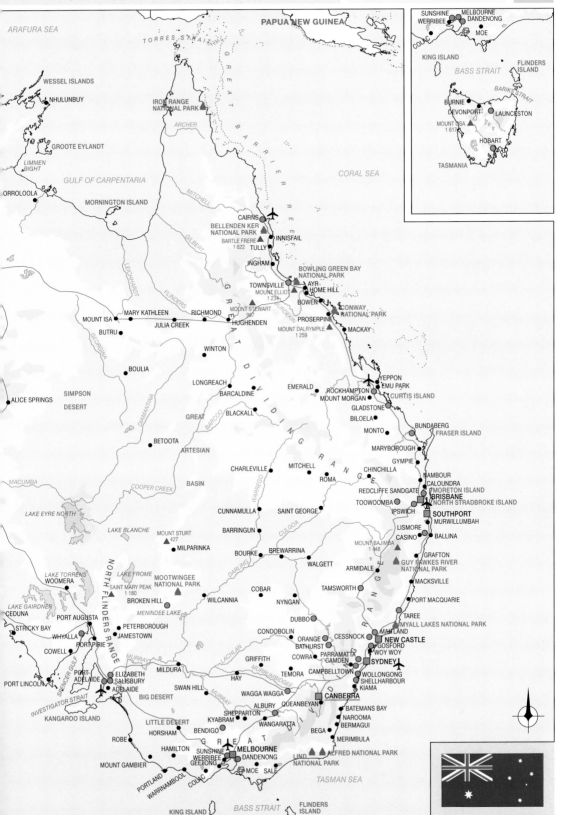

ARAFURA SEA

PAPUA NEW GUINEA

TORRES STRAIT

WESSEL ISLANDS

NHULUNBUY

GROOTE EYLANDT

LIMMEN BIGHT

ORROLOOLA

GULF OF CARPENTARIA

MORNINGTON ISLAND

ARCHER

IRON RANGE NATIONAL PARK

GREAT BARRIER REEF

CORAL SEA

SUNSHINE
WERRIBEE
MELBOURNE
DANDENONG
MOE
COLAC

KING ISLAND

BASS STRAIT

FLINDERS ISLAND

BANKS STRAIT

BURNIE
DEVONPORT
LAUNCESTON
MOUNT ISA
1 617

HOBART

TASMANIA

CAIRNS
BELLENDEN KER NATIONAL PARK
BARTLE FRERE 1 622
INNISFAIL
TULLY
INGHAM
BOWLING GREEN BAY NATIONAL PARK
TOWNSVILLE
MOUNT ELLIOT 1 234
AYR
HOME HILL
BOWEN
CONWAY NATIONAL PARK
MOUNT ISA
MARY KATHLEEN
RICHMOND
JULIA CREEK
HUGHENDEN
MOUNT STEWART 987
PROSERPINE
MOUNT DALRYMPLE 1 259
MACKAY

BUTRU

GEORGINA

GILBERT

LEICHHARDT

FLINDERS

MITCHELL

BURDEKIN

GREAT DIVIDING RANGE

WINTON

BOULIA

LONGREACH

BARCALDINE

BLACKALL

EMERALD

ROCKHAMPTON
MOUNT MORGAN
YEPPON
EMU PARK
CURTIS ISLAND
GLADSTONE
BILOELA
MONTO
BUNDABERG
FRASER ISLAND
MARYBOROUGH
GYMPIE

ALICE SPRINGS

SIMPSON DESERT

DIAMANTINA

BETOOTA

ARTESIAN

GREAT

BARCOO

BASIN

MACUMBA

COOPER CREEK

LAKE EYRE NORTH

LAKE BLANCHE

MOUNT STURT 427
MILPARINKA

CHARLEVILLE

MITCHELL

ROMA

WARREGO

CHINCHILLA

NAMBOUR
CALOUNDRA
REDCLIFFE SANDGATE MORETON ISLAND
BRISBANE
TOOWOOMBA
NORTH STRADBROKE ISLAND
IPSWICH
SOUTHPORT
MURWILLUMBAH
LISMORE
CASINO
BALLINA
GRAFTON
MOUNT BAJIMBA 1 448
GUY FAWKES RIVER NATIONAL PARK
ARMIDALE
MACKSVILLE
PORT MACQUARIE

CUNNAMULLA

SAINT GEORGE

BARRINGUN

CULGOA

BOURKE

BREWARRINA

WALGETT

DARLING

TAMWORTH

TAREE
MYALL LAKES NATIONAL PARK

LAKE TORRENS

WOOMERA

LAKE FROME

MOOTWINGEE NATIONAL PARK

NORTH FLINDERS RANGE

SAINT MARY PEAK 1 180

BROKEN HILL

MENINDEE LAKE

WILCANNIA

COBAR

NYNGAN

DUBBO

CONDOBOLIN

LAKE GAIRDNER

CEDUNA

STREAKY BAY

PORT AUGUSTA

WHYALLA

COWELL

PORT PIRIE

PETERBOROUGH

JAMESTOWN

SPENCER GULF

PORT LINCOLN

PORT ADELAIDE
ELIZABETH
SALISBURY
ADELAIDE

INVESTIGATOR STRAIT

KANGAROO ISLAND

MURRAY

MILDURA

SWAN HILL

BIG DESERT

ORANGE
CESSNOCK
BATHURST
MAITLAND
NEW CASTLE
GOSFORD
WOY WOY
COWRA
PARRAMATTA
CAMDEN
SYDNEY
GRIFFITH
TEMORA
CAMPBELLTOWN
WOLLONGONG
SHELLHARBOUR
KIAMA
HAY
MURRUMBIDGEE
WAGGA WAGGA
LACHLAN
ALBURY
QUEANBEYAN
CANBERRA
BATEMANS BAY
SHEPPARTON
WANGARATTA
NAROOMA
BERMAGUI
KYABRAM
BEGA
MERIMBULA
BENDIGO
LITTLE DESERT
HORSHAM
HAMILTON
ROBE
SUNSHINE
WERRIBEE
MELBOURNE
DANDENONG
GEELONG
MOE
SALE
LIND NATIONAL PARK
ALFRED NATIONAL PARK
MOUNT GAMBIER
PORTLAND
WARRNAMBOOL
COLAC

GREAT

ROBE

MURRAY

GREAT DIVIDING RANGE

TASMAN SEA

KING ISLAND
BASS STRAIT
FLINDERS ISLAND

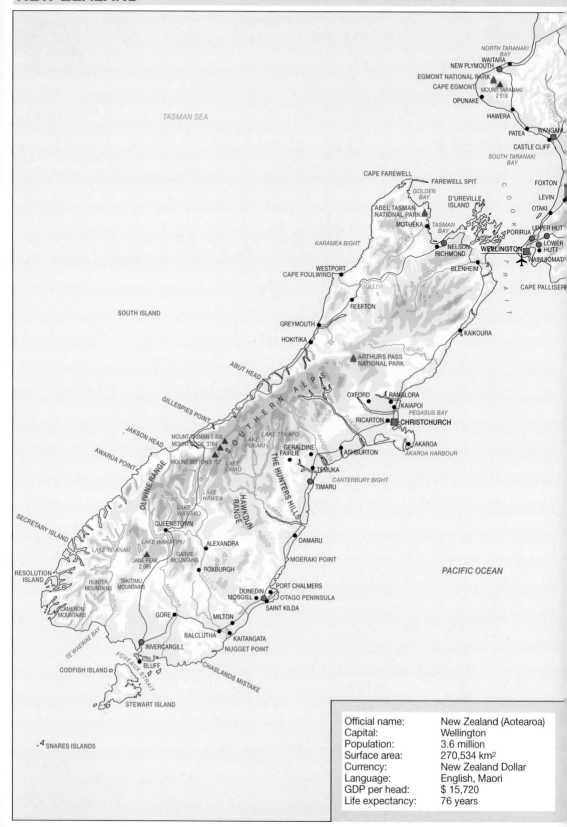

Official name:	New Zealand (Aotearoa)
Capital:	Wellington
Population:	3.6 million
Surface area:	270,534 km²
Currency:	New Zealand Dollar
Language:	English, Maori
GDP per head:	$ 15,720
Life expectancy:	76 years

THREE KINGS ISLAND

NORTH CAPE
CAPE MARIA VAN DIEMEN
PARENGARENGA HARBOUR

CAPE KARIKARI
DOUBTLESS BAY
AWANUI

BAY OF ISLANDS
CAPE BRETT

HOKIANGA HARBOUR

WHANGAREI
TARANGA
ISLAND

DARGAVILLE

GREAT BARRIER ISLAND

COLVILLE CHANNEL
CRADOCK CHANNEL

KAIPARA HARBOUR

EAST COAST BAYS
TAKAPUNA
HAURAKI
GULF
MERCURY ISLANDS
AUCKLAND
DEVONPORT
MOUNT ROSKILL
OTAHUHU
WAITEMATA
PAPATOETOE
NORTH ISLAND
MANUKAU
Manukau Harbour
FIRTH OF
THAMES
PAPAKURA
THAMES
LAKE WAIKARE
MAYOR ISLAND
WAIHI

TASMAN SEA

WAIKATO
MOUNT MAUNGANUI
TAURANGA
HAMILTON
TE PUKE
BAY OF PLENTY
TE AWAMUTU
PUTARURU
WAKATANE
KAWHIA HARBOUR
LAKE ROTORUA
ROTORUA
OPOTIKI
OTOROHANGA
LAKE TARAWERA
RAUKUMARA RANGE
TE KUITI
TOKOROA
WAIKATO
MANGAKINO

TAUPO
UREWERA NATIONAL
GISBORNE
PARK
LAKE TAUPO
Rangitaiki
POVERTY BAY
NORTH TARANAKI
BAY
TAUMARUNUI
LAKE WAIKAREMOANA
WAITARA
NEW PLYMOUTH
MOUNT NGAURUHOE
2 291
KAIMANAWA
EGMONT NATIONAL PARK
TONGARIRO
MOUNTAINS
CAPE EGMONT
NATIONAL
MOUNT TARANAKI
PARK
2 518
WAIROA
OPUNAKE
MOUNT RUAPEHU
OHAKUNE
2 797
TABLE CAPE
HAWERA
WANGANUI
NAPIER
HAWKE BAY
TAIHAPE
PATEA
HASTINGS
CASTLE CLIFF
WANGANUI
CAPE KIDNAPPERS
MARTON
HAVELOCK NORTH
SOUTH TARANAKI
BAY
WAIPUKURAU
RUAHINE RANGE
FIELDING
CAPE FAREWELL
FAREWELL SPIT
FOXTON
PALMERSTON
NORTH
CAPE TURNAGAIN
GOLDEN
BAY
D'UREVILLE
ISLAND
OTAKI
LEVIN
ABEL TASMAN
NATIONAL PARK
MASTERTON
TASMAN
KARAMEA
BAY
CARTERTON
BIGHT
MOTUEKA
PORIRUA
UPPER HUTT
MOTUEKA
NELSON
WELLINGTON
LOWER HUTT
RICHMOND
WAINUIOMATA
WAIRAU
VESTPORT
BLENHEIM
BULLER
CAPE PALLISER
PACIFIC OCEAN
REEFTON

KAIKOURA

ARTHURS PASS
NATIONAL PARK
WAIAU

OXFORD
RANGIORA
CHATHAM ISLANDS
KAIAPOI
PEGASUS BAY

COOK STRAIT

PAPUA NEW GUINEA

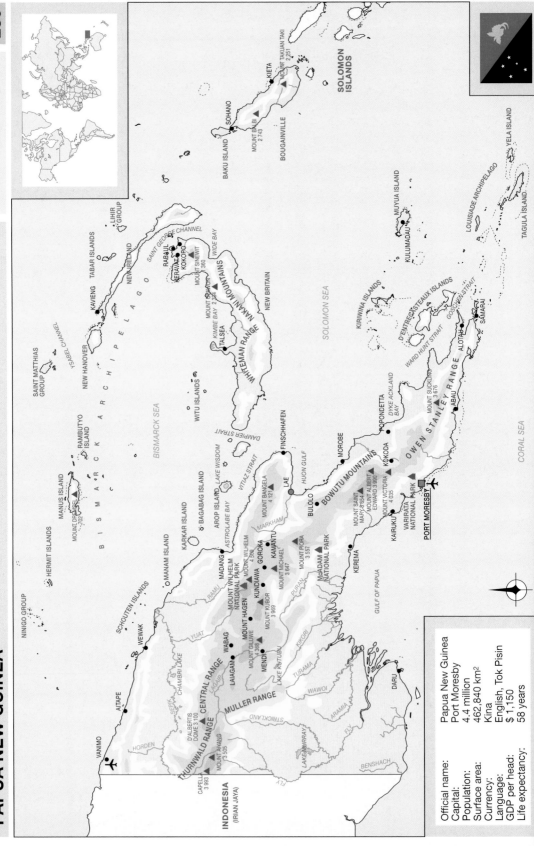

SOLOMON ISLANDS

MOUNT TAKUAN TAKI 2,251

KIETA

BOUGAINVILLE

SOHANO

BAKU ISLAND

MOUNT BALBI 2 743

SOLOMON SEA

YELA ISLAND

TAGULA ISLAND

LOUISIADE ARCHIPELAGO

GOSCHEN STRAIT

SAMARAI

ALOTAU

WARD HUNT STRAIT

D'ENTRECASTEAUX ISLANDS

MUYUA ISLAND

KULUMADAU

KIRIWINA ISLANDS

MOUNT SUCKLING 3 676

ABAU

OWEN STANLEY RANGE

DYKE ACKLAND BAY

POPONDETTA

KOKODA

VARIRATA NATIONAL PARK

MOUNT VICTORIA 4 035

MOUNT ALBERT EDWARD 3 990

KAIRUKU

PORT MORESBY

CORAL SEA

KEREMA

GULF OF PAPUA

MOROBE

BOWUTU MOUNTAINS

MOUNT SAINT MARY 3 664

BULOLO

LAE

HUON GULF

FINSCHHAFEN

MADAM NATIONAL PARK

MOUNT PIORA 3 557

PURARI

MOUNT MICHAEL 3 647

KAMANTU

GOROKA

KUNDIAWA

MOUNT WILHELM 4 509

MOUNT HAGEN

MOUNT GILUWE

MENDI

MOUNT KUBOR 3 969

LAKE KUTUBU

MARKHAM

MOUNT WILHELM NATIONAL PARK

MADANG

KARKAR ISLAND

ASTROLABE BAY

LAKE WISDOM

BAGABAG ISLAND

AROP ISLAND

MANAM ISLAND

RAMU

WITIAZ STRAIT

DAMPIER STRAIT

MOUNT BANGELA 4 121

WHITEMAN RANGE

NAKANAI MOUNTAINS

NEW BRITAIN

SOLOMON SEA

TALSEA

KIMBE BAY 2 206

MOUNT ULAWUN 2 360

MOUNT SINEWIT 3 360

KOKOPO

RABAUL

KERAVAT

NEW IRELAND

SAINT GEORGE CHANNEL

WIDE BAY

WITU ISLANDS

BISMARCK SEA

BISMARCK ARCHIPELAGO

YSABEL CHANNEL

KAVIENG

TABAR ISLANDS

LIHIR GROUP

NEW HANOVER

SAINT MATTHIAS GROUP

MANUS ISLAND

MOUNT DREMSEL 702

RAMBUTYO ISLAND

HERMIT ISLANDS

NINIGO GROUP

SCHOUTEN ISLANDS

WEWAK

AITAPE

VANIMO

SEPIK

YUAT

CHAMBRI LAKE

LAIGAP

LAIAGAM

WABAG

CENTRAL RANGE

MULLER RANGE

D'ALBERTIS DOME 3 100

THURNWALD RANGE

MOUNT IALIBU 3 505

CAPELLA 3 993

HORDEN

STRICKLAND

KIKORI

TURAMA

WAWOI

ARAMIA

FLY

LAKE MURRAY

BENSHACH

DARU

INDONESIA (IRIAN JAYA)

Official name:	Papua New Guinea
Capital:	Port Moresby
Population:	4.4 million
Surface area:	462,840 km²
Currency:	Kina
Language:	English, Tok Pisin
GDP per head:	$ 1,150
Life expectancy:	58 years

NEW CALEDONIA

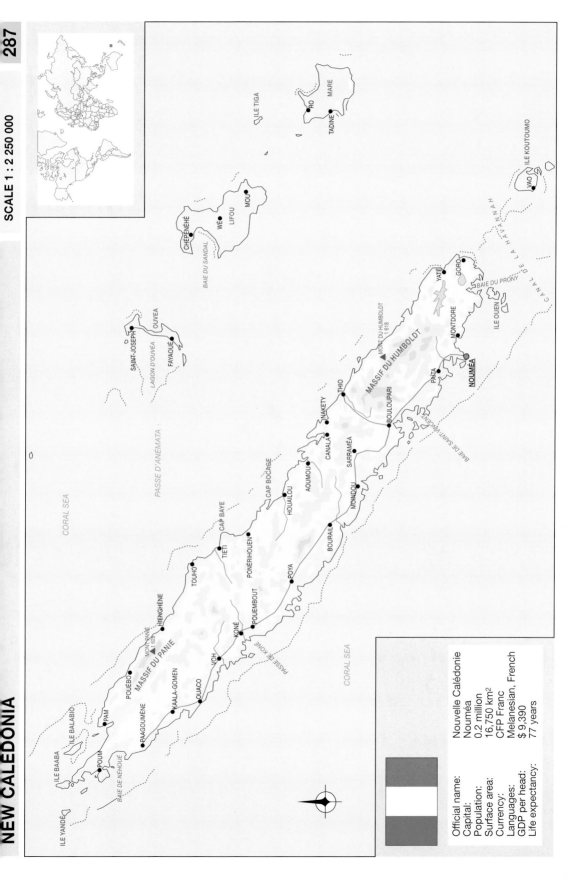

Official name:	Nouvelle Calédonie
Capital:	Nouméa
Population:	0.2 million
Surface area:	16,750 km²
Currency:	CFP Franc
Languages:	Melanesian, French
GDP per head:	$ 9,390
Life expectancy:	77 years

ILE YANDÉ

ILE BAABA

ILE BALABIO

BAIE DE NÉHOUÉ

POUM

PAM

PAAGOUMÈNE

POUEBO

KAALA-GOMEN

OUACO

VOH

MONT PANIÉ

MASSIF DU PANIE

HIENGHÈNE

TOUHO

KONÉ

POUEMBOUT

POYA

PONÉRIHOUEN

TIÉTI

CAP BAYE

CAP BOCAGE

HOUAILOU

PASSE DE KONÉ

BOURAIL

AOUMOU

MONDOU

SARRAMÉA

CANALA

NAKETY

THIO

BOULOUPARI

MASSIF DU HUMBOLDT

MONT DU HUMBOLDT
1 618

PAITA

MONTDORE

NOUMÉA

BAIE DE SAINT-VINCENT

ILE OUEN

BAIE DU PRONY

YATÉ

GORO

CANAL DE LA HAVANNAH

ILE KOUTOUMO

VAO

SAINT-JOSEPH

OUVÉA

LAGON D'OUVÉA

FAYAOUÉ

PASSE D'ANÉMATA

BAIE DU SANDAL

CHÉPÉNÉHÉ

WÉ

LIFOU

MOU

ILE TIGA

MARE

LIFOU

RO

TADINE

CORAL SEA

CORAL SEA

PACIFIC ISLANDS

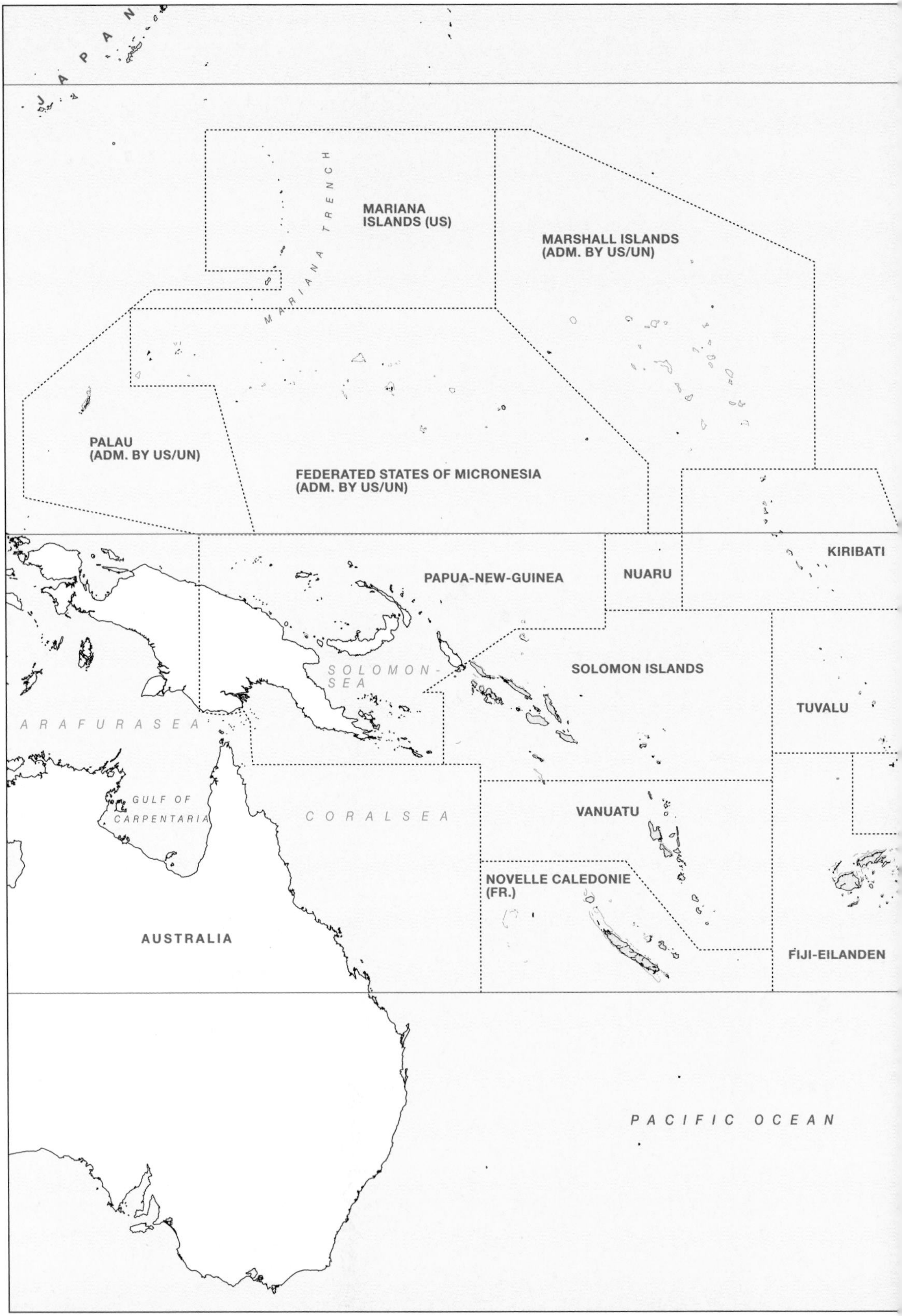

JAPAN

MARIANA TRENCH

MARIANA
ISLANDS (US)

MARSHALL ISLANDS
(ADM. BY US/UN)

PALAU
(ADM. BY US/UN)

FEDERATED STATES OF MICRONESIA
(ADM. BY US/UN)

KIRIBATI

PAPUA-NEW-GUINEA

NUARU

SOLOMON-
SEA

SOLOMON ISLANDS

TUVALU

ARAFURA SEA

VANUATU

GULF OF
CARPENTARIA

CORAL SEA

NOVELLE CALEDONIE
(FR.)

FIJI-EILANDEN

AUSTRALIA

PACIFIC OCEAN

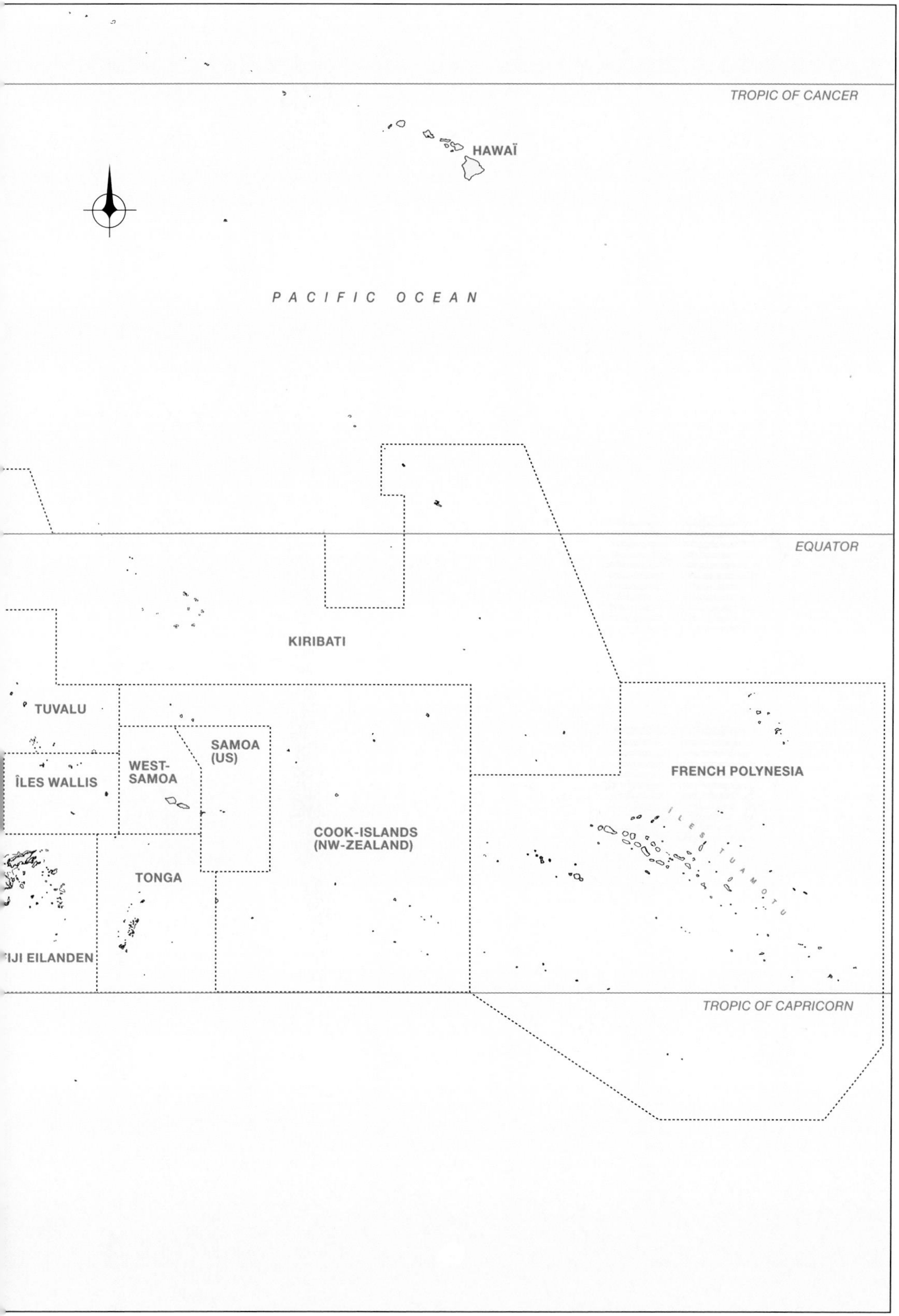

TROPIC OF CANCER

HAWAÏ

PACIFIC   OCEAN

EQUATOR

KIRIBATI

TUVALU

SAMOA
(US)

WEST-
SAMOA

ÎLES WALLIS

FRENCH POLYNESIA

ÎLES TUAMOTU

COOK-ISLANDS
(NW-ZEALAND)

TONGA

FIJI EILANDEN

TROPIC OF CAPRICORN

MARIANA ISLANDS / MARSHALL ISLANDS/ PALAU / MICRONESIA

TUVALU
NAMUMEA

KINGSMILL
GROUP

ABEMAMA

KIRIBATI

BAIRIKI
TARAWA
BUTARITARI

MARSHALL EILANDEN
(ADM. BY US/UN)

TAONGI

WAKE
(US)

RATAK CHAIN

BIKAR

WOTJE
MALOELAP
ULIGA
MAJURO
MILI

RONGELAP

RALIK CHAIN

BIKINI

KWAJALEIN

AILINGLAPALAP
JALUIT
EBON

YAREN

NUARU

SOLOMON EILANDEN

KÜSAIE

ENIWETOK

UJELANG

M I C R O N E S I E

MARIANA EILANDEN (US)

POHNPEI
POHNPEI
SENJAVIN IS.

KAPINGAMARANGI

NUKUMANU IS.
ONTONG JAVA

MARIANA TRENCH

ASUNCION

PAGAN

OROLUK

MORTLOCK

BOUGAINVILLE
ARAWA
CHOISEUL

SUSUPE
SAIPAN
ROTA

'HALL IS.

MOEN

TRUK IS.

FEDERATED STATES OF MICRONESIA
(ADM. BY US/UN)

9140
PLANET DEEP

NEW IRELAND

GUAM
(US)

MARIANA ISLANDS

NAMONUITO

C A R O L I N E   I S L A N D S

MELANESIË

PAPUA-NIEUW-GUINEA

NEW HANOVER

BISMARCK
ARCHIPEL

NEW BRITAIN

GAFERUT

LAMOTREK

IFALIK

ADMIRALITY IS.

MANUS IS.

MADANG

WEWAK

11034
CHALLENGER DEEP

SOROL

FAIS

YAP

JAYAPURA

PALAU
(ADM. BY US/UN)

BIAK

MAPI

KOROR
PALAU

SONSOROL

MERIR

TOBI

KEP.
ARU

EQUATOR

NAUARU / SOLOMON ISLANDS / TUVALU / CALEDONIA / FIJI

SCALE 1 : 22 670 000

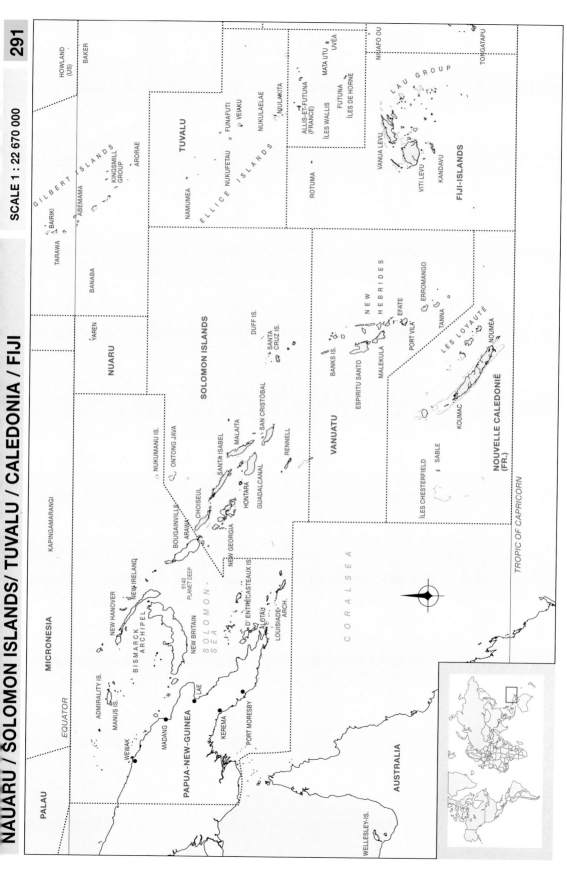

PALAU

MICRONESIA

KAPINGAMARANGI

HOWLAND (US)

BAKER

EQUATOR

GILBERT ISLANDS

TARAWA

BAIRIKI

ABEMAMA

KINGSMILL GROUP

ARORAE

TUVALU

NAMUMEA

FUNAFUTI

VEIAKU

NUKULAELAE

ELLICE ISLANDS

NUKUFETAU

ROTUMA

NIUAFO OU

TOÑGATAPU

UVÉA

MATA UTU

ALLIS-ET-FUTUNA (FRANCE)

ÎLES WALLIS

FUTUNA

ÎLES DE HORNE

NUKULAITA

LAU GROUP

VANUA LEVU

VITI LEVU

KANDAVU

FIJI-ISLANDS

BANABA

YAREN

NUARU

SOLOMON ISLANDS

DUFF IS.

SANTA CRUZ IS.

NEW HEBRIDES

EFATE

ERROMANGO

PORT VILA

TANNA

BANKS IS.

ESPIRITU SANTO

MALEKULA

VANUATU

LES LOYAUTÉ

NOUMÉA

KOUMAC

NOUVELLE CALEDONIË (FR.)

ÎLES CHESTERFIELD

SABLE

NUKUMANU IS.

ONTONG JAVA

SANTA ISABEL

MALAITA

SAN CRISTÓBAL

RENNELL

BOUGAINVILLE

ARAWA

CHOISEUL

HONIARA

GUADALCANAL

NEW GEORGIA

NEW HANOVER

NEW IRELAND

BISMARCK ARCHIPEL

NEW BRITAIN

9140 PLANET DEEP

SOLOMON-SEA

D'ENTRECASTEAUX IS.

ALOTAU

LOUISIADE ARCH.

ADMIRALITY IS.

MANUS IS.

WEWAK

MADANG

LAE

KEREMA

PORT MORESBY

PAPUA-NEW-GUINEA

CORAL SEA

TROPIC OF CAPRICORN

AUSTRALIA

WELLESLEY-IS.

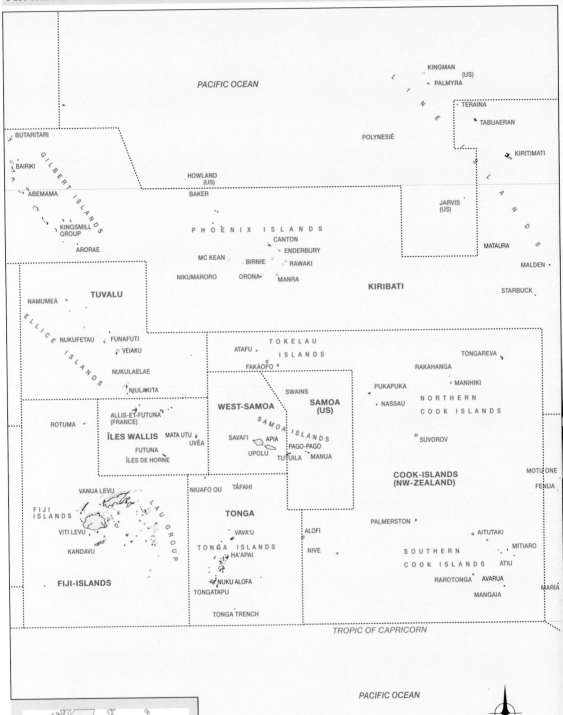

PACIFIC OCEAN

KINGMAN
(US)
PALMYRA

TERAINA

TABUAERAN

POLYNESIË

KIRITIMATI

BUTARITARI

GILBERT ISLANDS

BAIRIKI

HOWLAND
(US)

BAKER

JARVIS
(US)

ABEMAMA

KINGSMILL
GROUP

PHOENIX ISLANDS

CANTON

ENDERBURY

MATAURA

ARORAE

MC KEAN

BIRNIE

RAWAKI

MALDEN

NIKUMARORO

ORONA

MANRA

KIRIBATI

STARBUCK

NAMUMEA

TUVALU

TONGAREVA

ELLICE ISLANDS

NUKUFETAU

FUNAFUTI

VEIAKU

TOKELAU
ISLANDS

ATAFU

FAKAOFO

RAKAHANGA

MANIHIKI

PUKAPUKA

NORTHERN
COOK ISLANDS

NASSAU

NUKULAELAE

NIULAKITA

SWAINS

ROTUMA

ALLIS-ET-FUTUNA
(FRANCE)

WEST-SAMOA

SAMOA
(US)

SUVOROV

ÎLES WALLIS

MATA UTU

UVÉA

SAMOA ISLANDS

SAVAI'I

APIA

FUTUNA

ÎLES DE HORNE

UPOLU

PAGO-PAGO

TUTUILA

MANUA

COOK-ISLANDS
(NW-ZEALAND)

MOTUONE

FENUA

VANUA LEVU

NIUAFO OU

TÂFAHI

FIJI
ISLANDS

LAU GROUP

TONGA

PALMERSTON

AITUTAKI

VITI LEVU

VAVA'U

ALOFI

MITIARO

KANDAVU

TONGA ISLANDS

HA'APAI

NIVE

SOUTHERN
COOK ISLANDS

ATIU

FIJI-ISLANDS

NUKU ALOFA

RAROTONGA

AVARUA

MARIÁ

TONGATAPU

MANGAIA

TONGA TRENCH

TROPIC OF CAPRICORN

PACIFIC OCEAN

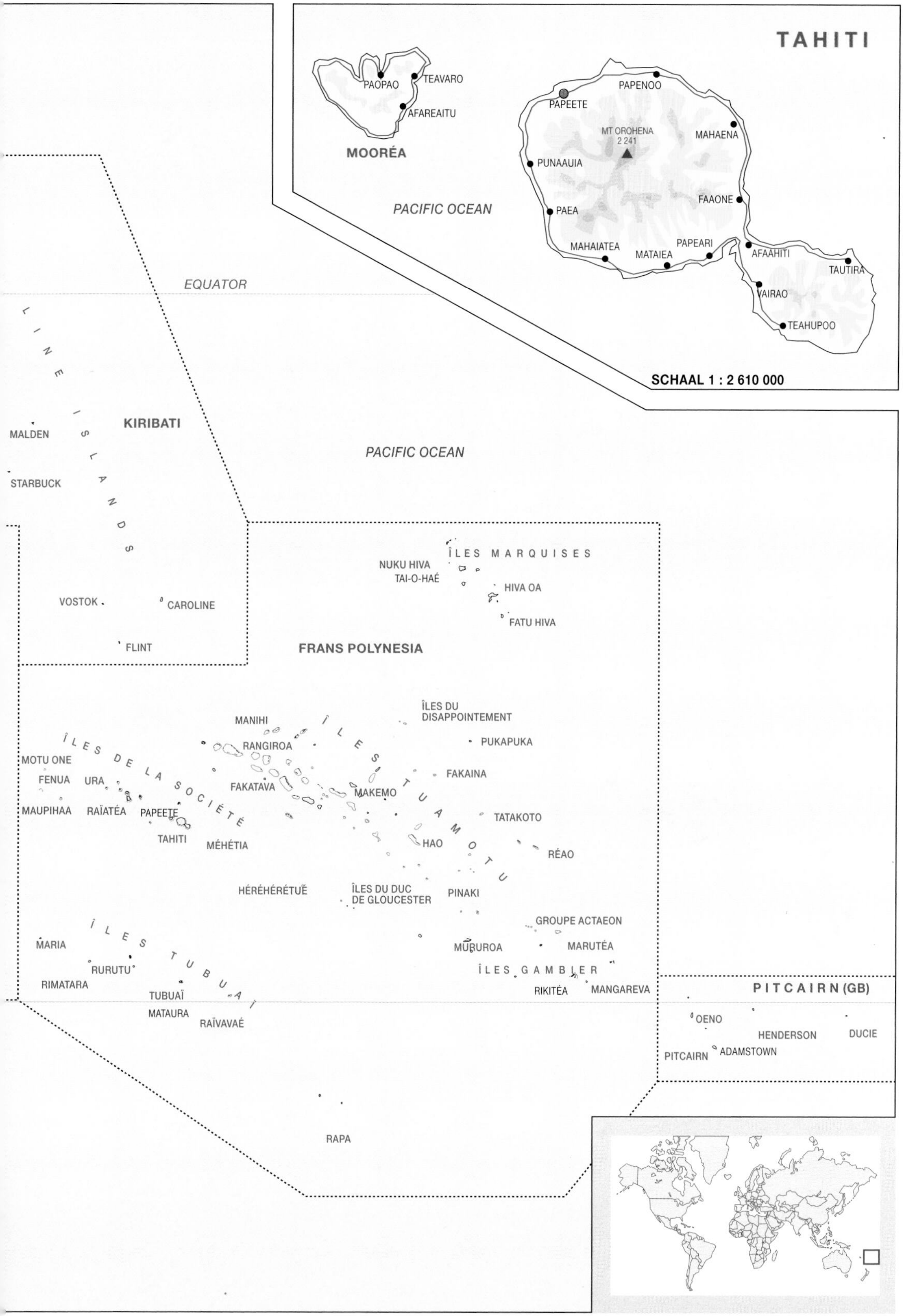

TAHITI

PAOPAO
TEAVARO
AFAREAITU

MOORÉA

PAPENOO
PAPEETE
MT OROHENA
2 241
MAHAENA
PUNAAUIA
FAAONE
PAEA
MAHAIATEA
PAPEARI
MATAIEA
AFAAHITI
TAUTIRA
VAIRAO
TEAHUPOO

PACIFIC OCEAN

SCHAAL 1 : 2 610 000

EQUATOR

L I N E   I S L A N D S

MALDEN

KIRIBATI

STARBUCK

PACIFIC OCEAN

VOSTOK
CAROLINE

FLINT

ÎLES MARQUISES

NUKU HIVA
TAI-O-HAÉ
HIVA OA

FATU HIVA

FRANS POLYNESIA

ÎLES DU
DISAPPOINTEMENT

MANIHI
ÎLES TUAMOTU
RANGIROA
PUKAPUKA
MOTU ONE
ÎLES DE LA SOCIÉTÉ
FAKAINA
FENUA   URA
FAKATAVA
MAKEMO
MAUPIHAA   RAÏATÉA   PAPEETE
TATAKOTO
TAHITI
MÉHÉTIA
HAO
RÉAO

HÉRÉHÉRÉTUÉ
ÎLES DU DUC
DE GLOUCESTER
PINAKI

GROUPE ACTAEON
MARIA
ÎLES TUBUAÏ
MURUROA
MARUTÉA
RURUTU
ÎLES GAMBIER
RIMATARA
RIKITÉA   MANGAREVA

PITCAIRN (GB)

TUBUAÏ
MATAURA   RAÏVAVAÉ
OENO
HENDERSON   DUCIE
PITCAIRN   ADAMSTOWN

RAPA

SOUTH AFRICA

ATLANTIC OCEAN

PRINCE EDWARD
ISLANDS

SOUTH GEORGIA

CAPE NORVEGIA

NEW
SCHWABENLAND

QUEEN MAUD LAND

CAPE ANN

ÎLES
KERGUÉLEN

FALKLAND ISLANDS

ENDERBY
LAND

ARGENTINA

WEDDELL SEA

COAST LAND

HEARD ISLAND

DRAKE PASSAGE

CHILE

MOUNT JACKSON
4 190

BERKNER
ISLAND

ALEXANDER ISLAND

AMERICAN
HIGHLAND

BELLINGHAUSEN SEA

VINSON MASSIF
4 897

SOUTH POLE

INDIAN OCEAN

EIGHTS COAST

THURSTON ISLAND

MOUNT KIRKPATRICK
4 528

MOUNT MARKHAM 4 351

MOUNT McCLINTOCK
3 497

ROCKEFELLER
PLATEAU

VICTORIA LAND

W I L K E S   L A N D

MARIE BYRD LAND

MOUNT SIDLEY
4 181

ROOSEVELT
ISLAND

CAPE POINSETT

AMUNDSEN SEA

CAPE COLBECK

PURPOISE BAY

ROSS SEA

CAPE ADARE

BALLENY
ISLANDS

PACIFIC OCEAN

NEW ZEALAND

AUSTRALIA